THE SCEPTER AND THE STAR:

THE MESSIAHS OF THE

DEAD SEA SCROLLS AND

OTHER ANCIENT LITERATURE

THE ANCHOR BIBLE REFERENCE LIBRARY is designed to be a third major component of the Anchor Bible group, which includes the Anchor Bible commentaries on the books of the Old Testament, the New Testament, and the Apocrypha, and the Anchor Bible Dictionary. While the Anchor Bible commentaries and the Anchor Bible Dictionary are structurally defined by their subject matter, the Anchor Bible Reference Library will serve as a supplement on the cutting edge of the most recent scholarship. The series is open-ended; its scope and reach are nothing less than the biblical world in its totality, and its methods and techniques the most up-to-date available or devisable. Separate volumes will deal with one or more of the following topics relating to the Bible: anthropology, archaeology, ecology, economy, geography, history, languages and literatures, philosophy, religion(s), theology.

As with the Anchor Bible commentaries and the Anchor Bible Dictionary, the philosophy underlying the Anchor Bible Reference Library finds expression in the following: the approach is scholarly, the perspective is balanced and fair-minded, the methods are scientific, and the goal is to inform and enlighten. Contributors are chosen on the basis of their scholarly skills and achievements, and they come from a variety of religious backgrounds and communities. The books in the Anchor Bible Reference Library are intended for the broadest possible readership, ranging from world-class scholars, whose qualifications match those of the authors, to general readers, who may not have special training or skill in studying the Bible but are as enthusiastic as any dedicated professional in expanding their knowledge of the Bible and its world.

David Noel Freedman
GENERAL EDITOR

THE ANCHOR BIBLE REFERENCE LIBRARY

JOHN J. COLLINS

THE SCEPTER AND THE STAR:

THE MESSIAHS OF THE

DEAD SEA SCROLLS AND

OTHER ANCIENT LITERATURE

DOUBLEDAY

NEW YORK   LONDON   TORONTO   SYDNEY   AUCKLAND

THE ANCHOR BIBLE REFERENCE LIBRARY
PUBLISHED BY DOUBLEDAY
a division of Bantam Doubleday Dell Publishing Group, Inc.
1540 Broadway, New York, New York 10036

THE ANCHOR BIBLE REFERENCE LIBRARY, DOUBLEDAY, and the portrayal
of an anchor with the letters ABRL are trademarks of Doubleday,
a division of Bantam Doubleday Dell Publishing Group, Inc.

Book Design by Patrice Fodero

Library of Congress Cataloging-in-Publication Data

Collins, John J. (John James), 1938–
    The scepter and the star: The messiahs of the Dead Sea scrolls
and other ancient literature / by John J. Collins. — 1st ed.
        p.   cm. — (The Anchor Bible reference library)
    Includes bibliographical references and index.
    1. Dead Sea scrolls—Criticism, interpretation, etc.   2. Messiah—
Prophecies.   3. Messiah—Judaism.   I. Title.   II. Series.
BM487.C57   1995
296/3'3—dc20   94-16886
                                                        CIP

ISBN 0-385-47457-1
Copyright ©1995 by John J. Collins
All Rights Reserved
Printed in the United States of America

April 1995
First Edition

10   9   8   7   6   5   4   3   2   1

PREFACE

Messianism is not a matter of ancient history. Two episodes that were featured in the media while I was writing this book serve to underline the continued vitality of the topic. In April 1993 a self-proclaimed messiah, David Koresh, and his followers, the Branch Davidians, committed mass suicide in Waco, Texas, after a fifty-one-day siege, rather than surrender to the Bureau of Alcohol, Tobacco and Firearms. The Davidian movement, an offshoot of Seventh Day Adventism, has been in existence since 1935. The Branch Davidians were born of a split in the movement in 1959. The messianic overtones of the movement are clear from the name. "Branch" is a title for the future Davidic king in the prophecies of Jeremiah and Zechariah. The name Koresh is the Hebrew for Cyrus, who is called God's anointed, or messiah, in Isa 45:1. David Koresh, who emerged as leader in 1987, was the first to claim to be a messiah. Earlier leaders had been content with the status of prophets. Koresh evidently departed from any biblical precedent in the sexual exploitation of his followers, but the movement as a whole claimed biblical foundations. Koresh was recognized as a leader because of his ability to quote Scripture.

David Koresh was not the only messiah in the news in 1993. On Sunday, August 29, 1993, *The New York Times* carried a full-page advertisement for "The International Campaign to Bring Moshiach." There was a photograph of Rabbi Menachem M. Schneerson, the Lubavitcher Rebbe Shlita, who "is telling us, as a prophecy, that the Moshiach is on his way." The Lubavitchers are Orthodox Jews, who trace themselves to a Hasidic movement in the Russian town of Lubavitch, in the early nineteenth century. Rabbi Schneerson, who died in 1994, was the seventh *rebbe* of the movement. His utterances heightened the expectation of the messiah among his followers. Some Lubavitchers believed that Schneerson himself was the messiah, although he did not make that claim for himself. The advertisement ended with an invitation to dial (718) 2-MOSHIACH. Messianic movements that advertise in *The New York Times* are evidently closer to the mainstream than the ill-fated messiah of Waco, but they share a common source in biblical texts.

The Dead Sea Scrolls have also received an unusual amount of media attention in recent years. Much of this attention was occasioned by the controversy over the publication of the Scrolls, and the eventual decision, in Fall 1991, to make all the photographs public. A good deal of the attention, however, was focused on a few fragments of messianic import. The most notable controversy, which was trumpeted in newspapers from Los Angeles to London, concerned a fragment that supposedly spoke of a slain messiah (see Chapter Three in this book). Other fragments that received widespread publicity concerned a figure who is called "Son of God" (Chapter Seven) and one that associated a messiah with the resurrection (Chapter Five). A headline in the English newspaper, the *Independent*, on September 1, 1992, p. 5, announced that a "Scroll fragment challenges basic tenet of Christianity." The reference was to the "Son of God" text, ·which turns out to be rather less momentous than the headline would lead one to expect. The more sensational claims about these fragments, such as the discovery of a dying messiah in a pre-Christian Jewish text, or the claim that the "Son of God" text undermines Christianity, turned out to be short-lived. The significance of the Scrolls for the understanding of messianism, however, is enormous.

In the wake of the debacle in Texas, many people have noted the failure of modern society, and in this case the United States government, to comprehend the mind-set of apocalyptic and messianic movements. The first step in such comprehension lies in the understanding of the historical origins of messianism, in the Bible, ancient Judaism and early Christianity. Granted that it is a long way from there to David Koresh, historical perspective is a necessary beginning. Not all messianism ends in conflagration. For better or worse, messianic expectation was a key

Preface

element in the foundation of Christianity, and the enduring vitality of messianism in Judaism is shown in the recent prominence of Rabbi Schneerson.

The Dead Sea Scrolls provide us with some of the oldest messianic texts in the Jewish tradition. Several of these texts have only recently been published. In the following pages we will attempt to explore the meanings of messianism in this ancient Jewish context.

In writing this book, I have drawn on a number of essays that were published previously. Chapter Three incorporates material from my essay, "Messiahs in Context: Method in the Study of Messianism in the Dead Sea Scrolls," in M. Wise, N. Golb, J. J. Collins, and D. Pardee, eds., *Methods of Investigation of the Dead Sea Scrolls and the Khirbet Qumran Site: Present Realities and Future Prospects* (New York: New York Academy of Sciences, 1994). Chapter Five draws on my essays "Teacher and Messiah" in Eugene Ulrich and James VanderKam, eds., *The Community of the Renewed Covenant. The Notre Dame Symposium on the Dead Sea Scrolls* (Notre Dame: University of Notre Dame Press, 1994) and "The Works of the Messiah," *Dead Sea Discoveries* 1(1994). Chapter Seven appeared in an earlier form in Martinus de Boer, ed., *From Jesus to John. Essays on Jesus and New Testament Christology in Honour of Marinus de Jonge* (Sheffield: JSOT, 1993) 65–82. An earlier form of Chapter Eight appeared as "The Son of Man in First Century Judaism" in *New Testament Studies* 38(1992) 448–66. I am grateful to the editors of these volumes for permission to reuse the material. Unless otherwise noted, all biblical translations are taken from the New Revised Standard Version Bible.

Adela Yarbro Collins read the entire manuscript and improved it in many ways. I also benefited from conversations with John Strugnell, and with colleagues too numerous to mention at a spate of Qumran conferences in the last few years. Last, but by no means least, I am indebted to David Noel Freedman for his inimitable editing and encouragement and to Michael Iannazzi of Doubleday for smoothing the way to publication.

John J. Collins
August 1994

CONTENTS

Contents

Albrecht Dürer woodcut, "St. John's vision of Christ and the seven candlesticks," *no. 107 in* The Complete Woodcuts of Albrecht Dürer, *ed. Willi Kurth (New York: Dover Publications, 1963).*

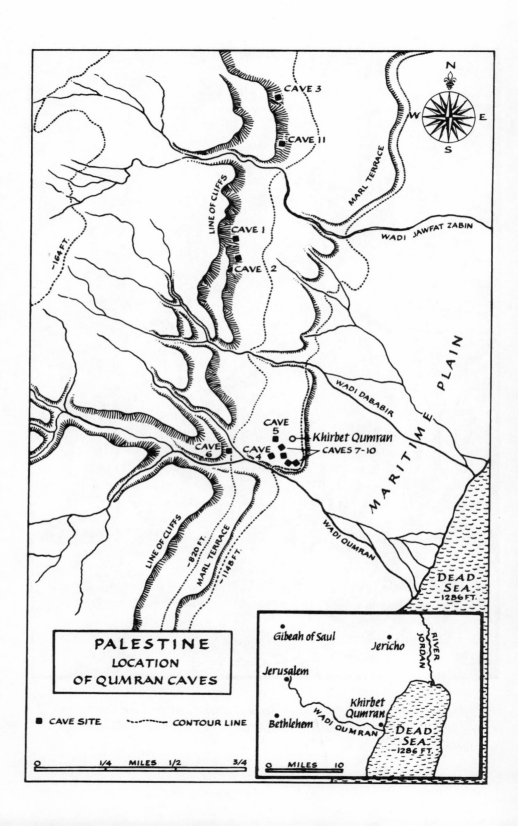

CAVE 3

CAVE 11

N
W   E
S

MARL TERRACE

WADI JAWFAT ZABIN

LINE OF CLIFFS

CAVE 1

CAVE 2

-164 FT.

WADI DABABIR

MARITIME PLAIN

CAVE 5

○ Khirbet Qumran

CAVES 7-10

CAVE 6

CAVE 4

LINE OF CLIFFS

-820 FT.

MARL TERRACE

-1145 FT.

WADI QUMRAN

DEAD SEA -1286 FT.

PALESTINE
LOCATION OF QUMRAN CAVES

■ CAVE SITE   .... CONTOUR LINE

Gibeah of Saul

Jericho

JORDAN RIVER

Jerusalem

Khirbet Qumran

Bethlehem

WADI QUMRAN

DEAD SEA -1286 FT.

0   1/4   MILES 1/2   3/4

0   MILES 10

MESSIANISM AND THE SCROLLS

"Any discussion of the problems relating to Messianism is a delicate matter, for it is here that the essential conflict between Judaism and Christianity has developed and continues to exist."[1] With these words Gershom Scholem began his famous study, *The Messianic Idea in Judaism.* According to Scholem, "a totally different concept of redemption determines the attitude to Messianism in Judaism and Christianity." Judaism "has always maintained a concept of redemption as an event which takes place publicly, on the stage of history, and within the community." Christianity, in contrast, locates redemption in "the spiritual and unseen realm, . . . in the private world of each individual."[2] To be sure, the contrast is overdrawn. Christianity has known its share of millenarian movements that expected a new earth as well as a new heaven, and Judaism has its traditions of inward spirituality. As a broad generalization, however, the contrast has merit, in underlining a dominant characteristic of each religion.[3]

Scholem was not concerned with the origin of messianism in antiquity, but with "the varying perspectives by which it became an effective force after its crystallization in historical Judaism."[4] By historical Judaism, he meant the religion codified by the rabbis, beginning in the late second century CE, and carrying on down to modern times. The "essential conflict" between Judaism and Christianity, however, was rooted more deeply than this, in the very origins of the Christian movement and its emergence from Judaism in the first century CE. For Christianity takes its name from Jesus Christ, and whether Christ be regarded as a title or, as it soon became, a proper name, it expresses the confession that Jesus of Nazareth was the messiah. In this confession lay the seed of the essential and continuing conflict that Scholem perceived between Judaism and Christianity. If we are to understand the roots of this conflict, it is essential to understand what a messiah was supposed to be, and why some fundamental differences in interpretation were possible in the first century CE.

Both the Jewish and the Christian understandings of messiah have been subjects of controversy in recent years. On the Christian side, we have had the astonishing claim that Paul, the earliest Christian writer, did not regard Jesus as the messiah.[5] The ecumenical intentions of such a claim are transparent and honorable, but also misguided since the claim is so plainly false. Jesus is called *Christos*, anointed, the Greek equivalent of messiah, 270 times in the Pauline corpus.[6] If this is not ample testimony that Paul regarded Jesus as messiah, then words have no meaning.[7] There is plenty of room for debate as to how various New Testament authors understood the messiahship of Jesus,[8] but that his messiahship was foundational for the Christian movement is beyond dispute.

Messianism has a more important place in the study of Christianity than in a comprehensive description of ancient Judaism. The Torah, rather than the messiah, is central to traditional Judaism, and one might argue that Paul's rejection of the Law precipitated the separation of Christianity from Judaism.[9] But the Christian abrogation of the Law was based on the belief that Jesus, as messiah, had ushered in a new age, so the issue comes back to messianism. Acceptance of a messiah was not in itself a heresy in Judaism. Rabbi Akiba allegedly hailed Bar Kochba as messiah, and is none the less venerated in Jewish tradition. In the case of Jesus of Nazareth, the issue was not just the claim of messiahship, but the understanding of what it entailed, and eventually the claim of divinity. As a broad generalization, however, Scholem's dictum stands. The separation of Christianity from Judaism, and the problematic relations between the two religions over the centuries, are rooted in Christian claims about Jesus as the Christ or messiah, which are unacceptable to Jews.

◈ *A Common Jewish Hope?*

My concern in this book, however, is primarily with Jewish messianism, both as an interesting phenomenon in the history of religion in its own right and as the context in which the earliest acclamation of Jesus as messiah must be understood. Jewish messianism too, has been a subject of controversy in recent years. The traditional assumption, at least in Christian circles, has been that messianic expectation was ubiquitous and had a consistent form. Consequently, the question of whether Jesus was the messiah admitted of a clearcut answer. There has been a growing recognition in recent years that this view of the matter is heavily influenced by Christian theology. The Gospels portrayed Jesus as the fulfillment of Old Testament prophecy.[10] Those who did not perceive the correspondences were "foolish and slow of heart" (Luke 24:25). Traditional Christianity construed Judaism as a religion in waiting, and this construing of the relationship between Judaism and Christianity has had long-lasting repercussions in Christian scholarship.[11] Its influence can still be seen in major scholarly, historical works in this century.

The classic scholarly view of these matters is presented in the handbooks of Emil Schuerer and George Foot Moore.[12] Both Schuerer and Moore proceeded on the assumption that there was a uniform system of messianic expectation in ancient Judaism. This approach is still in evidence in the revised edition of Schuerer's classic, which provides "a systematic outline of messianism."[13] The system, however, is inevitably constructed from late sources. Moore's discussion is primarily a description of the rabbinic sources.[14] The account in the revised Schuerer is "based on all the inter-Testamental sources, including the Dead Sea Scrolls, but presented according to the pattern emerging from the apocalypses of *Baruch* and *Ezra* since it is in these two late compositions that eschatological expectation is most fully developed."[15] The apocalypses in question, *4 Ezra* and *2 Baruch*, were written at the end of the first century CE. It is obviously problematic to infer from them the pattern of messianic belief throughout the so-called intertestamental period. Yet the sources available to (the original) Schuerer and Moore included little other evidence of messianism in this period. Only two other documents in the Jewish Pseudepigrapha refer to a messiah. One, the *Psalms of Solomon*, written after Pompey's conquest of Jerusalem in 63 BCE resembles *4 Ezra* and *2 Baruch* insofar as it speaks of a royal, Davidic, messiah. The other, the *Similitudes of Enoch*, is very different, and only uses the term "messiah" incidentally to refer to a preexistent, heavenly figure who is primarily patterned on the "one like a son of man" in Daniel 7.[16]

In recent years there has been a sweeping reaction against the kind of synthesis presented by Schuerer and Moore. James Charlesworth reports that "No member of the Princeton Symposium on the Messiah holds that a critical historian can refer to a common Jewish messianic hope during the time of Jesus. . . ."[17] J. D. G. Dunn discerns "four pillars of Second Temple Judaism," monotheism, election, covenant, and land. Future hope does not rank with the pillars, much less messianism.[18] E. P. Sanders provides an outline of the future hopes of "common Judaism," but he emphasizes that "the expectation of a messiah was not the rule."[19] Burton Mack warns that it is wrong "to think of Judaism in general as determined by messianism, the desire for a king."[20] Even the editors of a volume on messiahs find "powerful reasons to ditch" the established consensus, and emphasize instead the diversity of "Judaisms and their Messiahs."[21]

Several factors have contributed to this rather dramatic shift in the assessment of Jewish messianism around the turn of the era. Jews and Christians alike have been sensitized to the theological distortions of past generations. Liberal Christians are eager to avoid anything that might smack of supersessionism. Moreover, messianism, and eschatology in general, have become something of an embarrassment in modern culture. They conjure up images of David Koresh and the Branch Davidians, or, on a more respectable level, the Lubavitcher Rebbe and his followers. But there are also serious scholarly reasons for the shift. Our documentation for Judaism around the turn of the era is spotty, and explicit documentation of messianic expectation is relatively rare. Nonetheless, there are reasons to believe that the pendulum of scholarly opinion has swung too far.

The Dead Sea Scrolls

The primary reason for a reassessment of Jewish messianism at this time is the availability of new evidence from the Dead Sea Scrolls. To be sure, much of the evidence has been available now for forty years, but it has not been well integrated into the discussion. In the revised edition of Schuerer's *History*, the Qumran evidence is still fitted into a pattern derived from *4 Ezra* and *2 Baruch*. More often the various corpora, such as the Pseudepigrapha and the Dead Sea Scrolls, are studied separately, and not integrated with each other.[22] Moreover, the full corpus of Dead Sea Scrolls was only made generally available in Fall 1991, and a number of important texts have been published since then. These could not be taken into account in such syntheses as the revision of Schuerer's history, volume 2 (1979), or the Princeton symposium on the messiah (1987).

The failure to integrate the Scrolls into the discussion of Second Temple Judaism is bound up with a wider debate as to just what the Scrolls represent. Many scholars have regarded them as the writings of a secluded sect, which might then be deemed rather atypical of the Judaism of the time. This view, however, has become harder to maintain in view of the extent and diversity of the fragmentary remains from Qumran Cave 4, which have only recently come into public view.[23]

The view that the Dead Sea Scrolls were the library of an Essene settlement at Khirbet Qumran, by the Dead Sea south of Jericho, took hold within a few years of the first discoveries in 1947 and has remained the dominant hypothesis.[24] Two factors are fundamental to that hypothesis. First, the Roman writer Pliny, who died in the eruption of Vesuvius in 79 CE, refers to an Essene settlement between Jericho and En-Gedi.[25] No other plausible site for Pliny's reference has been identified. Second, the first batch of discoveries in Qumran Cave 1 included a *Community Rule* (1QS), which has several points of resemblance to the description of the Essenes by Josephus and Philo.[26] The caves where the Scrolls were found are in close proximity to the ruins of a settlement. The original excavator of the site, Roland de Vaux, argued that these ruins reflected a quasi-monastic settlement, and that the Scrolls were the library of that settlement, hidden in the caves at the time of the Jewish war against Rome.[27] The fact that pottery found at Qumran matched the jars in which the Scrolls were hidden has usually been taken as confirmation of that view. It is clear from the archeological evidence that Qumran was destroyed by the Roman army during the First Jewish Revolt (66–70 CE), probably in 68 CE. The beginning of the settlement is often put close to the middle of the second century BCE, but the evidence of the coins would seem to favor a date closer to 100 BCE. (143 coins were found from the reign of Alexander Jannaeus, 103–76 BCE, while only one was found from that of John Hyrcanus, 135–104 BCE.) The settlement was apparently in existence for more than a century and a half around the turn of the era.[28]

The use of such terms as "sect" or "sectarian" with reference to the Scrolls arises in part from the usual translation of the term *hairesis*, which Josephus uses to categorize the Essenes, Pharisees and Sadducees

(*Ant* 13.171–72).[29] It is reinforced by the regulations of the Community Rule, and to a lesser extent the Damascus Document (CD), which was originally published from manuscripts found in the Cairo Geniza in 1910,[30] and which has been found in several fragmentary copies at Qumran. Both the Community Rule and the Damascus Document posit an organization with its own procedures of admission, and which distinguishes itself from the rest of Judaism. Another important document known as the Halakhic Letter (4QMMT), formally published in 1994, also makes clear that it comes from a community that has separated itself from the rest of Judaism. It declares explicitly that "we have separated ourselves from the majority of the peo[ple . . .] from intermingling in these matters and from participating with them in these [matters]."[31] The view that the Scrolls are a sectarian collection assumes that the rule books and 4QMMT relate to the same movement (not necessarily to a single community) and that the other books were collected (though not all produced) by members of that movement. In this volume, I will use the words "sect" and "sectarian" with reference to this movement that had separated itself from the rest of Judaism.

In recent years, however, the consensus about the origin of the Scrolls has come into question. The most comprehensive challenge to the consensus has been formulated by Norman Golb, who disputes not only the character of the site and the Essene identification, but whether the Scrolls can be characterized as sectarian at all, and do not rather represent a random sampling of the Jewish literature of the period.[32]

Two factors weigh heavily against the view that the Qumran library was not sectarian. First, certain kinds of books are conspicuously absent from the caves. There are no writings that could be described as Pharisaic, or that conform to the teachings of the later Tannaim, who compiled the rabbinic corpus.[33] Even the *Psalms of Solomon*, which have often been characterized as Pharisaic, are unattested at Qumran. Equally there are no writings that reflect the views of the Maccabees, or their successors in the Hasmonean dynasty. There are no copies of 1 Maccabees, which surely existed in Hebrew, or of Judith, which is often thought to be pro-Hasmonean. One fragmentary document, 4Q448, which mentions "Jonathan the King," has been interpreted as a prayer for Alexander Jannaeus,[34] but the interpretation is disputed[35] and, in any case, it would constitute only a single exception out of some eight hundred documents. The paucity of pro-Hasmonean literature among the Scrolls remains striking. The omission of whole categories of writings cannot be dismissed as fortuitous. It is far more plausible that the people who collected the Scrolls had a quarrel with both the Hasmoneans and the Pharisees. In contrast, some of the most distinctively sectarian books are preserved in multiple copies. There are twelve copies of the sectarian Community Rule, seven copies of the Damascus Document, and six copies of the avowedly separatist Halakhic Letter (4QMMT).[36] Why should multiple copies of such sectarian works be preserved in a Jerusalem library? The view that the Scrolls represent a sectarian collection remains overwhelmingly probable.

Whether the sect in question should be identified as the Essenes, and whether they had a settlement at Qumran, are less pressing questions for our present purposes. The Community Rule and Damascus Document show more similarities to the Essenes than to any other known group.[37] It must be readily admitted that the correspondences are not complete. Josephus and Philo give no indication that the Essenes had any interest in messianism, or in a dualistic view of the world. There is also a discrepancy in the matter of celibacy, which is never required in the Scrolls.[38] It is possible, even probable, that the Greek accounts distorted the Essenes, by interpreting them in the light of Greek interests. In that case, however, these accounts cannot be regarded as reliable sources, and the Scrolls should not be assimilated to them in any way.[39] While I think the Essene identification is highly probable, I do not intend to press it. The Scrolls must be studied in their own right in any case.

The connection of the Scrolls with the Qumran site also seems to me very probable. There is a cemetery of over a thousand graves at Qumran. This can hardly be explained if Qumran was a military outpost, still less if it was a private residence of some sort. Pliny's reference to an Essene settlement in the area must still be taken into account. No one has yet identified a more plausible site for this settlement than Qumran. If the collection of Scrolls is indeed sectarian, then their proximity to Qumran can hardly be coincidental. Here again we do not need to press the point. The interpretation of the Scrolls seldom depends on the connection with the site, and some reservation is necessary in any case, pending the final archaeological publications.[40]

While the sectarian origin of the Scrolls remains highly probable, Golb must be credited with some significant observations. The Qumran library is strangely lacking in primary documents, such as legal memoranda, personal letters, and records of transactions.[41] This would be surprising if Qumran were the administrative center of a sect, as has often been supposed,[42] but it remains puzzling regardless of the provenance of the Scrolls.[43] There evidently was a settlement at Qumran, and it presumably had records, which either did not survive or have not been discovered. A more significant observation concerns the lack of autograph manuscripts among the Scrolls. Even the *pesharîm*, of which only single copies have been found, contain evidence of copying errors.[44] This observation raises questions as to whether Qumran was the scene of intense scribal activity. De Vaux had identified a collapsed upper room as a "scriptorium," on the basis of three tables and two inkwells found in the debris. In antiquity, however, scribes did not sit at tables,[45] and in any case two inkwells provide a very slim basis for identifying a scriptorium. Pauline Donceel-Voute, one of the archeologists engaged in completing the publication of de Vaux's excavations, has argued persuasively that the table came from a *triclinium* or dining room.[46] The disappearance of the scriptorium raises further questions about the extent of scribal activity at Qumran. These questions are intensified by the fact that several hundred different scribal hands can be detected in the Scrolls. Moreover, the ongoing publication of the Scrolls has made clear that the Scrolls include texts that are not sectarian in character (e.g. some wisdom texts; apocryphal psalms) and others that have sectarian tendencies but are considerably older than the settlement at Qumran (e.g. parts of *1 Enoch*). It is certain that some of the manuscripts were copied elsewhere; it is questionable whether any were actually written at Qumran. None of this is incompatible with the Essene hypothesis, but it shows that the Scrolls cannot be conceived as the product of a community sealed off from the outside world.

Scholars have always recognized that some of the books found at Qumran had been composed elsewhere, at an earlier time. Obviously, the biblical books are not sectarian. Even some of the copies found at Qumran date from the third century BCE, long before the settlement at the site.[47] Some nonbiblical compositions, such as the books of *Enoch* and *Jubilees*, have also been assumed to antedate the Qumran community. There is no doubt, however, that our consciousness of non-sectarian works at Qumran has increased considerably in recent years. If this was a sectarian library, the sectarians were widely read, even though they rejected certain kinds of literature. The library, then, may give us a wider sample of the Judaism of the time than has been generally supposed. This much, indeed, might have been inferred from the sheer size of the corpus. The collection included such books as Tobit and Sirach, which had wide currency but were not objectionable to the sect in the way 1 Maccabees probably was. The Psalms Scroll, which has been the focus of extended debate about the formation of the canon,[48] is significant precisely because it contains "noncanonical" psalms, some of which were known before the Dead Sea discoveries, and which show no sectarian traits. The sect also had its own literature, some of which may well have been esoteric, and which remained, as far as we can tell, unknown outside sectarian circles. It is now clear, however, that not all previously unknown works were specifically sectarian.

Moreover, even if the collection is a sectarian library, it is not necessarily the case that it was specifically the library of the Qumran settlement. We have seen that the evidence for a scriptorium at Qumran has been severely questioned. Besides, the Community Rule is not the only description of a sectarian community found in the Scrolls. There are also seven copies of the Damascus Document, which is clearly related to the Community Rule but also differs from it in significant ways. The most important difference for our purposes is that the Damascus Document contains explicit provision for those who "live in camps according to the rule of the Land . . . marrying and begetting children" (CD 7:6–7). This provision has often been compared to Josephus' account of the second order of Essenes, who were also said to marry (*Jewish War* 2.160). The way in which the provision is introduced, "and if they live in camps . . ." strongly suggests that not all members of the "new covenant" did so.[49] It is apparent that the sect allowed for some variety in lifestyle. The laws of the Damascus Document also provide for contact with Gentiles, which is not envisaged in the Community Rule. We must assume that the members of this movement were not isolated from other Jews either. It would seem, then, that the members of the sect were spread throughout the land and this, too, is in accordance with what Josephus says about the Essenes.[50]

It is at least possible that the collection of scrolls found near Qumran was not just the library of the Qumran community but had been brought there from various sectarian "camps" at the time of the war.[51] This would explain the multiple copies of the Damascus Rule, and might also help explain the diversity of the collection. On this hypothesis, then, we might expect to find in the Scrolls not only the distinctive compositions of the sect and "outside writings" that antedated its formation, but also diverse writings that had come into the possession of sectarians at any time prior to the Jewish war. There is still a principle of exclusion, which stamps the collection as sectarian, but this is by no means a principle of isolation. We should expect the Scrolls to reflect some notions that were widespread in the Judaism of their day, as well as those that were peculiar to the sect itself.

Much scholarship on the Scrolls has proceeded on the assumption that if a nonbiblical document was found at Qumran "its presence in the Essene library suggests that it was written by an Essene."[52] This assumption is obviously no longer tenable. Carol Newsom has suggested even that it should be reversed, and that the burden of proof always falls on whoever wants to posit sectarian provenance.[53] Newsom and Hartmut Stegemann have advanced some criteria for distinguishing sectarian compositions.[54] Stegemann cites recognition of the authority of the Teacher of Righteousness, or of the rule books, and formal or terminological connections with explicitly sectarian texts. Newsom also cites terminological relationships; e.g. 4Q 502, dubbed a "marriage ritual" by its editor,[55] is not conspicuously sectarian but appears to cite 1QS 4:4–6, and so belongs in the orbit of the sect. A text that follows the solar, 364-day calendar is also likely to be sectarian, but it is admitted that a book like *Jubilees*, which attaches great importance to this calendar, is older than the Qumran sect.

Both Newsom and Stegemann readily admit the limited value of these criteria. It is easy enough to arrive at a core group of sectarian texts: The Damascus Document (CD), the Community Rule (1QS), the so-called Messianic Rule (1QSa), the Scroll of Blessings (1QSb), the Thanksgiving Hymns or *Hodayot*, the biblical commentaries or *pesharîm*, the Rule for the War of the Sons of Light against the Sons of Darkness (1QM, 4QM), the Halakhic Letter (4QMMT). There is a large grey area, however, of texts that bear some terminological relationship to these core texts, but the terms in question are not always distinctive, and it is difficult to draw a line or determine what degree of correspondence is required. Members of the community (יחד) described in the Community Rule, or of the covenant described in the Damascus Document, still shared a wide range of traditions and observances with other Jews. We cannot expect even their own compositions always to display distinctive sectarian features.

In the matter of messianism, our objective here is not to isolate distinctively sectarian ideas, but rather to get a sense of the popularity and distribution of certain ideas in Judaism around the turn of the era. To this end, we will look not only for correspondences among the Scrolls, but also for their relation to other Jewish texts of the time. Parallels between the Scrolls and texts *not* found at Qumran, such as the *Psalms of Solomon*, are of particular interest. Such parallels may show not whether a text is sectarian, but whether an idea was current across sectarian boundaries and might be considered part of a common Jewish tradition of the time.

The discovery of the Dead Sea Scrolls considerably expanded the corpus of literature relevant to the study of messianism. The number of occurrences of מָשִׁיחַ, messiah, in its various forms is not great, but it illustrates well the range of reference of the term. One of the first scrolls published, the Community Rule, refers to the coming of "the prophet and the messiahs of Aaron and Israel" (1QS 9:2), and so testifies to the expectation of at least two messiahs, one priestly and one royal.[56] Since מָשִׁיחַ is also used in the plural with reference to prophets (CD 2:9; 1QM 11:7), and the Melchizedek scroll (11QMelchizedek) identifies the "herald" of Isa 52:7 as "the anointed of the spirit" (מְשִׁיחַ הָרוּחַ, cf. CD 2:9), it is possible that the prophet may be a messianic figure, too. The Scrolls, then, indicate a greater diversity of messianic expectations in Judaism around the turn of the era than was apparent before their discovery.[57]

◈ *The Terminological Issue*

The degree of diversity is inevitably bound up with the question of terminology. In modern parlance, the word "messiah" refers at the minimum to a figure who will play an authoritative role in the end time, usually the eschatological king. The Hebrew word מָשִׁיחַ, however, means simply "anointed" and does not necessarily refer to an eschatological figure at all. While it refers to a royal figure some thirty times in the Hebrew Bible, it can also refer to other figures, most notably the anointed High Priest.[58] The association of the term with an ideal Davidic king derives from Ps 2:2, which speaks of the subjugation of all the peoples to God's anointed. In the postexilic period, when there was no longer a king in Jerusalem, we occasionally find the hope for an ideal king of the future. Jer 23:5–6 can be read in this context: "The days are coming, says the Lord, when I will raise up for David a righteous Branch, and he shall reign as king and deal wisely, and he shall execute justice and righteousness in the land." The use of the term מָשִׁיחַ, messiah, for such a future king is not attested in the biblical period. In the late apocalyptic Book of Daniel, the only uses of מָשִׁיחַ refer to High Priests (Dan 9:25,26).

It is not helpful, however, to restrict the discussion of messianism too narrowly to occurrences of מָשִׁיחַ or its translation equivalents (*christos*, *unctus*, etc.). On the one hand, since the term "messiah" is commonly used in later tradition for the ideal Davidic king of the future, passages such as Jer 23:5–6, which clearly refer to such a figure, may reasonably be dubbed "messianic," even though the specific term does not occur. On the other hand, it is best to reserve the English term "messiah" for figures who have important roles in the future hope of the people. Even though historical High Priests are called משיח in Daniel 9, they are not "messiahs" in the eschatological, futurist, sense of the term. The term "messiah" may be used legitimately, however, for the High Priest in an eschatological context, and for other eschatological figures, such as the Enochic Son of Man, who are *sometimes* designated as משיח or its translation equivalents. The term cannot be extended at will. Many reviews of Jewish messianism include sections on such writings as the *Testament of Moses*, which have no provision for a messiah by any name.[59] In short, a messiah is an eschatological figure who sometimes, but not necessarily always, is designated as a משיח in the ancient sources.

It should be clear from these remarks, however, that "messiah," even as an eschatological term, can refer to different kinds of figures, and that to speak of "the messiah" without further qualification is to speak ambiguously. This is the valid insight that underlies the recent denials of any common messianism in ancient Judaism. One could, arguably, give a satisfactory account of Jewish future hope without using the word "messiah" at all. What matters is the expectation of a Davidic king, of an ideal priest, of an eschatological prophet. Besides, there was no Jewish orthodoxy in the matter of messianic expectation, and so we should expect some variation.

We shall argue, however, that the variation was limited, and that some forms of messianic expectation were widely shared. To be sure, we cannot go back to the single pattern of messianic expectation described by Schuerer and Moore. We shall find four basic messianic paradigms (king, priest, prophet, and heavenly messiah), and they were not equally widespread.[59a] We cannot be sure just how widespread messianic expectation was. Our sources do not permit us to speak with confidence about the majority of the Jewish people. It is possible, however, to show that some ideas had wide distribution and were current across sectarian lines. If we may accept Ed Sanders's notion of a common Judaism, in the sense of what was typical, though not necessarily normative, in the period 100 BCE–100CE, the expectation of a Davidic messiah was surely part of it.[60]

The history of Judaism in the Roman era is marked by a series of abortive movements led by individuals who claimed or aspired to be king.[61] The most conspicuous of these were Jesus of Nazareth, who was crucified as "King of the Jews" and was known to his followers as *Christos*, Greek for anointed one or messiah, at least after his death, and Simon Bar Kosiba, who was hailed by Rabbi Akiba as Bar Kochba, son of the star. The messianic character of some of the other pretenders is not explicit in the sources, but then our main source, Josephus, was not very sympathetic to failed uprisings. It is true, in a sense, that such movements were "not the rule," but neither can they be dismissed as aberrations. We should rather think of them as the tips of icebergs. Open rebellion only takes place when passions have built up to the point where they cannot be suppressed. It would be foolish to assume that only those who joined in messianic movements were familiar with and entertained messianic expectations.

It is unfortunate that we have no writings from the hands of messianic pretenders, or even from their followers, which would illuminate their ideology.[62] Only in the case of Jesus of Nazareth do we have extended narratives, and the multiplicity of these narratives is a problem in itself. Jesus is, moreover, an anomaly. Although the claim that he is the Davidic messiah is ubiquitous in the New Testament, he does not fit the typical profile of the Davidic messiah. This messiah was, first of all, a warrior prince, who was to defeat the enemies of Israel. The discrepancy between Jewish expectation and Christian fulfillment on this point has long been recognized. Sigmund Mowinckel went so far as to assert that "the Jewish Messianic idea was the temptation of Satan, which he had to reject."[63] Nonetheless, Jesus is hailed precisely as the messiah of Israel in the New Testament, and so the discrepancy poses a problem for any attempt to apply a schema of promise and fulfillment to the subject of messianism.

There were other paradigms of messianism besides the Davidic one, and some elements of these were found to be applicable to the Christian messiah. Attempts to find precedents in the Scrolls for a suffering or dying messiah have, I believe, been misguided. There are, however, significant precedents for the prophetic activity attributed to Jesus in the Gospels. We shall find, also, texts that envisage exaltation and enthronement in heaven and texts that apply certain attributes of divinity to a messianic figure. The statement attributed to the Jewish partner in Justin Martyr's *Dialogue with Trypho* 49.1, that "we all expect the messiah to be born a human being from human beings,"[64] holds true in most cases that we shall examine, but not in all. The messianic paradigm that was applied most successfully to Jesus in the Gospels was that of the heavenly messiah or Son of Man, if only because his manifestation still awaits eschatological verification.

We shall return to the question of messianic movements, and to the messianic claims concerning Jesus of Nazareth, in the closing chapter. Our main purpose, however, is to fill in the picture of Jewish messianism at the turn of the era, with special attention to the newly available evidence. In so doing we will endeavor to strike a balance between the extreme positions of modern scholarship, by giving due attention not only to the rich diversity of the trees but also the distinct contours of the forest.

NOTES

[1] Gershom Scholem, *The Messianic Idea in Judaism and Other Essays on Jewish Spirituality* (New York: Schocken, 1971) 1.

[2] Ibid.

[3] Scholem has been criticized by William Scott Green, "Introduction: Messiah in Judaism: Rethinking the Question," in J. Neusner, W. S. Green and E. S. Frerichs, eds., *Judaisms and their Messiahs* (Cambridge: Cambridge University Press, 1987) 1–2. It does not seem to me that Scholem "assumes the constant centrality of the messiah in the morphology and history of Judaism and in the Jewish-Christian argument," as Green claims, or that Scholem is discussing the morphology of Judaism in this essay at all. He is making a broad generalization about the root cause of the differences between Judaism and Christianity. Green himself recognizes that the use of the word *christos* in the Gospels was "pivotal in shaping later understanding" (p. 4).

[4] Ibid., 2.

[5] John G. Gager, *The Origins of Anti-Semitism. Attitudes Towards Judaism in Pagan and Christian Antiquity* (New York: Oxford University Press, 1983) 201, summarizing the views of Lloyd Gaston, which were expressed in a series of articles, most notably "Paul and the Torah," in A. Davies, ed., *Anti-Semitism and the Foundations of Christianity* (New York: Paulist, 1979) 48–71.

[6] See Martin Hengel, "Jesus, der Messias Israels," in I. Gruenwald, S. Shaked and G. G. Stroumsa, eds., *Messiah and Christos. Studies in the Jewish Origins of Christianity Presented to David Flusser* (Tübingen: Mohr-Siebeck, 1992) 155.

[7] Note also the clear messianic resonance of Romans 1:3–4: "the gospel according to his Son, who was descended from David according to the flesh and was declared to be Son of God with power according to the spirit of holiness by resurrection from the dead."

[8] See George MacRae, "Messiah and Gospel," in Neusner et al., eds., *Judaisms and their Messiahs*, 169–85.

[9] The separation of Christianity from Judaism is a complex issue. See James D. G. Dunn, *The Partings of the Ways Between Christianity and Judaism and Their Significance for the Character of Christianity* (Philadelphia: Trinity Press International, 1991).

[10] This point is made lucidly by Green, "Introduction," 5.

[11] It is an intriguing question, implied in Green's critique of Scholem, whether *Jewish* scholarship has also been distorted by the prevalent Christian stereotypes. Cf. Scholem's statement that "in Judaism the Messianic idea has compelled a life lived in deferment," (*The Messianic Idea*, 35).

[12] Emil Schuerer, *The History of the Jewish People in the Age of Jesus Christ* (rev. and ed. by G. Vermes, F. Millar and M. Black; 3 vols.; Edinburgh: Clark, 1973–87); G. F. Moore, *Judaism in the First Centuries of the Christian Era* (2 vols.; New York: Schocken, 1971, original copyright, 1927).

[13] Schuerer, *The History*, 2.514.

[14] G. F. Moore, *Judaism in the First Centuries of the Christian Era*, 2.323–76.

[15] Schuerer, *The History*, 3.514.

[16] See the review by J. H. Charlesworth, "The Messiah in the Pseudepigrapha," in H. Temporini and W. Haase, eds., *Aufstieg und Niedergang der Römischen Welt* (Berlin: de Gruyter, 1979) II.19.1 188–218. Charlesworth includes *3 Enoch* as a further Jewish pseudepigraphon, but this comes from a much later period.

[17] J. H. Charlesworth, "From Messianology to Christology: Problems and Prospects," in J. H. Charlesworth, ed., *The Messiah* (Minneapolis: Fortress, 1992) 5.

[18] Dunn, *The Partings of the Ways*, 18–36. Dunn freely admits that he is not attempting a complete taxonomy of early Judaism.

[19] E. P. Sanders, *Judaism. Practice and Belief. 63 BCE–66 CE* (Philadelphia: Trinity Press International, 1992) 295.

[20] B. L. Mack, *A Myth of Innocence. Mark and Christian Origins* (Philadelphia: Fortress, 1988) 36.

[21] Green, "Introduction," 10.

[22] Consequently Charlesworth's study of "The Messiah in the Pseudepigrapha" gives a misleading impression of the extent of messianic expectation in "intertestamental" Judaism.

[23] Photographs of most of the scrolls can be found in Rober H. Eisenman and James M. Robinson, eds., *A Facsimile Edition of the Dead Sea Scrolls* (2 vols.; Washington: Biblical Archaeology Society, 1991). The complete collection can be found in Emanuel Tov, ed., with the collaboration of Stephen J. Pfann, *The Dead Sea Scrolls on Microfiche* (Leiden: Brill, 1993).

[24] See the classic discussion of F. M. Cross, *The Ancient Library of Qumran and Modern Biblical Studies* (Garden City: Doubleday, 1961) 51–196; G. Vermes, *The Dead Sea Scrolls. Qumran in Perspective* (Philadelphia: Fortress, 1977) 116–36; J. J. Collins, "Essenes," David N. Freedman, ed., *The Anchor Bible Dictionary* (6 vols.; New York: Doubleday, 1992) 2.619–26. The Essenes were first introduced into the discussion by W. H. Brownlee, "A Comparison of the Covenanters of the Dead Sea Scrolls with Pre-Christian Jewish Sects," *Biblical Archeologist* 13(1950) 50–72 and A. Dupont-Sommer, *Aperçus préliminaires sur les manuscrits de la Mer Morte* (Paris: Maisonneuve, 1950). The identification has recently been reaffirmed by Émile Puech, *La Croyance des Esséniens en la Vie Future: Immortalité, Résurrection, Vie Éternelle?* (Études Bibliques 21; Paris: Gabalda, 1993) 14–20 and James C. VanderKam, *The Dead Sea Scrolls Today* (Grand Rapids, MI: Eerdmans, 1994) Chapter Three.

[25] Pliny, *Natural History* 5.15.73

[26] Josephus, *Jewish War* 2.8.2–13 §119–61, *Antiquities* 18.1.5 §18–22; Philo, *Quod omnis probus liber sit*, 75–91, *Hypothetica* 11.1–18. See also Hippolytus, *Refutation of All Heresies* 9.18–28. The parallels with the Scrolls are discussed by T. S. Beall, *Josephus' Description of the Essenes Illustrated by the Dead Sea Scrolls* (Studiorum Novi Testamenti Societas Monograph Series 58; Cambridge: Cambridge University Press, 1988) and much more briefly by Collins, "Essenes," in *The Anchor Bible Dictionary* 2.619–26 and by Geza Vermes and Martin D. Goodman, *The Essenes According to the Classical Sources* (Sheffield: Journal for the Study of the Old Testament, 1989).

[27] R. de Vaux, *Archaeology and the Dead Sea Scrolls* (London: Oxford University Press, 1973).

[28] De Vaux argued that the site was abandoned after an earthquake in 31 BCE and not reoccupied until 4 BCE, at the end of Herod's reign. Magen Broshi, in a postscript to de Vaux's article "Qumran, Khirbet and 'Ein Feshka," in E. Stern, ed., *The New Encyclopedia of Archaeological Excavations in the Holy Land* (New York: Simon and Schuster, 1993) 4.1235–41, expresses doubt that the site was abandoned for more than a few years.

[29] For a concise discussion of the category "sect" with reference to Judaism in this period see Anthony J. Saldarini, *Pharisees, Scribes and Sadducees in Palestinian Society. A Sociological Approach* (Wilmington: Glazier, 1988) 70–73. Saldarini draws on the typology of Bryan Wilson, *Magic and the Millennium* (London: Heinemann, 1973) 16–26.

[30] Solomon Schechter, *Fragments of a Zadokite Work* (Cambridge: Cambridge University Press, 1910).

[31] E. Qimron and J. Strugnell, *Qumran Cave 4. V. Miqṣat Maʿaśē Ha-Torah* (DJD 10; Oxford: Clarendon, 1994) 59.

[32] N. Golb, "The Problem of Origin and Identification of the Dead Sea Scrolls," *Proceedings of the American Philosophical Society* 124(1980) 1–24; "Who Hid the Dead Sea Scrolls?" *Biblical Archeologist* 48(1985) 68–82; "The Dead Sea Scrolls. A New Perspective," *The American Scholar* 58(1989) 177–207; "Khirbet Qumran and the Manuscripts of the Judaean Wilderness: Observations on the Logic of their Investigation," *Journal of Near Eastern Studies* 49(1990) 103–14.

[33] F. García Martínez and A. van der Woude, "A Groningen Hypothesis of Qumran Origins," *Revue de Qumran* 14(1990) 535. This is not to deny that the Scrolls agree with Pharisaic teachings on individual points.

[34] E. and H. Eshel and A. Yardeni, "A Scroll from Qumran Which Includes Part of Psalm 154 and a Prayer for King Jonathan and His Kingdom," (Hebrew) *Tarbiz* 60(1991) 295–324; (English) *Israel Exploration Journal* 42(1992) 199–229. R. H. Eisenman and M. Wise, *The Dead Sea Scrolls Uncovered. The First Complete Translation and Interpretation of 50 Key Documents Withheld for Over 35 Years* (Rockport, MA: Element, 1992) 273, claim that this text "completely disproves the Essene theory of Qumran origins at least as classically conceived."

[35] D. J. Harrington and J. Strugnell, "Qumran Cave 4 Texts: A New Publication," *Journal of Biblical Literature* 112(1993) 491–99, read "Rise up, O Holy One, against King Jonathan" (p. 498). Geza Vermes, "Brother James's heirs? The Community at Qumran and its relations to the first Christians," *Times Literary Supplement* 4 December 1992, 6–7, questions the reading "Jonathan." In a more recent study, "The So-Called King Jonathan Fragment (4Q448)," *Journal of Jewish Studies* 44(1993) 294–300, he accepts the reading but suggests that the reference is to Jonathan Maccabee, although he never

bears the title king in the ancient sources. These readings seem to be rather desperate attempts to avoid the reference to Jannaeus. On the problems presented by the syntax of the fragment, see the comments of P. S. Alexander, "A Note on the Syntax of 4Q448," *Journal of Jewish Studies* 44(1993) 301–2.

[36] Carol A. Newsom, "'Sectually Explicit' Literature from Qumran," in W. H. Propp, B. Halpern and D. N. Freedman, eds., *The Hebrew Bible and its Interpreters* (Winona Lake, IN: Eisenbrauns, 1990) 170. The pattern of multiple copies is more significant than the percentage of the entire collection that can be considered sectarian.

[37] See my article, "Essenes," in D. N. Freedman, ed., *The Anchor Bible Dictionary* 2.619–26 and Beall, *Josephus' Description of the Essenes.* Some scholars who have studied the halakah of the Scrolls, especially that of 4QMMT, have argued that it corresponds most closely to that of the Sadducees (Y. Sussman, "The History of the Halakha and the Dead Sea Scrolls: Preliminary Observations on the Miqsat Ma'ase Ha-Torah," *Tarbiz* 59(1990) 11–76 (Hebrew); L. H. Schiffman, "The Sudducean Origins of the Dead Sea Scroll Sect," in H. Shanks, ed., *Understanding the Dead Sea Scrolls* [New York: Random House, 1992] 35–49). This suggestion faces considerable difficulties, in view of the conspicuously non-Sadducean character of many of the Scrolls (note e.g. the prominence of angels and of deterministic notions). See the critique of the Sadducean hypothesis by J. C. VanderKam, "The People of the Dead Sea Scrolls: Essenes or Sadducees?" in Shanks, ed., *Understanding the Dead Sea Scrolls*, 50–62.

[38] See, however, the interesting argument of J. M. Baumgarten, "The Qumran-Essene Restraints on Marriage," in L. H. Schiffman, ed., *Archaeology and History in the Dead Sea Scrolls* (Sheffield: Journal for the Study of the Old Testament, 1990) 13–24, who argues that the provision for marriage in CD 7:6–7 ("But if they live in camps according to the rule of the land, marrying and begetting children . . .") implies that some members of the sect did not marry.

[39] This point is made forcefully by Roland Bergmeier, *Die Essener-Berichte des Flavius Josephus* (Kampen: Kok Pharos, 1993) 114–21. Puech, *La Croyance des Ésseniens*, 761, argues that the account of the Essenes in Hippolytus is reliable, but few would agree.

[40] Pauline Donceel-Voûte, one of the archeologists charged with completing the publication of the site, has argued that the material remains are too "luxurious" for a monastic community, and that Qumran was part private villa, part industrial estate. See her article, "The Archaeology of Qumran," in M. Wise, N. Golb, J. J. Collins, and D. Pardee, eds., *Methods of Investigation of the Dead Sea Scrolls and the Khirbet Qumran Site: Present Realities and Future Prospects* (New York: New York Academy of Sciences, 1994) 1–32. Her argument has met with considerable skepticism. (See VanderKam, *The Dead Sea Scrolls Today*, Chapter One.) The evidence for luxury at Qumran is modest indeed, and the poverty of a quasi-monastic life does not require destitution.

[41] A small number of such documents have been found in Cave 4. See 4Q341–59, E. Tov, *The Dead Sea Scrolls on Microfiche, Companion Volume* (Leiden: Brill, 1993) 40–41.

[42] De Vaux, *Archaeology and the Dead Sea Scrolls*, 113, used the term "mother-house." So also Vermes, *The Dead Sea Scrolls*, 108.

[43] García Martínez and van der Woude, "A Groningen Hypothesis," 530: "if the absence of documentary records can be an objection to the MSS coming from a library, the objection must equally apply to its coming from another library, from the temple library or from unspecified libraries of Jerusalem." Golb has tried to forestall this objection by

pointing out that the Jerusalem archives were destroyed during factional strife in 66 CE (Josephus, *Jewish War* 2.427–28; Golb, "The Problem of Origin," 23, n. 76) but it is scarcely possible that all primary documents were destroyed while only literary works survived.

[44] M. Horgan, *Pesharim: Qumran Interpretations of Biblical Books* (Catholic Biblical Quarterly Monograph Series 8; Washington, D.C.: Catholic Biblical Association, 1979) 3–4.

[45] B. Metzger, "The Furniture of the Scriptorium at Qumran," *Revue de Qumran* 1(1959) 509–15; Golb, "The Problem of Origin," 5.

[46] Pauline Donceel-Voûte, "'Coenaculum.' La Salle à l'Étage du Locus 30 à Khirbet Qumrân sur la Mer Morte," in *Banquets d'Orient. Res Orientales* 4(1992) 61–84.

[47] Cross, *The Ancient Library*, 42.

[48] See the review of the debate by G. H. Wilson, "The Qumran Psalms Scroll Reconsidered: Analysis of the Debate," *Catholic Biblical Quarterly* 47(1985) 624–42.

[49] Baumgarten, "The Qumran-Essene Restraints on Marriage," 19.

[50] Josephus, *Jewish War* 2.124: "They are not in one town only, but in every town several of them form a colony." Similarly Philo says that "they live in a number of towns in Judaea, and also in many villages and large groups" (Philo, *Hypothetica*, in Eusebius, *Praeparatio Evangelica* 8.6–7).

[51] This has been suggested orally by Michael O. Wise.

[52] So A. Dupont-Sommer, *The Essene Writings from Qumran* (Gloucester, MA: Smith, 1973) 306.

[53] Newsom, "'Sectually Explicit' Literature," 177.

[54] H. Stegemann, "Die Bedeutung der Qumranfunde für die Erforschung der Apokalyptik," in D. Hellholm, ed., *Apocalypticism in the Mediterranean World and the Near East* (Tübingen: Mohr-Siebeck, 1983) 511.

[55] M. Baillet, *Qumrân Grotte 4:3 (4Q482–4Q520)* (Discoveries in the Judaean Desert 7; Oxford: Clarendon, 1982) 81–105; cf. J. M. Baumgarten, "4Q502, Marriage or Golden Age Ritual?" *Journal of Jewish Studies* 34(1983) 125–35.

[56] The extent of this "bi-messianism" in the Scrolls has been much disputed. We will return to it in a later chapter.

[57] A point noted by Morton Smith, "What is Implied by the Variety of Messianic Figures?" *Journal of Biblical Literature* 78(1959) 66–72.

[58] F. Hesse, "*Chrio*, etc." G. Friedrich, ed., *Theological Dictionary of the New Testament* (Grand Rapids: Eerdmans, 1974) 9.501–9. Gerbern S. Oegema, *Der Gesalbte und sein Volk* (Göttingen: Vandenhoeck & Ruprecht, 1994) 26, lists several definitions of messiah that have been proposed.

[59] Schuerer, *The History of the Jewish People*, 2.506; J. Klausner, *The Messianic Idea in Israel* (London: Allen and Unwin, 1956) 325–29.

[59a] Compare F. García Martínez, "Messianische Erwartungen in den Qumranschriften," *Jahrbuch für Biblische Theologie* 8(1993) 171–208.

[60] Compare the remarks of Geza Vermes, *Jesus the Jew* (Philadelphia: Fortress, 1973) 134. Sanders's notion of common Judaism is spelled out in his book, *Judaism, Practice and Belief*.

[61] See R. A. Horsley and J. S. Hanson, *Bandits, Prophets, and Messiahs. Popular Movements at the Time of Jesus* (Minneapolis: Winston, 1985) 110–31.

[62] The letters of Bar Kosiba throw only a little light on his aims and self-understanding. See M. O. Wise, "Bar Kochba Letters," *The Anchor Bible Dictionary* 1.601–6.

[63] S. Mowinckel, *He That Cometh. The Messiah Concept in the Old Testament and in Later Judaism* (Nashville: Abingdon, 1955) 449–50.

[64] See A. J. B. Higgins, "Jewish Messianic Belief in Justin Martyr's Dialogue with Trypho," in Leo Landman, ed., *Messianism in the Talmudic Era* (New York: Ktav, 1979) 183.

2

THE FALLEN BOOTH OF DAVID:

MESSIANISM AND THE HEBREW BIBLE

▣ *The Emergence of a Canon*

Ancient Judaism did not have a creed that defined orthodoxy, in the manner of later Christianity. The reason that some notions, such as the expectation of a Davidic messiah, were widely shared, was that by this time (approximately 150 BCE to 70 CE) a corpus of scriptures had come to be accepted as authoritative in Judaism. Eventually, these scriptures took the form of the canonical Hebrew Bible that we know today. Whether one may properly speak of a canon in the period before 70 CE, however, is a matter of dispute.

There have been wide swings in the pendulum of scholarship on this subject. For a long time, the canon of Scripture was thought to have been closed at the so-called Council of Jamnia, about 90 CE.[1] This hypothesis now generally has been abandoned.[2] The deliberations of the sages at Jamnia did not constitute a council in the manner of the later church councils, and it is not apparent that any final decisions were reached about the canonical status of books. Some scholars have reacted to the demise of the Jamnia hypothesis by pushing back the closure to the second century BCE. Sid Leiman, in his book *The Canonization of Hebrew Scripture*, argued that the process was completed by Judas Maccabee. This position, however, is indefensible. The putative evidence, 2 Macc 2:14–15, says only that Judah collected all the books that had been lost on account of the war. It makes no claim that he canonized anything, or in any way set a limit to the number of sacred books.[3] In fact, a specific number of authoritative scriptures is not attested until the period after 70 CE, when Josephus (*Against Apion* 1.7) gives the number of sacred books as twenty-two and *4 Ezra* 14:45 gives it as twenty-four, probably counting the same books in a different way.[4]

The Dead Sea Scrolls provide ample evidence that the canon had not been closed around the turn of the era. Books such as *Enoch* and *Jubilees* are preserved in multiple copies and were evidently authoritative.[5] *Jubilees* is cited as a source in the Damascus Document (CD 16:4). In contrast, Chronicles is barely attested and Esther is absent from the library.[6] Some biblical books (notably Samuel and Jeremiah) circulated in widely different textual forms, and this also tells against the idea that the canon was closed.

There is also abundant evidence, however, that some writings were already established as authoritative, even if their text was fluid and the extent of the authoritative scriptures was uncertain. Most of our witnesses through the New Testament period attest a bipartite rather than a tripartite division of the scriptures: so Matt 5:17; 7:12; 11:13; 16:16; 22:40; Luke 16:29–31; Acts 13:15; 24:14; 28:23; Rom 3:21. The normal reference is to "The Law and the Prophets."[7] Luke 24:44 is exceptional in the New Testament in referring to "the law of Moses, the prophets and the psalms."[8] A similar division seems to be implied in 4QMMT, the Halakhic Letter from Qumran: "For on account of [these things] we have [written] for you that you may perceive in the book of Moses [and in the words of the pro]phets and in Davi[d . . .] from generation to generation." David was regarded as a prophet (Acts 2:30), and the psalms were interpreted by the *pesher* method at Qumran, just as the prophets were, and taken as prophecies of the history of the sect or of the eschatological time. The Qumran Community Rule begins with a reference to what God has commanded "by the hand of Moses and all His servants the Prophets." The path that the covenanters are to prepare in the wilderness is "the study of the Law which He commanded by the hand of Moses . . . and as the Prophets have revealed by His Holy Spirit." (1QS 8). At no point is there a clear line of demarcation between the Prophets and the books that later became known as the Writings, but it is clear that there was a corpus of authoritative scriptures.

There is no doubting the importance of the revealed Torah at

Qumran. In a passage known as the "Well midrash," the Damascus Document explains Num 21:18 as follows: "the Well is the Law, and those who dug it were the converts of Israel who went out of the land of Israel to sojourn in the land of Damascus.... The Stave is the Interpreter of the Law...."[9] Similarly, the Community Rule instructs the sectarians to prepare in the wilderness the way of the Lord, and specifies that "this is the study of the Law which He commanded by the hand of Moses."[10] It is amply clear that the major sectarian rule books regard the law of Moses as the fundamental norm. Some people have argued that the Temple Scroll had the status of Scripture, and that it was in effect a new Torah, but there is no evidence that it ever replaced the traditional Torah in authority.[11]

While the Qumran sect accepted some authoritative writings that were not accepted elsewhere, they also shared with all contemporary Jews a set of scriptures that included the Torah, prophetic writings and psalms. This common heritage is of enormous importance as a source of common traditions. To be sure, the sectarians had their own distinctive way of interpreting these scriptures, as is immediately evident from the *pesharîm*, the biblical commentaries that correlate the prophecies with the experiences and expectations of the sect. Nonetheless, it would be surprising if they did not also pick up some common exegetical traditions and as we shall see, these exegetical traditions are of fundamental importance for the formulation of messianic expectations.

The Royal Ideology

The Hebrew Scriptures provided a clear basis for the expectation of a royal messiah from the line of David, in passages that reflect the royal ideology of ancient Israel.[12] The classic formulation of this ideology is found in Nathan's oracle in 2 Samuel 7:

> "Moreover the Lord declares to you that the Lord will make you a house. When your days are fulfilled and you lie down with your ancestors, I will raise up your offspring after you, who shall come forth from your body, and I will establish his kingdom. He shall build a house for my name, and I will establish the throne of his kingdom forever. I will be a father to him, and he shall be a son to me. When he commits iniquity, I will punish him with a rod such as mortals use,

with blows inflicted by human beings. But I will not take my steadfast love from him, as I took it from Saul, whom I put away from
before you. Your house and your kingdom shall be made sure forever before me; your throne shall be established forever" (2 Sam
7:11–17).

The emphasis in this oracle is on the permanence of the Davidic line,
not on an individual king.[13] The permanence is guaranteed by divine
grant, and reflects the language of royal grants to faithful vassals in the
ancient Near East.[14] The king becomes the son of God by adoption but
the paternity of the human father is also essential to the ideology.
Nonetheless, the oracle reflects the common assumption throughout the
Near East that the king enjoys special status in the divine world. The
election of David is celebrated in generally similar terms in Psalms 89
and 132.[15]

The mythological aspects of the royal ideology emerge more clearly
in some other psalms and prophetic oracles. Psalm 2, which refers to the
king as the Lord's anointed (משיח) also tells of the decree of the Lord:
"You are my son; today I have begotten you. Ask of me, and I will make
the nations your heritage, and the ends of the earth your possession. You
shall break them with a rod of iron, and dash them in pieces like a potter's vessel." Ps 110:3, while textually difficult, probably also refers to the
divine birth of the king.[16] In the same psalm, God bids the king sit at his
right hand, and tells him that he is a priest forever according to the order
of Melchizedek. Isa 8:23–9:6 announces the birth of a royal child, who
is named "Wonderful Counselor, Mighty God, Everlasting Father,
Prince of Peace." These three texts (Psalms 2, 110, Isaiah 9) have all
been plausibly related to enthronement ceremonies in ancient Judah.[17]
The Israelite king was never identified with a deity in as full a sense,
unlike his counterpart in Egypt. Scholars generally assume that even
a passage like Psalm 2 should be understood in terms of adoption, like
2 Samuel 7. Nonetheless, the mythological claims should not be disre-
garded. In Psalm 45 the king is addressed as אלהים, "God:" "Your throne,
O God, endures forever and ever.... Therefore God, your God, has
anointed you...." Such direct address is exceptional (Psalm 45 is the
only hymn to the king in the Psalter) but it accords well with the designation of the king as son of God in Psalm 2.[18] While the king was not to
be confused with the Almighty, he was evidently exalted above the common rank of humanity.[19]

Predictions of an Ideal King

The passages we have considered thus far all have viewed the kingship, however idealized, as a present reality. Only later, when the monarchy no longer existed, would they be understood in an eschatological sense, as predictions of a future restoration. There are, however, also several passages in the Hebrew Scriptures that were originally written to predict an ideal ruler who is to come in the future. Some of these prophecies are clearly *ex eventu*, or after the fact. Two of the most influential texts in later tradition are of this type. Balaam's oracle, in Num 24:15–19, predicts that "a star shall come out of Jacob, and a scepter shall rise out of Israel; it shall crush the borderlands of Moab, and the territory of all the Shethites." This text has rightly been attributed to the early monarchy, and taken as a celebration of the victories of one of the early kings.[20] The promise in the "Blessing of Jacob" (Genesis 49), that "The scepter shall not depart from Judah nor the ruler's staff from between his feet," also surely presupposes the rise of the Davidic dynasty. *Ex eventu* predictions of this sort were a form of royal propaganda: the right of the king to rule was guaranteed by the promise of the deity. This device, of prophecy after the fact in the service of propaganda, is also found in ancient Babylon.[21] Like the biblical predictions, the Babylonian oracles can also envisage universal, everlasting rule. As an example we may cite a prophecy from Uruk, from the sixth century BCE, which says of a "good" king that "After him his son will arise as king in Uruk and rule the entire world. He will exercise authority and kingship in Uruk, and his dynasty will stand forever. The kings of Uruk will exercise authority like gods." The king in question, who would inaugurate this dynasty, appears to be none other than Nebuchadnezzar II, the king who destroyed Jerusalem and took its people into exile.[22]

A more difficult problem is presented by the predictions of a future ruler in the books attributed to the eighth-century prophets. The conclusion of the book of Amos, which promises to "raise up the booth of David that is fallen," (Amos 9:11) contrasts so sharply with the prophet's message of doom and destruction that we must suspect an editorial addition, after the southern kingdom had actually fallen.[23] Micah 5:2–5, which speaks of a ruler from Bethlehem of Ephrathah, David's hometown, is also commonly regarded as postexilic.[24] The authenticity of Isa 11:1–9 ("A shoot shall come out of the stump of Jesse") is also widely disputed.[25] The reference to the "stump" of Jesse naturally leads one to suppose that the line had been cut off when this oracle was composed. It is possible, however, that the oracle reflects the distress of the Assyrian invasions at the end of the eighth century BCE and expresses a longing for the golden days of the Davidic empire.[26] In that case, these prophecies "suggest a new David is needed and thus imply a serious criticism of the current occupant of the Davidic throne as less than an adequate heir to David."[27] Throughout the ancient Near East, the ideal king was envisaged as a shepherd, who would rule with wisdom and righteousness. The hope for such an ideal king was not necessarily confined to situations where there is no king at all. Whether or not Isaiah 11 comes from the time of the monarchy, we will find that messianic expectation could imply dissatisfaction with actual Jewish kings in the Hellenistic and Roman periods. It is possible that the dream of a utopian monarchy had arisen in Israel before the Babylonian Exile, but in any case that hope emerges much more clearly in the postexilic period. Isaiah 11 becomes an important proof-text for messianic expectation in the period of the Dead Sea Scrolls.

A similar uncertainty surrounds the messianic oracles in the books of Jeremiah and Ezekiel. Jer 23:5–6 rivals Isaiah 11 in its importance for later messianic expectation:

> "The days are surely coming, says the Lord, when I will raise up for David a righteous Branch,[28] and he shall reign as king and deal wisely, and shall execute justice and righteousness in the land. In his days, Judah will be saved and Israel will live in safety. And this is the name by which he will be called: 'The Lord is our righteousness.'"

Again, the authenticity of the passage is open to question. It stands in stark contrast to Jer 22:30, which declares emphatically that no offspring of Jehoiakin would succeed in sitting on the throne of David and ruling again in Judah, and so, in effect, that the Davidic line was terminated. The introductory formula ("the days are surely coming . . .") also gives rise to suspicion that what follows is a redactional insertion. Such formulae ("on that day," "a day is coming") often introduce editorial expansions in the prophetic books.[29] Yet it is also possible to argue for authenticity here. This passage concludes with a play on the name of Zedekiah ("Righteousness of Yahweh"), the last king of Judah (597–587 BCE), and can be read as a rejection of that monarch: Zedekiah has failed to live up to his name, so God will send a new king who will implement righteousness in the land.[30] In that case, it might be appropriate in the mouth of Jeremiah, despite the inconsistency with chapter 22. The

metaphor of the "branch" (צמח) is similar to the shoot (חטר, נצר) of Isa
11:1, but not necessarily derived from it. The motif was not peculiar to
Israel. The Assyrian king Esarhaddon was called "a precious branch of
Baltil...an enduring shoot."[31] The expression צמח צדק (legitimate
branch) appears in a Phoenician inscription of the third century BCE.[32]
The image of a branch with reference to royalty must be regarded as a
common Near Eastern motif.

While Jer 23:5–6 may have originated in criticism of Zedekiah, the
original context was soon lost from view. Already within the book of Jeremiah we find an exegetical transformation of the prophecy.[33] In Jer
33:14–16 we find virtually the same oracle, but with an insertion. Where
chapter 23 reads "I shall raise up for David·a righteous branch...,"
chapter 33 reads "I shall establish the good word which I proclaimed to
the House of Judaea and Israel. In those days and at that time I shall
cause to sprout for David a righteous branch...." This passage is not
found in the Greek text of Jeremiah and is almost certainly a late addition to the book.[34] The insertion shows a concern with the nonfulfillment
of prophecy. This concern that the word of the Lord not go unfulfilled is
increasingly prominent in the postexilic period.[35] At the same time, the
revised prophecy is still not overly specific: it will come to pass "in those
days and at that time." It would be difficult ever to say that the prophecy
had failed.

The concern for the fulfillment of prophecy is also evident in the passage that follows:

> "For thus says the Lord: David shall never lack a man to sit on the
> throne of the house of Israel, and the levitical priests shall never lack
> a man in my presence to offer burnt offerings, to make grain offer-
> ings, and to make sacrifices for all time.... If any of you could break
> my covenant with the day and my covenant with the night, so that
> day and night would not come at their appointed time, only then
> could my covenant with my servant David be broken, so that he
> would not have a son to reign on his throne, and my covenant with
> my ministers the Levites ..." (Jer 33:17–22).

The prophecy affirms the reliability of the divine promise. The covenant
with David cannot be broken, and neither can the covenant with Levi.
(Compare Mal 2:5). The passage implicitly recognizes that the promises
have not been fulfilled in any satisfactory way as yet. It has been argued
that such a passage could only have been written during the exile, before

the restoration of the High Priesthood[36] but this is not necessarily so. We know of various groups in the Second Temple period who found the restored temple cult unsatisfactory.[37] The concern for both kingship and priesthood points rather to the situation after the exile, when the prophet Zechariah hailed Zerubbabel and the High Priest Joshua as "two sons of oil."[38] What is important for our present purpose, however, is the light this passage sheds on one factor that contributed to messianic speculation. The promises must be fulfilled. If they are not seen to be fulfilled in the past or present, the fulfillment must be projected into the future.

The imagery of a young tree underlies the Isaianic passage about the shoot of David and Jeremiah's branch of David. This imagery is also found in Ezekiel. In Ezek 17:3–4, the Davidic king is "the crown of a cedar, its topmost shoot, (ראש יניקותיו)" which an eagle, representing the king of Babylon, carried off. The Lord promises, however, in 17:22–23: "I will take of the lofty crown of a cedar and put it; of its topmost shoots I will pluck a tender one; and I will plant—on a high and towering mountain in the mountainous heights of Israel I will plant it. It will bear branches and produce fruit and become a noble cedar."[39] The more typical Ezekielian designation for the future king, however, is the term "prince" (נשיא). So in Ezek 34:23–24 we read:

> "I will set up over them one shepherd, my servant David, and he shall feed them: he shall feed them and be their shepherd. And I, the Lord, will be their God, and my servant David shall be prince among them."

Again in Ezekiel 37, the restoration of the "dry bones" of Israel concludes with the promise that "my servant David" will be "king" and "prince" (Ezek 37:24, 25).

The term "prince" is used extensively in the Priestly strand of the Pentateuch to refer to the lay leaders of the tribes.[40] Martin Noth argued that it was an amphictyonic term from the period of the judges,[41] but the whole hypothesis, that Israel had been organized in the form of an amphictyony in that period, has now been widely rejected.[42] The antiquity of the term need not concern us here. It may suffice to note that the term is not inherently monarchic. It is, however, used repeatedly in Ezekiel for the Davidic ruler.[43] In Ezekiel 34 and 37, in the predictions of a future ruler, the term "prince" clearly designates royal rank, and refers to a member of the Davidic line, granted that Ezekiel envisaged a chastened monarchy, shorn of much of the traditional royal ideology.[44]

The term "prince" is used repeatedly for the lay leader of the restored Israel in Ezekiel 40–48, chapters that often are thought to be an appendage to the book.[45] The royal status is not explicit in these chapters, which emphasize rather the prince's role in supporting the cult.[46] Nonetheless, there is no good reason to suppose that the understanding of the prince in these chapters is fundamentally different from what we find in Ezekiel 1–37.[47] The point is rather that the role of the king is overshadowed by the interest in the temple and the sacrifices. In this respect, Ezekiel 40–48 anticipates some aspects of what we will find in the Dead Sea Scrolls, where נשיא, prince, is also a prominent messianic term. It is of interest to note that the first Jewish governor after the exile, Sheshbazzar, is also called a נשיא (Ezra 1:8).

A Gentile "Messiah"

Not every prophet of the exilic period dreamed of a branch of David. The anonymous prophet whom we know as Second Isaiah transferred the promises to David to the whole Jewish people: "I will make with you an everlasting covenant, my steadfast, sure love for David. See, I made him a witness to the peoples, a leader and commander for the peoples. See, you shall call nations that you do not know, and nations that do not know you shall run to you" (Isa 55:3–4).[48] For Second Isaiah, Israel is the servant of the Lord, the light to the nations (Isa 49:1–6).[49] The prophet who celebrated the deliverance of Israel by the Persians had no role for a Davidic king.[50]

He did, however, have a role for an "anointed of the Lord." The משיח in question was Cyrus, king of Persia: "Thus says the Lord to his anointed, to Cyrus, whose right hand I have grasped to subdue nations before him . . ." (Isa 45:1).[51] Cyrus is also called "my shepherd," a traditional metaphor for king, which has a future, messianic nuance in Ezek 34:23 ("I will set up over them one shepherd, my servant David").[52] Cyrus is, then, portrayed in terms reminiscent of the Israelite royal ideology. He is not, however, depicted as the heir to the Davidic promises. In the words of Antti Laato, "Isa 40–55 does not place all of its messianic hopes upon Cyrus."[53] The Jewish people were, or rather the faithful remnant was, heir to the covenant with David. Nonetheless, Cyrus was accorded a crucial role in the Jewish restoration. This fact may be attributed to the political realities of the time. It was Cyrus who allowed and enabled the Jewish exiles to return to their homeland when he conquered Babylon in 539 BCE.

Cyrus was not the only Gentile king chosen by Yahweh, according to the prophets of the exilic period. Jeremiah 27:6 designates Nebuchadnezzar of Babylon, destroyer of Jerusalem, as "my servant," and decrees that all nations should serve him.[54] This passage, too, is shaped by political realism. Nebuchadnezzar in fact enjoyed sovereignty over the entire Near East. Cyrus, however, has a more positive role: "he shall build my city and set my exiles free . . ." (Isa 45:13). He is cast as the deliverer of Israel. This role is exceptional for a Gentile monarch and is remarkable both for its confidence in the benevolence of the Persian king and for its acceptance of Jewish dependence on a foreign power. We shall find a similar example of hopes placed in a Gentile king, in the Hellenistic Diaspora, on the testimony of the *Sibylline Oracles*.

A *Messianic Movement in the Persian Period?*

The image of the branch appears again in the book of Zechariah. In this case we have a far clearer view of the context than was the case with the texts from Jeremiah. Haggai and Zechariah were active in Jerusalem about 520 BCE, and were instrumental in the building of the Second Temple. There was a period of instability in the Persian empire between the death of Cambyses in 522 BCE and the consolidation of power by Darius I, and there were a number of uprisings, notably one by a royal pretender, Nebuchadnezzar IV, in Babylon. The atmosphere of unrest is captured at the end of the book of Haggai, in an oracle addressed to Zerubbabel, governor of Judah:

> "I am about to shake the heavens and the earth, and to overthrow the throne of kingdoms; I am about to destroy the strength of the kingdoms of the nations. . . . On that day, says the Lord of hosts, I will take you, O Zerubbabel my servant, son of Shealtiel, says the Lord, and make you like a signet ring; for I have chosen you, says the Lord of hosts" (Hag 2:21–24).

Zerubbabel ("offspring of Babylon" or "seed of Babylon") was of Davidic descent, being a grandson of King Jehoiachin (1 Chron 3:16–19).[55] The reference to the signet ring suggests that he would be the Lord's authorized representative.[56] The analogy of a signet ring is used with reference to King Jehoiachin in Jer 22:24–30. The chosenness of Zerubbabel surely implied for Haggai the imminent restoration of the Davidic monarchy.[57] His enthronement would follow the overthrow of the Gentile kingdoms, and so usher in a new age.

Zerubbabel also figures prominently in the prophecies of Zechariah. He is given a key role in the rebuilding of the temple, and told that before him a mountain will become a plain (4:7). Zechariah also reassures the High Priest Joshua by promising that "I am going to bring my servant the Branch" (3:8). The term Branch (צמח) is an allusion to Jeremiah's prophecy and must be understood as messianic, in the sense that it implies the restoration of the Davidic line. In Zechariah's time, the hopes for such restoration rested with Zerubbabel.[58] The objection that he was a Persian appointee, and that a return of the kingship was unlikely under Persian rule,[59] is beside the point. The text does not speak for Zerubbabel, but for a prophet who was a visionary, not a political realist. There is, of course, no evidence that Zerubbabel ever played the role for which Haggai and Zechariah cast him, but the prophetic texts attest to hopes that can reasonably be called messianic. They would entail the fulfillment of the promise to David and the dawn of a new, utopian age.

Zerubbabel and the High Priest Joshua are the "two sons of oil" represented by two shoots of olive trees in 4:12.[60] A further reference in chapter 6 is problematic. The prophet is told: "Take the silver and gold and make a crown and set it on the head of Joshua son of Jehozadak; say to him: Thus says the Lord of hosts: Here is a man whose name is Branch: for he shall branch out in his place, and he shall build the temple of the Lord" (6:11–12). The passage continues "There shall be a priest by his throne with peaceful understanding between the two of them." The Branch, then, is not a priest, and cannot be identified with Joshua, despite the latter's coronation in vs. 11. Here again there can be no doubt that he should be identified with Zerubbabel, the heir to the Davidic line. In fact, the MT of 6:12 reads the plural "crowns" (עטרות); the versions read the singular (עטרת). If the MT is correct, then presumably crowns were envisaged for both Joshua and Zerubbabel.[61] If a single crown was original, it must have been meant for Zerubbabel.[62] Either the text suffered corruption, or, more plausibly, an editor excised the coronation of Zerubbabel because of its revolutionary implications.[63] There is good reason, then, to hold that Haggai and Zechariah regarded Zerubbabel as a messianic figure.

Despite the relatively high number of texts that could be interpreted in a messianic sense, only very rarely do we find an actual historical figure in whom such hopes are invested. Cyrus of Persia is called "his anointed" (משיחו) in Isa 45:1. While he obviously was not thought to restore the Davidic kingship, he was regarded as an agent of deliverance for the Jewish people. Zerubbabel is the only potential Jewish messiah of whom we hear in the Persian period. For another Jewish figure for whom messianic status is claimed we have to come all the way down to the Roman era.

The prophecies of Zechariah are notable in another respect, however. They speak of two "sons of oil," and envisage a dual leadership of priest and king. This qualification of the monarchy was not without precedent. Deut 17:18 clearly specifies that the king should have a copy of the Law "written for him in the presence of the levitical priests," implying that he is bound by the priests' interpretation. Jer 33:14–26 reaffirms not only the covenant with David but also "my covenant with my ministers the Levites" (33:21).[64] The Zadokite priests are as prominent as the prince in Ezekiel 40–48. Zechariah's formulation, however, is determined not so much by scriptural precedent as by the social structure of the early postexilic community, in which the High Priest was no less important than the governor. In fact, the prominence of the priesthood was more enduring than that of the Davidic line in the Second Temple period. As we have noted, the two anointed offices appear to be collapsed into one in Zech 6:12. For most of the postexilic period, with exceptions in the times of Ezra and Nehemiah, the High Priest was sole leader in Judah.[65]

▨ *The Absence of Messianism in the Second Temple Period*

After the time of Zerubbabel, messianism does not figure prominently in Second Temple Judaism. A few passages in Zechariah 9–14 require comment. The first is Zechariah 9:9–10:

"Rejoice greatly, O daughter Zion! Shout aloud, O daughter Jerusalem!
Lo, your king comes to you; triumphant and victorious is he,
humble and riding on a donkey, on a colt, the foal of a donkey.
He will cut off the chariot from Ephraim and the war horse from Jerusalem;
and the battle bow shall be cut off, and he shall command peace to the nations;

his dominion shall be from sea to sea, and from the River to the
ends of the earth."

As in many of the passages we have considered, the kingship here is
chastened and is, in some respects, a throwback to the period of the
Judges.[66] The proclamation of peace and destruction of the weapons of
war recall Isa 2:1–4; 11:1–9; Mic 5:2–5, etc. Nonetheless, the royal status of this figure is explicit, and he is given universal rule from sea to sea.

The provenance of this oracle is quite uncertain. Zechariah 9 is often
related to the campaign of Alexander the Great in 333 BCE.[67] This dating
is influenced by Zech 9:13: "I will arouse your sons, O Zion, against your
sons, O Greece." This reading, however, is suspect on textual grounds.
It appears intrusive on grounds of meter and parallelism, and it can easily be explained as resulting from dittography.[68] While these arguments
are not conclusive, they raise some doubt about the Greek dating.
Roberts has argued that the oracle contains a number of elements that
strongly suggest an original eighth-century context.[69] If the reference to
Greece is original, the oracle could still be either earlier or later than
Alexander.[69a] Greeks were active along the Syrian-Palestinian coast
throughout the Persian period. We know virtually nothing of the Jewish reaction to Alexander[70] and have no independent indication of any
messianic sentiment at that time. If the reference to Greece is not original, it should still not be dismissed simply a mistake. However it was introduced, the reference made very good sense in the Hellenistic period,
when the Greeks became the dominant power in the area.[71] We may have
here a case of an old oracle updated to fit new circumstances.

There may also be a reflection of messianic hope in Zechariah 11–13.
These oracles are extremely obscure, and there is no consensus about
their historical setting. Zech 12:8, however, looks forward to a time when
the house of David will be like a god (אלהים) and like an angel of the Lord,
and Zech 13:1 speaks of a day when "there shall be a fountain opened
for the house of David to cleanse them from sin and uncleanness." Much
of the material in these chapters indicates dissatisfaction with the "shepherds," who were evidently the rulers of the day, whether priestly or
lay.[72] The passage speaks of the house of David in conjunction with the
inhabitants of Jerusalem, in a way that suggests that it was in existence
and in need of purification. If the reference here is to the royal line, this
would probably require a date early in the Persian period, as we have no
record of the Davidic line thereafter. The text stops short of speaking explicitly of a restoration of the kingship.

A particularly intriguing statement is found in Zech 12:10:

"And I will pour out on the house of David and the inhabitants of Jerusalem a spirit of compassion and supplication, so that, when they look on him whom they have pierced, they shall mourn for him, as one mourns for an only child, and weep bitterly over him, as one weeps over a firstborn."

The "one whom they have pierced" has been identified with a range of historical figures from Josiah to Simon Maccabee.[73] More probably, it refers to some incident that is no longer known to us, near the time of composition.[74] Inevitably, it has also been interpreted in a messianic sense. So some scholars find in this passage "a martyrdom of the eschatological good shepherd or Davidic king."[75] There is nothing in the text, however, to confirm that the one who was pierced was a king. Since there is no parallel for such a notion of messianic martyrdom in Second Temple Judaism, it seems unwise to derive it from such a cryptic and controversial text as Zech 12:10.

In all, then, we have very little evidence of messianism in Judaism in the period 500–200 BCE, but our evidence for Judaism in this period is scanty in any case.

We have much fuller documentation for the period 200–150 BCE. One indication of popular Jewish beliefs at the beginning of the second century BCE is provided by the book of Sirach. Sirach wrote before the Maccabean revolt, and has little interest in eschatology of any sort. The prayer for divine intervention in Sir 36:1–17 is so different in tone from the rest of the book that its authenticity must be questioned. Yet even here there is no reference to a messiah. Ben Sira praises David at some length (47:1–11) but does not use the occasion to speak of the restoration of his line. The statement that God exalted his horn forever (47:11) does not necessarily imply that the dynasty will last forever. In 49:4–5 Sirach states that the "horn" of the Davidic kings was given to others because all but three were sinful. Only in the Hebrew psalm inserted in chapter 51, between vss. 12 and 13 do we find the hope for the restoration of the Davidic line (line h: "Give thanks to him who makes a horn to sprout for the house of David"), but this psalm is almost certainly a later addition and of uncertain provenance. For Sirach, the glory of David belongs to the past. Moreover, Sir 45:25 contrasts the Davidic covenant with that of Aaron and suggests that it is inferior in some respects. The covenant with Aaron is elaborated at greater length than that of David (45:6–22). There is no doubt that Sirach viewed the High Priest Simon as the main mediator of God's blessing in his own time (50:1–21). The sage's lack of interest in Davidic messianism is a consequence of his satisfaction with the priestly theocratic regime.

The early second century was a period of great upheaval, which gave rise to what Martin Hengel has called "the first climax of Jewish apocalyptic."[76] Messianic expectation, however, in the sense of hope for the restoration of the Davidic line, is conspicuously absent in the early apocalypses. The *Animal Apocalypse* in *1 Enoch* 85–90 is exceptional among the apocalypses in its apparent support for the armed rebellion of the Maccabees. (Judas Maccabee is allegorized as a ram with "a big horn.") It also envisages some kind of leader in the eschatological period, but the precise kind of leader is obscure because of the allegorical language. After the enemies of the "sheep" have been defeated, and a large house has been built, the visionary continues: "I saw how a white bull was born, and its horns were big, and all the wild animals and all the birds of heaven were afraid of it and entreated it continually" (*1 Enoch* 90:37). It has been suggested that this "bull" is a Davidic messiah, on the grounds that "his person and those of the remiss angelic shepherds of God's flock in *1 Enoch* 89:59–90:25 are derived from Ezekiel 34, where 'David' will rule over the Chosen People after God delivers them from evil."[77] This is too simple, however. The imagery of the *Animal Apocalypse* is not simply derived from Ezekiel 34, or any one source.[78] In *1 Enoch* 85, Adam and the antediluvian patriarchs are represented as white bulls.[79] All that is said of the "bull" in 90:37 is that all the wild animals and birds were afraid of it and entreated it. It is not clear that it represents a king. In fact, all the sheep are transformed into white bulls in *1 Enoch* 90:38. Moreover, this "bull" is not the agent of salvation. That role is filled by Judas Maccabee ("that ram," 90:13), with angelic and divine assistance.[80] There is, then, little role for a messiah in this apocalypse.

The Transformation of Messianism in Daniel

The term מָשִׁיחַ occurs twice in the book of Daniel. In Daniel 9, Jeremiah's prediction of seventy years of desolation is reinterpreted as seventy weeks of years. The first seven weeks end with the advent of "an anointed ruler" (מָשִׁיחַ נָגִיד). The reference is most probably to Joshua the postexilic High Priest, who was one of the two "sons of oil" in Zechariah. Then, after sixty-two weeks, "the anointed one will be cut off" (9:26).

Modern critics generally recognize here a reference to the murder of the High Priest Onias III about 171 BCE, which is recorded in 2 Macc 4:23–28. There is a long line of traditional exegesis that reads both Dan 9:25 and 26 in terms of an eschatological messiah. For traditional Christian exegesis, the anointed one who was cut off was obviously Christ.[81] The original reference, however, was neither to a king nor to a savior figure at all, but to a High Priest. Daniel accepted the theocratic organization of the postexilic community, as surely as did Ben Sira.

Unlike Ben Sira, however, Daniel is greatly concerned with future deliverance, and "kingdom" is one of the central symbols that runs through the book. The book in its canonical form dates from the time of the Maccabean rebellion (168–64 BCE), but chapters 2–6 preserve older Aramaic stories that have their roots in the eastern Diaspora. In chapter 2, Daniel interprets Nebuchadnezzar's famous dream of a statue with a head of gold, breast and arms of silver, loins and thighs of bronze, legs of iron and feet of iron and clay, which is destroyed by a stone that strikes its feet. Daniel interprets the metals in terms of a succession of four kingdoms, which must be interpreted, in the context of the book, as Babylon, Media, Persia, and Greece. The stone that destroys the statue is interpreted by the statement that "in those days the God of heaven will set up a kingdom which will never be destroyed," and which will bring all previous kingdoms to an end.[82]

The schema of four kingdoms, followed by a fifth of definitive character, is well known from Roman historiography.[83] The typical sequence is Assyria, Media, Persia, and Greece. Roman historians regarded Rome as the definitive, fifth, kingdom. Many scholars have argued, however, that the schema did not originate in Rome, but in the Near East, and that it expressed Near Eastern resistance to Hellenism.[84] The fourth kingdom, Greece, is not the last. The schema implies that it will be overthrown, and so carries at least an implicit polemic against Hellenism. The main evidence for this anti-Hellenistic usage is Jewish. Daniel 2 is no later than the early second century BCE and shows no Roman influence. The *Fourth Sibylline Oracle* also preserves a four-kingdoms sequence, ending with Greece.[85] A Persian oracle, the *Bahman Yasht*, has four periods, symbolized by metals, of which the fourth is "the evil sovereignty of the 'divs' having dishevelled hair," probably a reference to the Greeks, and has been taken as evidence of widespread resistance to Hellenism in the Near East.[86]

Daniel 2, however, is not revolutionary. In fact, it is remarkable for its lack of emphasis on the eschatological motif. The primary emphasis falls on Daniel's ability to tell and interpret the king's dream, while the Chaldean wise men fail. The king reacts with admiration but pays no attention to the content of the interpretation, which might have been expected to cause him consternation. The reader is invited to consider the dream from the perspective of the king. To be sure, his kingdom will pass, but its destruction is not imminent. The irruption of the kingdom of God is still far in the future, in the time of a later kingdom. Eschatology is deferred.[87]

Daniel 2–6 make no allusion whatever to a future Jewish king. The Gentile rulers are not contrasted with a Davidic ideal, but with God. In Dan 3:33 Nebuchadnezzar praises the God of Daniel: "His kingdom is an everlasting kingdom, and his dominion is from generation to generation." The kingship of God is compatible with the reign of a human monarch. The Babylonian kings reign because God has given them the kingship. These tales, however, show no interest in the restoration of a native Jewish dynasty.

The four-kingdom schema is taken up again in Daniel 7, with much greater eschatological urgency, in a passage that would play a prominent part in later messianic expectation. This is Daniel's famous vision of "one like a son of man" who comes on the clouds of heaven (Dan 7:13). For much of Jewish and Christian history, this figure was interpreted as the messiah.[88] We will see in a later chapter that the earliest adaptations of this vision, in the *Similitudes of Enoch* and *4 Ezra* 13, use messianic language with reference to the "Son of Man" figure, even though he is a transcendent figure rather than an earthly king. Rabbi Akiba is said to have explained the plural "thrones" in Dan 7:9 as "one for Him, and one for David."[89] The messianic interpretation remained standard in both Jewish and Christian traditions down to the Enlightenment but is rarely defended in recent times.[90] There are, to be sure, elements in the vision that lend themselves to a messianic interpretation and provided the basis for the traditional understanding. The vision begins with four great beasts coming up out of the sea. These beasts are interpreted as kings or kingdoms. The human figure on the clouds in 7:13 is set over against the beasts. Their kingdoms are taken away, while he is given dominion and glory and kingship (7:14). It is natural enough, then, to infer that the figure on the clouds is the king of a restored Jewish kingdom. Moreover, the imagery of this vision, which sets the sea and its monsters over against a "rider of the clouds" and a white-headed "Ancient of Days," has old associations with kingship. The imagery is rooted in ancient Canaanite mythology, where a rebellious deity, Yamm (Sea), rises up against

Baal, the rider of the clouds and god of fertility and rain, while El, the High God, is a venerable white-headed figure.[91] The royal ideology of preexilic Israel derived much of its imagery from this Canaanite mythology. Psalm 89 celebrates Yahweh's rule over the raging of the sea, and also says of David, "I will set his hand on the sea and his right hand on the rivers." The "one like a son of man" in Daniel takes the place occupied by Baal in the Canaanite myth, and by the Davidic king in the mythology of preexilic Israel.[92]

Nonetheless, there is no clear reference in Daniel to the restoration of the Davidic line. Where the word משיח appears in chapter 9, the reference is to the anointed High Priest. The only savior figure, under God, in the book of Daniel, is the archangel Michael, the "prince" (שׂר) of Israel (Dan 12:1). The kingdom that is given to the "one like a son of man" in 7:13 is also given to the "holy ones of the Most High" (7:18). The holy ones, in the vast majority of instances in ancient Hebrew and Aramaic literature, are the heavenly host.[93] I have argued at length elsewhere that "the one like a son of man" is not a collective symbol for Israel, as many scholars hold, but should be identified as Michael, the leader of the heavenly host.[94] Even though Daniel anticipates that "the kingship and dominion and the greatness of the kingdoms under the whole heaven shall be given to the people of the holy ones of the Most High" (7:27), there is no unambiguous reference in the book to a restored Davidic king. The nature of the earthly kingdom remains vague. Daniel, like the early *Enoch* apocalypses, looks beyond this world to the triumph of Michael and the holy ones, and ultimately to the resurrection and exaltation of the righteous (Dan 12:1–3). There is no reason, then, to call the future kingdom messianic.

Rather than messianic expectation, then, what we have in Daniel is a transformation of the royal mythology. There is no role here for the Davidic king, and little for any human deliverer. The Maccabees are, at most, "a little help" (Dan 11:34). There is a deliverer under God, but he operates on the heavenly level: the fate of Israel is determined by the battle between Michael and the princes of Greece and Persia (Dan 10:20–21). This kind of transcendent, heavenly deliverer plays an increasingly important role in Jewish eschatology in the following centuries. It also provides a paradigm for messianic expectation that is quite different from the Davidic paradigm, although the two are sometimes combined. In this paradigm the "messiah" is a heavenly figure, more like an angel than a human being. This paradigm is developed in the *Similitudes of Enoch* and in the apocalypse of *4 Ezra* in the first century CE. It is a paradigm that would be crucially important for the Christian affirmation of Jesus as messiah, despite his evident failure to restore the earthly kingdom of Israel.

The Savior King in Egyptian Judaism

The literature of the Egyptian Diaspora in the Hellenistic period deals only rarely with political eschatology. An important exception, however, is found in the Jewish *Sibylline Oracles*, the earliest of which were most probably composed in Egypt in the middle of the second century BCE.[95] These *Oracles* are greatly concerned with the rise and fall of kingdoms, and refer repeatedly to a definitive change that was expected in the reign of "the young seventh king of Egypt . . . numbered from the line of the Greeks" (*Sib Or* 3:608–9, cf. vss. 193–94, 318). The king in question must be identified either as Ptolemy VI Philometor (180–164 and 163–145 BCE),[96] if Alexander the Great is counted as the first king, or Philometor's short-lived successor, Ptolemy VII Neos Philopator (145–144 BCE). Philometor's benevolence to the Jews is well known. When Onias IV, the legitimate heir to the Zadokite line and to the High Priesthood, fled from Jerusalem after the murder of his father, shortly before the outbreak of the Maccabean revolt, Philometor gave him permission to build a temple at Leontopolis. Josephus claims that Philometor set Onias and Dositheus over all his army,[97] and even if we allow for some exaggeration, it is clear that Onias enjoyed high rank.[98] Aristobulus, the Jewish philosopher, was allegedly the teacher of Philometor.[99] It is understandable, then, that some Jews, especially those who had fled from Jerusalem with Onias on the eve of the Maccabean revolt, would pin their hopes on a Ptolemaic king.

The references to the "seventh king" in *Sib Or* 3 say only that a great change will come in his reign and do not give a clear picture of the role the king will play. There is, however, one passage that ascribes a more active role to the king. Vss. 652–56 predict: "then God will send a king from the sun, who will stop the entire earth from evil war, killing some, imposing oaths of loyalty on others; and he will not do all these things by his private plans but in obedience to the noble teachings of the great God." Many scholars have assumed that the reference is to a Jewish messiah and translated it as "from the east," by analogy with Isa 41:25 (LXX) where the phrase is "from the rising of the sun."[100] In Isaiah, however, the reference is not to a Jewish messiah, but to Cyrus the Persian.

The Fallen Booth of David

There was no tradition that the messiah should come from the east, and in any case the phrase in the Sibyl is not "from the east" but "from the sun." In an Egyptian context a "king from the sun" evokes Egyptian mythology, where the pharaoh was understood as the son of the sun god Re.

In fact the same phrase, "a king from the sun," occurs in a nearly contemporary Egyptian oracle called *The Potter's Oracle*.[101] This oracle, which survives in Greek but was probably translated from Demotic, is attributed to a legendary figure, a potter in the reign of King Amenhotep (eighteenth dynasty, 1550–1300 BCE), who acts as the incarnation of the creator god Khnum. He predicts the destruction of "the city of the followers of the evil god Typhon-Seth," that is, Alexandria. Then "Egypt will prosper, when the king from the sun who is benign for fifty-five years comes, the giver of good things sent by the great goddess Isis, so that those who survive will pray that those who have already died may rise to share in the good things."

The Potter's Oracle belongs to a tradition of native Egyptian prophecy, which is also exemplified in the Demotic *Oracle of the Lamb to Bocchoris*, from the Persian period and in the *Demotic Chronicle* from the early Hellenistic era.[102] *The Potter's Oracle* is directed against the Ptolemies, and it looks for the restoration of native Egyptian kingship and the end of Greek rule. The old ideology of the pharaohs, however, was not the exclusive property of Egyptian nationalists in the Ptolemaic period. The Ptolemies also laid claim to the pharaonic titles.[103] These titles were translated into Greek under Ptolemy IV Philopator and were applied in abundance to Ptolemy V Epiphanes on the Rosetta Stone. Both these kings were called "son of the Sun." The Ptolemy of the day is also called "son of Re" in the texts inscribed at the temple of Edfu and identified as Horus.[104] A "king from the sun," then, was not necessarily a native Egyptian king. The title could equally well be applied to "a king of Egypt from the line of the Greeks." In view of the importance attached to the reign of the seventh king in *Sib Or* 3, it is very probable that the king expected by the Sibyl was a benevolent Ptolemy.

The Sibyl, then, resembles Deutero-Isaiah in endorsing a Gentile king as the agent of deliverance. The hopes of most Jews in the period 550–150 BCE were for a benevolent overlord who would protect and promote the Jewish people, rather than for national independence. This is the attitude we find in the court tales of Esther and Daniel 1–6.[105] It remained the norm in the Diaspora down to the late first century CE, when relations with the Roman authorities began to deteriorate, about the time of the revolt in Judea (66–70 CE).[106] In the land of Israel, however, circumstances were changed fundamentally by the Maccabean revolt and the rise of the Hasmoneans as a native Jewish dynasty.[107]

Conclusion

The absence of any messianic hope, in the sense of expectation of a Davidic restoration, in the early apocalypses is striking and undermines some common assumptions about the nature of messianism. It is natural enough to assume that the loss of native kingship underlies messianic hope, and in a sense this is inevitably true.[108] There are a few other instances from the Hellenistic Near East of the hope for restoration of a native king. The Babylonian "Dynastic Prophecy" predicts a succession of good and bad kings. The last column is badly preserved, but appears to deal negatively with the capture of Babylon by Seleucus I.[109] This would create a good setting for the restoration of native kingship, but unfortunately, the end of the prophecy is lost. There is better evidence for a quasi-messianic tradition in Egypt, exemplified in *The Potter's Oracle*. In Judea, however, we find no aspiration to restore the native kingship, even in the throes of the Maccabean revolt against the Seleucids. When messianic expectation reemerges, it is certainly nationalistic and emphasizes the overthrow of foreign power. But resistance to foreign power was not enough in itself to call forth messianism. As we shall see in the following chapters, the renewed interest in monarchy in the first century BCE was largely in reaction to the flawed restoration of Jewish kingship by the non-Davidic Hasmoneans.

It is often assumed that there was an unbroken tradition of Jewish messianism from the biblical period to postbiblical Judaism. Franz Hesse is typical of many when he writes, after admitting the difficulty of reconstructing a "messianic movement" in Israel and postexilic Judaism, "There undoubtedly must have been such a movement. This is shown by the examples given and may also be concluded from the fact that Messianism emerges into the clear light of history in later centuries, not merely as a trend that has just arisen in Judaism, but as a movement with hundreds of years of history behind it."[110] But the emergence of messianism in the first century BCE does not warrant any inference about a messianic movement at an earlier time. As we have seen, the evidence suggests that messianism was virtually dormant from the early fifth to the late second century BCE.[111]

The Fallen Booth of David

The older biblical texts, however, were very important for the resurgence of messianism in the Hasmonean era. The biblical texts provide a number of messianic paradigms, which informed the imagination of postbiblical Judaism and lent themselves to actualization in certain circumstances. No would-be messiah was motivated only, or primarily, by the desire to act out a textual paradigm. Political and especially social factors provided the obvious occasions of most of the messianic movements of the Roman era. But actions are also shaped by ideologies,[112] and in Judaism at the turn of the era the available ideologies were predominantly shaped by scriptural traditions.

NOTES

[1] On the origin of this idea, see D. E. Aune, "On the Origins of the 'Council of Yavneh' Myth," *Journal of Biblical Literature* 110(1991) 491–93, who traces the idea of "a council of Pharisees" to Spinoza, and the location at Yavneh to Heinrich Graetz.

[2] J. P. Lewis, "What Do We Mean by Jabneh?" *Journal of Bible and Religion* 32(1964) 125–32; S. Z. Leiman, *The Canonization of Hebrew Scripture* (Hamden, CT: Archon Books, 1976) 120–24; G. Stemberger, "Die sogenannte 'Synode von Jabne' und das frühe Christentum," *Kairos* 19(1977) 14–21; R. Beckwith, *The Old Testament Canon of the New Testament Church and its Background in Early Judaism* (Grand Rapids: Eerdmans, 1985) 276–77; J. Barton, *Oracles of God: Perceptions of Ancient Prophecy in Israel after the Exile* (Oxford: Oxford University Press, 1986) 24.

[3] Nonetheless, Leiman is followed by Beckwith, *The Old Testament Canon* and E. Earle Ellis, *The Old Testament in Early Christianity* (Tübingen: Mohr-Siebeck, 1991).

[4] Some later authorities, such as Origen and Jerome, count Judges-Ruth and Jeremiah-Lamentations each as one book. See Leiman, *The Canonization of Hebrew Scripture*, 32. David Noel Freedman observes that twenty-two is the number of letters in the Hebrew alphabet, while the Greek alphabet has twenty-four. The correspondence between the number of sacred books and the number of letters in the alphabet showed that the canon was full.

[5] J. C. VanderKam, *The Dead Sea Scrolls Today* (Grand Rapids, MI: Eerdmans, 1994), Chapter 5, section C.

[6] Some fragments related to Esther have been identified by J. T. Milik, "Les Modèles Araméens du Livre d'Esther dans le Grotte IV de Qumrân," *Revue de Qumran* 15(1992) 321–99, but these are not part of the Book of Esther as we know it.

[7] J. Barton, *Oracles of God: Perceptions of Ancient Prophecy in Israel after the Exile* (Oxford: Oxford University Press, 1986) 35.

[8] Cf. Philo, *De vita contemplativa* §25 on the Therapeutae.

[9] CD 6:2–11 (trans. G. Vermes, *The Dead Sea Scrolls in English* [London: Penguin, 1987] 87). The translation of the phrase שבי ישראל (here: "converts of Israel") is disputed. Alternative renderings are "returnees of Israel" or "captivity of Israel."

[10] 1QS 8:14–15.

[11] Contra B. Z. Wacholder, *The Dawn of Qumran: The Sectarian Torah and the Teacher of Righteousness* (Cincinnati: Hebrew Union College, 1983) 228, who holds that it was the Torah of Qumran. We will return to the Temple Scroll in a later chapter.

[12] Sigmund Mowinckel, *He That Cometh. The Messiah Concept in the Old Testament and Later Judaism* (Nashville: Abingdon, 1955); T. N. D. Mettinger, *King and Messiah. The Civil and Sacral Legitimation of the Israelite Kings* (Lund: Gleerup, 1976).

[13] See the commentary by P. K. McCarter, *2 Samuel* (Anchor Bible 9; Garden City: Doubleday, 1984) 205–8.

[14] M. Weinfeld, "The Covenant of Grant in the Old Testament and in the Ancient Near East," *Journal of the American Oriental Society* 90(1970) 184–203.

[15] In Ps 132:12, however, the promise appears to be conditional: "If your sons keep my covenant and my decrees that I shall teach them, their sons also, forevermore, shall sit on your throne." See the discussion of the royal ideology in F. M. Cross, *Canaanite Myth and Hebrew Epic* (Cambridge, MA: Harvard University Press, 1973) 241–65. Unlike Cross, however, I would argue that the covenantal, conditional formulation is a late, Deuteronomic development, rather than "Israel's earliest royal theology."

[16] Reading with H. J. Kraus, בהררי קדש מרחם שחר כטל ילדתיך ("on the holy mountains, out of the womb of Dawn, like dew I have begotten you," *Psalms 60–150. A Commentary* [Minneapolis: Augsburg, 1989] 344). The MT reads: "to you the dew of your youth."

[17] J. J. M. Roberts, "The Old Testament's Contribution to Messianic Expectations," in J. H. Charlesworth, ed., *The Messiah. Developments in Earliest Judaism and Christianity* (Minneapolis: Fortress, 1992) 42–43; M. B. Crook, "A Suggested Occasion for Isaiah 9,2–7 and 11,1–9," *Journal of Biblical Literature* 68(1949) 213–24; A. Alt, "Jesaja 8,23–9,6. Befreiungsnacht und Krönungstag," *Kleine Schriften zur Geschichte des Volkes Israel* (Munich: Kaiser, 1953) 2.206–25; S. Morenz, "Ägyptische und davidische Königstitular," *Zeitschrift für ägyptische Sprache* 79(1954) 73–74.

[18] See H. J. Kraus, *Psalms 1–59. A Commentary* (Minneapolis: Augsburg, 1988) 451, 455. Kraus notes that the divinity of the king was commonplace in the ancient Near East, but that this psalm is exceptional in the Hebrew Bible.

[19] See further the classic account of Israelite kingship in its ancient Near Eastern context by Mowinckel, *He That Cometh*, 21–95 and *The Psalms in Israel's Worship* (Nashville: Abingdon, 1967) 1.50–60. See also Mettinger, *King and Messiah*, 254–93.

[20] Roberts, "The Old Testament's Contribution," 41.

[21] A. K. Grayson, *Babylonian Historical-Literary Texts* (Toronto: University of Toronto Press, 1975) 13–22.

[22] S. A. Kaufman, "Prediction, Prophecy, and Apocalypse in the Light of New Akkadian Texts," A. Shinan, ed., *Proceedings of the Sixth World Congress of Jewish Studies 1973* (Jerusalem: World Union of Jewish Studies, 1977) 1.221–28.

[23] H. W. Wolff, *Joel and Amos* (Hermeneia; Philadelphia: Fortress, 1977) 353. Other scholars argue, however, that Amos only preached destruction to the northern kingdom and hoped for the restoration of Davidic rule over all Israel. See S. Paul, *Amos* (Hermeneia; Minneapolis: Fortress, 1991) 288–95.

[24] J. Blenkinsopp, *A History of Prophecy in Israel* (Philadelphia: Westminster, 1983) 120. There is an explicit reference to the Babylonian exile in Mic 4:10. The authenticity of Micah 5 is defended, however, by H. Seebass, *Herrscherverheissungen im Alten Testament* (Neukirchen-Vluyn: Neukirchener Verlag, 1992) 48. D. Hillers, *Micah* (Hermeneia;

Philadelphia: Fortress, 1984) 3–4 sweepingly rejects attempts to identify late redactional insertions in the book.

[25] H. Wildberger, *Isaiah 1–12* (Minneapolis: Augsburg, 1991) 465–69.

[26] So Roberts, "The Old Testament's Contribution," 45; cf. Seebass, *Herrscherverheissungen*, 34–36. Hillers, *Micah*, 65–69, suggests a similar setting for Micah 5.

[27] Roberts, ibid.

[28] Or: "a Branch, a Righteous One." So David Noel Freedman, who points out that in Zechariah the messianic title is simply "Branch."

[29] Isa 7:18, 20, 21, 23; 26:1; 27:2, 12; Joel 3:1, 18; Zech 12:6; 13:2; 14:1, 6, 8, 9, 20. Blenkinsopp, *A History*, 256–67.

[30] Roberts, "The Old Testament's Contribution," 46. The authenticity of the passage is defended by W. Holladay, *Jeremiah I* (Philadelphia: Fortress, 1986) 616–20.

[31] R. Borger, *Die Inschriften Asarhaddons König von Assyrien* (Archiv für Orientforschung 9; Graz: published by the editor, 1956) §20.17; See M. Fishbane, *Biblical Interpretation in Ancient Israel* (Oxford: Oxford University Press, 1985) 472.

[32] H. Donner and W. Rollig, *Kanaanäische und aramäische Inschriften* (3 vols.; Wiesbaden: Harrassowitz, 1962–64) I,10, no. 43; W. Beyerlin, *Near Eastern Religious Texts Relating to the Old Testament* (Philadelphia: Westminster, 1978) 232–4. See Holladay, *Jeremiah I*, 618–19.

[33] Fishbane, *Biblical Interpretation*, 471–74.

[34] Y. Goldman, *Prophétie et royauté au retour de l'exil. Les origines littéraires de la forme massorétique du livre de Jérémie* (Orbis Biblicus et Orientalis 118; Freiburg: Universitätsverlag/Göttingen: Vandenhoeck & Ruprecht, 1992) 226, argues that the insertion derives from the time of Zerubbabel after the return from exile.

[35] Compare the concern for the interpretation of Jeremiah's prediction of restoration after 70 years in Daniel 9.

[36] Roberts, "The Old Testament's Contribution," 47.

[37] See M. Knibb, "The Exile in the Literature of the Intertestamental Period," *Heythrop Journal* 17(1976) 253–72.

[38] Zech 4:14. See further below.

[39] Trans. Moshe Greenberg, *Ezekiel 1–20* (Anchor Bible 22; Garden City: Doubleday, 1983) 309. Botanic imagery for monarchy can be found already in Jotham's fable in Judges 9.

[40] Exod 16:22; Num 4:34; 31:13; 32:2. See H. Niehr, "נשׂיא," in G. J. Botterweck and H. Ringgren, eds., *Theologisches Wörterbuch zum Alten Testament* (Stuttgart: Kohlhammer, 1986) 5.647–57.

[41] M. Noth, *Das System der Zwölf Stämme Israels* (Stuttgart: Kohlhammer, 1930) 151–63.

[42] See A. D. H. Mayes, "Amphictyony," in D. N. Freedman, ed., *The Anchor Bible Dictionary* 1.212–16.

[43] Ezek 7:27; 12:10, 12; 19:1; 21:30; 34:24. See Jon D. Levenson, *Theology of the Program of Restoration of Ezekiel 40–48* (Harvard Semitic Monographs 10: Missoula: Scholars Press, 1976) 64.

[44] Levenson, *Theology of the Program of Restoration*, 75–101.

[45] Walther Zimmerli, *Ezekiel 2* (Hermeneia; Philadelphia: Fortress, 1983) 547–53, argues for complex redactional growth but allows that a core may derive from Ezekiel.

[46] Ezek 46:12–15.

[47] See Levenson, *Theology of the Program of Restoration*, 75–101.

[48] See Richard J. Clifford, *Fair Spoken and Persuading. An Interpretation of Second Isaiah* (New York: Paulist, 1984) 192.

[49] Despite the explicit identification of Israel as the servant in Isa 49:3, many scholars dispute whether this identification is valid throughout Isaiah 40–55, especially in the so-called "Servant Songs" (Isa 42:1–4; 49:1–7; 50:4–9; 52:13–53:12). Isa 49:6 seems to distinguish between Israel and the servant. Nonetheless, it is agreed that "it is generally Israel represented by the diasporic 'remnant' which is the Servant of Yahweh" (Blenkinsopp, *A History*, 215).

[50] David Noel Freedman contends that Second Isaiah may still have envisaged a role for a vassal kingship, presumably from the Davidic line, but if this was so, he remains remarkably reticent about it.

[51] R. G. Kratz, *Kyros im Deuterojesaja-Buch* (Tübingen: Mohr-Siebeck, 1991) 25–33, argues that the latter part of the verse, beginning with the words "to Cyrus," is part of a redactional expansion. The mention of Cyrus in Isa 44:28 is also assigned to this redactional stage. In the original oracles, Cyrus was God's instrument in judging the nations. In the redactional stage he is the agent of the salvation of Israel. Kratz dates the redactional stage to the time of the rebuilding of the Temple under Darius I, and suggests that it was partly intended to counter messianic hopes centered on Zerubbabel (pp. 183–91). Kratz's methodology, which routinely explains shifts in emphasis in the text by positing source and redactional distinctions, seems to me very dubious.

[52] See Antti Laato, *The Servant of YHWH and Cyrus* (Stockholm: Almqvist & Wiksell, 1992) 181.

[53] Laato, *The Servant of YHWH and Cyrus*, 244.

[54] In the Greek this passage is found in chapter 34. The designation "servant" is missing, but the subjugation of all nations to Nebuchadnezzar is attested.

[55] C. L. and E. M. Meyers, *Haggai, Zechariah 1–8* (Anchor Bible 25B; Garden City: Doubleday, 1987) 9. For a recent summary of the discussion see also Janet E. Tollington, *Tradition and Innovation in Haggai and Zechariah 1–8* (Journal for the Study of the Old Testament Supplement 150; Sheffield: Journal for the Study of the Old Testament, 1993) 133–34.

[56] Meyers and Meyers, *Haggai, Zechariah 1–8*, 69: "The use of such a seal was the way of carrying out the authority of the person to whom the seal belonged." Cf. Tollington, *Tradition and Innovation*, 141.

[57] Blenkinsopp, *A History of Prophecy*, 233, speaks of "a messianic movement." Tollington, *Tradition and Innovation*, 136, emphasizes that the restoration is not by human military action, but its political implications are none the less significant for that.

[58] Cf. D. Petersen, *Haggai and Zechariah 1–8* (Philadelphia: Westminster, 1984) 210. David Noel Freedman comments that the Persian empire did not seem so formidable during the transition between the reigns of Cambyses and Darius, and so the prophet's expectation may not have been unrealistic, even though it was eventually disappointed.

[59] Meyers and Meyers, *Haggai, Zechariah 1–8*, 203.

[60] "Sons of oil" surely indicates that they were anointed, despite the demurral of Petersen, *Haggai and Zechariah 1–8*, 231.

[61] Petersen, *Haggai and Zechariah 1–8*, 275.

[62] Blenkinsopp, *A History of Prophecy*, 238. This interpretation goes back to Wellhausen.

[63] Meyers and Meyers, *Haggai, Zechariah 1–8*, 350–57, defend the MT at great length. In

their view, only Joshua is crowned and the Branch is not Zerubbabel but a Davidic figure in the indefinite future. The prophecy, so understood, would underline the inadequacy of Zerubbabel. Such a view, however, is difficult to reconcile with the prophet's explicit enthusiasm for Zerubbabel in chapter 4.

[64] Roberts, "The Old Testament's Contribution," 50.

[65] Contrary to what is sometimes claimed (e.g. K. Koch, "Ezra and the Origins of Judaism," *Journal of Semitic Studies* 19[1974] 190–93), Ezra was not High Priest in Jerusalem. See Ezra 8:33 where Ezra defers to Meremoth, son of Uriah, the priest.

[66] Cf. Judges 5:10: "you who ride on white donkeys." Also the "messianic" oracle in Gen 49:8–12 ("binding his foal to the vine, and his donkey's colt to the choice vine").

[67] Blenkinsopp, *A History of Prophecy*, 260.

[68] Paul D. Hanson, "Zechariah 9 and an Ancient Ritual Pattern," *Journal of Biblical Literature* 92(1973) 45. "Your sons, O Greece," בָּנַיִךְ יָוָן, lacks only one letter of "your sons, O Zion," בָּנַיִךְ צִיּוֹן.

[69] Roberts, "The Old Testament's Contribution," 44. The linking of Hadrach, Damascus, Israel, Hamath, and the Phoenician cities (Zech 9:1–2) recalls Tiglath-pileser's campaign in 738 BCE. (Compare Abraham Malamat, "The Historical Setting of Two Biblical Prophecies on the Nations [Zech 9:1–6, Jer 47]," *Israel Exploration Journal* 1(1951) 149–59. In contrast, Seebass, *Herrscherverheissungen*, 65, argues for a postexilic date, but his arguments are impressionistic.

[69a] Carol L. Meyers and Eric M. Meyers, *Zechariah 9–14* (Anchor Bible 25C; New York: Doubleday, 1993) 148, defend the reading "Greece" and argue for a mid-fifth century BCE date.

[70] The account of Alexander's visit to Jerusalem (*Antiquities* 11.317–47) is blatantly legendary.

[71] H. Gese, "Anfang und Ende der Apokalyptik, dargestellt am Sacharjabuch," *Zeitschrift für Theologie und Kirche* 70(1973) 20–49 argues that in the final redaction of Zechariah, the campaign of Alexander in chapter 9 marks the beginning of the end time. The sequence of events in Zechariah 9–14 is too unclear to support such a far-reaching interpretation.

[72] Paul Redditt, "Israel's Shepherds: Hope and Pessimism in Zechariah 9–14," *Catholic Biblical Quarterly* 51(1989) 631–42. Stephen L. Cook, "The Metamorphosis of a Shepherd: The Tradition History of Zechariah 11:17 + 13:7–9," *Catholic Biblical Quarterly* 55(1993) 453–66, holds that "the shepherds of Deutero-Zechariah represent civil, not religious leaders" (p. 457).

[73] Blenkinsopp, *A History of Prophecy*, 262.

[74] Otto Ploeger, *Theocracy and Eschatology* (Richmond: Knox, 1968) 85: "One has the impression that there is a definite historical event behind this mysterious description." He goes on to cite an incident from Josephus (*Antiquities* 11.7.1 §297–301) where a High Priest Johannes murdered his brother Jesus in the Temple precinct in the Persian period, as a possible background for Zechariah's prophecy.

[75] So Cook, "The Metamorphosis of a Shepherd," 462. Cook reads Zech 13:7–9 ("Awake, o sword against my shepherd") in conjunction with 12:10 as a reference to this supposed martyrdom. See also P. Lamarche, *Zacharie IX–XIV: Structure littéraire et messianisme* (Paris: Gabalda, 1961) 108; Gese, "Anfang und Ende der Apokalyptik," 44–48. Gese speaks of the martyred messiah as "Josiah redivivus."

[76] Martin Hengel, *Judaism and Hellenism* (Philadelphia: Fortress, 1974) 1.175.

[77] Jonathan A. Goldstein, "How the Authors of 1 and 2 Maccabees Treated the 'Messianic' Promises," in J. Neusner, W. S. Green and E. S. Frerichs, eds., *Judaisms and their Messiahs* (Cambridge: Cambridge University Press, 1987) 72. R. H. Charles, *The Book of Enoch, or 1 Enoch* (Oxford: Clarendon, 1912) 215–16, also identifies the bull as a messiah.

[78] J. C. VanderKam, *Enoch and the Growth of an Apocalyptic Tradition* (Catholic Biblical Quarterly Monograph Series 16; Washington, D.C.: Catholic Biblical Association, 1984) 164–67, argues that the most important source is Jeremiah 25. On the broader context of the "root metaphors" of sheep and predators, see Paul A. Porter, *Metaphors and Monsters. A Literary-Critical Study of Daniel 7 and 8* (Lund: Gleerup, 1983) 46–60.

[79] On the white bull as a new Adam, see Patrick A. Tiller, *A Commentary on the Animal Apocalypse of 1 Enoch* (Atlanta: Scholars Press, 1993) 20, 384.

[80] G. W. Nickelsburg, "Salvation without and with a Messiah," in Neusner et al., eds., *Judaisms and their Messiahs*, 55–56.

[81] On the traditional interpretation of Daniel 9 see Franz Fraidl, *Die Exegese der Siebzig Wochen Daniels in der alten und mittleren Zeit* (Graz: Leuschner & Lubensky, 1883). Louis E. Knowles, "The Interpretation of the Seventy Weeks of Daniel in the Early Church Fathers," *Westminster Theological Journal* 7(1944) 136–60.

[82] For full discussion see John J. Collins, *Daniel* (Hermeneia; Minneapolis: Fortress, 1993) 166–70.

[83] Aemilius Sura, in Velleius Paterculus; Polybius 38.22, Dionysius of Halicarnassus 1.2.2–4; Tacitus, Hist 5.8–9, Appian, Preface, 9. See Doron Mendels, "The Five Empires. A Note on a Hellenistic Topos," *American Journal of Philology* 102(1981) 330–37.

[84] J. W. Swain, "The Theory of the Four Monarchies: Opposition History under the Roman Empire," *Classical Philology* 35(1940) 1–21; David Flusser, "The Four Empires in the Fourth Sibyl and in the Book of Daniel," *Israel Oriental Studies* 2(1972) 148–75.

[85] *Sib Or* 4 also has an oracle against Rome, but this appears to be a redactional addition. See J. J. Collins, "The Place of the Fourth Sibyl in the Development of the Jewish Sibyllina," *Journal of Jewish Studies* 25(1974) 365–80.

[86] S. K. Eddy, *The King is Dead. Studies in the Near Eastern Resistance to Hellenism 334–32 B.C.* (Lincoln: University of Nebraska Press, 1961) 19.

[87] See further J. J. Collins, "Nebuchadnezzar and the Kingdom of God. Deferred Eschatology in the Jewish Diaspora," in C. Elsas and H. G. Kippenberg, eds., *Loyalitäts-konflikte in der Religionsgeschichte. Festschrift für Carsten Colpe* (Würzburg: Königshausen & Neumann, 1990) 252–57.

[88] Collins, *Daniel*.

[89] b. Ḥag. 13a; b. Sanh. 38b.

[90] For a recent defender, see G. R. Beasley-Murray, "The Interpretation of Daniel 7," *Catholic Biblical Quarterly* 45(1983) 44–58.

[91] See my essay "Stirring up the Great Sea: The Religio-Historical Background of Daniel 7," in A. S. van der Woude ed., *The Book of Daniel in the Light of New Findings* (Bibliotheca Ephemeridum Theologicarum Lovaniensium 106; Leuven: Leuven University Press, 1993) 121–36.

[92] Paul Mosca, "Ugarit and Daniel 7: A Missing Link," *Biblica* 67(1986) 496–517.

[93] For full documentation, see Collins, *Daniel*, 313–17.

[94] Ibid.

[95] J. J. Collins, *The Sibylline Oracles of Egyptian Judaism* (Society of Biblical Literature

The Fallen Booth of David

Dissertation Series 13; Missoula: Scholars Press, 1974) 24–33; "The Sibylline Oracles," in Charlesworth, ed., *Old Testament Pseudepigrapha* 1.354–61. The earliest stratum of *Sib Or* 3 is found in vss. 97–294 and 545–808.

[96] Throughout much of his reign Philometor was engaged in a struggle with his brother, Ptolemy VIII Euergetes (Physcon). They were joint rulers in 170–164. Euergetes was sole ruler in 164–163. He withdrew to Cyrene in 163 and returned to Egypt after the death of Philometor in 145 BCE.

[97] *Against Apion* 2.49.

[98] Aryeh Kasher, *The Jews in Hellenistic and Roman Egypt* (Tübingen: Mohr-Siebeck, 1985) 8.

[99] 2 Macc 1:10.

[100] So Valentin Nikiprowetzky, *La Troisième Sibylle* (Paris: Mouton, 1970) 133; Arnaldo Momigliano, "La Portata Storica dei Vaticini sul Settimo Re nel Terzo Libro degli Oracoli Sibillini," in *Forma Futuri. Studi in Onore del Cardinale Michele Pellegrino* (Turin: Erasmo, 1975) 1081; Schuerer, *History*, 2.517.

[101] For the text see Ludwig Koenen, "Die Prophezeiungen des 'Töpfers'," *Zeitschrift für Papyrologie und Epigraphik* 2(1968) 178–209. Koenen identifies two recensions, which he dates soon after 129 and 116 BCE respectively, but neither of these represents the original form of the oracle. See further J. J. Collins, "The Sibyl and the Potter," in L. Bormann, K. Del Tredici, and A. Standhartinger, eds., *Religious Propaganda and Missionary Competition in the New Testament World. Essays in Honor of Dieter Georgi* (Leiden: Brill, 1994) 57–69.

[102] See F. Dunand, "L'Oracle du Potier et la formation de l'apocalyptique en Égypte," in F. Raphael, ed., *L'Apocalyptique* (Paris: Geuthner, 1977) 39–67; J. Gwyn Griffiths, "Apocalyptic in the Hellenistic Era," in D. Hellholm, ed., *Apocalypticism in the Mediterranean World and the Near East* (Tübingen: Mohr-Siebeck, 1983) 273–93.

[103] Ludwig Koenen, "Die Adaptation Ägyptischer Königsideologie am Ptolemäerhof," in W. Peremans, ed., *Egypt and the Hellenistic World* (Studia Hellenistica 27; Leuven: Leuven University Press, 1983) 152–70.

[104] Griffiths, "Apocalyptic in the Hellenistic Era," 289.

[105] See Lawrence M. Wills, *The Jew in the Court of the Foreign King* (Harvard Dissertations in Religion 26; Minneapolis: Fortress, 1990). Wills speaks of a "ruled ethnic perspective."

[106] Louis H. Feldman, *Jew and Gentile in the Ancient World* (Princeton: Princeton University Press, 1993) 106, speaks of a "vertical alliance" between the Jews and foreign governments. On alleged indications of messianism in the Septuagint see Johan Lust, "Messianism and Septuagint," in J. A. Emerton, ed., *Congress Volume Salamanca (1983)* (VTSup 36; Leiden: Brill, 1985) 174–91.

[107] See Doron Mendels, *The Rise and Fall of Jewish Nationalism* (New York: Doubleday, 1992) 55–79.

[108] See the comments of Jonathan Z. Smith, "A Pearl of Great Price and a Cargo of Yams: A Study in Situational Incongruity," *History of Religions* 16(1976) 1–19.

[109] Grayson, *Babylonian Historical-Literary Texts*, 17.

[110] F. Hesse, "Chrio, etc.," in G. Friedrich, ed., *Theological Dictionary of the New Testament* (1974) 9.509.

[111] Joachim Becker, *Messiaserwartung im Alten Testament* (Stuttgarter Bibelstudien 83; Stuttgart: Katholisches Bibelwerk, 1977) 74, speaks of "das messianologische Vakuum" in the Second Temple period, exemplified by the work of the Chronicler.

[112] Cf. the illuminating study of David Frankfurter, "Lest Egypt's City Be Deserted: Religion and Ideology in the Egyptian Response to the Jewish Revolt (116–117 C.E.)," *Journal of Jewish Studies* 43(1992) 203–20, and more generally, S. Trump, ed., *Millennial Dreams in Action* (Hague: Mouton, 1962); Victor Turner, *Dramas, Fields, and Metaphors* (Ithaca, NY: Cornell University Press, 1974); Bruce Lincoln, *Discourse and the Construction of Society* (New York: Oxford University Press, 1989) 15–50.

3

A SHOOT FROM THE STUMP OF JESSE

The expectation of a king from the Davidic line, which is dormant for much of the postexilic era, resurfaces after the restoration of native, non-Davidic, Jewish kingship in the Hasmonean period (late second to early first centuries BCE). It then reappears in more than one setting. By the first century CE it can fairly be said to be part of the common heritage of Judaism.

▨ *The* Psalms of Solomon

Prior to the discovery of the Dead Sea Scrolls, the only clear evidence from the last two centuries before the turn of the era for the use of the term messiah (χριστός) with reference to a future Davidic king, and indeed for the expectation of a Davidic messiah in any terms, lay in the *Psalms of Solomon*. This document is a collection of eighteen psalms preserved in Greek and Syriac. It is sometimes listed with the Apocrypha, such as the books of Maccabees and the Wisdom of Solomon, in ancient canonical lists, and it is printed in modern editions of the Septuagint.[1] While the real author is unknown, and it is not certain that all the psalms are by the same author, the psalms betray their original setting more clearly than do most of the Pseudepigrapha. Three of the psalms, 2, 8 and 17, contain clear historical allusions, and one of these, *Ps Sol* 17, articulates messianic expectation. The messiah is also a focus of attention in *Ps Sol* 18.

The historical allusions relate to the Hasmonean dynasty (17:5–9), the invitation to a foreign conqueror to enter Jerusalem (8:15–20), the profanation of the temple by foreigners (2:2) and the death of the foreign invader "on the mountains of Egypt" (2:26). The latter passage is a transparent allusion to the death of Pompey in Egypt in 48 BCE,[2] and the other allusions relate to Pompey's conquest of Jerusalem in 63 BCE. The sequence of events originated in the civil war between Hyrcanus II, who was the eldest son of Salome Alexandra (queen of Judea 76–67 BCE) and had been appointed High Priest during her reign, and his brother Aristobulus II.[3] After his victory over Mithridates in 66 BCE, Pompey was waging a campaign in Asia. In spring of 63 BCE, he came to Damascus. Here three Jewish parties appeared before him, not only the representatives of Hyrcanus and Aristobulus but also a delegation of the Jewish people who wished Hasmonean rule to be abolished and the older priestly theocracy to be restored.[4] When Aristobulus departed suddenly, Pompey became suspicious and marched against him. When Pompey encamped outside Jerusalem, Aristobulus came to him with gifts, but the people refused to admit the Romans to the city. Pompey then took Aristobulus prisoner, and the followers of Hyrcanus opened the gates to him. The followers of Aristobulus were besieged on the Temple mount. The siege ended in a massacre, in which some twelve thousand Jews allegedly were killed.[5] Afterwards, Pompey insisted on entering the Holy of Holies, where only the High Priest was allowed to go. He did not, however, pillage the Temple or further disrupt the sacrifices. Judea was then placed under the jurisdiction of the Roman province of Syria. Hyrcanus remained as High Priest, without royal title. He remained in office until he was captured and mutilated by the Parthians in 40 BCE. Pompey took Aristobulus to Rome as a prisoner. The Jewish king was compelled to walk in front of the Roman general's chariot in his triumphal procession. The messianic expectation of the *Psalms of Solomon* must be read against the background of these events.

Ps Sol 17:16 says that at the time of Pompey's invasion "those who loved the assemblies of the devout (οἱ ἀγαπῶντες συναγωγὰς ὁσίων) fled from them as sparrows fled from their nest." There is little doubt that the authors of the *Psalms* belonged to these conventicles of the pious. The identity of the assemblies is less certain. The *Psalms* have often been identified as Pharisaic, and they are indeed compatible with the description of Pharisaic beliefs in Josephus,[6] but most scholars are now reticent about such identifications.[7] The themes in question, such as the importance of the Law and the belief in resurrection, are not distinctive enough to warrant a firm identification and, in any case, we know too little about Pharisaic beliefs in the first century BCE. The *Psalms* cannot, however, be taken as representative of Judaism at large. Not all Jews of the time accepted resurrection. We can also say with confidence that the *Psalms of Solomon* do not represent the supporters of the Hasmoneans, of whom they are severely critical. Since no trace of them has been found at Qumran, it also seems safe to say that they did not originate in the Dead Sea sect.

▨ *The Political Context*

The seventeenth *Psalm of Solomon* is devoted to the subject of kingship. It begins with the confession that "Lord, you are our king forevermore" and that "we hope in God our savior." The kingship of God, however, is implemented through human kingship. *Ps Sol* 17:4 hearkens back to the covenant with David: "Lord, you chose David to be king over Israel, and swore to him about his descendants forever, that his kingdom should not fall before you." In fact, however, David's kingdom had fallen several hundred years before this psalm was written. The psalm follows traditional Deuteronomic theology in attributing the blame for this to Israel's sinfulness: "but because of our sins, sinners rose up against us." The sinners in question, however, are not the Gentile rulers who brought the Davidic dynasty to an end, but "those to whom you did not make the promise," who "took away by force" and "despoiled the throne of David" (17:5–6).[7a] God overthrew these people, by raising up against them "a man alien to our race." It is clear, then, that the sinners who despoiled the throne of David were not "alien to our race," but were Jewish kings who were not of the Davidic line, that is, the Hasmonean dynasty that ruled Judea prior to the arrival of Pompey. Simon Maccabee had been proclaimed "leader and High Priest forever, until a trustworthy prophet should arise" (1 Macc 14:41). His titles are further specified as "High Priest, commander and ethnarch of the Jews and priests, and protector of them all" (14:47). He had *not* been proclaimed king. Likewise, John Hyrcanus (135/4–104 BCE), who "was accounted by God worthy of three of the greatest privileges, the rule of the nation, the office of high priest, and the gift of prophecy,"[8] did not claim to be king. According to Josephus, the first Hasmonean ruler to assume the royal title was Aristobulus I, who reigned briefly in 104–103 BCE: "After their father's death, the eldest son, Aristobulus, saw fit to transform the government into a kingdom, which he judged the best form, and he was the first to put a diadem on his head, four hundred and eighty-one years and three months after the time when the people were released from the Babylonian captivity and returned to their own country."[9] Even Aristobulus, however, did not claim royalty on his coins, which read "Judas the High Priest and the Congregation of the Jews."[10] Only with Alexander Jannaeus (103–76 BCE) do we find the explicit claim of royal status. While some of his coins have the same form as those of Aristobulus ("Yehonathan the High Priest and the Congregation of the Jews"), others read, in Hebrew and Greek "Yehonathan the King — King Alexander."[11] The non-Davidic Jewish kingship, judged illegitimate by the psalmist, had lasted about forty years. It had already been overthrown for some fifteen years when the psalmist wrote (after the death of Pompey in 48 BCE) but its memory was vivid.[12]

The offense of the Hasmoneans was, in part, the usurpation of the Davidic throne. They are probably also the sinners denounced in *Ps Sol* 1:4–8:

> "Their wealth was extended to the whole earth, and their glory to the end of the earth. They exalted themselves to the stars, they said they would never fall. They were arrogant in their possessions and they did not acknowledge (God). Their sins were in secret, and even I did not know. Their lawless actions surpassed the gentiles before them; they completely profaned the sanctuary of the Lord."

The Hasmoneans are probably also in view in *Ps Sol* 8:11–13:

> "They stole from the sanctuary of God as if there were no redeeming heir. They walked on the place of sacrifice of the Lord (coming) from all kinds of uncleanness; and with menstrual blood, they defiled the sacrifices as if they were common meat. There was no sin they left undone in which they did not surpass the gentiles."

The sinners in question are Jews, not Gentiles, and had control of the temple. The same psalm alleges that "In secret places underground was their lawbreaking, provoking (him), son involved with mother and father with daughter. Everyone committed adultery with his neighbor's wife; they made agreements with them with an oath about these things" (8:9–10).

The *Psalms of Solomon* are highly polemical, and do not necessarily give an accurate picture of the conduct of the Hasmoneans. The themes sounded in the critique, wealth, fornication, impurity, profanation of the temple, are very similar to those found in the Damascus Document columns 4–5, which also probably reflect the Hasmonean era. There the "three nets of Belial" are fornication, riches, and profanation of the Temple, and abuses involving menstrual blood and sexual relations with relatives are also condemned. In the case of the Damascus Document there is good reason to believe that the complaints rested in part on a distinctive, sectarian, interpretation of the Law. There may also be factional considerations underlying the opposition of the psalmists. Alexander Jannaeus and Aristobulus II were notoriously at odds with the Pharisees.[13] If the authors of the psalms were Pharisees, or belonged to a likeminded group, this may have been a factor in their condemnation of the Hasmoneans.

In the view of the psalmist, the termination of the Hasmonean line reflected the just judgment of God. Pompey had been the Lord's instrument, as kings of Assyria and Babylon had been in the past.[14] But the cure was even worse than the ailment. Pompey is described as "the lawless one"[15] or even as "the dragon."[16] He was "a stranger and his heart was alien to our God, he acted arrogantly" (17:12–13). His downfall is celebrated at length in *Ps Sol* 2:26–30 and taken as evidence that God is "king over the heavens, judging even kings and rulers."

The Davidic Hope

Both the Hasmoneans and the Romans represented unacceptable violations of the divine order. Accordingly, the psalmist prays for the restoration of the Davidic monarchy:

"See, Lord, and raise up for them their king,
    the son of David, to rule over your servant Israel
    in the time known to you, O God.
Undergird him with the strength to destroy the unrighteous rulers,
    to purge Jerusalem from gentiles
    who trample her to destruction;

in wisdom and in righteousness to drive out
    the sinners from the inheritance;
to smash the arrogance of sinners
    like a potter's jar;
to shatter all their substance with an iron rod
to destroy the unlawful nations with the word of his mouth;
at his warning the nations will flee from his presence;
and he will condemn sinners by the thoughts of their hearts"
(17:21–25).

This prayer is replete with biblical allusions. The primary influence is from Isa 11:2–4.[17] The future king will be endowed with wisdom (Isa 11:2a) and strength (Isa 11:2b). The statement that he will destroy the unlawful nations with "the word of his mouth" is drawn from the Septuagint translation of Isa 11:4 (the Hebrew has the more familiar "rod of his mouth"). Other phrases are drawn from Psalm 2, especially vs. 9: "you shall break them with a rod of iron, and dash them in pieces like a potter's vessel." The "unrighteous rulers" to be destroyed include both Jews and Gentiles, but at this time Jerusalem was under Gentile power.[18] The language of Isa 11:1–4 also figures prominently in the description of the "Lord Messiah" in *Ps Sol* 18:6–8:

> "Blessed are they who shall be in those days, seeing the good things of the Lord which he will perform for the generation that is to come, under the rod of discipline of the Lord's anointed in the fear of his God, in wisdom of spirit, and of justice and of might, so as to direct every man in works of righteousness in the fear of God."

The initial role of this king is undeniably violent. He is "to destroy the unrighteous rulers, to purge Jerusalem from gentiles" (17:22). It is surprising that some scholars have denied the warlike character of this messiah.[19] Charlesworth contrasts the portrayal of the messiah in Targum Pseudo-Jonathan to Genesis 49:11:

> "How beautiful is the king, Messiah, who is destined to arise from the house of Judah! He has girded his loins and gone down to battle against his enemies, destroying kings and their power, and there is neither king nor power that can withstand him. He reddens the mountains with the blood of their slain. His garments are saturated with blood, like those of him who presses grapes."[20]

The imagery in *Ps Sol* 17 is certainly less bloody, but it is scarcely less violent. He will destroy the unlawful nations with the word of his mouth, but the destruction is none the less for that. "To smash the arrogance of sinners like a potter's jar," and "to shatter all their substance with an iron rod" implies militant, violent action. Klausner's claim that "there is no suggestion of wars and bloodshed in his time"[21] fails to account for the clear implications of the text.

Klausner summarized the messianic expectations of the psalm as follows: "There is indeed *a political and national side* to the Messianic kingdom; but *the spiritual side* is emphasized more." Klausner's "spiritual side" is evidenced by an emphasis on righteousness and holiness. "He will gather a holy people whom he will lead in righteousness, and he will judge the tribes of the people that have been made holy by the Lord their god" (17:26). The holiness of Israel is understood in the priestly tradition of separation from the Gentiles: "The alien and the foreigner will no longer live near them" (17:28).[22] Gentile nations will serve under the yoke of the messiah (17:30). The contrast between political and national, on the one side, and spiritual, on the other, is anachronistic. The spirituality of the psalms is rooted in political and national conceptions and requires the exaltation of Israel above all other nations.

This is not to deny that the spiritual concerns of the psalms are profound. The king will not rely on horse and rider, or on a multitude for war (cf. Deut 17:16). God is his hope and his strength, and "the Lord himself is his king" (*Ps Sol* 17:34, cf. 17:38). He is compassionate to the nations that stand before him in fear. Most striking of all is the assertion that he is "pure from sin" (καθαρὸς ἀπὸ ἁμαρτίας, 17:36). There is no indisputable Jewish parallel for such a statement about the messiah. (*Testament of Judah* 24:1, "a star will arise to you from Jacob . . . and no sin whatever will be found in him," is Christian in its present context). In contrast, the sinlessness of Christ is an important motif in the New Testament.[23] Yet the notion of a sinless human being is not unknown in the Jewish tradition. The LXX of Isa 53:9 says that the Servant "did nothing unlawful."[24] Ezek 36:25 promises Israel that "I will sprinkle clean water upon you, and you shall be clean from all your uncleannesses." It may be that the sinlessness of the king is required by the purity of the people in the eschatological age.[25] All the people are children of their God in the end time (17:27). Klausner rightly concludes that "the Jewish Messiah, no matter how noble and how spiritual, is nevertheless a human being, a king of flesh and blood of the house of David, and is only an instrument for the great work of the God of Israel, the God of the universe."[26]

We have, then, a distinct picture of the Davidic messiah in the *Psalms of Solomon*. He is first of all the one who will liberate Jerusalem, and defeat and subjugate the Gentiles. He will then usher in an era of peace and reign in a kingdom marked by holiness and righteousness. This picture draws its warrants from biblical prophecy, especially Isaiah 11 and Psalm 2.

It is unlikely that the authors of the *Psalms of Solomon* were the first Jews to see in Isaiah 11 or Psalm 2 the promise of a future glorious king. As we have seen, the hope for a future Davidic king was explicit in several prophetic passages. It had simply lain dormant, until it was evoked here by the disintegration of Hasmonean rule. It is quite likely that the messianic expectations attested in the Dead Sea Scrolls also originated in the Hasmonean era, and they, too, were formulated with reference to familiar biblical passages.

The Davidic Messiah in the Scrolls

The Dead Sea Scrolls have greatly expanded the corpus of messianic texts from around the turn of the era. This corpus is still modest in proportion to the entire corpus of the Scrolls. Claims that the Scrolls represent "the Messianic Movement in Palestine"[27] involve considerable exaggeration. The Halakhic Letter, 4QMMT, which lists some of the issues that led the Dead Sea sect to separate from the rest of Judaism, makes no mention of messianism. Neither does the Damascus Document treat it as part of the *raison d'être* of the sect. Nonetheless, the messianic passages in the Scrolls constitute a significant body of evidence and throw considerable new light on the subject.

The messianism of the Scrolls is a complex subject, whose study is impeded by a number of factors. One is the lack of firm dates for the composition of individual documents, with the result that theories of development within the Scrolls are inevitably hypothetical. Another is uncertainty as to how far the Scrolls constitute a coherent corpus, and whether specific documents should be regarded as sectarian in the sense that applies to the Community Rule. In the matter of coherence, it is necessary to proceed inductively, and to note the correspondences that in fact exist among the various texts. There is also the perennial problem of terminology. The word משיח can refer to prophets and priests as well as to kings, and to figures from the past as well as the future. Our concern here is with eschatological figures who are sometimes called מְשִׁיח, but who can also be designated by other terms.

◨ *The* Pesher *on Isaiah*

The Scrolls provide ample documentation for the expectation of a Davidic messiah, envisaged along the lines of the Anointed of the Lord in the *Psalms of Solomon*. As in the *Psalms*, the messianic expectations are drawn from biblical prophecy. Isaiah 11:1–5, a key passage for the *Psalms*, also figures prominently in the Scrolls. This passage is treated in a fragmentary *pesher*, or commentary, from Cave 4, 4QpIs^a, which is based on Isaiah chapters 10 and 11. While the extant text is very fragmentary, the context is clear. There are several parallels to the *Rule of the War of the Sons of Light against the Sons of Darkness* (1QM, 4QM), which gives instructions for a final battle against Belial and the *Kittim*, or Westerners.[28] One passage in the *pesher* fragments 2–6, column 2, line 18 reads "when they return from the wilderness of the p[eopl]es," recalling 1QM 1:3.[29] The following line mentions "the Prince of the Congregation."[30] This passage gives little information about him, except that "afterward he will depart from [them]." Another fragment refers to the battle of the *Kittim*, and there are several other mentions of the *Kittim* in the context of battle.[31] Fragment 7 goes on to cite Isa 11:1–5. The interpretation is fragmentary. Only two-and-a-half words are preserved on the first line: [דויד עומד באח]. The line is plausibly restored to read:

פשר הפתגם על צמח] דויד העומד באח[רית הימים

"The interpretation of the matter concerns the Branch of] David, who will arise at the en[d of days. . . ."[32]

Whatever the precise wording, there can be little doubt that the reference is to an eschatological Davidic king. The *pesher* goes on to speak of a throne of glory and (victory over) the nations and Magog,[33] and says that his sword will judge the peoples.

The *pesher* clearly envisages a role for the Davidic messiah in the final battle against the *Kittim*. The name *Kittim* is derived from Citium in Cyprus, and is applied to Westerners in Jewish sources.[34] In Dan 11:30, the *Kittim* are the Romans. In 1 Macc 1:1, Alexander the Great comes from the land of *Kittim*. There is universal agreement that in the *pesharîm* the *Kittim* are the Romans: there is a clear allusion in the *pesher* on Habakkuk, 1QpHab 6:1–8, where they sacrifice to their standards.[35] The *pesher* on Nahum contains clearly identifiable references to the reigns of Alexander Jannaeus (103–76 BCE), Salome Alexandra (76–67 BCE) and Hyrcanus II and Aristobulus II (67–63 BCE). The notion of a "war of the *Kittim*" in 4QpIsaᵃ probably presupposes the Roman intervention in Jerusalem under Pompey. The setting of the *pesher*, then, is very close in time to the *Psalms of Solomon*.

Because of its fragmentary state, the *pesher* on Isaiah permits few inferences about the Branch of David, apart from the fact that he is associated with the eschatological war. We should note, however, a tendency to correlate messianic titles and prophetic allusions. The "Branch of David," mentioned by Jeremiah, is identified with the shoot from the stump of Jesse, foretold in Isa 11:1–5. We will find ample corroboration that the title "Prince of the Congregation" also has a messianic nuance, which it derives from Ezekiel's use of נשׂיא, prince.

The Messiah in the War Rule

Both these titles, "Branch of David" and "Prince of the Congregation" are found again in the context of Isaiah's prophecy in another fragmentary text from Qumran Cave 4, 4Q285, better, though inaccurately, known as the "Dying Messiah" text. The controversy surrounding this text has by now been essentially resolved. Initial claims reported in the media, that this text reported the death of a messianic figure,[36] have been shown to be unwarranted.[37] What is decisive in this case is not the grammar or syntax, which can be construed in different ways, but the context. The fragment begins with a reference to "Isaiah the prophet" and line 2 contains the beginning of Isa 11:1: "there shall come forth a shoot from the stump of Jesse." The third line reads

". . .] the Branch of David and they will enter into judgment with ["

The Branch here is surely taken as the fulfillment of Isaiah's prophecy about the shoot from the stump of Jesse. Branch and shoot are closely related images in any case. The passage then continues with the controversial line

[והמיתו נשׂיא העדה צמ]ח דויד

which has been variously translated as "they will put to death the Leader of the Community, the Bran[ch of David],"[38] or "the Prince of the Congregation, the Bran[ch of David] will kill him."[39] Even though the mem of צמח is only partially visible, the restoration seems very probable, so that the Branch of David is further identified with the Prince of the Congregation. In view of the association with Isaiah 11, where the shoot of Jesse will strike the earth with the rod of his mouth and kill the wicked with the breath of his lips, it seems beyond reasonable doubt that the Prince/Branch is the subject of the verb to kill, not its object.[40]

In 1972, J. T. Milik identified 4Q285 as a fragment of the War Rule.[41] The identification is suggested by the reference to killing and by an apparent reference to "the slain of the *Kittim*" in line 6. The other fragments on the plate, which come from the same hand and most probably from the same document, make further reference to the *Kittim*, to the archangel Michael, and to the Prince of the Congregation, all of whom are mentioned in the War Rule.[42] The War Rule had a complicated literary history, and it is not yet clear how 4Q285 should be related to the Scroll as found in 1QM.[43] But it is surely clear that the two are related, and that 4Q285 is part of a tradition about the eschatological war. Presumably these fragments belong toward the end of the War Rule, since the figure who is killed is evidently a figure of importance, possibly the king of the *Kittim* (who is mentioned in 1QM 15:2).[44]

It is now clear that the Davidic messiah/Branch of David had a role in the traditions about the eschatological war at some stage. The title "Prince of the Congregation" also occurs in 1QM 5:1, where his name is written on his shield as part of the preparation for battle. Also, Balaam's oracle is cited without interpretation in 1QM 11. (In the Damascus Document column 7, the scepter of Balaam's oracle is identified as "the Prince of the whole Congregation.") In view of the messianic overtones of both the prince and Balaam's oracle, the burden of proof falls on anyone who would claim that the Davidic messiah was absent at any stage of the War Rule tradition.

The appearance of the Branch of David/Prince of the Congregation in the War Rule is of some significance for our understanding of the extent of messianic expectation. In a major survey of Jewish practice and belief between 63 BCE and 66 CE, E. P. Sanders writes that "What is most striking about the sect's messianic expectation is that there is no Davidic messiah in the War Rule, where one would expect him to take the leading role."[45] He goes on to offer explanations for this absence: the ambiguous attitude toward kings in the Hebrew Bible, and the fact that "the stage had become too large for a mere king." Such speculation is now seen to be needless. The Dead Sea sect did indeed have its own distinctive attitude to messianism and indeed did look for supernatural deliverance in the final war, but the Davidic king had a well-established place in their expectations.

Wise and Eisenman at least deserve credit for recognizing that the figure in question in 4Q285 is messianic, although the word משיח does not occur.[46] The Branch of David (צמח דויד, mentioned clearly in the third line of the fragment) cannot be other than an anointed eschatological king,[47] and is in fact explicitly identified as "the righteous messiah" (משיח הצדק) in another Qumran *pesher*, 4QpGen (= 4QPatriarchal Blessings, 4Q252). In fact, the correlation of various epithets and titles that may be applied to the same figure is an essential step in the interpretation of the Scrolls.

Diverse Titles of the Messiah

4Q285, the so-called "Dying Messiah" text appears to identify the Branch of David with נשיא העדה, Prince of the Congregation, a title we have also seen in 4QpIs[a]. (The reservation about the identification arises because of the fragmentary state of the text.) The messianic connotations of the prince are shown in another Qumran document, the Scroll of Blessings, 1QSb. This scroll contains a series of blessings, apparently intended for the messianic age. The first blessing applies to all the faithful; the second to an individual priest (perhaps the messiah of Aaron); the third to "the sons of Zadok, the priests." Finally there is a blessing for "the Prince of the Congregation," that God will raise up for him the kingdom of his people (1QSb 5:21). The blessing that follows is heavily indebted to Isaiah 11:

> ". . . to dispense justice with [equity to the oppressed] of the land (Isa 11:4a).

> (May you smite the peoples) with the might of your hand and ravage the earth with your scepter; may you bring death to the ungodly with the breath of your lips! (Isa 11:4b) . . . and everlasting might, the spirit of knowledge and of the fear of God (Isa 11:2); may righteousness be the girdle (of your loins) and may your reins be girded (with faithfulness) (Isa 11:5)."

The blessing goes on to compare the prince to a young bull with horns of iron and hooves of bronze, and (probably) to a lion (cf. Gen 49:9).[48] Also notable is the phrase כיא אל הקימכה לשבט, "for God has established you as the scepter" (1QSb 5:27), an allusion to the "scepter" of Balaam's oracle in Num 24:17.

In view of the clear application of Isaiah 11 to the Prince of the Congregation in 1QSb, there can be little doubt about the identification with the "Branch of David" in 4Q285 and 4QpIsa[a]. All three texts have the same scriptural base in Isaiah 11 and share a common view of the warrior messiah.

Both "Branch of David" and "Prince of the Congregation" appear in a number of other texts. The Branch also appears in the Florilegium (4Q174). This fragmentary text strings together commentaries on 2 Sam 7:10–14; Pss 1:1 and 2:1. 2 Sam 7:14 ("I will be a father to him and he will be a son to me") is interpreted as referring to "the Branch of David, who shall arise with the Interpreter of the Law in Zion at the end of days." This text is further correlated with Amos 9:11 ("I will raise up the tent of David that is fallen"): "the fallen tent of David is he who shall arise to save Israel."[49] The rather minimal description of the role of the Branch of David at least indicates that he has an active role in restoring the fortunes of Israel. Brief though this notice is, it throws important light on several aspects of messianic expectation. The exegesis of 2 Sam 7:14 identifies the Branch of David as the son of God. We shall return to this point in a later chapter. The activity of the messiah is linked with that of another figure, the Interpreter of the Law, a title also known from the Damascus Document. This figure will also detain us in a later chapter. Finally, the association of the Davidic messiah with the "end of days" is important not only for our understanding of the messiah, but also for the use of the expression "end of days" in the Scrolls: the "end of days" is marked, among other things, by the coming of the messiah.

The "Branch of David" appears in another biblical commentary, 4Q252. This document is variously known as the Patriarchal Blessings or the *Pesher* on Genesis (4QpGen). Whether this text is properly called a *pesher* is a matter of dispute.[50] It resembles other *pesharîm* in some respects. It follows sections of Genesis, the biblical text is sometimes atomized and interpreted in the usual *pesher* style, and the formula פשרו אשר ("its interpretation is") is used at least once. Yet other passages, especially the discussion of the Flood, read like a biblical paraphrase such as we find in *Jubilees*. The text, then, is not primarily a messianic prophecy. The messianic reference comes in an interpretation of Gen 49:10.

The biblical text of Gen 49:10 reads: "The scepter (שבט) shall not depart from Judah, nor the ruler's staff (מחקק) from between his feet, until he comes to whom it belongs (עד כיא יבא שילה). And the peoples shall be in obedience to him (ולו יקהת עמים)."

The *pesher* (4Q252 frag. 1, col. 5) cites an abbreviated form of the verse: "A ruler (שליט) will not depart from the tribe (שבט) of Judah." The word שבט can mean either scepter or tribe in Hebrew. The *pesher*, in effect, takes it both ways, substituting ruler for scepter.[51] Then the interpretation continues:

"Whenever Israel rules there shall [not] fail to be a descendant of David upon the throne. For the ruler's staff is the covenant of kingship, [and the clans] of Israel are the feet, until the Messiah of Righteousness comes, the Branch of David. For to him and to his seed was granted the covenant of kingship over his people for everlasting generations...."[52]

The titles Messiah of Righteousness and Branch of David reflect the "righteous Branch" (צמח צדיק\צדקה) of Jer 23:5 and 33:15, and show beyond doubt that Jeremiah's "Branch" could also be called "messiah" at Qumran. In the exegesis of Gen 49:10, this figure is identified with the obscure Hebrew word שילה, Shiloh, which is usually rendered "to whom it belongs" in modern translations. Shiloh is also taken as a name for the messiah, however, in Targum Onkelos to Gen 49:10, the midrash Genesis Rabbah 98:8 and most explicitly in the Talmudic tractate Sanhedrin 98b.[53] The *pesher*, then, is not giving a peculiarly sectarian interpretation but is drawing on a tradition that was (or eventually became) widely known.

There are indications, nonetheless, that 4Q252 is a sectarian text. The line following the passage quoted above contains the words... תורה עם אנשי היחד ...(...Law, with the men of the Community...) and the solar calendar is used in the chronology of the Flood.[54] By analogy with the Florilegium, we might suppose that here also there was a reference to the Interpreter of the Law, who is to arise with the Branch of David at the "end of days."[55]

This *pesher* on Genesis 49 was distinctive in one respect. The word for staff (מחקק) also occurs in the Damascus Document, CD 6:3–9, where it is cited, not from Genesis 49, but from Num 21:18 ("the well which the princes dug, which the nobles of the people delved with the staff"). In the Damascus Document (CD), however, it is given a different interpretation: "the staff is the Interpreter of the Law," not the

covenant of kingship as here. There was, then, some variation in the exegetical traditions of the sect. Nonetheless, there is also a remarkable degree of consistency in the way different messianic titles are combined and
associated in different texts among the Scrolls.

❖ *Star and Scepter in the Damascus Document*

The Prince of the Congregation also appears with messianic overtones
in CD 7:19, in the context of a citation of Balaam's oracle from Numbers
24. The two manuscripts of the Damascus Document that were found in
the Cairo Geniza have different texts at this point.[56] Balaam's oracle is
found only in MS A. The passage begins with the citation and interpretation of Amos 5:26–27, but then introduces Num 24:17: "The star is the
Interpreter of the Law who shall come to Damascus; as it is written, A
star shall come forth out of Jacob and a scepter shall rise out of Israel.
The scepter is the Prince of the whole congregation, and when he comes
he shall smite all the children of Sheth."

The messianic interpretation of Balaam's oracle is well attested. Perhaps the most famous attestation is in the legend of Akiba's recognition
of Bar Kochba: "Rabbi Akiba interpreted, 'A star has come forth out of
Jacob' as '[Kosiba] has come forth out of Jacob.' When Rabbi Akiba
saw bar [Kosiba] he said: This is the King Messiah. Rabbi Yohanan ben
Torta replied: 'Akiba, grass will grow out of your cheekbones before the
son of David comes.'"[57] The messianic interpretation of Num 24:17 was
also current in Greek-speaking Judaism. The LXX read "man"
(ἄνθρωπος) for scepter, and Philo interprets this "man" as a warrior, who
"leading his host to war, will subdue great and populous nations."[58] The
messianic interpretation of this passage in Philo is all the more remarkable because Philo generally shows very little messianic or eschatological fervor.[59] A similar interpretation of Balaam's oracle appears in the
Testament of Judah 24:1–6, which is a Christian text but probably preserves Jewish traditions:

> "And after this a star will come forth for you out of Jacob in peace,
> and a man will rise from among my descendants like the sun of righ-
> teousness. . . . Then will the scepter of my kingdom shine forth, and
> from your root will come a stem. And from it will spring a staff of
> righteousness for the Gentiles, to judge and to save all that invoke
> the Lord."[60]

There can be little doubt that the prince who is identified with the scepter in CD 7 is also a messianic figure. Balaam's oracle is also cited without interpretation in the Testimonia (4Q175), which is apparently a collection of passages with eschatological significance,[61] and in 1QM11:6–7, again in an eschatological context. In CD 7, at least, the star and the scepter refer to two distinct figures. We will return to the issue of bi-messianism, the expectation of two messiahs, in the following chapter. For the present, it is sufficient to establish that Balaam's oracle was widely understood in a messianic sense, and that "Prince of the Congregation" was a messianic title.

Thus far we have traced allusions to the titles "Branch of David" and "Prince of the Congregation," which are juxtaposed in 4Q285 and in the *pesher* on Isaiah. What we have found is a network of interlocking references, in which messianic titles and biblical allusions are combined in various ways. This network includes two major rule books, the Damascus Document and the War Rule, several exegetical texts (*pesharîm* on Isaiah and Genesis 49, the Florilegium)[62] and a liturgical collection of benedictions (1QSb). The references are tied to a few biblical texts, sometimes linked together, sometimes in separate passages. Chief of these passages are Isaiah 11 and Numbers 24, and the expression צמח דויד from Jeremiah 23 and 33 (where it appears as לדויד צמח). Each of these passages occurs several times. Genesis 49, 2 Samuel 7 and Amos 9 are also interpreted with reference to a Davidic messiah at least once. These passages by no means exhaust the references to the Davidic messiah in the Scrolls. We should also take into account messianic references in the Community Rule and the so-called Messianic Rule, and some other texts such as 4Q246 (the "Son of God" text). The network of interlocking references, however, throws some important light on the nature of messianic expectation in the Scrolls.

▦ *Exegetical Traditions*

Joseph Fitzmyer concludes his thorough study of biblical quotations in the Scrolls with the declaration that "There is no evidence at Qumran of a systematic, uniform exegesis of the Old Testament. The same text was not always given the same interpretation (see the variants in CD 7 and 19 and compare the use of Num 24:17 and Amos 9:11 in different contexts)."[63] That there is some variation is certainly true. Amos 9:11 provides a clear example that bears on our subject. In the Florilegium, the booth of David that is fallen is equated with the Branch that will arise to save Israel at the end of days. In CD 7:15–16, however, the booth is identified with the books of the Torah.[64] Another pertinent example is the מחוקק (staff) of Num 21:18, which is variously interpreted as the Interpreter of the Law (CD 6:7) and as "the covenant of the kingdom" (4Q252, "*Pesher* on Genesis").

To say that there was variation, however, is not to deny that there were any fixed traditions. Isaiah 11:1–5 is cited with reference to a Davidic messiah in 4Q285, 4QpIsaᵃ and 1QSb, and no non-messianic interpretation is attested. Moreover, the same passage is echoed in *Ps Sol* 17:22–24 with reference to the future Davidic king. The *Psalms of Solomon* are roughly contemporary with the Scrolls, but are conspicuously absent from the caves. If sectarian scrolls such as the *pesher* on Isaiah and the War Scroll share a common understanding of Isaiah 11 with the psalms of a different sect, it is reasonable to assume that this interpretation was widespread. The same text is reflected, a century and a half later, in the account of the messianic "man from the sea" in *4 Ezra* 13, who "sent forth from his mouth as it were a stream of fire, and from his lips a flaming breath" (*4 Ezra* 13:10).[65] It is also applied to the "Chosen One" in the *Similitudes of Enoch* (*1 Enoch* 49:3–4; 62:2–3) in the first century CE.[66] It is routinely referred to as "the king messiah" in the *targumim* and *midrashim*.[67] Here again there is some variation: the messiahs in the *Similitudes of Enoch* and *4 Ezra* are rather different figures from the king in the *Psalms of Solomon*. There is, however, a very strong and widespread tradition that interpreted Isaiah 11 with reference to a Davidic messianic king, and this tradition is already reflected in the Scrolls.

The same is very probably true of Balaam's oracle in Numbers 24, which Fitzmyer cites as an example of variation in interpretation. We have already noted the explicit identification of the scepter with the "Prince of the Congregation" in CD 7:19. Num 24:17–19 is cited without interpretation in 1QM 11:5–7. The context emphasizes that victory in battle is by the power of God, not of human beings. Fitzmyer infers that "the promise of messianic figures, which is the normal understanding of the verse, is here completely set aside in the new context."[68] I see no basis for this statement. The power of God may be exercised through a messiah. While the messianic interpretation of Balaam's oracle is not explicit in 1QM 11, there is nothing to exclude it, and this interpretation now seems more likely in view of the role of the Branch of David in 4Q285. Balaam's oracle is also cited without interpretation in the Testimonia, but the context has generally been taken to imply a messianic interpretation. In the *Testaments of the Twelve Patriarchs* we find the star related to Judah in *T. Judah* 24, but it is also said of Levi that his star will rise in heaven like a king (*T. Levi* 18:3). Here again, we may speak of a strong and widespread tradition that identified the scepter with the Davidic messiah but not of strict exegetical orthodoxy that would exclude all variation.

The exegetical traditions pertaining to the messiah were surely not confined to Isaiah 11 and Numbers 24. Genesis 49 and 2 Samuel 7, both cited at Qumran, later enjoy an illustrious history in messianic exegesis. Other texts such as Psalm 2, which are important both in the New Testament and in later Jewish tradition, may also have been used more widely around the turn of the era.

In this connection, it is instructive to note the way Isaiah 9 is used in the Thanksgiving Hymns or Hodayot. In 1QH 3, the hymnist compares his own travail to that of a woman in childbirth:

"For the children have come to the breakers of death
  and she who bears a man labors in her pains.
For amid the breakers of Death
  she shall deliver a male,
and amid the pains of Sheol
  there shall spring from the crucible of the pregnant one
a wonderful counselor in his strength,
  and a man shall be brought forth from the birth canal."[69]

The hymn goes on to contrast the pregnancy of one who is pregnant with אפעה, which is variously translated as "wickedness," "nothingness," or "asp or viper."[70] This pregnancy ends in terror and destruction:

"the doors of the pit close behind her that is pregnant with mischief and the bars of eternity behind all the spirits of wickedness."

The hymn contrasts the distress of one individual, which will have a happy outcome, with that of another, which will end in disaster. The contrast is drawn, however, with imagery that has mythological and eschatological overtones. The phrase "wonderful counselor" is taken from Isa 9:5 and evokes the birth, not just of any child, but of one "through whom the house of David is assured that the line of succession will continue."[71] Birth imagery is often associated with the coming of the messiah. Revelation 12, with its vivid imagery of a woman giving birth, is an obvious example.[72] In the rabbinic tradition, the time of distress that precedes the redemption is known as "the birth pangs of the messiah" (חבלי המשיח).[73] The manner in which this imagery is used in the Thanksgiving Hymn, as a metaphorical illustration of the distress of an individual, suggests that both the messianic connotations of Isaiah 9 and the notion of the "birth pangs of the messiah" were well-known in the first century BCE.

It is unfortunate that the *pesharîm* on the psalms are not more fully preserved. The extant evidence, however, lends support to the position of Vermes that there were exegetical traditions relating to the Davidic messiah that were known across sectarian lines by the first century BCE.[74] The fact that even Philo seems to be familiar with a messianic understanding of Balaam's oracle shows the widespread diffusion of such exegesis in the first century CE. Whether we may therefore speak of a "general messianic *expectation*"[75] is another matter. We do not know how important these traditions were to the populace at large; interest probably fluctuated with historical circumstances. When interest in messianic expectation arose, however, there was at hand a body of tradition that could be used to articulate it.

The Character and Role of the Davidic Messiah

The portrait of the ideal king that emerges from this corpus is sketchy but consistent. He is the scepter who will smite the nations, slay the wicked with the breath of his lips, and restore the Davidic dynasty. Hence his role in the eschatological war. He is also the messiah of righteousness, who will usher in an era of peace and justice. He is presumably a human figure, although he is endowed with the spirit of the Lord. He is expected to restore a dynasty rather than rule forever himself. Most of the passages we have considered, however, are brief and elliptic, and the picture could be filled out in various ways.

The main features of this picture of the messiah persist in the apocalypses of *4 Ezra* and *2 Baruch*, which can certainly not be associated with the Dead Sea sect at the end of the first century. In *4 Ezra* 11–12, Ezra sees a vision of an eagle and a lion.[76] The eagle represents Rome. The lion is explicitly "the Messiah whom the Most High has kept until the end of days, who will arise from the posterity of David" (12:32). He will rebuke the wicked, then "set them living before his judgment seat, and when he has reproved them he will destroy them." He will then "restore the remnant of my people." Similarly in *2 Baruch* 40, the messiah will convict the last ruler of all his wicked deeds and then kill him but protect "the rest of my children." Again in *2 Baruch 72*, when "the time of my Messiah is come, he will call all the nations together, and some of them he will spare, and some of them he will destroy. . . . Every nation that has not exploited Israel and has not trampled the race of Jacob underfoot will be spared. . . . But all those who have had dominion over you, or have exploited you, will be given over to the sword."[77]

The concept of the messiah in these late first-century apocalypses is considerably more complex than this, however.[78] Both envisage an extended, but not everlasting, messianic reign (400 years in *4 Ezra* 7:28–29), followed by general resurrection, rather than the restoration of a dynasty. The messiah is said to be "revealed" rather than born (*4 Ezra* 7:28). He is apparently pre-existent: the Most High has kept him for many ages (13:26). Yet he dies, after his 400-year reign. *4 Ezra* 13 speaks of a messianic "man" who will rise from the sea on clouds, and then take his stand on a mountain and destroy the wicked with the breath of his lips. The messiah here is modeled on the paradigm of the "one like a son of man" of Daniel 7 as well as that of the traditional Davidic messiah.[79] The passages we have referred to, however, show that these apocalypses shared the expectation of a warlike Davidic messiah, which was common to various strands of Judaism in the first century CE. The same conception survives in the *targumim* and *midrashim* of later Jewish tradition.[80]

This concept of the Davidic messiah as the warrior king who would destroy the enemies of Israel and institute an era of unending peace constitutes the common core of Jewish messianism around the turn of the era. In the following chapters, we will consider some of the other messianic paradigms that are less widely attested. These are the eschatological High Priest, or messiah of Aaron, who figures prominently in the Scrolls, the eschatological prophet, and the heavenly messiah or "Son of Man."

NOTES

[1] R. B. Wright, "Psalms of Solomon," in James H. Charlesworth, ed., *The Old Testament Pseudepigrapha* (Garden City, N.Y.: Doubleday, 1985) 2.639; Schuerer, *The History of the Jewish People* 3/1.192.

[2] Note especially the lack of proper burial in *Ps Sol* 2:26, cf. Dio Cassius 42.5.

[3] Schuerer, *The History of the Jewish People* 1.233–42. See also William W. Buehler, *The Pre-Herodian Civil War and Social Debate* (Basel: Reinhardt, 1974).

[4] Josephus, *Antiquities* 14.41–45; Diodorus 40.2.

[5] So Josephus, *Antiquities* 14.71.

[6] H. E. Ryle and M. R. James, *Psalmoi Salomontos. Psalms of the Pharisees commonly called The Psalms of Solomon* (Cambridge: Cambridge University Press, 1891) xliv–lii; G. B. Gray, "The Psalms of Solomon," in R. H. Charles, ed., *Apocrypha and Pseudepigrapha of the Old Testament* (Oxford: Clarendon, 1913) 2.630; J. Schüpphaus, *Die Psalmen Salomos: Ein Zeugnis Jerusalemer Theologie und Frömmigkeit in der Mitte des vorchristlichen Jahrhunderts* (Leiden: Brill, 1977) 158.

[7] R. B. Wright, "Psalms of Solomon," 2.642; J. H. Charlesworth, "From Jewish Messianology to Christian Christology: Some Caveats and Perspectives," in Neusner et al., eds., *Judaisms and their Messiahs*, 234; A. Chester, "Jewish Messianic Expectations and Mediatorial Figures," in M. Hengel and U. Heckel, eds., *Paulus und das antike Judentum* (Tübingen: Mohr, 1991) 29.

[7a] Johannes Tromp, "The Sinners and the Lawless of Psalm of Solomon 17," *Novum Testamentum* 35(1993) 344–61, is exceptional in holding that the sinners are foreigners here.

[8] So Josephus, *Antiquities* 13.300.

[9] Josephus, *Antiquities* 13.301. The number of years is too large, but would be roughly accurate for the time elapsed since the fall of Jerusalem in 586.

[10] Schuerer, *The History of the Jewish People*, 1.217.

[11] Schuerer, *The History of the Jewish People*, 1.227.

[12] On the Hasmonean ideology of kingship, see Doron Mendels, *The Rise and Fall of Jewish Nationalism* (New York: Doubleday, 1992) 55–79.

[13] For Jannaeus, see Josephus, *Antiquities* 13.400. For Aristobulus, *Antiquities* 13.423.

[14] Compare Isa 10:5; Jer 27:6.

[15] *Ps Sol* 17:11. Some MSS read "the storm" here.

[16] *Ps Sol* 2:25. On the mythological connotations of the "dragon" see A. Yarbro Collins, *The Combat Myth in the Book of Revelation* (Harvard Dissertations in Religion 9; Missoula: Scholars Press, 1976) 76–79.

[17] G. L. Davenport, "The 'Anointed of the Lord' in Psalms of Solomon 17," in J. J. Collins and G. W. Nickelsburg, eds., *Ideal Figures in Ancient Judaism* (Chico, CA: Scholars Press, 1980) 72.

[18] Davenport's claim ("The 'Anointed of the Lord,'" 73) that the content of Ps 2:9 has been modified so that it refers to sinners rather than Gentiles cannot be sustained in light of the passage as a whole.

[19] J. Klausner, *The Messianic Idea in Israel* (London: Bradford and Dickens, 1956) 323; M. Delcor, "Psaumes de Salomon," *Supplément au Dictionnaire de la Bible*, fasc. 48(1973) 214–45; Charlesworth, "The Messiah in the Pseudepigrapha," 199; Chester, "Jewish Messianic Expectations," 28; J. D. Crossan, *The Historical Jesus* (San Francisco: Harper, 1991) 108: "And this messianic leader does not use violence, neither the actual violence of normal warfare nor the transcendental violence of angelic destruction."

[20] Samson H. Levey, *The Messiah: An Aramaic Interpretation. The Messianic Exegesis of the Targum* (Monographs of the Hebrew Union College 2; Cincinnati, OH: Hebrew Union College/Jewish Institute of Religion, 1974) 9. The bloody allusions are drawn from Isa 63:1–6. Cf. Rev 19:11–15.

[21] Klausner, *The Messianic Idea*, 323.

[22] Contrast Ezek 47:22, where the aliens are included in the land with the Israelites.

[23] John 8:46; 2 Cor 5:21; Heb 4:15; 7:26; 9:14; 1 Pet 1:19; 2:22. J. Ephron, *Studies on the Hasmonean Period* (Leiden: Brill, 1987) 278, argues that the *Psalms of Solomon* are Christian, but this view is eccentric.

[24] The Hebrew reads "committed no violence."

[25] So Davenport, "The 'Anointed of the Lord,' in Psalms of Solomon 17," 80.

[26] Klausner, *The Messianic Idea*, 324.

[27] Eisenman and Wise, *The Dead Sea Scrolls Uncovered*, 11.

[28] *Kittim* is the normal form of the word in scholarly literature, but the name is properly to be transliterated as *Kittiyyim*, and this is the form found in the Scrolls.

[29] 4QpIsa^a fragments 2–6, column 2, line 18.

[30] M. P. Horgan, *Pesharim. Qumran Interpretations of Biblical Books* (Catholic Biblical Quarterly Monograph Series 8; Washington, D.C.: Catholic Biblical Association, 1979) 79, restores the line to read השבט הוא [א] נשׂיא העדה "the rod is the Prince of the Congregation," in light of CD 7:20, where the prince is identified with the שבט of Num 24:17. The text being interpreted here is Isa 10:24–27, which mentions how the Lord's rod (מטה) will be over the sea. The word שבט also occurs in the passage with reference to the rod with which Assyria will smite Israel. מטה rather than שבט would seem to be the more apt restoration here.

[31] Fragment 7, column 3, line 11.

[32] Horgan, *Pesharim*, 80, following the suggestion of J. Strugnell.

[33] The fragmentary *pesher* sheds no light on the identification of Magog. From the context, the name seems to refer to a nation or place, as in Ezekiel 38–39, rather than to a person as in Rev 20:8. Gog is also mentioned in 1QM 11:16 as someone chastised by God in the final war. See Horgan, *Pesharim*, 86.

[34] Yigael Yadin, *The Scroll of the War of the Sons of Light against the Sons of Darkness* (Oxford: Oxford University Press, 1962) 23–26.

[35] Horgan, *Pesharim*, 8. George Brooke, "The Kittim in the Qumran Pesharim," in L. Alexander, ed., *Images of Empire* (Sheffield: Journal for the Study of the Old Testament, 1991) 135–59, emphasizes the role of biblical stereotypes in the *pesharîm*, and discounts their historical value. The method of the *pesharîm*, however, involves correlation of the biblical language with historical events. The recognition of these events, where possible, is an essential element in the understanding of the texts. See my essay, "Prophecy and Fulfillment in the Qumran Scrolls," *Journal of the Evangelical Theological Society* 30(1987) 267–78.

[36] *The New York Times*, November 8, 1991, *The Times* (London), November 8, 1991, *The Chicago Tribune*, November 11, 1991, and the *Independent* (London), December 27, 1991. The claims were attributed to R. Eisenman and M. O. Wise. Eisenman and Wise are more tentative in their subsequent publication, *The Dead Sea Scrolls Uncovered*, 24–27, but they still defend their original interpretation as possible.

[37] G. Vermes, "The Oxford Forum for Qumran Research Seminar on the Rule of War from Cave 4 (4Q285)," *Journal of Jewish Studies* 43(1992) 85–90; M. Bockmuehl, "A 'Slain Messiah' in 4Q Serekh Milhamah (4Q285)?" *Tyndale Bulletin* 43(1992) 155–69. The objections of James D. Tabor, "A Pierced or Piercing Messiah? — The Verdict is Still Out," *Biblical Archeology Review* (November/December 1992) 58–59, are easily refuted by Vermes, ibid., 59.

[38] Eisenman and Wise, *The Dead Sea Scrolls Uncovered*, 29.

[39] Vermes, "The Oxford Forum," 88.

[40] Vermes, "The Oxford Forum," 88–89.

[41] J. T. Milik, "Milkî-sedeq et Milkî-rešaʿ dans les écrits juifs et chrétiens," *Journal of Jewish Studies* 23(1972) 143. M. G. Abegg has reconstructed the place of this and other frag-

ments at the end of the War Rule ("Messianic Hope and 4Q385: A Reassessment," *Journal of Biblical Literature* 113[1994] 81–91).

[42] Abegg, "Messianic Hope and 4Q285," claims that only 7 percent of the vocabulary of 4Q285 is not found in the War Scroll, and that this extremely low percentage indicates an almost certain relationship.

[43] See the fragments from Cave 4, published by M. Baillet, *Qumrân Grotte 4. III (4Q482–4Q520)* (Discoveries in the Judean Desert 7; Oxford: Clarendon, 1982) 12–45, which show considerable divergence from 1QM.

[44] Vermes, "The Oxford Forum," 89. Abegg, "Messianic Hope," offers the following reconstruction of the events in 4Q285: "The High Priest blesses God before the assembly reflecting the imminent age of peace and prosperity (fragment 1). Fragments 6 and 4 appear to describe a campaign beginning in the mountains of Israel. The final battle is then fought on the Mediterranean (?) Sea. The evil forces are routed with the help of the angelic hosts and the wicked leader is brought before the Prince of the congregation for judgment (4:6). He is found guilty and put to death in fulfillment of Isaiah 10:33–11:5. The daughters of Israel then celebrate with timbrel and dance and the High Priest orders the cleansing of the land from the corpses of the Kitians."

[45] Sanders, *Judaism. Practice and Belief*, 296. Compare P. R. Davies, "War Rule (1QM)," in D. N. Freedman, ed., *The Anchor Bible Dictionary* 6.875.

[46] J. H. Charlesworth, "Sense or Sensationalism? The Dead Sea Scrolls Controversy," *The Christian Century*, (January 29, 1992) 97, denies that the text is messianic.

[47] J. A. Fitzmyer, "4Q246: The 'Son of God' Document from Qumran," *Biblica* 74 (1993) 172–73, tries to maintain a distinction between a future Davidic king and a messiah, but his position rests on a refusal to speak of a messiah unless the word מֹשׁיח is explicitly used.

[48] Only the first letter of אַ[ריה], lion, is legible, but the word טרף, prey, occurs on the next line.

[49] See the discussion of this passage by G. J. Brooke, *Exegesis at Qumran. 4QFlorilegium in its Jewish Context* (Journal for the Study of the Old Testament Supplement 29; Sheffield: Journal for the Study of the Old Testament, 1985) 197–205.

[50] See Timothy H. Lim, "The Chronology of the Flood Story in a Qumran Text (4Q252)," *Journal of Jewish Studies* 43(1992) 288–98; George H. Brooke, "4Q252, Pesher Genesis: Structure and Themes," *Jewish Quarterly Review*, forthcoming.

[51] See F. García Martínez, "Nuevos Textos Mesiánicos de Qumran y el Mesias del Nuevo Testamento," *Communio* 26(1993) 9–11; García Martínez, "Messianische Erwartungen in den Qumranschriften," *Jahrbuch für Biblische Theologie* 8(1993) 175.

[52] Trans. G. Vermes, *The Dead Sea Scrolls in English* (London: Penguin, 1987) 260.

[53] S. H. Levey, *The Messiah: An Aramaic Interpretation*, 7–11. A more general messianic interpretation is found in Targum Pseudo-Jonathan and in Genesis Rabbah 98:8.

[54] While the solar calendar is found in pre-Qumran documents such as *1 Enoch* and *Jubilees*, it may at least be taken as an indication that the text does not derive from the Jerusalem temple.

[55] Eisenman and Wise, *The Dead Sea Scrolls Uncovered*, 89, translate: "to him and his seed was given the covenant of the Kingdom of His people in perpetuity, because he kept . . . the Torah with the men of the Community," and comment that the messiah's observance of the Torah is important "not only for Qumran messianic notions, but for Qumran ideology as a whole and its overtones with early Christianity of the Jamesian mould" (p. 85). The word "kept" (שמר) is not clear in the photograph, and in any case the lacuna before

"the Torah" invalidates the Eisenman-Wise translation. The passage says nothing about the relation of the messiah to the Torah.

56 For a recent discussion see M. Knibb, "The Interpretation of Damascus Document VII,9b–VIII,2a and XIX,5b–14," *Revue de Qumran* 15(1991) 243–51.

57 jTaᶜanit 68d. G. Vermes, *Jesus the Jew* (Philadelphia: Fortress, 1981) 134.

58 Philo, *De Praemiis et Poenis*, 95. On the LXX, see P. Volz, *Die Eschatologie der Jüdischen Gemeinde* (Tübingen: Mohr, 1934; reprint, Hildesheim: Olms, 1966) 188. On Philo, see P. Borgen, "'There Shall Come Forth a Man': Reflections on Messianic Ideas in Philo," in Charlesworth, ed., *The Messiah*, 341–61.

59 R. D. Hecht, "Philo and Messiah," in *Judaisms and their Messiahs*, 139–68; B. Mack, "Wisdom and Apocalyptic in Philo," *The Studia Philonica Annual. Studies in Hellenistic Judaism* 3(1991) 21–39. Philo takes the "man" as a symbolic reference to Israel at its best in *Mos* 2.263–99.

60 See A. Hultgård, *L'Eschatologie des Testaments des Douze Patriarches I. Interprétation des Textes* (Stockholm: Almqvist & Wiksell, 1977) 204–13. For further Christian references, see H. W. Hollander and M. de Jonge, *The Testaments of the Twelve Patriarchs. A Commentary* (Leiden: Brill, 1985) 228.

61 See J. A. Fitzmyer, "'4QTestimonia' and the New Testament," in Fitzmyer, *Essays on the Semitic Background of the New Testament* (Missoula: Scholars Press, 1974) 59–89.

62 I do not understand how Charlesworth can say that "None of the Pesharim contains messianic exegesis," especially as he goes on to recognize the allusion to the Branch of David in the *pesher* on Isaiah (*The Messiah*, 25).

63 J. A. Fitzmyer, "The use of explicit Old Testament quotations in Qumran literature and in the New Testament," in *Essays on the Semitic Background of the New Testament* (Missoula: Scholars Press, 1974) 55. Cf. F. M. Cross, *The Ancient Library of Qumran and Modern Biblical Studies* (Garden City, NY: Doubleday, 1961) 229.

64 This passage begins with Amos 5:26–27, which refers to "the booth of your king," but introduces Amos 9:11 as a supporting citation.

65 For further allusions see Volz, *Die Eschatologie*, 176.

66 J. Theisohn, *Der auserwählte Richter* (Göttingen: Vandenhoeck & Ruprecht, 1975) 58–63.

67 Levey, *The Messiah*, 49–52 (T. Jonathan); *Midrash Rabbah: Genesis* (trans. H. Freedman and M. Simon; London: Soncino, 1939) 2.902; *Midrash on Psalms* (trans. W. G. Braude; New Haven, CT: Yale University Press, 1959) 1.36–37; *Pesikta Rabbati* (trans. W. G. Braude; New Haven, CT: Yale University Press, 1968) 2.641–42 (Piska 33); *Pirke de Rabbi Eliezer* (trans. G. Friedlander; New York: Hermon, 1965) 19. There was also a tradition that related Isaiah 11 to the historical Hezekiah (Klausner, *The Messianic Idea*, 464). This tradition is attested in Justin's *Dialogue with Trypho*, 43, 67, 68, 71, 77.

68 Fitzmyer, "Old Testament Citations," 43.

69 The translation of this passage is made difficult by the density of poetic double meanings. The word משבר is variously translated as "breaker," (mišbār) or "birth canal" (mašbēr). The word חבל means "pain," but can also mean "snare." כור, "crucible," is here a metaphor for the womb. See S. Holm-Nielsen, *Hodayot: Psalms from Qumran* (Aarhus: Universitets-vorlaget, 1960) 51; J. J. Collins, "Patterns of Eschatology at Qumran," in B. Halpern and J. D. Levenson, eds., *Traditions in Transformation. Turning Points in Biblical Faith* (Winona Lake: Eisenbrauns, 1981) 366–70.

[70] See especially A. Dupont-Sommer, "La mère du Messie et la mère de l'Aspic dans un hymne de Qoumrân," *Revue de l'Histoire des Religions* (1955) 174–88.

[71] Wildberger, *Isaiah 1–12*, 399. In its original context, the oracle was concerned with the present, not the eschatological future.

[72] See Yarbro Collins, *The Combat Myth in the Book of Revelation*, 101–55.

[73] Klausner, *The Messianic Idea*, 440–50; Schuerer, *A History*, 2.514.

[74] "The disclosure of a body of interpretative tradition prior to, and free from any sectarian bias is one of the most important contributions made by Qumran literature to our knowledge of Palestinian religious thought," G. Vermes, *Post-Biblical Jewish Studies* (Leiden: Brill, 1975) 47.

[75] So Vermes, *Jesus the Jew*, 130. Vermes also cites the "Blessing concerning David" from the Eighteen Benedictions, but it is not clear that this can serve as evidence for the period before 70 CE.

[76] See A. Lacocque, "The Vision of the Eagle in 4 Esdras: A Rereading of Daniel 7 in the First Century CE," in K. H. Richards, ed., *Society of Biblical Literature 1981 Seminar Papers* (Chico, CA: Scholars Press, 1981) 237–58.

[77] See Charlesworth, "The Messiah in the Pseudepigrapha," 200–5.

[78] See M. E. Stone, "The Question of the Messiah in 4 Ezra," in Neusner et al., eds., *Judaisms and their Messiahs*, 209–24; Ulrich B. Müller, *Messias und Menschensohn in jüdischen Apokalypsen und in der Offenbarung des Johannes* (Gütersloh: Mohn, 1972) 107–56.

[79] See further Chapter Eight (of this book).

[80] See Levey, *The Messiah*.

4

THE MESSIAHS OF AARON AND ISRAEL

One or Two Messiahs?

The expectation of a Davidic messiah was part of the common Judaism of the last century BCE and the first century CE. This, however, is only one aspect of the messianic expectation reflected in the Dead Sea Scrolls.

One of the first scrolls published, the Community Rule or Manual of Discipline (1QS) contains a famous passage, which is widely regarded as a summary of the messianic expectations of the Qumran sect:[1] "They shall depart from none of the counsels of the Law to walk in the stubbornness of their hearts, but shall be ruled by the primitive precepts in which the men of the Community were first instructed until there shall come the Prophet and the Messiahs of Aaron and Israel" (1QS 9:11). The scriptural underpinning for this expectation was found in the Testimonia (4Q175), which strings together a series of biblical passages without interpretation. Exod 20:21 (Samaritan text = Deut 5:28–29 + Deut 18:18–19) promises that "I will raise up for them a prophet like you from among their brethren," Num 24:25–27 (Balaam's oracle about the star and the scepter), Deut 33:8–11 (the blessing of Levi) and a passage from the Psalms of Joshua, including Josh 6:26 ("Cursed be the man who rebuilds this city"), which refers to "an accursed man, a man of Belial." The passages from Exodus 20 (Samaritan text = Deuteronomy 18), Numbers 24 and Deuteronomy 33 have usually been understood with reference to the prophet and messiahs of Israel and Aaron, respectively.[2]

The eschatological prophet is an elusive figure in the Qumran scrolls, but the binary messianism of priest and king, Aaron and Israel, is usually taken to be the norm at Qumran and to be the most distinctive feature of Qumran messianism. Like much of the received wisdom about Qumran, this view has come under attack in the wake of the release of the unpublished Scrolls. The expression "messiahs of Aaron and Israel" in 1QS is actually unique. A closely related expression, "the messiah of Aaron and Israel" (משיח אהרון וישראל), is found three times in the Damascus Document (CD 12:23, 14:19, and 19:10), and in CD 20:1 we have the expression "a messiah from Aaron and from Israel" (משיח מאהרון ומישראל). In these cases, however, there is a long-standing dispute, to which we will return below, as to whether one or two messiahs is involved. If the expressions in CD are taken to refer to a single messiah, then we have only one text that speaks explicitly of two messiahs, and so some scholars have argued that dual messianism is the exception rather than the rule.[3] Their argument is bolstered by the fact that a number of the newly available texts (4Q246, the "Son of God text"; 4Q521, which speaks of "the messiah of heaven and earth") speak of a single messianic figure, with no implication of a second.

The question of dual messianism in the Scrolls cannot, however, be reduced to the occurrence of the expression "messiah(s) of Aaron and Israel." Just as the royal messiah is the eschatological king of Israel, by whatever name he is called, so the priestly messiah is the eschatological High Priest. The use of the term משיח with reference to this figure in the phrase "messiahs of Aaron and Israel" implies that his rank in the eschatological period is at least comparable to that of the King Messiah. The issue, then, is not how many texts speak explicitly of two messiahs, but how many involve the presence of another figure of authority equal to or greater than that of the Davidic messiah. If the issue is viewed in these terms, the evidence for a "priestly messiah" is considerably more extensive than the revisionist critics allow, since it includes any text that subordinates the King Messiah to priestly authority.

A classic illustration of the issue is found in the so-called "Messianic Rule" (1QSa). The second column of this document contains a rule for assemblies in the messianic age. The introductory sentence is fragmentary, and the restoration has been very controversial. Some scholars read אם יו[לי]ד [אל] א[ת] המשיח אתם "when God begets the messiah with them;"[4]

others "when God sends the Messiah to be with them," reading יוליך, sends, instead of יוליד, begets;[5] yet others read "when the messiah shall assemble with them."[6] The passage continues:

> "[The priest] shall enter [at] the head of all the congregation of Israel and [all his brethren the sons of] Aaron, the priests, [who are invited] to the feast, men of renown, and they shall sit be[fore him, each] according to his importance. Afterwards, [the messiah] of Israel [shall enter] and the heads of the [thousands of Israel] shall sit before him [ea]ch according to his importance.... [no] one [shall extend] his hand to the first (portion) of the bread and [the wine] before the priest. Fo[r he shall extend] his hand to the bread first. Afterwa[rds,] the messiah of Israel [shall exten]d his hand to the bread. [Afterwards,] all of the congregation of the community [shall ble]ss, ea[ch according to] his importance...."[7]

The priest in this text is not clearly called a משיח, although the messiah in the controversial opening verse may arguably be a priest-messiah.[8] It is quite clear, however, that the "messiah of Israel" here is not a priest, and that the priest takes precedence over him in the strictly hierarchical proceedings. It is reasonable, then, to refer to the chief priest in this passage as "the messiah of Aaron," even though he is not explicitly so called in the extant text.

Several other texts indicate that the royal messiah must defer to priestly authority. In 4QpIsa[a], the biblical phrase, "He shall not judge by what his eyes see" (Isa 11:3), is taken to mean that the messiah will defer to the teachings of "the priests of renown." 4Q285 (the "dying messiah" text), line 5, after the reference to the Prince of the Congregation, reads "and a priest will command...." The High Priest in the War Scroll enjoys greater prominence than the Prince of the Congregation in any case. In the Scroll of Blessings (1QSb) the blessing of the High Priest precedes that of the Prince of the Congregation. Further, in *Florilegium* 1:11, the Branch of David is accompanied by the Interpreter of the Law, and likewise in CD 7:18 the Prince of the Congregation is linked with the Interpreter, who can plausibly, though not certainly, be identified as a priestly messiah.[9] In fact, all the major rule and law books, the Community Rule, the Messianic Rule, the Damascus Document, and the War Rule, support the bifurcation of authority in the messianic era. We might add that the Temple Scroll, which some scholars regard as the Torah for the end of days, clearly subjects the king to the authority of the High

Priest: "on his instructions he shall go out and on his instructions he shall return home."[10] We shall argue in Chapter Five that the Temple Scroll does not in fact relate to the end of days and is not messianic, but nonetheless it supports the general pattern of bifurcation of authority in the Dead Sea Scrolls.

There is, then, impressive evidence that the Dead Sea sect expected two messiahs, one royal and one priestly. This binary messianism had, of course, its biblical precedent in Zechariah's "two sons of oil,"[11] and indeed the model of dual leadership can be traced further back, to the roles of king and High Priest in the preexilic community, and even to Moses and Aaron in the Pentateuch. There is also evidence of dual leadership in the organization of the sect. The "rule for the assembly of the camps" in CD 14 singles out two authoritative figures, the priest who enrolls the congregation and "the guardian (מבקר) of all the camps." On a lower level, CD 13 says that wherever there are ten people in a "camp" there should be a priest in charge, and the passage goes on to define the role of the "guardian of the camp," who is clearly a different figure. The Community Rule also distinguishes between the priest and the guardian, in the Rule for the Assembly of the Congregation.[12] While it is not clear that the role of the guardian corresponds in any way to that of the royal messiah in the end time, the bifurcation of authority between priestly and lay leadership was embedded in the life of the sect.[13]

Theories of Development

Since the Dead Sea Scrolls are thought to span a period of a century and a half, it is natural to expect some development in messianism as in other matters over that period. Several developmental theories have been proposed. All have focused on the expression "messiah(s) of Aaron and Israel" in the Damascus Document. If this phrase is construed as referring to one messiah rather than two, then we can distinguish at least two stages in the messianism of the Dead Sea sect, one stage that envisaged a single messiah and another that envisaged two.

In 1963, Jean Starcky proposed a four-stage theory of development, which he correlated with the stages of the history of the Qumran community proposed by Roland de Vaux on the basis of the archeology of the site.[14] In the first stage (Maccabean) the settlement was quite small, and there was no evidence of messianic expectation. The second (Hasmonean) stage was marked by an influx of members and an expansion of the settlement. According to Starcky, the community envisaged two messiahs at this stage, with the priestly one taking precedence. The third stage (Pompeian) is represented by the Damascus Document, which is understood to have only one messiah from Aaron and Israel. The fourth (Herodian) is marked by a revival of expectation of a Davidic messiah, in addition to the priestly one. This theory has been widely criticized.[15] It depends heavily on the palaeographic dating of documents and, even if one accepts these dates without reservation, they only give us the date at which a manuscript was copied, not the date at which the text was composed. Starcky assigned a relatively late date to the Damascus Document (CD). Recent scholarship has favored an earlier date for CD and posited a complex redactional history for the document, which is known in two recensions from the Cairo Geniza in addition to the fragments from Qumran.[16]

These recent trends are reflected in a new proposal by George Brooke.[17] Building on the work of P. R. Davies, Brooke reconstructs three stages in the evolution of CD:

First, there was a "pre-Qumran" core (supposedly composed before the settlement at Qumran) that spoke consistently of one "messiah of Aaron and Israel," who was priestly in character. This figure would be the anointed High Priest, but his coming would mark the advent of a messianic age. This stage is reflected in MS B from the Cairo Geniza in a midrash on Zech 13:7 and Ezek 9:4 (CD 19:7–13), which speaks of a "messiah of Aaron and Israel."

In the second stage, this document was edited at Qumran. The "Qumran recension" replaced this Zechariah-Ezekiel midrash with one on Amos 5:26–27 and Num 24:17 (CD 7:14–21; MS A from the Geniza). The insertion cites Balaam's oracle about the star and the scepter. The star is identified as the Interpreter of the Law, who was already present in the Qumran community. Brooke reasons that if the Interpreter was known to have already come, then the prophecy was believed to be already being fulfilled, and it was introduced into CD to show that the eschatological period had begun.[18] The scepter of Balaam's oracle is, however, interpreted as a separate figure, the Prince of the Congregation, who is still to come. Consequently we have two messianic figures in the "Qumran recension," one of whom has already come.[19]

The third stage, placed "around the turn of the era," reverts to the notion of a single, priestly messiah. This is attributed to "some of the Levitical circle," who had been the original core of the movement reflected in CD. They now replaced the citations from Amos and Numbers by reinserting the Zechariah-Ezekiel midrash (= CD Text B) with its reference to a "messiah of Aaron and Israel," which Brooke takes to be "a clear presentation of the singular Aaronic Messiah."[20] The main point at issue in the B recension is "the pre-eminence amongst eschatological figures of the single Messiah of Aaron."[21]

Brooke's developmental theory is no less problematic than Starcky's. It presupposes a theory of multiple stages in the Damascus Document that is itself highly dubious. We will confine our remarks here to the issues that bear directly on messianism.

The expression משיח אהרון וישראל ("messiah of Aaron and Israel" or "messiahs of Aaron and Israel") provides only a precarious foundation for any theory of messianic development. Before any Qumran Scrolls were discovered, no less an authority than Louis Ginzberg had argued that the reference was to two messiahs rather than one.[22] For many scholars, this interpretation seemed to be confirmed by the plural in 1QS 9:11 (משיחי אהרון וישראל, "messiahs of Aaron and Israel").[23] Grammatically, the phrase may refer to either two messiahs or one,[24] although the singular interpretation is often taken as the more natural. The strongest argument in favor of the single reference here is found in CD 14:18–19, where the reference to the coming of the messiah of Aaron and Israel is followed by the singular verb יכפר, which is most naturally translated as an active (piel) "he will atone." This would imply that the subject is a single figure, and that he is a priest.[25] It is possible, however, to take it as a passive (pual), so "atonement will be made."[26] The singular interpretation, despite its recent popularity, is difficult to reconcile with other considerations.

First, there is the form of the expression, "Aaron and Israel," which is found in conjunction with messiahs only in CD and 1QS. It would be a remarkable coincidence if the sectarians had first coined the reference to "Aaron and Israel" and only later developed the notion of a dual messiahship. CD elsewhere uses Aaron and Israel to distinguish priesthood and laity as the twin sources of its community. God "raised from Aaron men of discernment and from Israel men of wisdom" (CD 6:2–3; cf. 1:7). It is conceivable that one messiah could represent both strands of the community, but then one wonders why the distinction between Aaron and Israel should be emphasized. After all, a messiah from Aaron was inevitably also "from Israel."[27] Indeed, F. M. Cross has argued that the reference to Aaron and Israel necessarily implies two messiahs, since a single, priestly messiah would simply be called "messiah of Aaron."[28]

Another obstacle to the view that CD originally envisaged a single, priestly, messiah is presented by the exposition of Balaam's oracle in

CD 7, MS A. Since the scepter of Balaam's oracle is identified as the Prince of the Congregation, there is a clear reference here to a royal messiah. Those who argue that the document originally expected only a priestly messiah have to argue that the passage dealing with Balaam's oracle is a secondary insertion.

EXCURSUS: THE DAMASCUS DOCUMENT

The passage in question is exceptionally complicated, as two quite different texts are preserved in the two manuscripts, A and B, of the Geniza document. The context is a warning about future punishment. Both manuscripts have midrashic passages at this point, but they cite different texts. MS A cites Isa 7:17, followed by Amos 5:26–27 (with a subsidiary citation of Amos 9:11) and Numbers 24:17, as follows:

> "... when the saying shall come to pass which is written among the words of the Prophet Isaiah son of Amoz: *He will bring upon you, and upon your people, and upon your father's house, days such as have not come since the day that Ephraim departed from Judah* (Isa 7:17). When the two houses of Israel were divided, Ephraim departed from Judah. And all the apostates **were given up to the sword**, but those who held fast escaped to the land of the north; as God said, *I will exile the tabernacle of your king and the bases of your statues from my tent to Damascus* (Amos 5:26–27). The Books of the Law are the tabernacle of the king; as God said, *I will raise up the tabernacle of David which is fallen* (Amos 9:11). The king is the congregation; and the bases of the statues are the Books of the Prophets whose sayings Israel despised. The star is the Interpreter of the Law who shall come to Damascus; as it is written, *A star shall come forth out of Jacob and a sceptre shall rise out of Israel* (Num 24:17). The sceptre is the Prince of the whole congregation, and when he comes *he shall smite all the children of Seth* (Num 24:17). At the time of the former visitation they were saved, whereas the apostates **were given up to the sword**; ..." (trans. Vermes, emphasis added. Biblical quotations italicized).

MS B cites Zech 13:7 and Ezek 9:4, as follows:

> "... by the hand of the prophet Zechariah: *Awake, O Sword, against my shepherd, against my companion, says God. Strike the shepherd that the flock may be scattered and I will stretch my hand over the little ones* (Zech 13:7). The humble of the flock are those who watch for Him. They shall be saved at the time of the Visitation whereas the others **shall be delivered up to the sword** when the Anointed of Aaron and Is-

rael shall come, as it came to pass at the time of the former Visitation concerning which God said by the hand of Ezekiel: *They shall put a mark on the foreheads of those who sigh and groan* (Ezek 9:4). But the others **were delivered up to the avenging sword** of the Covenant" (trans. Vermes, emphasis added).

Both manuscripts contain messianic allusions. The scepter of Balaam's oracle is explicitly identified as the Prince of the Congregation in MS A, and the star also invites interpretation as a messianic figure.[29] MS B refers to "the messiah(s) of Aaron and Israel" at the end of the midrash on Zechariah.

There have been several attempts to sort out the relationship between these two passages. One of the most influential has been that of J. Murphy-O'Connor, who argued that the original text consisted of CD 7:9b–13a from MS A (the Isaiah midrash) plus 19:7b–14 from MS B (the Zechariah-Ezekiel midrash).[30] The Isaiah midrash was lost accidentally from MS B. In MS A the Zechariah-Ezekiel midrash was replaced by the Amos-Numbers midrash. Murphy-O'Connor later changed his mind and defended the originality of the Amos-Numbers midrash, suggesting rather that the Zechariah material is secondary.[31] Nonetheless Davies, Knibb, and Brooke remain persuaded that the Amos-Numbers midrash is an insertion.[32] Davies then goes on to suggest that the B text deliberately replaced the entire Isaiah-Amos-Numbers passage with the Zechariah-Ezekiel midrash, thereby "replacing a 'Prince' (a clearly military figure) by a more innocuous messiah."[33] He quite rightly ends by acknowledging the speculative character of any explanation. Brooke's theory of development is essentially the same as that of Davies: the Zechariah-Ezekiel passage was original, then it was taken out and replaced by the Amos-Numbers passage, and finally it was reinserted and the Amos-Numbers passage was taken out.

All of these redactional arguments are undercut by Sidnie White, who proposes that all the midrashic passages are original, and that both MSS suffered losses by mechanical error.[34] One of the main arguments for the interpolation theory lies in the fact that the midrash is framed by the nearly identical words "were given over to the sword," הוסגרו לחרב (7:13) and "gave them over to the sword," הסגירו לחרב (8:1),[35] which are then taken as a redactional seam. The interpolator supposedly repeated the words that preceded the insertion at the end as he picked up the original text. The same phrase occurs at the end of the Zechariah-Ezekiel midrash in 19:13. White suggests, on the contrary, that the repetition was original, but that it gave rise to haplography, that is, the copyist's eye jumped from one phrase to another that was identical with it. The near-identical phrases that could give rise to haplography are emphasized in the translation above. White posits two haplographies. The first, between the words אשר כתוב ("which is written") introducing the Zechariah quotation and the same words introducing the Isaiah quotation, resulted in the loss of the Zechariah-Ezekiel midrash in MS A. The second, between the words הסגרו לחרב ("were given up to the sword") at the end of the Zechariah-Ezekiel midrash and הסגירו לחרב ("gave them up to the sword") at the end of the Amos-Numbers midrash, resulted in the loss of the Amos-Numbers midrash in MS B. On this argument, all the passages in question are original, and the losses are accidental. While this explanation is also speculative, it has the advantage that it involves least resort to dubious redactional intentions.[36]

It is difficult, then, to entertain with confidence the view that the Amos-Numbers midrash, with its clear reference to a princely messiah, is secondary. It should also be noted that only the reading of MS A (the Isaiah-Amos-Numbers midrash) is attested in the fragments found at Qumran.[37] The theory of Brooke and Davies requires us to give a manuscript known only from the Cairo Geniza priority over the fragments found at Qumran, which are several centuries older. Brooke's further argument that the Zechariah-Ezekiel midrash was original, then replaced in the "Qumran recension," then reinserted around the turn of the era, seems gratuitous. The Zechariah-Ezekiel midrash is not extant in the Dead Sea Scrolls. It may have had a place in the early form of CD, and subsequently been lost as White supposes, but there is no evidence that it was "reinserted" at Qumran.

The various redactional proposals have yielded no consensus as to whether the Amos-Numbers midrash or the Zechariah-Ezekiel midrash is the more original. If White is right, and both are original, then both the Prince of the Congregation and the messiah(s) of Aaron and Israel belong to the original text. In that case, the original text has two messiahs. The phrase משיח אהרון וישראל ("messiah[s] of Aaron and Israel") must surely refer to two messiahs, at least in this instance, and the Amos-Numbers midrash reinforces this idea by mention of the star and the scepter of Balaam's oracle. All this is admittedly tentative, but it shows how fragile is the attempt to extract from CD a stage where only a priestly messiah was expected.

The evidence now at our disposal clearly attests both a messianic "Prince of the Congregation" and a messianic priest in the Damascus Document. Suggestions that this was not the case in certain hypothetical redactional stages of the document are ultimately unpersuasive.

We have noted already that the Community Rule contains a clear ref-

erence to the coming of the prophet and the messiahs of Aaron and Israel (1QS 9:11). J. T. Milik has claimed that this passage is not found in
the oldest copy of the Community Rule, 4QSᵉ, which copies 1QS 9:12
directly after 1QS 8:16.[38] This claim has been disputed by Larry Schiffman, who claims that Milik joined two fragments incorrectly.[39] Even if
Milik is correct, however, the significance of his observation is uncertain.
It is quite possible that messianism was not a factor in the earliest for-
mative stage of the community. The issue that concerns us here is the
kind of messianic expectation that eventually arose. 1QS 9:11 shows a
clear expectation of two messiahs, in addition to the prophet. No fragment of the document suggests the expectation of a single messiah. In no
case does the Community Rule lend any support to the kind of developmental theory of messianism that has been advanced in relation to CD.[40]
Insofar as the Community Rule speaks of messianism at all, it speaks of
two messiahs.

This is not to suggest that there was a requirement of orthodoxy in
the matter of messianism at Qumran. Individual authors or members of
the community may have focused their attention on one messiah, or on
none at all. The authoritative rule books, however, which are surely our
best guide to the general beliefs of the sect, reflect the expectation of both
a royal messiah of Israel and a priestly messiah of Aaron.

The Origins of Priestly Messianism

While it is not possible to trace development within the Dead Sea Scrolls
on this issue with any confidence, it may be possible to shed some light
on the earlier development of priestly messianism.

The notion of a priestly messiah has its roots in the expression
הכהן המשיח, the anointed priest, in Leviticus.[41] We have noted that after
the Babylonian exile the High Priest Joshua and the Davidic heir
Zerubbabel (Zechariah's "two sons of oil") shared the leadership of the
Jewish community. For most of the postexilic period, however, the High
Priest alone was supreme in Judea. This situation is reflected in Ben
Sira, who extols Aaron (Sir 45:6–22) at greater length than David
(47:2–11) and eulogizes the High Priest of his day, Simon the Just, as
"the leader of his brothers and the pride of his people" (50:1). We have
noted earlier the use of משיח (anointed one) for historical High Priests in
Daniel 9. The expectation of a priestly messiah in the eschatological
sense, however, involves more than the exaltation of the office of High

Priesthood. It implies a dissatisfaction with the current exercise of the office. If CD looks forward to a messiah of Aaron who will atone for iniquity, the implication is that the current Temple cult is ineffective and that a new, messianic priest is needed to restore it.

Alienation from the Temple cult was one of the root causes of Jewish sectarianism in the Hellenistic era. The 364-day calendar in the *Enoch* literature, *Jubilees*, and the Dead Sea Scrolls was probably at variance with the official calendar of the Jerusalem Temple, and those who followed it would be out of line with the temple in the celebration of the liturgical festivals.[42] The *Animal Apocalypse* in *1 Enoch* declared all the offerings in the Second Temple impure (*1 Enoch* 89:73), a judgment that may have been colored by the manifest corruption of the priesthood at the time of the Maccabean revolt. Nonetheless, the *Enoch* literature that flourished in the late third and early second centuries BCE did not envisage a priestly messiah to put things right. This fact may be an indication that the *Enoch* books were not the product of priestly circles.[43] There were, however, traditions about an ideal priest or Levite in the second century BCE in the *Jubilees* and in Aramaic fragments related to Levi from Qumran.

◈ Jubilees

Jubilees is immediately relevant to a discussion of the Damascus Document, since it is cited as authoritative scripture in CD 16:3–4. There is no consensus on the date. R. H. Charles, writing early in this century, favored a date around 100 BCE. More recent scholars have pushed the date back to the time of the Maccabean revolt[44] or shortly thereafter.[45] The arguments, however, are far from compelling.[46] *Jubilees* is demonstrably later than the early *Enoch* books (the Book of the Watchers, Astronomical Book)[47] and earlier than CD, where it is cited as an authoritative work. The fragments of *Jubilees* in the Dead Sea Scrolls require a date no later than 100 BCE.[48] The parameters for dating the book, then, are approximately 170–100 BCE. The most persuasive arguments for a more specific date have been advanced by Doron Mendels, based on the extent of the territory of Israel in the book.[49] *Jub* 38:12–14, which says that "the children of Edom have not ceased from the yoke of servitude which the twelve sons of Jacob ordered upon them until today," would seem to presuppose the final conquest of Idumea by John Hyrcanus in 125 BCE, and Mendels would date the book shortly thereafter. For the present discussion, it is important to note that *Jubilees* is not necessarily older than the Hasmonean period.

Levi is the subject of a number of stories in *Jubilees* 30–32. *Jubilees* 30 tells the story of the rape of Dinah, and the vengeance of Levi and Simeon on Shechem. *Jubilees* is emphatic that the deed of the patriarchs "was reckoned to them as righteousness" (30:17). Immediately after this we are told that "the descendants of Levi were chosen for the priesthood, and to be Levites, that they might minister before the Lord continually; and Levi and his sons are blessed forever, for he showed zeal to execute righteousness and judgment and vengeance on all those who rose up against Israel." Mention of zeal recalls Numbers 25, and the story of Phinehas, who pierced an Israelite and a foreign woman and was rewarded with a covenant of peace and eternal priesthood. The story of the destruction of Shechem provided a convenient opportunity to link the motif of zeal also with the priestly figure of Levi.

The priestly zeal of Phinehas was noted by Ben Sira, at the beginning of the second century BCE,[50] but it was especially associated with the Maccabees. Mattathias, father of the Maccabees, was said to burn with zeal for the Law, just as Phinehas did, when he took up arms to resist the persecution under Antiochus Epiphanes (1 Macc 2:26). His descendants, the Hasmoneans, were also militant, and they were also priests, like Phinehas and Levi. The Shechem story was attractive to the Hasmoneans, because they were in conflict with the Samaritans, and Genesis 34 could serve as a virtual *Magna Carta* for violence against Shechem.[51] John Hyrcanus ravaged Shechem, destroyed the Samaritan temple on Mount Gerizim, and finally besieged and destroyed Samaria in 107 BCE.[52] He could claim that he was following in the footsteps of the patriarchs Levi and Judah. The zeal of Levi, then, was a motif that could be used for propaganda purposes by the militant Hasmonean priests. The motif was not, however, the exclusive property of the Hasmoneans, as it could have been derived easily enough from the Bible, by reading the story of Shechem in conjunction with that of Phinehas.[53]

In *Jubilees* 31, two of Jacob's sons are singled out for special blessing: first Levi, and then Judah. Levi is told: "May the Lord give you and your descendants greatness and great glory, and set you and your descendants apart from all mankind to minister to him and to serve him in his sanctuary like the angels of the presence and the holy ones ..." (31:14). The blessing continues with a loose paraphrase of Deut 33:9–11 (Moses' blessing of Levi): "they shall declare my ways to Jacob and my paths to Israel. May all who hate you fall before you, and all your enemies be uprooted and perish."[54] The choice of Deuteronomy 33 is of interest here, since it is one of the texts cited in the Testimonia from Qumran, which is usually taken to be a collection of messianic proof-texts. It is also of interest that the blessing of Levi is paired with a blessing of Judah. Judah is promised: "a prince shall you be (you and one of your sons) over the sons of Jacob: may your name and your son's name go out and spread through every land and region. Then shall the Gentiles fear you, and all nations quake and all peoples stand in awe of you. In you shall be Jacob's help and in you shall be found Israel's salvation" (*Jub* 31:18). These blessings are not necessarily eschatological. They were presumably fulfilled in the historical priesthood and Davidic monarchy. At the least, however, they also represent an ideal structure of Jewish leadership. While it might be possible to arrive at this structure by reflection on biblical texts, it is more likely that it was prompted by developments in Jewish society, specifically by the combination of temporal and priestly power by the Hasmoneans. In the context of the second century BCE, the point to note is the inclusion of Judah. Leadership is not left to Levi alone, and the two offices are not combined. If *Jubilees* represents the kind of circles from which the movement described in the Damascus Document emerged, we should expect that dual messianism, rather than priestly messianism alone, was the norm from the start.[55]

Aramaic Levi

There are, however, other traditions that exalt Levi without providing a corresponding role for Judah. The patriarch Levi was the subject of an apocryphal writing, which later became a source for the *Testament of Levi* in the *Testaments of the Twelve Patriarchs*. Fragments of this document, in Aramaic, are preserved in the Dead Sea Scrolls and in the Cairo Geniza, and, in Greek, in an eleventh-century Greek manuscript from Mount Athos. The Aramaic fragments include the report of a vision, in which Levi is told "now, see how we elevated you above all and how we gave you the anointing of eternal peace."[56] He is then invested and consecrated by Jacob as a priest of El Elyon.[57] This goes beyond what is said of Levi in Genesis, but has a parallel in *Jubilees* 32, where Levi has a dream at Bethel "that they had ordained him and made him the priest of the Most High God, him and his sons forever." There was some biblical precedent for the ordination of Levi in Mal 2:4, which speaks of a covenant with Levi, but the texts from the Hellenistic period are at pains to justify his elevation to the priesthood in various ways. *Jubilees* 32 suggests that Levi was given to God as a tithe, since he was the tenth son.[58]

The consecration of Levi as a priest of El Elyon recalls another figure from Genesis. Melchizedek, king of Salem, to whom Abraham gave a tithe, was priest of El Elyon (Gen 14:18; cf. Ps 110:4). The question arises whether Levi was also given royal rank in the Aramaic Levi document. The association with Melchizedek is not developed in the extant fragments. A few passages, however, associate Levi with kingship. A small fragment, 4QTLevi 1 reads "the kingdom of priesthood is greater than the kingdom...."[59] The notion of a priestly kingdom is familiar from Exod 19:6 and may mean that priestly sovereignty or authority is greater than some other power, without necessarily implying that priests become kings.[60] The Greek Mount Athos manuscript says of Kohath (second son of Levi, grandfather of Aaron and Moses) that "he and his seed will be the beginning of kings, a priesthood for Israel," and thus applies the blessing of Judah explicitly to Kohath. If we ask when in Israelite and Judean history the line of Levi could be regarded as "the beginning of kings," only one situation comes to mind: the Hasmonean dynasty, which combined the offices of priest and king. The statement about "the beginning of kings," however, is not found in the Aramaic, and may not have been part of the original text. It may have been inserted into the text as a pro-Hasmonean gloss.[61]

Two other passages use language drawn from (what later became) classic messianic biblical passages, with reference to the priesthood. One passage foresees that Kohath "would have an assembly of all [the peoples and that] he would have the highpriesthood for all Israel."[62] There is an allusion here to Gen 49:10 (the blessing of Judah), which concludes with the difficult phrase ולו יקהת עמים. The NRSV translates as "the obedience of the people is his," but in antiquity the phrase is sometimes interpreted as "and to him an assembly of the people."[63] The word יקהת lent itself to a wordplay on the name Kohath.[64] We have seen in Chapter Three, with reference to the *"Pesher* on Genesis" (4Q252 = 4Q Patriarchal Blessings) that Gen 49:10 was often interpreted as a messianic prediction. Usually, however, the messianic reference hangs on the phrase עד כי יבא שילה, "until Shiloh comes," taking Shiloh as a name for the messiah. It is not clear that an allusion to the "assembly of the peoples," without reference to Shiloh, necessarily has any messianic implications, or that it confers royal status on Kohath.

There is an allusion to another classic messianic passage in the Prayer of Levi, which is found in Aramaic in 4QTLevi[a] and in Greek after *T. Levi* 3:2 in manuscript *e* of the *Testaments of the Twelve Patriarchs*. Levi asks: "Show me, O Lord, the holy spirit, and counsel and wisdom and knowledge and strength grant me." The formulation echoes Isa 11:2, but again it is not clear that there is any messianic implication in this context. The attributes in question emphasize the wisdom of the ideal priest.[65] They do not require that he also be a king.

Michael Stone has described the Aramaic Levi document as "subsuming all the messianic functions, both priestly and royal, under the priestly figure."[66] It is not clear, however, that the functions in question are understood in an eschatological or messianic sense in Aramaic Levi. Genesis 49 is applied to Kohath, not to a figure of the future, and Isaiah 11 is applied to Levi himself in his prayer. Neither passage is cited to predict a definitive, eschatological priest. On the basis of these passages it is not apparent that Aramaic Levi had any messianic expectation at all.

An eschatological priest does, however, figure prominently in another fragmentary Aramaic text, 4Q541, otherwise known as 4QAhA or 4QAaron A.[67] This work survives in twenty-four fragments. Fragment 9 contains the following passage:

"He will atone for the children of his generation, and he will be sent to all the children of his people. His word is like a word of heaven, and his teaching conforms to the will of God. His eternal sun will shine, and his fire will blaze in all the corners of the earth. Then darkness will disappear from the earth and obscurity from the dry land."

The passage goes on to speak of the opposition which this figure will encounter.

Emile Puech has drawn attention to the similarity between this passage and the *Testament of Levi* in the Greek *Testaments of the Twelve Patriarchs*, which are Christian in their present form[68] but are widely thought to incorporate an older Jewish work.[69] *T. Levi* 18:2–5 reads:

"(2) Then the Lord will raise up a new priest, to whom all the words of the Lord will be revealed; and he will execute a judgment of truth upon the earth in course of time. (3) And his star will arise in heaven, as a king, lighting up the light of knowledge as by the sun of the day; and he will be magnified in the world until his assumption. (4) He will shine as the sun on the earth and will remove all darkness from under heaven, and there will be peace on all the earth. (5) The heavens will exult in his days, and the earth will be glad, and the clouds will rejoice, and the knowledge of the Lord will be poured out upon the earth as the water of the seas, and the angels of the glory of the presence of the Lord will rejoice in him."

The similarities between the two passages lie in the theme of instruction, and the motifs of light and the sun. The priestly character of the figure in 4QAhA is established by the function of atonement. The motif of light has its origin in the priestly blessing of Num 6:25, but the shared reference to the sun suggests a close relationship between the two texts. Both passages are describing an eschatological High Priest[70] and at least draw on a common tradition, even if the Christian author of *T. Levi* 18 did not necessarily have this specific passage before him.

Long before the publication of 4Q541, Nickelsburg and Stone suggested that *T. Levi* 18 corresponds to the lost climax of the Aramaic Levi document.[71] They point to parallels with the call of Levi in *T. Levi* 4:2–6, especially in 18:3, 7; to the emphasis on knowledge and teaching, which is also found in Aramaic Levi; and to allusions to Isaiah 11 in 18:2, 5, 7 (compare the Prayer of Levi, line 8). They do not deny that the passage has undergone development and that some Christian motifs have been added (e.g. a transparent reference to the baptism of Jesus in 18:7), but suggest that there is an underlying Aramaic text that applies language from the classic royal messianic text, Isaiah 11, to an eschatological priest. Puech now argues that 4Q541 is part of *T. Levi*, pointing especially to the parallels with *T. Levi* 18.[72]

Unfortunately, we do not have the ending of the Aramaic Levi apocryphon. De Jonge concludes: "We are, therefore, not in a position to know whether the author of T. L. 18 had any consistent picture of an eschatological priest before him or not, let alone what it looked like."[73] At issue here is the vexed question of the degree to which the Greek *Testaments of the Twelve Patriarchs* preserve Jewish material from the pre-Christian era.

◩ *The* Testaments of the Twelve Patriarchs

The *Testaments of the Twelve Patriarchs* are indubitably Christian in their extant forms but, equally undeniably, make heavy use of Jewish material. In the case of the *Testament of Levi*, we now have some idea of the traditional material that was available. In some other cases it is possible to identify material that addresses an issue that was of importance in a Jewish context, but not in Christianity. The emphasis on dual leadership, from Levi and Judah, is one such case. We must tread carefully here, however, since many of the Levi-Judah passages in the *Testaments* actually speak of only one figure, who must be identified as Christ.[74]

The picture of Levi in *T. Levi* 5–6 corresponds to that of the Aramaic Levi apocryphon. Here the blessings of the priesthood are closely related to the action of Levi and Simeon against Shechem, and the Phineas-like zeal of Levi (*T. Levi* 6:3).[75] The distinction between priesthood and kingship plays no part in this passage, nor indeed is there any mention of kingship at all. In contrast, the distinction is drawn clearly in *T. Judah* 21, where Judah tells his children:

> "And now, my children, love Levi, that you may abide, and do not exalt yourselves against him that you may not be destroyed utterly. For to me the Lord gave the kingship and to him the priesthood, and he set the kingship beneath the priesthood. To me he gave the things upon the earth, to him, the things in the heavens. As heaven is higher than the earth, so is the priesthood of God higher than the kingship on the earth unless it falls away from the Lord through sin and is dominated by the earthly kingship" (*T. Judah* 21:1–4).

There follows a passage on the failure of the kingship of Judah, "until the salvation of Israel comes, until the appearing of the God of righteousness" (22:2), which is quite probably Christian.[76] The initial distinction between the kingship and the priesthood, however, addresses no situation in Christianity, whereas it has an obvious *Sitz-im-Leben* in Judaism. The warning that the priesthood falls away from the Lord when it lets itself be dominated by the kingship is surely a criticism of the Hasmoneans.

The relation of the *Testaments* to the Hasmoneans is a subject of long-standing controversy. R. H. Charles argued that "It was the priestly character of the Maccabean priest-kings that gave rise to the expectation that the messiah was also to be a priest as well as a king."[77] Charles supposed that in the original *Testaments* there was only one messiah from the tribe of Levi, who was both king and priest. The prototype of this figure was John Hyrcanus. Only after Hyrcanus broke with the Pharisees were passages about the kingship of Judah added. Charles found confirmation for this view in *T. Levi* 8, where Levi's seed is divided into three offices. The first is greater than all,[78] the second is the priesthood and the third "will be called with a new name because a king will arise from Judah and will establish a new priesthood after the fashion of the Gentiles for all the Gentiles. And his presence will be marvelous as that of a high prophet from the seed of Abraham our father."[79] Charles saw here a reference to John Hyrcanus, who was temporal ruler, High Priest, and, alone of the Hasmoneans, was credited with the gift of prophecy.[80]

Against this, however, there are signs of Christian influence, if not authorship, in this passage. There is a textual variant in the case of the first office. The shorter reading preferred by Charles, ("the first portion shall be great; yea, greater than it shall none be") fails to identify the office in question. The longer reading, defended by de Jonge, ("he who believes will be the first; no portion will be greater than he") is probably Christian: the primacy of faith is more likely to be affirmed by a Christian than a Jewish author. The fact that the new priesthood is "after the fashion of the Gentiles for all the Gentiles" also points to Christian authorship and has to be bracketed out by Charles. The combination of king-priest-prophet is well attested in early Christianity.[81] The evidence for a pro-Hasmonean stratum of the *Testaments* in this passage is tenuous at best.

T. Judah 21, which makes a clear distinction between kingship and priesthood, is not eschatological in focus and cannot be said to speak of any messiah. The classic passages for the expectation of two messiahs in the *Testaments* are found in *T. Levi* 18 and *T. Judah* 24. Both passages refer to Balaam's oracle of the star and the scepter. *T. Judah* 24 reads:

"(1) And after these things a star will arise to you from Jacob in peace and a man will arise from my seed like the sun of righteousness, walking with the sons of men in meekness and righteousness, and no sin whatever will be found in him. (2) And the heavens will be opened to him to pour out the blessing of the spirit of the holy Father, and he will pour out the spirit of grace upon you; (3) and you will be sons to him in truth and you will walk in his commandments from first to last. (4) This (is) the branch of God Most High, and this is the fountain unto life for all flesh. (5) Then the scepter of my kingdom will shine, and from your root a stem will arise; (6) and in it a rod of righteousness will arise to the nations to judge and save all who call upon the Lord."

The Christian character of this passage is clear in the meekness and sinlessness of the messianic figure, and in the transparent allusion to the baptism of Jesus (Matt 3:16–17; Mark 1:9–11; Luke 3:21–22; John 1:33–34). The question is whether there is an underlying Jewish oracle that can be identified. Charles ignored the Christian elements and distinguished "two messianic fragments." The first, in vss. 1–3, originally identified the star as a messiah from Levi (taking "from my seed," which should refer to *Judah's* seed, as a gloss). The second, in vss. 5–6, identified the scepter as a messiah from Judah.[82] This analysis was inspired in large part by the parallels between vss. 1–3 and *T. Levi* 18. The star and the scepter of Balaam's oracle are often interpreted with reference to two different figures, and since the scepter is necessarily the king, the star is readily interpreted as a priestly figure. Charles' theory of "two messianic fragments," however, is untenable in view of the Christian elements we have noted in vss. 1–3. The Christian elements, however, are found only in vss. 1–3. The remaining verses, with their allusions to the familiar messianic motifs of branch, scepter, root and stem (or shoot), and rod, are entirely appropriate to a Jewish prediction of a messiah from Judah. We may suggest, then, that the Jewish core of this passage lies in *T. Judah* 24:4–6, and is a prediction of one messiah, a royal one from Judah. Vss. 1–3 are best understood, not as a vestige of an original oracle about a Levitical messiah, but as a Christian addition, which associates the messiah of Judah with the messiah of Levi, so as to suggest that both have their fulfillment in the one person, Christ.

T. Levi 18 also shows some transparent Christian influence. The new priest "will be magnified in the world until his assumption" (vs. 3). Vss. 6–7 allude to the baptism of Jesus and vs. 9 predicts that "the Gentiles will be multiplied in knowledge upon the earth" while Israel will be diminished. The parallels we have noted above with 4Q541 (4QAhA) show that *T. Levi* 18 is indebted to Jewish tradition, and so here again we should think in terms of a Jewish core, expanded by a Christian redactor. The differences between 4Q541 and *T. Levi* 18, however, are not confined to those elements that are clearly Christian. While the language of 4QAhA is eschatological (cf. Isaiah 60 for the motif of light and darkness), it is not overtly messianic. There is no star, and there is no reference to kingship. In short, the fusion of royal and priestly imagery that we find in the Greek *T. Levi* 18 is not present in the older Aramaic document. If we use 4QAhA as a guide to the Jewish elements in *T. Levi* 18, it would seem that here, too, there was only one eschatological figure, in this case a priest. The explicit motif of kingship may have been introduced by the Christian author or redactor, who saw both strands of messianism fulfilled in Christ.

In summary, then, it would seem that *T. Levi* 18 builds on a Jewish text that envisaged an eschatological priest, and *T. Judah* 24 incorporated a Jewish prediction of an eschatological king. The combination of priest and king in a single messianic figure in the Greek *Testaments of the Twelve Patriarchs* was the work of the Christian redactor.

⊠ *The Development of the Levi Tradition*

The Greek *Testaments*, then, certainly preserve Jewish traditions, including traditions about an eschatological priest and a messianic king, but these traditions have been reworked by a Christian redactor and cannot be easily separated out. It is unsafe to assume that the pre-Christian Apocryphon of Levi must have had the same shape as the Christian *Testament of Levi*,[83] or to infer that 4Q541 must have been part of the Levi apocryphon because it parallels *T. Levi* 18. The fact that parallels to *T. Levi* are only found in one fragment of 4Q541, and that there is no overlap between 4Q541 and the other fragments of the Levi apocryphon, makes it likely that 4Q541 is distinct both from the Aramaic Levi document and from *T. Levi*. The Greek *T. Levi* had more than one Aramaic source.

The Aramaic Levi Apocryphon, to judge from the extant fragments, was not an eschatologically oriented work and did not predict a messiah of any kind. Stone has argued that this document dates from the third century BCE, because some of the Qumran fragments have been dated to the second century on palaeographic grounds,[84] and because it is likely to have been a source for the *Jubilees*.[85] Neither of these considerations requires quite so early a date. It is not certain that it was a source for *Jubilees*; the two works could have drawn on common traditions.[86] In any case, if we date *Jubilees* to the 120s, an earlier date for Aramaic Levi can be found in the second century. Stone has also observed that Aramaic Levi is remarkably free from polemics, even in its use of the 364-day calendar, which is the subject of vigorous polemics in *Jubilees*. The nonpolemical tone may be taken to reflect the period before rather than after the Maccabean revolt. In that case Aramaic Levi might be roughly contemporary with Sirach, but an earlier date is also possible.

Milik and Puech have argued that Aramaic Levi belonged to a series of testaments of priestly patriarchs, together with the testaments of Kohath and ᶜAmram.[87] While the genre of Aramaic Levi is uncertain, the three works are certainly related.[88] The testaments of Kohath and ᶜAmram are also no later than the mid-second century BCE.[89] These works surely belong to the tradition from which the idea of a priestly messiah later emerged. They are also part of the older literature inherited by the Dead Sea sect.

It is not at all clear that 4Q541 was part of the same document as the Aramaic Levi fragments from the Geniza. Only one fragment of 4Q541 shows significant parallels to the Levi material. Puech dates the manuscript of 4Q541 towards the end of the second century, or about 100

BCE.[90] This document is not necessarily older than the Dead Sea sect. In the following chapter we will note some indications that it reflects the career of the Teacher of Righteousness. The extant fragments speak only of an eschatological priest, not of a messianic king. They do not in any way exclude a royal messiah, however, and could easily have been harmonized with the expectation of two messiahs at Qumran.

The prominence of both Levi and Judah in *Jubilees* suggests that the theme of dual leadership had emerged in the second century, before the crystallization of the Dead Sea sect. It is unfortunate that we do not have a more precise date for *Jubilees*. If Mendels is right, then *Jubilees* is no older than the reign of John Hyrcanus, and so it may already be reacting against the combination of temporal and priestly power by the Hasmoneans. In fact, the assumption of both civil and priestly power by the Hasmoneans provides by far the most plausible setting for the insistence on a distinction between royal and priestly offices. The clear distinction between priest and king in *T. Judah* 21 should also be understood in this context. It is probably also in this context that the interest in Davidic messianism revived. At least, we have no evidence of messianic expectation in the second century before the rise of the Hasmoneans as a native, non-Davidic, Jewish dynasty.

The Qumran texts that speak of messiahs contain regrettably few allusions to historical events. Most of the references to the messiahs or messiah of Aaron and Israel are simply eschatological markers, and are extremely terse. A rare window on historical circumstances may be provided by the Testimonia. As noted earlier, this text strings together quotations from Deuteronomy 18 (the prophet like Moses), Deuteronomy 33 (the blessing of Levi) and Balaam's oracle. The series concludes, however, with a passage of no messianic significance, from the *Psalms of Joshua*.[91] It begins with a citation of the curse on Jericho from Josh 6:26: "Cursed be the man who rebuilds this city! At the cost of his firstborn he will found it, and at the cost of his youngest son he will set up its gates. Behold, an accursed one, a man of Belial. . . ." It now appears, from the excavations conducted by E. Netzer in 1987–88, that the man who rebuilt Jericho was none other than John Hyrcanus.[92] According to Josephus, Hyrcanus "was accounted by God worthy of three of the greatest privileges, the rule of the nation, the office of high-priest, and the gift of prophecy" (*Antiquities* 13.299–300). In contrast, the Testimonia lays out the biblical basis for three distinct eschatological figures, king, priest, and prophet. The citation from the *Psalms of Joshua* becomes intelligible if the author saw the fulfillment of Joshua's curse in the death of

Hyrcanus' sons, Antigonus and Aristobulus I, in 103 BCE, within a year of their father's death.[93]

It has often been remarked that the references to "messiahs of Aaron and Israel" tell us nothing about the messiahs except that they were expected to come. The plurality of the messianic figures in question, however, was in itself a political statement, since it implicitly rejected the combination of royal and priestly offices by the Hasmoneans.

▧ *Conclusion*

The expectation of a Davidic messiah had a clear basis in the Scriptures, and became very widespread in various sectors of Judaism in the last century before the Common Era, in reaction to the rule of the Hasmoneans. (Presumably it had less appeal for the Hasmoneans than for their critics.) The notion of a priestly messiah was not so obvious from the scriptures and flourished mainly among people with a strong priestly ideology. It was not confined to the Qumran settlement, but it is only attested in literature that is related to the Dead Sea sect as exemplified in the Damascus Document, even if some of that literature (*Jubilees*) belongs to the forerunners of the sect. It is well known that the "sons of Zadok" were at one time a leading force in the sect, and so the movement had a strong priestly ideology.[94] The notion of a priestly messiah implies some dissatisfaction with the current High Priest and the operation of the Temple cult. The insistence of dual messianic offices of priest and king implies a critique of the combination of these offices by the Hasmoneans. The Dead Sea sect was not the only group that was dissatisfied with the Hasmonean rule, as can be seen from the *Psalms of Solomon*. The expectation of two messiahs, however, appears to have been a distinctive trait of that movement, rather than something common to the Judaism of the day.

The enigmatic Teacher of Righteousness, who evidently played a crucial role in the development of the Dead Sea sect, was also a priest. We will consider the relevance of this figure for the messianic expectations of the sect in the following chapter.

NOTES

[1] For standard treatments, see Vermes in the revised Schuerer, *The History of the Jewish People* 2.550–54; S. Talmon, "Waiting for the Messiah at Qumran," in *The World of Qum-*

ran from Within (Leiden: Brill, 1989) 273–300; S. Talmon, "The Concept of Māšîaḥ and Messianism in Early Judaism," in Charlesworth, ed., *The Messiah*, 79–115.

[2] E.g. F. M. Cross, *The Ancient Library of Qumran and Modern Biblical Studies* (Garden City: Doubleday, 1961) 219–21. See further, George J. Brooke, *Exegesis at Qumran. 4QFlorilegium in its Jewish Context* (Journal for the Study of the Old Testament Supplement 29; Sheffield: Journal for the Study of the Old Testament, 1985) 309–10.

[3] M. O. Wise and J. D. Tabor, "The Messiah at Qumran," *Biblical Archeology Review* (November/December 1992) 60–65.

[4] So E. Lohse, *Die Texte aus Qumran* (Darmstadt: Wissenschaftliche Buchgesellschaft, 1971) 50. Cf. the remarks of P. Skehan, "Two Books on Qumran Studies," *Catholic Biblical Quarterly* 21(1979) 74.

[5] So Cross, *The Ancient Library of Qumran*, 87.

[6] So L. H. Schiffman, *The Eschatological Community of the Dead Sea Scrolls* (Society of Biblical Literature Monograph Series 38; Atlanta: Scholars Press, 1989) 54, following a suggestion of J. Licht, מגילת הסרכים (Jerusalem: Mosad Bialik, 1965) 267.

[7] Trans. Schiffman, *The Eschatological Community*, 54–55.

[8] So G. Vermes, *The Dead Sea Scrolls in English* (3rd ed.; London: Penguin, 1987) 102.

[9] The eschatological Interpreter will be discussed in Chapter Five below.

[10] Temple Scroll 58:19. For the eschatological character of the Scroll see M. O. Wise, *A Critical Study of the Temple Scroll from Qumran Cave 11* (Chicago: The Oriental Institute of the University of Chicago, 1990) 167–94, but see the discussion in Chapter Five below.

[11] S. Talmon, "Types of Messianic Expectation at the Turn of the Era," in idem, ed., *King, Cult and Calendar in Ancient Israel* (Jerusalem: Magnes, 1986) 202–24; "Waiting for the Messiah," 290–93.

[12] In the Community Rule, the מבקר, guardian, is probably identical with the official designated פקיד, overseer, and משכיל, master, in view of the similarity of their functions.

[13] For further indications of dual leadership in the Dead Sea sect, see Vermes, *The Dead Sea Scrolls in English*, 1–18; J. J. Collins, *The Apocalyptic Imagination* (New York: Crossroad, 1984) 123–24.

[14] J. Starcky, "Les quatres étapes du messianisme à Qumrân," *Revue Biblique* 70(1963) 481-505. Cf. A. Caquot, "Le messianisme Qumrânien," in M. Delcor, ed., *Qumrân. Sa piété, sa théologie et son milieu* (Bibliotheca Ephemeridum Theologicarum Lovaniensium 46; Leuven: Leuven University Press, 1978) 231–47. Concise summaries of de Vaux's stages can be found in R. de Vaux, "Qumran, Khirbet and 'Ein Feshka," in E. Stern, ed., *The New Encyclopedia of Archaeological Excavations in the Holy Land*, 4.1235–41; and J. Murphy-O'Connor, "Qumran, Khirbet," in Freedman, ed., *The Anchor Bible Dictionary* 5.590–93.

[15] See the prompt critique by R. Brown, "J. Starcky's Theory of Qumran Messianic Development," *Catholic Biblical Quarterly* 28(1966) 51–57. Gerbern S. Oegema, *Der Gesalbte und sein Volk* (Göttingen: Vandenhoeck & Ruprecht, 1994) 88, accepts Starcky's theory.

[16] So especially P. R. Davies, *The Damascus Covenant. An Interpretation of the 'Damascus Document'* (Journal for the Study of the Old Testament Supplement 25; Sheffield: Journal for the Study of the Old Testament, 1983).

[17] George J. Brooke, "The Messiah of Aaron in the Damascus Document," *Revue de Qumran* 15(1991) 215–30.

[18] Brooke, "The Messiah of Aaron," 225.

[19] Brooke, "The Messiah of Aaron," 229.

[20] Ibid., 227. Brooke supposes that the citation of Isa 7:17 at CD 7:10–12 was lost from MS B when the Zechariah-Ezekiel midrash was reinserted.

[21] Ibid., 230.

[22] L. Ginzberg, *An Unknown Jewish Sect* (New York: Jewish Theological Seminary, 1976, trans. of the German 1922 edition) 209–56.

[23] K. G. Kuhn, "The Two Messiahs of Aaron and Israel," in K. Stendahl, ed., *The Scrolls and the New Testament* (New York: Harper, 1957) 54–64; Talmon, "Waiting for the Messiah," in *The World of Qumran from Within*, 288. The dual reading was recently defended by Hartmut Stegemann, "Some Remarks to 1QSa, 1QSb, and Qumran Messianism," at the meeting of the *International Organization of Qumran Studies* in Paris in July 1992.

[24] A. S. van der Woude, *Die messianischen Vorstellungen der Gemeinde von Qumrân* (Assen: van Gorcum, 1957) 29; R. Deichgräber, "Zur messiaserwartung der Damaskusschrift," *Zeitschrift für die Alttestamentliches Wissenschaft* 78(1966) 333–43.

[25] Caquot, "Le messianisme Qumrânien," 241. See the discussion by van der Woude, *Die messianischen Vorstellungen*, 32.

[26] So recently F. M. Cross, "Some Notes on a Generation of Qumran Studies," in J. Trebolle Barrera and L. Vegas Montaner, eds., *The Madrid Qumran Congress* (Leiden: Brill, 1992) 14. Ginzberg also considered the possibility that the subject of יכפר is God (*An Unknown Jewish Sect*, 252).

[27] Ginzberg, *An Unknown Jewish Sect*, 227.

[28] Cross, "Some Notes on a Generation of Qumran Studies," 14.

[29] Several scholars dispute the messianic understanding of the star in this passage. For references see M. A. Knibb, "The Interpretation of Damascus Document VII,9b–VIII,2a and XIX,5b–14," *Revue de Qumran* 15(1991) 247. Knibb defends the view that the Amos-Numbers midrash refers to two messiahs.

[30] J. Murphy-O'Connor, "The Original Text of CD 7:9–8:2 = 19:5–14," *Harvard Theological Review* 64(1971) 379–86.

[31] J. Murphy-O'Connor, "The Damascus Document Revisited," *Revue Biblique* 92(1985) 225–45.

[32] P. R. Davies, *Behind the Essenes. History and Ideology in the Dead Sea Scrolls* (Brown Judaic Studies 94; Atlanta: Scholars Press, 1987) 39; Knibb, "The Interpretation of Damascus Document VII,9b–VIII,2a and XIX,5b–14," 247; Brooke, "The Messiah of Aaron," 225.

[33] Davies, *Behind the Essenes*, 40.

[34] S. A. White, "A Comparison of the 'A' and 'B' Manuscripts of the Damascus Document," *Revue de Qumran* 48(1987) 537–53.

[35] The translation by Vermes, quoted above, emends this phrase to read "were given up to the sword."

[36] Brooke objects that White "does not sufficiently account for how exegetical redactional activity employs techniques that in the modern eye can look like scribal error" ("The Messiah of Aaron," 216). The objection can be reversed. Scribal phenomena that in the modern eye look like redactional techniques may be mere scribal errors. Where explanation as mechanical error is possible, it is surely to be preferred.

[37] F. García Martínez, *Textos de Qumrán* (Madrid: Trotta, 1992) 99.

[38] J. T. Milik, *Ten Years of Discovery in the Wilderness of Judaea* (London: SCM, 1959) 123.

[39] See Charlesworth, *The Messiah*, 26–27. At the meeting of the Studiorum Novi Testamenti Societas in Chicago in August 1993, however, Charlesworth repudiated Schiffman's claim and agreed with Milik.

[40] It should be noted that the oldest copy of the rule does not necessarily preserve the original text. Many scholars have argued that part of the omitted passage, 9:3–11, belongs to the oldest stratum of the Community Rule, e.g. J. Murphy-O'Connor, "La genèse littéraire de la Règle de la Communauté," *Revue Biblique* 76(1969) 528–49; J. Pouilly, *La Règle de la Communauté de Qumrân. Son évolution littéraire* (Paris: Gabalda, 1976).

[41] Lev 4:3, 5, 16; 6:15.

[42] For different views on this issue see J. C. VanderKam, "The Origin, Character and Early History of the 364-Day Calendar: A Reassessment of Jaubert's Hypotheses," *Catholic Biblical Quarterly* 41(1979) 390–411; P. R. Davies, "Calendrical Change and Qumran Origins: An Assessment of VanderKam's Theory," *Catholic Biblical Quarterly* 45(1983) 80–89, and VanderKam, "The 364-Day Calendar in the Enoch Literature," in K. H. Richards, ed., *Society of Biblical Literature 1983 Seminar Papers* (Chico, CA: Scholars Press, 1983) 157–65.

[43] Even though Enoch is admitted, in effect, to the heavenly temple in *1 Enoch* 14, he is never said to be a priest, but a "scribe of righteousness" (*1 Enoch* 12:4). See J. J. Collins, "The Sage in Apocalyptic and Pseudepigraphic Literature," in J. G. Gammie and L. Perdue, eds., *The Sage in Israel and the Ancient Near East* (Winona Lake, IN: Eisenbrauns, 1990) 344–45.

[44] G. W. E. Nickelsburg, *Jewish Literature Between the Bible and the Mishnah* (Philadelphia: Fortress, 1981) 77.

[45] James C. VanderKam, *Textual and Historical Studies in the Book of Jubilees* (Harvard Semitic Monographs 14; Missoula: Scholars Press, 1977) 217–38.

[46] Robert Doran, "The Non-Dating of Jubilees: Jub 34–38; 23:14–32 in Narrative Context," *Journal for the Study of Judaism* 20(1989) 1–11.

[47] J. C. VanderKam, "Enoch Traditions in Jubilees and Other Second Century Sources," in P. J. Achtemeier, ed., *Society of Biblical Literature 1978 Seminar Papers* (Missoula: Scholars Press, 1978) 1.229–51.

[48] J. C. VanderKam and J. T. Milik, "The First Jubilees Manuscript from Qumran Cave 4: A Preliminary Publication," *Journal of Biblical Literature* 110(1991) 246.

[49] D. Mendels, *The Land of Israel as a Political Concept in Hasmonean Literature* (Tübingen: Mohr-Siebeck, 1987) 57–88.

[50] Sir 45:23–24: "Phinehas son of Eleazar... for being zealous in the fear of the Lord, and standing firm, when the people turned away, in the noble courage of his soul; and he made atonement for Israel" and was given "the dignity of the priesthood forever."

[51] This is the phrase of H. G. Kippenberg, *Garizim und Synagoge* (Berlin: de Gruyter, 1971) 90. See J. J. Collins, "The Epic of Theodotus and the Hellenism of the Hasmoneans," *Harvard Theological Review* 73(1980) 91–104.

[52] *Antiquities* 13.254–58, 275–81; *Jewish War* 1.62–65. See J. D. Purvis, *The Samaritan Pentateuch and the Origin of the Samaritan Sect* (Cambridge, MA: Harvard, 1968) 112–13; Kippenberg, *Gazirim und Synagoge*, 85–87.

[53] This point is emphasized by James Kugel, "The Story of Dinah in the Testament of Levi," *Harvard Theological Review* 85(1992) 1–34.

[54] See J. C. VanderKam, "Jubilees and the Priestly Messiah of Qumran," *Revue de Qumran* 13(1988) 363–64.

[55] VanderKam, "Jubilees and the Priestly Messiah," 365, makes the interesting observation that neither *Jubilees* nor the Damascus Document ever invoke Zechariah's two sons

of oil as a model for dual leadership. This text is cited, however, in 4Q254, which is another manuscript of 4Q252, the *"Pesher* on Genesis."

[56] Bodleian MS a (from the Cairo Geniza), 1QTest Levi, fragments 3 and 4. See J. C. Greenfield and M. E. Stone, "The Aramaic and Greek Fragments of a Levi Document," in H. W. Hollander and M. de Jonge, *The Testaments of the Twelve Patriarchs. A Commentary* (Leiden: Brill, 1985) 461.

[57] The Geniza text has עלמא, eternity, but this appears to be written over Elyon. See J. C. Greenfield and M. E. Stone, "Remarks on the Aramaic Testament of Levi from the Geniza," *Revue Biblique* 86(1979) 220.

[58] See further James Kugel, "Levi's Elevation to the Priesthood in Second Temple Writings," *Harvard Theological Review* 86(1993) 1–64; on Levi as a human tithe, see pp. 13–17.

[59] מלכות כהנותא רבא מן מלכות. Greenfield and Stone, "The Aramaic and Greek Fragments," 461. Note, however, J. Liver, "The Doctrine of the Two Messiahs in Sectarian Literature in the Time of the Second Commonwealth," *Harvard Theological Review* 52(1959) 171, who construes as "[to you and your sons] kingship. The priesthood is superior to the kingship. . . ." Liver points to *T. Judah* 21:2 as a parallel: "For to me the Lord gave the kingdom and to him the priesthood, and he set the kingdom beneath the priesthood." Cf. Pierre Grelot, "Notes sur le Testament araméen de Levi," *Revue Biblique* 63(1956) 391–406.

[60] Another reference to "priests and kings" occurs in a passage too fragmentary to be evaluated, 4Q213 7 ii–8 13–18.

[61] A. Hultgård, *L'Eschatologie des Testaments des Douze Patriarches. I. Interprétation des textes* (Stockholm: Almqvist & Wiksell, 1977) 43. Hultgård argues that this Levitical ideology was not invented by the Hasmoneans, but could have been easily adopted and adapted by them.

[62] Cambridge MS c, from the Geniza. Greenfield and Stone, "The Aramaic and Greek Fragments," 466. (Greenfield and Stone restore the singular "people," but the text of Genesis has the plural "peoples.") The Mount Athos passage, which refers to "the beginning of kings," is a longer variant of this passage.

[63] See J. C. Greenfield and M. E. Stone, "Remarks on the Aramaic Testament of Levi from the Geniza," 223. Instances include Aquila and Bereshit Rabba 99. Whether mention of "assembly (כנסת) of the men of . . ." in 4Q252 (Patriarchal Blessings) should be considered another instance is uncertain, because of the fragmentary nature of the text, but the phrase occurs in the context of the interpretation of Gen 49:10. The LXX reads "and he is the expectation of the nations."

[64] J. C. Greenfield and M. E. Stone, "Remarks on the Aramaic Testament of Levi," 223–24; M. de Jonge, "The Testament of Levi and 'Aramaic Levi,'" *Revue de Qumran* 13(1988) 371.

[65] This point is emphasized by M. E. Stone and J. C. Greenfield, "The Prayer of Levi," *Journal of Biblical Literature* 112(1993) 252–53.

[66] So M. E. Stone, "Enoch, Aramaic Levi and Sectarian Origins," *Journal for the Study of Judaism* 19(1988) 168.

[67] Emile Puech, "Fragments d'un apocryphe de Lévi et le personnage eschatologique. 4QTestLévi[c–d](?) et 4QAJa," in J. Trebolle Barrera and L. Vegas Montaner, eds., *The Madrid Qumran Congress* (Leiden: Brill, 1992) 2.449–501.

[68] M. de Jonge, *The Testaments of the Twelve Patriarchs. A Study of their Text, Composition and Origin* (2nd ed.; Assen: van Gorcum, 1975); Hollander and de Jonge, *The Testaments of*

the Twelve Patriarchs, 82–85. The Armenian version of the *Testaments*, which is shorter than the Greek at some places and has sometimes been used to isolate Christian additions, is still Christian.

[69] Recent attempts to distinguish a Jewish stage in the *Testaments* include Hultgård, *L'Eschatologie des Testaments des Douze Patriarches* and J. H. Ulrichsen, *Die Grundschrift der Testamente der zwölf Patriarchen* (Stockholm: Almqvist & Wiksell, 1991).

[70] Starcky, "Les quatre étapes du messianisme," 492, gave a brief description of this document, in which he said that it concerned "une figure eschatologique qui est certainement le grand prêtre de l'ère messianique."

[71] G. W. E. Nickelsburg and M. E. Stone, *Faith and Piety in Early Judaism* (Philadelphia: Fortress, 1983) 168, 199.

[72] Puech, "Fragments d'un apocryphe de Lévi," 490–91.

[73] M. de Jonge, "Two Messiahs in the Testaments of the Twelve Patriarchs?" in de Jonge, *Jewish Eschatology, Early Christian Christology and the Testaments of the Twelve Patriarchs* (Leiden: Brill, 1991) 199.

[74] See especially de Jonge, "Two Messiahs," 191–203.

[75] In *T. Levi* 5, Levi destroys Shechem after he is ordained a priest, but this is not necessarily the order of events in Aramaic Levi. *T. Levi* 12:5 puts the destruction of Shechem before Levi became priest.

[76] So de Jonge, "Two Messiahs," 197.

[77] R. H. Charles, "The Testaments of the Twelve Patriarchs," in Charles, ed., *Apocrypha and Pseudepigrapha of the Old Testament*, 2.294.

[78] There is a textual problem here. Hollander and de Jonge read "he who believes will be the first."

[79] Trans. Hollander and de Jonge, *The Testaments*, 149.

[80] Josephus, *Antiquities*, 13.299–300.

[81] Hollander and de Jonge, *The Testaments*, 154.

[82] Charles, *Apocrypha and Pseudepigrapha of the Old Testament*, 2.323. Charles dismissed vs. 4 as a gloss. Van der Woude also sees two messiahs in this passage (*Die messianische Vorstellungen*, 205), as does Hultgård, *L'Eschatologie*, 1.204–13.

[83] Ulrichsen, *Die Grundschrift der Testamente der Zwölf Patriarchen*, 186, denies that there is literary dependence of *T. Levi* on the older documents, although he recognizes a traditiohistorical relationship.

[84] See J. T. Milik, *The Books of Enoch* (Oxford: Oxford University Press, 1976) 23.

[85] Stone, "Enoch, Aramaic Levi and Sectarian Origins," 159.

[86] Kugel, "Levi's Elevation to the Priesthood," 52–58, argues for a complex relationship between the two documents, wherein *Jubilees* was influenced by source documents that were incorporated later into *Aramaic Levi*, but the extant form of *Aramaic Levi* was influenced by *Jubilees*.

[87] J. T. Milik, "4Q Visions de 'Amram et une citation d'Origène," *Revue Biblique* 79(1972) 77–97; E. Puech, "Le Testament de Qahat en Araméen de la Grotte 4 (4QTQah)," *Revue de Qumran* 15(1991) 23–54.

[88] The strongly dualistic character of *T. Amram* is not, however, paralleled in the other two documents.

[89] Puech, "Le Testament de Qahat," 51.

[90] Puech, "Fragments d'un apocryphe de Lévi," 452.

[91] C. Newsom, "The 'Psalms of Joshua' from Qumran Cave 4," *Journal of Jewish Studies* 39(1988) 56–73.

[92] H. Eshel, "The Historical Background of the Pesher Interpreting Joshua's Curse on the Rebuilder of Jericho," *Revue de Qumran* 15(1992) 409–20.

[93] For the death of the brothers Antigonus and Aristobulus, see Josephus, *Antiquities* 13.301–19. Aristobulus succeeded John Hyrcanus but ruled for only one year. He had his brother Antigonus murdered, but subsequently, according to Josephus, died of remorse.

[94] Davies, *Behind the Essenes*, 51–72, argues that the influence of Zadokite priests on the Qumran community was short-lived. The role of the "sons of Zadok," however, must now be reevaluated in light of the evidence from Cave 4. The authoritative role of the sons of Zadok in 1QS5 appears to be an interpolation into the text as preserved in 4QS. See G. Vermes, "Preliminary Remarks on Unpublished Fragments of the Community Rule from Qumran Cave 4," *Journal of Jewish Studies* 42(1991) 250–55.

5

TEACHER, PRIEST AND PROPHET

▨ *The Teacher at the End of Days*

In the interpretation of Balaam's oracle in the Damascus Document (CD 7, MS A), the scepter is interpreted as the Prince of the Congregation, which, as we have seen, is a title for the Davidic messiah. The star is not identified explicitly as a priest, as we might expect by analogy with the "messiahs of Aaron and Israel." Rather, it is interpreted as "the Interpreter of the Law who shall come to Damascus." Similarly in the Florilegium (4Q174) the Branch of David is expected to arise with the Interpreter of the Law "at the end of days" (אחרית הימים). In another passage, however, CD refers to an Interpreter of the Law as a figure from the past, and distinguishes him from another figure who is to teach righteousness at the end of days. In CD 6:7–11, Num 21:18, "the well which princes dug, which the nobles of the people delved with the staff," is expounded as follows: "The well is the Law, and those who dug it were the converts of Israel who went out of the land of Judah to sojourn in the land of Damascus.... The staff (מחקק) is the Interpreter of the Law of whom Isaiah said, He makes a tool for His work; and the nobles of the people are those who come to dig the well with the staffs with which the staff ordained that they should walk in all the age of wickedness—and without them they shall find nothing—until he comes who shall teach righteousness at the end of days."[1]

The reference to "one who will teach righteousness at the end of days" has been especially controversial. The controversy centers on the relation between this figure, who is clearly future, and the Teacher of Righteousness, who appears elsewhere in the document as a figure from the past, and also on the relation of this eschatological figure to the "Interpreter of the Law." If all references to a Teacher of Righteousness and to an Interpreter of the Law are to the same person, then the Teacher must have been expected to rise from the dead in the end of days, and would provide an astonishing parallel to Christian belief about Jesus.

The notion that the Teacher was expected to come again as a messiah was first put forward by the Jewish scholar Solomon Schechter, in the original publication of the Damascus Document from the Cairo Geniza in 1910.[2] This interpretation was rejected by Louis Ginzberg and others,[3] and was virtually forgotten until the discovery of the Dead Sea Scrolls. Then it was taken up by Dupont-Sommer,[4] and J. M. Allegro.[5] Both Dupont-Sommer and Allegro identified the Teacher with the priestly messiah. For a time, this view won wide support.[6] Scholars who subscribed to it, with minor variations, included Krister Stendahl[7] and W. D. Davies.[8] It also encountered prompt criticism.[9] There is a clear distinction between the Teacher, who is already dead, and the messiahs who are to come in CD 19:35–20:1. Nowhere else is there any suggestion that the historical Teacher had messianic status. A consensus developed that the figure expected at the end of days cannot be identified with the Teacher who played a role in the beginning of the community. Rather, that historical Teacher (the quasi-founder of the community) is referred to in this passage as the Interpreter of the Law, and the eschatological teacher remains in the future.[10]

This consensus was challenged by Philip Davies, who argued that this passage (CD 6:11) comes from an earlier stratum of CD than the other references to the Teacher of Righteousness. In his view, the core of CD was written before the Teacher came along, and the references to the Teacher were inserted later as part of a "Qumran redaction." The historical Teacher claimed to be the one who would teach righteousness at the end of days, as predicted in CD 6:11, and so might be described loosely as a messianic figure.[11] The Interpreter of the Law would then be another, less significant figure from the early days of the movement before the true Teacher came along. Davies then supposes that the dispute between the Teacher and the Man of the Lie, or the Scoffer, who rejected his teaching, was in effect a disagreement as to whether the Teacher was the fulfillment of eschatological expectations.

There are obvious problems with Davies' proposal, many of which have been pointed out by Michael Knibb.[12] The title "Interpreter of the Law," which clearly refers to a figure of the past in CD 6, appears as an eschatological title, for a figure who is to appear with the Branch of David at the end of days, in the Florilegium, a document that is closely related to CD.[13] It also appears in CD 7:18 with reference to the star of Balaam's oracle, which usually has eschatological connotations. This usage suggests that such titles as Interpreter of the Law and Teacher of Righteousness could be variously used to refer to figures past or future, and that they are interchangeable. Indeed, the Community Rule requires that every group of ten should include a man who interprets the Law (איש דרש בתורה) so the title Interpreter of the Law obviously could have more than one referent. The expectation of "one who will teach righteousness at the end of days" is retained in the final redaction of CD, even though the career of the historical Teacher is clearly past. The document clearly envisages two teachers, one of whom was dead at the time of the final redaction and one who was still to come. It is gratuitous to multiply teachers without cause, by identifying the Interpreter of the Law as yet a third figure who preceded the historical Teacher.

Davies has been supported, however, by Michael Wise, who argues in his dissertation not only that the Teacher was the one who had been expected, but that the Temple Scroll is the new law that he wrote for the end of days.[14] Since many scholars have argued for various reasons that the Temple Scroll was authored by the Teacher of Righteousness[15] or that it is a law for the eschatological period,[16] this argument deserves some consideration. There are three issues here that concern us. First, it is necessary to clarify what is meant in the Dead Sea Scrolls by the "end of days." Second, we must consider how the Temple Scroll relates to the "end of days." Finally, we will return to the figure of the Teacher and consider how his career was thought to relate to the "end of days."

The Understanding of the End of Days

The expression אחרית הימים, conventionally translated "end of days," occurs many times in the Hebrew Bible, and typically refers to some decisive change at a future time. Horst Seebass has argued that in the Pentateuch the expression is not eschatological at all, but that "the reference is to a limited future time."[17] Two of the Pentateuchal passages, however, Gen 49:1 and Num 24:14, occur in conjunction with classical messianic passages. The reference to the "end of days" is not part of the ancient poetry in either chapter, but is part of a prose introduction, and may already reflect a reorientation of the old prophecies to the more distant future. Whether or not the expression "end of days" was originally intended in an eschatological sense in these passages, it was surely read this way in the Hellenistic period. The Dead Sea Scrolls typically reinterpret older prophecy in this way, regardless of its original intention.[18] In Deut 4:30 and 31:29 the reference is to future turning points in Israel's history, in relation to the observance of the covenant. The phrase is more specifically eschatological in the prophets. In Isa 2:2 (= Mic 4:1) the reference is to a definitive transformation of Israel in the distant future. In Ezek 38:16 the reference is to the coming of Gog, as part of the drama that precedes the final transformation. In Dan 2:28 Daniel interprets the statue of Nebuchadnezzar's dream with reference to "the end of days," when "the king of heaven will set up a kingdom that shall never be destroyed" (Dan 2:44). In Dan 10:14 the phrase is used in anticipation of the final revelation of the book, which concludes with resurrection and judgment. The translation "end of days" derives from the Septuagint (ἐπ᾽ ἐσχάτων τῶν ἡμερῶν). It is somewhat misleading, since an end of history or of the world is not envisaged. In all the prophetic texts, the reference is rather to the end of one era and the beginning of another.

The phrase "end of days" occurs one other time in CD, in 4:4, which interprets the "sons of Zadok" of Ezek 44:15 as "the elect of Israel, the men called by name who (shall) stand at the end of days." The verb "stand" is a participle (עמדים) and so it is uncertain whether the reference is present or future.[19] It should be noted, however, that the same verb (עמד) is used of the figure who will teach righteousness in CD 6:11, of the "Prince of the Congregation" who is the scepter of Balaam's oracle in CD 7:20, and of the "Branch of David" who will arise with the Interpreter of the Law in Florilegium 1:11. In each of these cases the reference is to the eschatological future. The most significant parallel to CD 6:11 is found in the Florilegium, which refers to the "Branch of David" who will arise with the Interpreter of the Law at the end of days. Since there is no evidence that the Branch of David was thought to have come already, the "end of days" is surely future from the perspective of the Florilegium.

Nonetheless, George Brooke has argued that "This future time, this time before the end, is already being experienced. The latter days herald and anticipate, even inaugurate the end, but they are not the end, except proleptically. . . ."[20] One may grant, however, that the "latter days" are not the end, or the final culmination of history, without granting that they are already being experienced. Wise also takes the "end of days" as referring to a time before the end, but he sees this as the first stage of a two-stage eschatology. Against Brooke, he argues that there is no unambiguous use of "end of days" that refers to the present, but many that refer to the future.[21] 4QMMT is an exception here, insofar as it claims that some of the blessings and curses foretold in the book of Moses have come about, and that "this is the end of days."[22] It is very doubtful, however, whether the Damascus Document, the *pesharîm*, Florilegium or Catena regard the "end of days" as already inaugurated. The difference between 4QMMT and these documents might be explained in various ways. They may reflect different periods in the history of the sect, or different contemporaneous viewpoints but, in any case, 4QMMT appears to be exceptional on this point.

The eschatological expectations of the Florilegium have been much debated, and no consensus has been reached. The extant fragments of this composition begin with an exposition of 2 Sam 7:10. The beginning of the verse is not preserved, but it is the basis of the following interpretation. The verse reads "And I will appoint a place for my people Israel and will plant them, so that they may live in their own place and be disturbed no more." The interpretation follows:

"That is the house which [he will build] for him in the latter days, as it is written in the book of [Moses], 'The sanctuary of the Lord which thy hands have established' (Exod 15:17). . . . And foreigners shall not make it desolate again, as they desolated formerly the sanctuary of Israel because of their sin. And he said to build for him a sanctuary of men (מקדש אדם), for there to be in it for him smoking offerings. . . ."[23]

Much of the debate has centered on the various temples mentioned in this text.[24] The house that God will build in the latter days is explicitly identified with sanctuary mentioned in Exodus 15. Two further temples are mentioned: the sanctuary of Israel, which was made desolate because of sin, and the "sanctuary of men," which is to be built. The main point of debate is the meaning of the phrase "sanctuary of men" and whether this sanctuary is identical with the temple for the latter days. In my judgment, the "sanctuary of men" cannot be identified with the "sanctuary of the Lord" and is not a temple for the end of days. Even if it is identified with the Qumran community itself, it does not require that the end of days had already come.

Teacher, Priest and Prophet

EXCURSUS: THE SANCTUARY OF MEN

The "sanctuary of men" has been variously interpreted as the Qumran community or as a physical temple, and has often been identified with the sanctuary of the Lord, mentioned in the citation from Exodus 15 earlier in the passage, and so with the house for the latter days. Wise, who envisages a physical temple, points out that the sentence "and he said to build for him a מקדש אדם" is not preceded by a new citation of a biblical passage. Where, then, did God say this? Wise argues that this passage still refers back to 2 Sam 7:10–11, which was earlier interpreted as the temple that would be built in the latter days. But this is not the only possibility. Daniel Schwartz has plausibly suggested that this sentence is a paraphrase of 2 Sam 7:13a ("he will build me a temple"), which in its original context promises that Solomon will build the temple.[25] If this is correct, then the מקדש אדם is not necessarily identified with the "sanctuary of the Lord" which is promised for the end of days, since it is related to a different biblical passage. Even if we do not accept Schwartz's suggestion, however, and suppose that the "sanctuary of men" is an "additional explication" of 2 Sam 7:10, as Wise suggests,[26] it does not necessarily follow that the two temples should be identified. A scriptural verse may have more than one referent, as can be seen clearly from 1QpHab 2:1–10, àpropos of Hab 1:5, which we will cite later. It seems to me, moreover, that the "sanctuary of men," however understood, by its very terminology implies a contrast with the "sanctuary of the Lord," which will be built in the "latter days."[27] It should also probably be distinguished from the "temple of Israel" that was defiled (presumably Solomon's temple). I suggest, then, that the "sanctuary of men," whether understood as a real temple or as "a sanctuary consisting of men," is not an eschatological temple that belongs to the end of days. Rather it is an interim arrangement, pending the construction of the "sanctuary of the Lord" in the end of days. It may possibly refer to the sectarian community, as Brooke and others have argued, but it does not imply that the end of days has been inaugurated in the history of the community.

Yigael Yadin drew attention to a possible parallel between the temples of the Florilegium and those of 11QTemple col. 29,[28] and the parallel has been pursued by Wise. 11QTemple column 29 speaks of "the house upon which I will cause my name to d[well] . . . ," on which God will cause his glory to dwell "until the day of creation, when I myself shall create my temple, to establish it for me forever, according to the covenant which I made with Jacob at Bethel." The Temple Scroll does not use the expression "end of days," but Wise argues that the period of the temple where God causes his glory to dwell, or the period immediately prior to the "day of creation," is in fact the period called the "end of days" in the Florilegium.[29] This argument depends on his identification of the penultimate temple of the Temple Scroll (that is, the temple prior to the day of creation) with the "sanctuary of men" (Florilegium 1:6), on the one hand, and the "sanctuary of the Lord" that is to be made in the end of days (Florilegium 1:3, citing Exod 15:17) on the other. This argument, however, forces him to reject the plain meaning of the quotation from Exod 15:17, which implies that the "sanctuary of the Lord" will be made directly by God ("the sanctuary of the Lord which thy hands have established").[30] This sanctuary is more naturally correlated with the new temple that God himself will make on the day of creation, according to 11QTemple 29 (if indeed the Florilegium and the Temple Scroll should be so correlated at all). It seems to me, then, that only one temple in the Temple Scroll, the final one on the day of creation, can properly be called eschatological: the new temple that God will make on the day of creation is the same as the one promised in the Florilegium for the end of days. This has implications both for the supposed eschatological character of the Temple Scroll and for its possible authorship by the one who would teach righteousness at the end of days.

Up to this point, we have argued that the end of days is still in the future from the perspective of the Damascus Document (at all stages of its redaction) and of the Florilegium. We are told only a few important characteristics of this period. It will be a time of refining (עת מצרף, 4QFlor 2:1). It will be marked by the coming of the Branch of David and the eschatological Interpreter of the Law, and by the sanctuary made by God. This picture can be elaborated only to a slight extent from other texts. The time of testing is reflected in 4QCatena[a] 2:9–10, which also speaks of the purification of the hearts of the men of the community and of the conflict between the lots of light and darkness.[31] It is also reflected in the *pesher* on Habakkuk, which refers to traitors and ruthless ones at the end of days (1QpHab 2:5–6; cf. 4QpNah 3–4 ii 2). The Branch of David is also associated with the end of days in the *pesher* on Isaiah (4QpIsa[a]), and the messiah of Israel, who is presumably to be identified with the Branch of David, appears in the "Rule for all the congregation of Israel in the end of days" (1QSa).[32] This latter document, also known as the "Messianic Rule," shows that the end of days is not the end of history and does not imply a perfect world. There is still provision for marriage and for the education of children, and there are still laws to limit the roles of simpletons and of people smitten with various forms of uncleanness. The *pesharîm* also allude to the activity of the *Kittim* in this period (1QpHab 9:6–7) and to war and turmoil (4QpIsa[a] 7–10. 22–25; 4QpIsa[b] 2:1; 4QCatena[b] 3:7–8). The end of days, then, is not a period of perfection and peace, but it includes the final turmoil and at least the dawn of the messianic age, as well as the building of the eschatological temple.

The Temple Scroll and the End of Days

Is this characterization of the end of days reflected in the Temple Scroll? A crucial part of Wise's argument rests on his redactional study of the use of Deuteronomy in 11QTemple.[33] He argues that the Scroll did not draw directly from Deuteronomy, but from a source D that had already excerpted portions of the biblical book.[34] The redactor of the Temple Scroll left out portions of D that would cease to function at the end of days. So it omits laws relating to aliens, in accordance with their exclusion from the eschatological temple in the Florilegium. Passages on lending to Israelites are omitted, as are laws relating to slaves. Yet, as Wise recognizes, the Temple Scroll does not omit everything we would expect to be irrelevant to the end of days. It retains laws on adultery and rape, expiation for an unknown murderer and the stoning of a rebellious youth.[35] Wise's explanation, that inconsistency is human, and that the author's concept of righteousness allows for some individual lapses, is weak. If Wise is right that the author of the Temple Scroll was working with a D source rather than with the book of Deuteronomy itself, then we do not know whether these laws were already omitted from the source. It would also seem that many of the omissions could be explained by the author's relative lack of concern for social issues. While it is true that the end of days does not necessarily imply a perfect world, the argument that relevance to the end of days is a redactional principle in the Temple Scroll is not compelling.

One of the most consistent trademarks of the end of days is the coming of the messiah. We should expect then that the portrayal of the king in the Temple Scroll, in the so-called "Law of the King" (11QTemple 57:1–59:11),[36] would show some messianic traits. But this is not the case. We should not be surprised that the king is subordinated to the authority of the High Priest ("at his word he shall go and at his word he shall come," 58:19). The Branch of David is also subjected to priestly authority in the *pesher* on Isaiah, and this arrangement is compatible with the expectation of two messiahs elsewhere in the Scrolls.[37] It is surprising, however, to find that the reign of this king is conditional, and that the law envisages the possibility that his posterity would be cut off forever (59:14–15). Where else is such a possibility raised with reference to a messianic king? There is no hint here that this king is engaged in an eschatological war, no mention of the *Kittim* or of a time of testing. Most striking of all is the lack of any allusion to messianic prophecy, that might link the kingship as envisaged here with the end of days.

It is instructive to contrast the portrayal of the king with such messianic passages as *Psalms of Solomon* 17 and the Scroll of Blessings, 1QSb. Wise has argued that the threefold emphasis on the king as warrior, judge, and man of purity in the Temple Scroll is reminiscent of the psalm.[38] The two texts share a peculiarity insofar as they add the words "for war" in their adaptations of Deuteronomy 17.[39] The psalm, however, is resonant with messianic imagery: the king will "smash the sinners' arrogance like a potter's vessel" and "with a rod of iron break in pieces all their substance" (*Ps Sol* 17:23–24, cf. Ps 2:9). God has created him strong in the holy spirit, and wise in prudent counsel, together with strength and righteousness, like the shoot of David foretold in Isaiah 11 (*Ps Sol* 17:37). The blessing of the Prince of the Congregation in 1QSb 5 also draws heavily on Isaiah 11. There are no such allusions in the Temple Scroll. Neither the psalm nor the blessing contains any hint that the line of the messianic king could be discontinued. Instead the psalm declares confidently that "there will be no unrighteousness among them in his days, for all shall be holy, and their king shall be the Lord Messiah" (*Ps Sol* 17:32). The functions of the king remain substantially the same whether a passage is eschatological or not. There is a huge qualitative difference, however, between the fallible king of the Temple Scroll and the messianic king of the psalm, who is declared "pure from sin" (17:36).

Perhaps the aspect of the Temple Scroll that most strongly suggests that it is an eschatological law is the gargantuan size of the temple.[40] As is well known, the temple envisaged is too large for the site of Jerusalem, being about three times the size of the Herodian enclosure. Nonetheless, Wise has argued that there are some indications of compromise between the ideal dimensions of the temple, which were probably derived from an earlier source, and the necessities of real life — e.g. the distance of the latrine from the city is disproportionately short in relation to the width of the city. He infers that the "redactor of TS was probably willing to make such compromises because he really intended to build his temple."[41]

Johann Maier has also argued that the design is not entirely outside the range of possibility, noting that "the Qumran community, in its opposition to the cultic reality of Jerusalem, naturally favored ideal norms (as does every opposition group) and therefore concentrated ... on traditions that stressed the differences from the existing situation."[42] In any case, the temple described in the Temple Scroll is not the final temple that God will create on the day of creation according to 11QTemple 29:9, but rather an ideal temple for the interim period. This temple is obviously utopian, insofar as it is an ideal temple, not a pragmatic blueprint for construction. Whether it is eschatological is perhaps a matter of definition, but I have argued that it should not be identified with the temple that the Florilegium assigns to the end of days. That temple is more likely to correspond to the one that God will create on the day of creation. It seems to me then that the Temple Scroll is not a law for the end of days, and is reformist rather than eschatological. However unrealistic it may be, it would seem to be intended as an ideal for this age, prior to the final tribulation and the coming of the messiah.

▨ *The Teacher and the End of Days*

Both CD 6:11 and the Florilegium locate the eschatological Teacher/Interpreter of the Law firmly in the end of days. If this figure were to come, the end of days would presumably be underway. If Wise is right, as I think he is, that the end of days refers to a future time in these Scrolls,[43] it follows that the eschatological Teacher/Interpreter had not yet come, from their perspective. This applies not only to CD and the Florilegium, but also to the *pesharîm*, which make frequent reference to the Teacher of Righteousness as an historical figure[44] and to the end of days.[45] In the *pesher* on Habakkuk we read, apropos of Hab 1:5:

> "[The interpretation of the passage concerns] the traitors together with the Man of the Lie, for [they did] not [believe the words of] the Teacher of Righteousness (which were) from the mouth of God. And it concerns the trai[tors to] the new [covenant,] f[o]r they were not faithful to the covenant of God [but they profaned] his holy name. Likewise, the interpretation of the passage [concerns the trai]tors at the end of days. They are the ruthless [ones of the coven]ant who will not believe when they hear all that is going to co[me up]on the last generation from the mouth of the priest into [whose heart] God

put [understandi]ng to interpret all the words of his servants the prophets. . . ."

This passage clearly looks back to the Teacher of Righteousness, and forward to the end of days. The author of the *pesher*, then, cannot have viewed the historical teacher as the one who would teach righteousness at the end of days according to CD 6:11. There is, in fact, no evidence anywhere in the Scrolls that the historical Teacher was so regarded. The Teacher may or may not have been the author or redactor of the Temple Scroll, but he was not an eschatological figure and the Scroll was not an eschatological law. In fact, the notion of a new law for the eschatological period remains very poorly attested in ancient Judaism.[46]

The use of such titles as Interpreter of the Law and Teacher of Righteousness for figures of the historical past and the eschatological future underlines a feature of the eschatology of the Scrolls that has often been noted. This eschatology has a restorative aspect and involves the fulfillment and perfection of the institutions of past and present.[47] This is true of the offices of king and High Priest. It is also true of the office of Teacher. The homologies between past, present, and future sometimes engender confusion on the part of modern interpreters. The situation is rendered all the more confusing by the fact that the relationships of Teacher/Interpreter to other offices, present or future, are not clearly defined.

Teacher and Prophet

The historical Teacher was a priest. This is explicit in the *pesher* on Ps 37:23–24 (4QpPs[a] 1–10.iii.15). There is no evidence that he was ever High Priest in Jerusalem, despite frequent claims to the contrary,[48] but we should expect that he was regarded as an ideal priest by his followers. It is more difficult to say whether he was also regarded as a prophet. He is a priest to whom God has given the power "to interpret all the words of his servants the prophets" (1QpHab 2:8–9), "to whom God made known all the mysteries of the words of his servants the prophets" (1QpHab 7:4–5). Despite some lacunae, it appears that the same *pesher* also claims that the words of the Teacher were from the mouth of God (1QpHab 2:2–3), which is reminiscent of Num 12:6–8, where Moses is distinguished from the prophets by the fact that God speaks to him "mouth to mouth."[49] Yet he is never called a prophet, while he is called a priest.

Teacher, Priest and Prophet

Ever since the early years of research on the Scrolls, scholars have repeatedly put forward the view that the Teacher was the prophet like Moses, envisaged in the passage from Deuteronomy 18 cited in the Testimonia, and in the famous reference to "the prophet and the messiahs of Aaron and Israel" in 1QS 9.[50] This view encounters some difficulties, however. It implies that the passages in question were written before the historical Teacher came on the scene. The context in 1QS 9 bears considerable similarity to the passage in CD 6 which we considered at the beginning of this chapter. It refers to "the primitive precepts in which the men of the Community were first instructed," which will remain in effect "until there shall come the prophet and the messiahs of Aaron and Israel." Similarly CD 6 refers to the ordinances of the "Interpreter of the Law," which will remain in effect "until he comes who shall teach righteousness at the end of days." If, as is generally assumed, these passages refer to the same sect or movement, then the historical Teacher/Interpreter should be associated with the "primitive precepts" rather than with the coming of the messiahs. If he was the "Interpreter of the Law," who laid down the precepts in which people "should walk in all the age of wickedness" (CD 6:10), then he was indeed, in a sense, a "new Moses" but he was not necessarily the prophet like Moses, expected at the end of days.[51] We should also expect that if the Teacher were regarded as the eschatological prophet, this would have been made explicit at some point.

A much stronger case can be made for identifying the eschatological prophet with the one who will teach righteousness at the end of days, of CD 6:11. The biblical source of the prophet like Moses is Deut 18:18, which is quoted in the Testimonia: "A prophet like you I shall raise up for them from the midst of their brothers, and I shall put my words in his mouth, and he will tell them all that I command him. Whoever does not listen to my words, which the prophet will speak in my name, I shall seek a reckoning from him."[52] It is certainly possible to view this prophetic figure as a teacher. Moreover, Hos 10:12, "until he comes and teaches righteousness for you," the passage from which the language of CD 6:11 is drawn, is applied to Elijah in later Jewish tradition.[53] Van der Woude argued that the eschatological Interpreter of the Law should be identified with Elijah.[54] CD 7:18 identifies the star of Balaam's oracle as "the Interpreter of the Law who will come (הבא) to Damascus."[55] Van der Woude argued that this was an allusion to 1 Kgs 19:15, where Elijah is told "Go, return on your way to the wilderness of Damascus; when you arrive you shall anoint Hazael as king over Aram."[56] The wilderness of Damascus could be taken to suggest Qumran, and the fact that Elijah is charged to anoint someone recalls a later tradition, according to which Elijah would anoint the messiah.[57] Whether van der Woude is justified in inferring that the Interpreter of the Law here is identified with Elijah seems less than certain. The allusion hangs entirely on the mention of Damascus. The Interpreter is not said to anoint anyone in CD. Nonetheless, the suggestion is an attractive one, and strengthens the case for viewing the eschatological Teacher as the prophet who was to come.

Teacher and Priest

A case can also be made, however, for viewing the eschatological Teacher/Interpreter as a priest, who should be identified with the messiah of Aaron. George Brooke has argued that "The essential link between the functions of this eschatological figure as Interpreter of the Law and as priest is provided by the fortunate preservation among the fragments of 4QFlor (6–11) of a section of Deuteronomy 33."[58] Deut 33:10 says of the descendants of Levi: "They teach Jacob your ordinances and Israel your law." This passage is also cited in the Testimonia, which is usually taken as a string of eschatological proof-texts, so that the blessing of Levi would refer to the eschatological priest.[59] The teaching function of Levi is noted, in language reminiscent of Deuteronomy 33, in Isaac's blessing of Levi in Jubilees 31.[60]

The eschatological High Priest, then, could aptly be described as "Interpreter of the Law" or "Teacher of Righteousness." In light of this, the Interpreter of the Law and Branch of David in the Florilegium may be plausibly equated with the figures known elsewhere as the messiahs of Aaron and Israel.[61] This understanding of the eschatological Interpreter also fits the citation of Balaam's oracle at the end of CD 7: "The star is the Interpreter of the Law who shall come (הבא) to Damascus; as it is written, a star shall come forth out of Jacob and a scepter shall rise out of Israel. The scepter is the Prince of the whole congregation, and when he comes he shall smite all the children of Sheth." Since the scepter here is clearly eschatological, the star is most naturally interpreted in this sense, too. In the *Testaments of the Twelve Patriarchs*, the star is associated with the "new priest" of *T. Levi* 18, while the scepter is associated with kingship and the descendant of Judah in *T. Judah* 24. In CD 7, then, we have the familiar messianic duality.[62] The Prince of the Congregation is the figure elsewhere called the Branch of David or the messiah of Israel. The Interpreter of the Law is the eschatological High Priest or messiah of Aaron.

Corroboration for the notion that the eschatological High Priest would also function as Teacher comes now from 4Q541 (4QAaronA).[63] In fragment 9 i, it is said of the figure who "will atone for all the sons of his generation" that "his word is like a word of heaven and his teaching is in accordance with the will of God." The role of atoning for sin is expressly assigned to the messiah(s) of Aaron and Israel (משיח אהרון וישראל) in CD 14:19 (whether the reference be to one figure or two).[64] The passage in 4QAaronA goes on to say that he will encounter lies and adversity, which suggests a parallel between his career and that of the historical Priest/Teacher in his struggle with the Man of the Lie. The motif of priestly instruction also figures prominently in the *Testament of Kohath* (e.g. 2:1–2: "I have taught you in truth . . . every word of truth will come upon you").

While it is not certain that 4QAaronA refers to the same figure as CD or the Florilegium, it is certainly closer in time and setting to the Dead Sea Scrolls than the medieval Jewish traditions about Elijah. There seems then to be more reason to identify the "one who will teach righteousness at the end of days" with the messiah of Aaron, or eschatological High Priest, than with the "prophet like Moses," although admittedly the priestly interpretation does not clarify the association with Damascus in CD 7. I do not, however, claim that the expectations of the Dead Sea sect were necessarily consistent in this matter. We know little as yet of the historical development of eschatological ideas in the corpus of the Scrolls.[65] The prophet and eschatological priest may not always have been clearly distinguished. In fact, Elijah, the prototypical eschatological prophet, was also identified as eschatological High Priest in later Jewish tradition, through an association with Phineas and their shared motif of zeal.[66] Even in the biblical narrative, Elijah builds an altar and offers sacrifice (1 Kings 18:30–39). The association with Elijah, then, could imply a priestly motif as well as a prophetic one, and an eschatological High Priest could also have a prophetic persona.[67]

The historical Teacher evidently anticipated to some degree the roles of his eschatological counterpart. He is explicitly said to have been a priest, and he also had some prophetic characteristics (his words were from the mouth of God). He was, in a sense, a new Moses. If our analysis is correct, however, he was not himself regarded as the fulfillment of eschatological expectation, either as the "prophet like Moses" or as the "messiah of Aaron," and he did not write a law for the end of days. There was yet a more definitive Teacher to come, and this, perhaps, is a reason why the historical Teacher remains such a shadowy figure in the Dead Sea Scrolls.

The Eschatological Prophet

The eschatological prophet is a shadowy figure, not only in the Scrolls, but generally in the Judaism of the time.[68] There was a biblical basis for such a figure. In addition to the Deuteronomic "prophet like Moses," there is the promise in Mal 3:1, "See I am sending my messenger to prepare the way before me," which is specified in Mal 4:5: "Lo, I will send you the prophet Elijah before the great and terrible day of the Lord comes."[69] Ben Sira 48:10 says that Elijah is destined "to calm the wrath of God, to turn the hearts of parents to their children and to restore the tribes of Jacob," but otherwise Malachi's prophecies are rarely picked up in the literature of the Hellenistic period. When the Jewish people in 1 Macc 14:41 resolve that Simon Maccabee "should be their leader and high priest forever, until a trustworthy prophet should arise," it is clear that such a prophet is not expected any time soon.[70]

The older handbooks often assert that "it was the universal belief that shortly before the appearance of the Messiah Elijah should return."[71] To a great degree this view is inferred from the New Testament. When the disciples ask Jesus "why do the scribes say that Elijah must come first?" they are told "Elijah is indeed coming first to restore all things." Jesus goes on to say that Elijah has already come, presumably with reference to John the Baptist.[72] The notion that Elijah should return *as precursor of the messiah* may well have been a Christian development,[73] but we have seen that he had an eschatological role even in Ben Sira, and this role is developed at length in later Jewish tradition.[74] Yet there are surprisingly few references to this role in the Pseudepigrapha.[75] There is a clear reference to the return of Elijah in *Sib Or* 2:187–89, but while this oracle incorporates Jewish materials, it is Christian in its present form.[76] The Coptic *Apocalypse of Elijah* also incorporates Jewish material, but it is also Christian and dates from the third century CE.[77] The Hebrew *Book of Elijah* is later still.[78]

The expectation of Elijah as eschatological prophet was known at Qumran, even though it is not widely attested. In his article on Qumran messianism in 1963, Jean Starcky reported a papyrus fragment from Cave 4 that reads "therefore I will send Elijah be[fore ...]"[79] Starcky dated the script to the period 50–25 BCE. Several small scraps of this papyrus survive, but the context is unclear. The preceding line contains the words "the eighth as an elect one and behold." The line after the reference to Elijah contains the word "lightning" (ברקא), perhaps a sign of the day of the Lord. The reference to Elijah does not appear to be accompanied by a quotation from Malachi.

Teacher, Priest and Prophet

There is, however, a more substantial text from Qumran that does not mention the name of Elijah but may nonetheless throw some light on the expectations associated with an Elijah-like eschatological prophet. This text is 4Q521, dubbed "a messianic apocalypse" by Emile Puech[80] and entitled "The Messiah of Heaven and Earth" by Eisenman and Wise.[81]

◈ *4Q521*

4Q521 is a Hebrew text that survives in a single exemplar. Seventeen fragments have been identified. An eighteenth is possible but less sure. The handwriting dates from the Hasmonean period.[82] Many of the fragments are too small to be intelligible, but a few important passages are reasonably clear. The first of these (fragment 2 ii) is the longest:

> "... heaven and earth will obey his messiah, (2) [and all th]at is in them will not turn away from the commandments of holy ones. (3) You who seek the Lord, strengthen yourselves in his service. (4) Is it not in this that you will find the Lord, all who hope in their hearts. (5) For the Lord will seek out the pious and call the righteous by name, (6) and his spirit will hover over the poor and he will renew the faithful by his might. (7) For he will glorify the pious on the throne of an eternal kingdom, (8) releasing captives, giving sight to the blind and raising up those who are bo[wed down]. (9) Forever I will cleave to [those who] hope, and in his kindness. . . . (10) The fru[it of a] good [wor]k will not be delayed for anyone (11) and the glorious things that have not taken place the Lord will do as he s[aid] (12) for he will heal the wounded, give life to the dead and preach good news to the poor (13) and he will [sat]isfy the [weak] ones and lead those who have been cast out and enrich the hungry ... (14) ... and all of them. . . ."

This passage is heavily dependent on Psalm 146, in lines 1–8. It departs from the psalm, however, at one significant point. The psalm refers to the Lord "who made heaven and earth, the sea and all that is in them," but it has no mention of a messiah. The purpose of this innovation is not immediately apparent, as the Qumran text goes on to say that God will release captives, give sight to the blind, etc., just as he does in the psalm. Again at vs. 12, it is God who will heal the wounded, give life to the dead and preach good news to the poor.[83] The Lord, of course, is normally the one who raises the dead (cf. the second of the Eighteen Benedictions: "Lord, you are almighty forever, who makes the dead to live. . . . And you are faithful to make the dead alive. Blessed are you, Lord, who makes the dead alive"). It is surprising, however, to find God as the subject of preaching good news. This is the work of a herald or messenger.

The phrase in question is taken from Isa 61:1: "The spirit of the Lord God is upon me, because the Lord has anointed me; he has sent me to preach good news to the poor, to bind up the brokenhearted, to proclaim liberty to the captives and release to the prisoners; to proclaim the year of the Lord's favor, and the day of vengeance of our God." In Isaiah 61 the speaker is a prophet, who makes his proclamation in the name of God. He also claims to be anointed, and so he is a משיח, or anointed one. There is little evidence for the anointing of prophets in the Hebrew Bible. In 1 Kings 19:6 Elijah is told to anoint Elisha as prophet after him, but the actual anointing of Elisha is never reported. In the Dead Sea Scrolls, however, the prophets are called "anointed ones" in CD 2:12 and 1QM 11:7, and so the understanding of the prophet as an anointed one presents no problem in the context of the Scrolls. The anointing in Isaiah 61 endows the prophet with the authority to make his proclamation.[84]

In view of the introduction of a messiah in the first line of the fragment ("heaven and earth will obey his messiah") it is likely that God acts through the agency of a prophetic messiah in line 12.[85] There is another reference to messianic agency in 4Q521 fragment 9, in a very fragmentary passage, which apparently reads "you will abandon by the power of (your) messiah (or messiahs?)" (. . .]תעזוב ביד משיח[. . .).[86] There is also a plural reference to "all her anointed ones" (וכל משיחיה) in fragment 8. Puech suggests that the reference here is to priests, in view of a reference to "holy vessels" in the previous line.[87] The feminine suffix might then refer to Zion. Where the plural "anointed ones" occurs elsewhere in the Scrolls, however, the reference is to prophets. In CD 2:12 and 6:1 the expression is used with reference to the prophets of the past. (In CD 2:12 they are called "the anointed of your holy spirit.") In 1QM 11:7 the reference is again to the prophets of the past.

The most interesting parallel to 4Q521 on this point, however, is found in 11QMelchizedek, a text that weaves together allusions to Isaiah 61 and several other texts. "The year of the Lord's favor" (Isa 61:2) becomes "Melchiz[edek]'s year of favor" (11QMelch 2:9). The verb "to preach good news" (בשר) is picked up in a quotation from Isa 52:7:

"[How] beautiful on (the) mountains are the feet of the heral[d who pro]claims peace, the her[ald of good ..." (11QMelch 2:15–16). The herald (מבשר) is then identified as "[the one an]ointed of the spir[it about] whom Dan[iel said ...]." The quotation from Daniel is usually completed from Dan 9:25: "Until an anointed, a prince, (there will be) seven weeks."[88] Daniel also mentions an anointed one in 9:26. The herald, however, is clearly a prophetic figure, and the expression "anointed of the spirit" is similar to the phrase used for the prophets in CD 2:12. In 11QMelchizedek the role of this herald is to proclaim salvation and comfort the mourners of Zion.[89]

The anointed figure in Isaiah 61 is not said to give life to the dead. As we have seen, that function is usually reserved for God. 4Q521 fragment 7:6 refers to "the one who gives life to the dead of his people" (המחיה את מתי עמו).[90] The reference is presumably to God. It is quite possible that God should use an agent in the resurrection, but this agent is unlikely to be a royal messiah.[91] The resurrection is sometimes associated with the messianic age in writings of the first century CE. In *2 Bar* 30 we are told that when the earthly career of the messiah has run its course, he will return in glory. Then "all who have died and set their hopes on him will rise again" (*2 Bar* 30:2). In *4 Ezra 7*, the messiah dies, and the resurrection follows after seven days of primeval silence. In neither case does the messiah raise the dead. Also in the New Testament, Christ is the firstfruits of the resurrection, not the agent, in 1 Corinthians 15. In Revelation 20 the martyrs come to life and reign with Christ for a thousand years, but Christ is not said to raise them. In later Jewish tradition we find the notion that "the dead will first come to life in the time of the Messiah" (j. Ketubot 12:3). But the resurrection does not come through the (royal) messiah. Rather, "the resurrection of the dead comes through Elijah" (m. Soṭa 9, end; j. Sheqalim 3:3).[92] Elijah was credited with raising the dead during his historical career (1 Kings 17, cf. the story of Elisha in 2 Kings 4). So we read in Pesikta de R. Kahana 76a: "Everything that the Holy One will do, he has already anticipated by the hands of the righteous in this world, the resurrection of the dead by Elijah and Ezekiel, the drying of the Dead Sea by Moses...."[93] The association of Elijah with an eschatological resurrection may be attested already in Ben Sira. The versions of Sir 48:11 speak clearly of resurrection, and Puech restores the Hebrew text from the Cairo Geniza to read: "Blessed is he who sees you before he dies, f[or] you give l[if]e and he will live."[94] Puech takes this to mean that the righteous who die after the return of Elijah will be raised. In view of Ben Sira's skeptical attitude toward life after death, however, there must be doubt as to whether such a belief was part of the original, pre-Maccabean book.[95]

I suggest, then, that the messiah, whom heaven and earth will obey, is an anointed eschatological prophet, either Elijah or a prophet like Elijah. Elijah's command of the heavens was legendary. In the words of Sirach, "By the word of the Lord he shut up the heavens and also three times brought down fire" (Sir 48:3). The "two olive trees" in Revelation 11, who have authority to shut up the sky so that no rain may fall and to turn the waters into blood, are usually identified as Elijah and Moses.[96] The "two olive trees" of course, recall the "two sons of oil" or anointed ones of the prophet Zechariah.

Some support for the identification of the messiah of heaven and earth as Elijah may be found in another fragment of 4Q521 (fragment 2 iii).[97] The fragmentary text reads:

> "(1) and the precept of your mercy   ואת חק חסדך
> and I will liberate them . . .   ואתר אותם...
> (2) for it is sure: נכון
> 'the fathers will return to the sons.' "   באים אבות על בנים

Puech rightly recognizes in the last line a citation of Mal 3:24, which says that God will send Elijah before the day of the Lord and "he will turn the hearts of fathers to their children and the hearts of children to their fathers."[98] The same phrase is cited in the praise of Elijah in Sir 48:10. That verse begins with a statement that Elijah is "prepared for the time," נכון לעת, using the same word נכון translated above as "it is sure" in 4Q521.

Puech's conclusion from these parallels is that the speaker in this fragment, and the subject of the verb "I will liberate," is the new Elijah (Mal 3:24) or the new Moses (3:22). Puech distinguishes this figure from the messiah, who is referred to in the third person in other fragments.[99] The only other occurrence of a verb in the first person in 4Q521 is in the long passage from fragments 2 ii+4 cited above: "forever will I cleave to [those who] hope." In that case the subject is presumably the author of the composition. Puech suggests that in fragment 2 iii the subject is also the author of the text "in a sort of vision," perhaps the Teacher of Righteousness speaking as the new Elijah or new Moses. The messiah in 4Q521, then, is "clearly the kingly messiah, whom the prophet announces."[100]

It is unlikely, however, that the Teacher or any other human author would claim in the first person to be the liberator. The most plausible subject in this fragment is surely God, just as God is the subject who sets captives free in fragment 2 ii (which begins with the reference to the messiah whom heaven and earth will obey). It is true that the first person referent in fragment 2 ii+4 is the human author, but it is not unusual to have vacillation between God and a human author in a prophetic text. Isaiah 61 provides a relevant example. The speaker in Isa 61:1 is evidently human ("The spirit of the Lord God is upon me") but 61:6 reads "I the Lord love justice." If we take God as the speaker in 4Q521 fragment 2 iii, then Elijah, or an Elijah-like figure, is the one predicted, not the one making the prediction. The passage concerns the return of Elijah, who will turn the hearts of children to their fathers, and by whose hand God will bring about the liberation. Fragment 2 ii+4 can be interpreted in the same context. Elijah is the messiah whom heaven and earth obey, in whose time the sick are healed and the dead are raised.

It is not certain whether 4Q521 should be regarded as a product of the Dead Sea sect. The sectarian literature is notoriously lacking in references to resurrection,[101] and has relatively few references to the eschatological prophet. In favor of a sectarian origin, however, are several parallels in vocabulary, especially with the Hodayot and the interest in the poor, עניים, which suggest a common cultural context.[102] The question must be left open.

The most fascinating parallel to 4Q521, however, does not come from the other Scrolls but from the New Testament, in a passage that derives from the Sayings Source, Q, and is attested in Matthew and Luke. In response to the question from the Baptist, "Are you the one who is to come, or are we to look for another?" Jesus answers: "Go and tell John what you hear and see: the blind receive their sight, the lame walk, the lepers are cleansed, the deaf hear, the dead are raised, and the poor have good news brought to them" (Matt 11:2–5; Luke 7:22). Both Gospel passages go on to identify John with the messenger sent to prepare the way in Mal 3:1. Fitzmyer comments that "Jesus is depicted as rejecting the role of *Elias redivivus*, in which John had originally cast him (see [Luke] 3:15–18). Rather than understanding his mission as that of a fiery reformer of the eschaton, Jesus sees his role as the embodiment of the divine blessings promised to be shed on the unfortunate of human society by Isaiah."[103] But the relevant passage in Isaiah 61 does not promise raising of the dead, a motif that recalls precisely Elijah and Elisha.[104] The signs in Matt 11:5/Luke 7:22 could easily be taken to suggest that Jesus was *Elijah redivivus*. The pericopes in Matt 11:7–15 and Luke 7:24–28 identifying John as the messenger are placed at this point to undo that impression and affirm that Jesus was greater than the Baptist.[105] The possibility that Jesus might be Elijah is also voiced in Mark 6:14–15, where various people identify Jesus to Herod as John raised from the dead, Elijah or "a prophet," and again in Mark 8:27, where Jesus' question, "who do people say that I am?" receives the answer "John the Baptist; and others, Elijah; and still others, one of the prophets."

The parallel between 4Q521 and the New Testament text is intriguing since both go beyond Isaiah 61 in referring to the raising of the dead. This can hardly be coincidental. It is quite possible that the author of the Sayings Source knew 4Q521; at the least he drew on a common tradition. 4Q521 was somewhat atypical of the sectarian literature in any case. The reference to resurrection is exceptional in the Scrolls. If we are correct that the "messiah" in this text is an eschatological prophet, that, too, is exceptional. *Elijah redivivus* was not a distinctively sectarian figure, in the sense that the messiah of Aaron, or the Teacher at the end of days, was. The Elijah-like eschatological prophet had a clear scriptural basis and did not require a sectarian perspective. He did not, however, figure as prominently as the Davidic messiah in the literature of the time, and presumably he was not as well established in popular belief.

Conclusion

The identity and role of the one who would teach righteousness at the end of days is not as clearly defined in the Scrolls as that of the Davidic warrior messiah. The role was not necessarily less important, however. Both the priestly messiah and the "prophet like Moses" are teacher figures. Teaching and the Law carried enormous importance for the Dead Sea sect. It occupied far more of the sectarians' attention than preparation for the eschatological war. Authentic teaching would be an essential component of the messianic end of days. Whether the eschatological Teacher was prophet, priest or both, the important thing was that there would be a Teacher of Righteousness in the messianic age.

This doctrinal, prophetic aspect of messianic expectations, both in the Dead Sea sect and in the broader context of the Judaism of the time, is an important counterpart to the expectation of a militant messiah. Jewish hopes for the future were not completely focused on the restoration of Israel. There were also widely held aspirations to a life of holiness and justice. This was certainly true of the Dead Sea sect, but also of the authors of the *Psalms of Solomon*, and of most Jews of the time. Ultimately, the teachers would be more important for the survival of Judaism than the would-be messiahs. While Jesus of Nazareth taught a view of righteousness that was very different from those held at Qumran, he, too, was a teacher, and his success as messiah lay in his success as a teacher rather than in restoring the kingdom of Israel.

EXCURSUS: THE SUFFERING SERVANT AT QUMRAN?

One of the most controversial points in the Jewish-Christian debate over messianism concerns the notion that the messiah should suffer before he entered into his glory (Luke 24:26). Justin's *Dialogue with Trypho* has the Jew concede this point but refuse to accept the crucifixion: "for we know that he should suffer and be led as a sheep. But prove to us whether he must be crucified and die so disgracefully and so dishonourably the death cursed in the law. For we cannot bring ourselves even to think of this" (90:1; cf. 36:1; 39:7). Modern scholars view Justin's attribution of these views to a Jewish speaker with considerable skepticism. In the words of A. J. B. Higgins, "The messianic ideas expressed by Trypho bristle with inconsistencies which no amount of ingenuity can resolve into a harmonious picture."[106] Nonetheless, there have been many attempts in modern scholarship to find evidence of a suffering messiah in pre-Christian Judaism. The argument turns on the interpretation of Isa 52:13–53:12, which portrays a "servant of the Lord" who "has borne our infirmities and carried our diseases... was wounded for our transgressions, crushed for our iniquities," and was "led like a lamb to the slaughter."[107]

The view that Isa 52:13–53:12 was interpreted with reference to a suffering messiah by some Jews before the rise of Christianity is associated above all with Joachim Jeremias.[108] Subsequent scholarship has largely moved away from that position and admits that it is difficult to demonstrate either the notion of a suffering servant in Judaism or the influence of Isaiah 52–53 in the New Testament.[109] Jean Starcky, however, claimed to find "a suffering messiah, in the perspective opened up by the Servant poems" in 4Q541 (4QAaronA),[110] and the claim has been endorsed by Emile Puech.[111]

A few points should be clarified at the outset.

First, "servant" is not necessarily "suffering servant." Servant (עבד) is often used as a title for the king in the Hebrew Bible, both for historical kings ("my servant David" in 2 Sam 3:18; "King Nebuchadnezzar of Babylon, my servant," Jer 27:6) and with reference to an ideal king of the future ("my servant David," Ezek 34:23–24; 37:24–25; "my servant the branch," Zech 3:8).[112] In *4 Ezra* the Latin "my son" (filius) as a messianic title may reflect Greek *pais*, which in turn may mean servant rather than son,[113] and the messiah is also called "my servant" in *2 Bar* 70:9. In none of these cases does the term servant imply suffering.

Second, modern scholarship distinguishes four "servant songs" in Deutero-Isaiah, 42:1–7; 49:1–7; 50:4–9; and 52:13–53:12. These passages were not grouped together in antiquity.[114] Consequently, allusions to the other "servant songs" do not necessarily imply the kind of suffering described in Isaiah 53. The Son of Man figure in the *Similitudes of Enoch*, who will concern us in a later chapter, is called "the light of the nations" in *1 Enoch* 48:4. The same phrase is used of the servant of the Lord in Isa 42:6; 49:6. The Son of Man is also hidden like the servant (*1 Enoch* 48:6, cf. Isa 49:2). But the Son of Man is not a suffering figure, and carries no allusions to the notion of vicarious suffering as found in Isaiah 53.

Third, in the late-first-century CE apocalypses of *4 Ezra* and *2 Baruch*, the messiah dies. His death, however, does not involve suffering and has no atoning significance. In *4 Ezra* 7:29–30 the death of the messiah marks the end of a four-hundred-year reign and is the prelude to seven days of primeval silence, followed by resurrection. In *2 Bar* 30:1, "when the time of the appearance of the messiah has been fulfilled" he "returns in glory, and then all who sleep in hope of him rise." Neither scenario bears any similarity to Isaiah 53.

Fourth, some of the servant passages in Deutero-Isaiah (42:1; 43:10; 52:13) are construed messianically in the *targum*. In the case of Isaiah 52–53, however, the *targum* systematically subverts the references to the suffering of the servant. So the "man of sorrows" is taken to refer to the Gentile kingdoms (vs. 3); the sanctuary was desecrated because of our transgressions, delivered up because of our sins, but the messiah will rebuild it, (vs. 5) and he will lay on the Gentiles the transgressions of which Israel was guilty (vs. 8). Only a couple of traces of the suffering servant remain.[115] Jeremias supposed that the *targum* represents a reaction against the Christian interpretation of this passage. The reaction admits Isaiah 53 as a messianic prophecy, but virtually eliminates the suffering of the messiah. There is still no evidence for a Jewish interpretation of Isaiah 53 in terms of a suffering messiah.

The argument for a suffering messiah in 4Q541 rests on two fragments, 9 and 24. Fragment 9 reads:

> "He will atone for all the children of his generation and he will be sent to all the children of his [pe]ople. His word is like a word of heaven and his teaching is in accordance with the will of God. His eternal sun will shine, and his light will be kindled in all the corners of the earth, and it will shine on the darkness. Then the darkness

will pass away [fro]m the earth, and thick darkness from the dry land. They will speak many words against him, and they will invent many [lie]s and fictions against him and speak shameful things about him. Evil will overthrow his generation. . . . His situation will be one of lying and violence [and] the people will go astray in his days, and be confounded."

The figure described in 4Q541 is said to atone for the children of his generation. The obvious implication is that he is a priest and makes atonement by means of the sacrificial cult. He does not atone by his suffering and death, as is the case with Isaiah's servant. The motif of light recalls the "light to the nations" of Isa 42:6 and 49:6, but as we have seen these passages were not singled out as "servant songs" in antiquity. Finally the figure in this passage undergoes suffering, but it is mental anguish, brought on by lies and calumnies, and so is of quite a different sort from the suffering described in Isaiah 53. The trials described in 4Q541 are rather reminiscent of the trials of the Teacher of Righteousness, who endured the opposition of the "Man of the Lie."[116] According to CD 1: "The Scoffer arose who shed over Israel the waters of lies. He caused them to wander in a pathless wilderness. . . ." A hymn that is usually thought to be the work of the Teacher complains: "Teachers of lies [have smoothed] Thy people [with words], and [false prophets] have led them astray," and again "they, teachers of lies and seers of falsehood, have schemed against me a devilish scheme."[117] The eschatological priest of 4Q541 (Aaron A) is more likely to have been modeled on the career of the historical Teacher of Righteousness than on the suffering servant of Isaiah.

4Q541 fragment 24 is an obscure and difficult passage: "Do [not] grieve for [him]. . . . God will set many thing[s] right . . . many revealed things. . . . Examine and seek and know what the dove (or Jonah?) sought (?) and do not afflict the weak by wasting or hanging. . . . [Let] not the nail approach him. So you will establish for your father a name of joy, and for your brothers a proven foundation. . . . You will see and rejoice in the eternal light, and you will not be an enemy."[118]

The allusions to hanging (or crucifixion) and "the nail" are intriguing. The word translated nail (ṣṣ') is unknown in western Aramaic, and is translated on the basis of its Syriac usage.[119] If we may assume, however, that the text does refer to crucifixion, there is still no question of a messianic figure being crucified. Rather, the person addressed in the text is told not to afflict the weak by crucifixion. Puech asks, nonetheless, whether there might not be a "negative reference" to the violent death of a "Priest-Servant," i.e. the idea of crucifixion was suggested to the author by the story of the suffering servant, even though he is not actually referring to the servant here.[120] Such a "negative reference" is extremely speculative. There are no solid grounds for supposing that there is any reference to Isaiah 53 in 4Q541 fragment 24.

Insofar as this fragment makes any sense at all, it would seem to be a warning to a descendant of Levi not to afflict the poor and defenseless. It does not suggest that the descendant of Levi might be subjected to suffering and death. The possible, but very uncertain, reference to crucifixion inevitably brings Jesus to mind, but as Puech quite properly points out, crucifixion was widely used as a means of punishment in the Roman era.[121] The Hasmonean priest-king Alexander Jannaeus is said to have crucified 800 of his Jewish opponents (probably Pharisees).[122] There is a well-known reference to this incident in the *pesher* on Nahum, which speaks of "the lion of wrath who hangs men alive."[123] 4Q541 fragment 24 can be read as a condemnation of, or warning against, such behavior. A descendant of Levi should not do such things. There is no reference here to a suffering servant.

The alleged allusions to a suffering messiah in the Scrolls disappear under examination.[124] The Christian belief in such a figure, and discovery of prophecies relating to him, surely arose in retrospect after the passion and death of Jesus of Nazareth. There is no evidence that anyone in first-century Judaism expected such a figure, either in fulfillment of Isaiah 53 or on any other basis.

The notion of a suffering and dying messiah eventually found a place in Judaism.[125] In the Babylonian Talmud, tractate Sukkah 52, Zech 12:10 ("they will look on him whom they pierced") is explained with reference to "the slaying of the Messiah the son of Joseph." While the origin of this figure is obscure, he most probably reflects in some way the defeat and death of Bar Kokhba, whom Rabbi Akiba had hailed as messiah.[126] The messiah ben Joseph, however, is killed in battle, and his death has "no atoning power whatever."[127] There is also a strange passage in Sanhedrin 98 that tells of the messiah sitting among the lepers at the gate of Rome. The association with lepers is probably derived from the verb נגוע (afflicted) in Isa 53:4.[128] Here again there is no suggestion of an atoning function. Whatever the origin of this legend, it is clearly much later than the time of the Dead Sea Scrolls and the New Testament, and it does not represent the messiah as a suffering servant in the sense that this notion was developed in Christianity.

NOTES

[1] Trans. Vermes. The word מחקק, staff, also occurs in Gen 49:10. In 4Q252 (Patriarchal Blessings) it is interpreted as "the covenant of the kingdom." The expression translated

"converts of Israel," שבי ישראל, has been the subject of much debate. It could also be translated "returnees of Israel" (so J. Murphy-O'Connor) or "captivity of Israel" (so P. R. Davies). See Davies, *The Damascus Covenant*, 93–94.

[2] S. Schechter, *Fragments of a Zadokite Work*, xiii.

[3] Ginzberg, *An Unknown Jewish Sect*, 221, identifies the future teacher as Elijah.

[4] A. Dupont-Sommer, *Aperçus préliminaires sur les manuscrits de la Mer Morte* (Paris: Maisonneuve, 1950) 73–78. He repeated his view in several subsequent publications.

[5] J. M. Allegro, "Further Messianic References in Qumran Literature," *Journal of Biblical Literature* 75(1956) 176–77.

[6] For a summary of the early debate see G. Jeremias, *Der Lehrer der Gerechtigkeit* (Göttingen: Vandenhoeck & Ruprecht, 1963) 275–81; J. Carmignac, "Le Retour de Docteur de Justice à la fin des jours?" *Revue de Qumran* 1(1958–59) 235–48.

[7] K. Stendahl, *The Scrolls and the New Testament* (New York: Harper, 1957) 12.

[8] W. D. Davies, *Torah in the Messianic Age and/or the Age to Come* (Society of Biblical Literature Monograph Series 7; Philadelphia: Society of Biblical Literature, 1952) 46–47: "The Messiah will be none other than the Teacher of Righteousness *redivivus*, and it is difficult not to agree with Schechter in this."

[9] Jeremias, *Der Lehrer*, 279–80. The first critique of this interpretation after the discovery of the Scrolls was by M. Black, "Theological Conceptions in the Dead Sea Scrolls," *Svensk Exegetisk Årsbok* 18–19(1953/54) 86.

[10] Jeremias, *Der Lehrer*, 287. G. Vermes, *The Dead Sea Scrolls. Qumran in Perspective* (Philadelphia: Fortress, 1981) 185–86, identifies the historical Teacher with the prophet and the "one who will teach righteousness at the end of days" with the priestly messiah. The prophet was no longer expected, because he was thought to have already come.

[11] Davies, *The Damascus Covenant*, 124; Davies, "The Teacher of Righteousness at the End of Days," *Revue de Qumran* 49–52 (Mémorial J. Carmignac; 1988) 313–17.

[12] M. Knibb, "The Teacher of Righteousness—A Messianic Title?" in P. R. Davies and R. T. White, eds., *A Tribute to Geza Vermes. Essays on Jewish and Christian Literature and History* (Journal for the Study of the Old Testament Supplement 100; Sheffield: Journal for the Study of the Old Testament, 1990) 51–65.

[13] On the relationship between the Florilegium and CD, see George J. Brooke, *Exegesis at Qumran. 4QFlorilegium in its Jewish Context* (Journal for the Study of the Old Testament Supplement 29; Sheffield: Journal for the Study of the Old Testament, 1985) 206–9.

The Interpreter of the Law is also mentioned in the Catena (4QCatena[a] 2:5; F. García Martínez, *Textos de Qumrán* [Madrid: Trotta, 1992] 261) but the passage is too fragmentary to show whether the reference is past or future.

[14] Michael O. Wise, *A Critical Study of the Temple Scroll from Qumran Cave 11* (Studies in Ancient Oriental Civilization 49; Chicago: The Oriental Institute of the University of Chicago, 1990) 184; and "The Temple Scroll and the Teacher of Righteousness," in Z. J. Kapera, ed., *Mogilany 1989. Papers on the Dead Sea Scrolls, Vol. 2* (Kraków: Enigma, 1991) 121–47.

[15] So Y. Yadin, *The Temple Scroll: The Hidden Law of the Dead Sea Sect* (London: Weidenfeld and Nicolson, 1985) 226–28; B. Z. Wacholder, *The Dawn of Qumran: The Sectarian Torah and the Teacher of Righteousness* (Cincinnati, OH: Hebrew Union College, 1983) passim; F. García Martínez, "Qumran Origins and Early History: A Groningen Hypothesis," *Folia Orientalia* 25(1989) 121.

[16] M. Fishbane, "Use, Authority and Interpretation of Mikra at Qumran," in M. J. Mul-

der, ed., *Mikra. Text, Translation, Reading and Interpretation of the Hebrew Bible in Ancient Judaism and Early Christianity* (Compendia Rerum Iudaicarum ad Novum Testamentum 2.1; Philadelphia: Fortress, 1988) 365. Fishbane takes the Temple Scroll as a Torah for the New Age, after the final war, and so for a later point in the eschatological timetable than the "end of days" as understood by Wise.

[17] H. Seebass, "אחרית/'acharîth," G. J. Botterweck and H. Ringgren, eds., *Theological Dictionary of the Old Testament* (Grand Rapids, MI: Eerdmans, 1974) 1.207–12, J. van der Ploeg, "Eschatology in the Old Testament," *Oudtestamentische Studiën* 17(1972) 89–99, and J. Carmignac, "La Notion d'eschatologie dans la Bible et a Qumrân," *Revue de Qumran* 7(1969) 17–31, have also argued that the phrase only refers to the indefinite future.

[18] Cf. the explicit statement in 1QpHab 7:1–5 that God told Habakkuk to write what will happen to the last generation, but did not make known to him the fulfillment of the end. In contrast, God revealed to the Teacher of Righteousness "all the mysteries of his servants the prophets."

[19] See Davies, *The Damascus Covenant*, 91, for a discussion of the various scholarly positions.

[20] Brooke, *Exegesis at Qumran*, 176.

[21] M. O. Wise, "4QFlorilegium and the Temple of Adam," *Revue de Qumran* 15(1991) 115 n.45. See, however, Annette Steudel, *Der Midrasch zur Eschatologie aus der Qumrangemeinde (4QMidrEschat^{a,b})* (Leiden: Brill, 1994) 161–63, who argues that references can be past, present, or future. The messianic references are admittedly future.

[22] 4QMMT C 21.

[23] Trans. Brooke, *Exegesis at Qumran*, 92.

[24] For a summary of research, see Wise, "4QFlorilegium," 107–10.

[25] Daniel R. Schwartz, "The Three Temples of 4QFlorilegium," *Revue de Qumran* 10(1979–81) 88. Schwartz infers that the reference in the Florilegium is to Solomon's temple, but this does not necessarily follow. By omitting the actual citation, the author avoids the question of who will build this temple.

[26] Wise, "4QFlorilegium," 120.

[27] Other scholars who have argued that the "sanctuary of men" is human made include Michael Knibb, *The Qumran Community* (Cambridge: Cambridge University Press, 1987) 258–62, and Devorah Dimant, "4QFlorilegium and the Idea of the Community as Temple," in A. Caquot, M. Hadas-Lebel and J. Riaud, eds., *Hellenica et Judaica: Hommage à Valentin Nikiprowetzky* (Paris/Leuven: Peeters, 1986) 165–89.

[28] Y. Yadin, "Le Rouleau du Temple," in M. Delcor, ed., *Qumrân: Sa piété, sa théologie et son milieu* (Bibliotheca Ephemeridum Theologicarum Lovaniensium 46; Leuven: Leuven University Press, 1978) 115–19; and *The Temple Scroll, Volume One: Introduction* (Jerusalem: Israel Exploration Society, 1977) 140–44.

[29] Wise, "4QFlorilegium," 115. Wise translates the מקדש אדם as "the temple of Adam," implying a return to a paradisiac state.

[30] Contrast the MT, which reads "thy sanctuary, O Lord." Wise admits this problem ("4QFlorilegium," 115) but dismisses it in light of his other arguments.

[31] F. García Martínez, *Textos de Qumrán*, 261; cf. J. Strugnell, "Notes en marge du volume V des 'Discoveries in the Judaean Desert of Jordan,'" *Revue de Qumran* 7(1970) 244. Annette Steudel, "4QMidrEschat: 'A Midrash on Eschatology' (4Q174 + 4Q177)," in J. T. Barrera and L. V. Montaner, eds., *The Madrid Qumran Congress* 2.531–41, argues that the Catena and the Florilegium are two parts of the same composition. See now her fuller treatment, *Der Midrasch zur Eschatologie*, 127–57.

[32] On this text see Schiffman, *The Eschatological Community of the Dead Sea Scrolls*.

[33] Wise, *A Critical Study of the Temple Scroll*, 167–79; Wise, "The Eschatological Vision of the Temple Scroll," *Journal of Near Eastern Studies* 49(1990) 155–72.

[34] Wise, *A Critical Study of the Temple Scroll*, 35–38. See the critique of this position by L. H. Schiffman, "The Deuteronomic Paraphrase of the Temple Scroll," *Revue de Qumran* 15(1992) 543–67.

[35] Wise, *A Critical Study of the Temple Scroll*, 175.

[36] Wise attributes the Law of the King to a "Midrash to Deuteronomy" source (ibid., 101). Schiffman also regards the Law of the King as "pre-existent material" ("The Deuteronomic Paraphrase of the Temple Scroll," 567).

[37] See my essay, "Method in the Study of Messianism," in M. Wise, N. Golb, Collins, D. Pardee, eds., *Methods of Investigation of the Dead Sea Scrolls* (1994) pp. 213–29.

[38] Wise, "The Eschatological Vision of the Temple Scroll," 167–68.

[39] *Ps Sol* 17:33: "Nor shall he increase his store of gold and silver for war." 11QTemple 56:16: "nor lead the people back to Egypt to war." See D. Rosen and A. Salvesen, "A Note on the Qumran Temple Scroll 56:15–18 and Psalm of Solomon 17:33," *Journal of Jewish Studies* 38(1987) 99–101.

[40] M. Broshi, "The Gigantic Dimensions of the Visionary Temple in the Temple Scroll," *Biblical Archeology Review* 13(1987) 36–37.

[41] Wise, *A Critical Study of the Temple Scroll*, 84.

[42] J. Maier, "The Temple Scroll and Tendencies in the Cultic Architecture of the Second Commonwealth," in L. H. Schiffman, ed., *Archaeology and History in the Dead Sea Scrolls* (Sheffield: Journal for the Study of the Old Testament, 1990) 68. Compare also Hartmut Stegemann, "The Institutions of Israel in the Temple Scroll," in D. Dimant and U. Rappaport, eds., *The Dead Sea Scrolls. Forty Years of Research* (Leiden: Brill, 1992) 162: "the author of the *Temple Scroll* did indeed have in mind the actual temple in Jerusalem, not some utopian or heavenly model of it."

[43] Wise, "4QFlorilegium," 115.

[44] 1QpHab 1:13; 2:2; 5:10; 7:4; 8:3; 9:9–10; 11:5; 4QpPss^a 1–10 iii 15, 19; iv 8, 27; 4QpPss^b 1:4; 2:2.

[45] 1QpHab 2:5–6; 9:6; 4QpIsa^a 2–6 ii 26; 7–10 iii 22; 4QpIsa^b 2:1; 4QpIsa^c 6–7 ii 14; 13:4; 23 ii 10; 4QpNah 3–4 ii 2; 3–4 iii 3; 4QpMic 6:2.

[46] W. D. Davies, *Torah in the Messianic Age and/or the Age to Come* (Society of Biblical Literature Monograph Series 7; Philadelphia: Society of Biblical Literature, 1952) adduces very little evidence for it. The clearest passage is the medieval Yalqut Shimoni on Isaiah 26 (Davies, p. 74; cf. Wise, "The Temple Scroll and the Teacher of Righteousness," 146).

[47] See the remarks of S. Talmon, "Waiting for the Messiah: the Spiritual Universe of the Qumran Covenanters," in Neusner et al., eds., *Judaisms and their Messiahs at the Turn of the Christian Era*, 125.

[48] The view that the Teacher was High Priest was proposed by H. Stegemann, *Die Entstehung der Qumrangemeinde* (Bonn: published privately, 1971) 102, notes 328–29, and supported by J. Murphy-O'Connor, "The Damascus Document Revisited," *Revue Biblique* 92(1985) 239. See the critique of this position in my article "The Origin of the Qumran Community. A Review of the Evidence," in M. P. Horgan and P. J. Kobelski, eds., *To Touch the Text. Biblical and Related Studies in Honor of Joseph A. Fitzmyer, S.J.* (New York: Crossroad, 1989) 166, and the fuller treatment of the issue by M. Wise, "The Teacher of Righteousness and the High Priest of the Intersacerdotium: Two Approaches," *Revue de Qumran* 14(1990) 587–613.

[49] Wise, "The Temple Scroll and the Teacher of Righteousness," 144, regards this as "a transparent claim that the T of R was a typological Moses."

[50] N. Wieder, "The 'Law Interpreter' of the Sect of the Dead Sea Scrolls: The Second Moses," *Journal of Jewish Studies* 4(1953) 158–75; A. S. van der Woude, *Die messianischen Vorstellungen der Gemeinde von Qumrân* (Assen: van Gorcum, 1957) 186; H. M. Teeple, *The Mosaic Eschatological Prophet*, 54; G. Vermes, *The Dead Sea Scrolls. Qumran in Perspective*, 185–6; Wise, "The Temple Scroll and the Teacher of Righteousness," 142.

[51] See the comments of G. Jeremias, *Der Lehrer*, 274–5.

[52] Brooke, *Exegesis at Qumran*, 317, notes that the Testimonia follows the Samaritan text of Exod 20:21 in combining Deut 5:28b–29 and Deut 18:18–19. This was initially pointed out by P. W. Skehan, "The Period of the Biblical Texts from Khirbet Qumran," *Catholic Biblical Quarterly* 19(1957) 435.

[53] So e.g. Rashi, interpreting b. Bekhorot 24a. See Ginzberg, *An Unknown Jewish Sect*, 211–22, who notes that "in no fewer than eighteen passages in the Talmud Elijah appears as one who, in his capacity of precursor of the Messiah, will settle all doubts on matters ritual and juridical"; G. Molin, "Elijahu der Prophet und sein Weiterleben in den Hoffnungen des Judentums und der Christenheit," *Judaica* 8(1952) 81; J. Jeremias, " Ἡλ(ε)ίας," in G. Kittel, ed., *Theological Dictionary of the New Testament* (Grand Rapids, MI: Eerdmans, 1964) 2.932; H. M. Teeple, *The Mosaic Eschatological Prophet* (Society of Biblical Literature Monograph Series 10; Philadelphia: Society of Biblical Literature, 1957) 54–55; G. Jeremias, *Der Lehrer*, 286.

[54] Van der Woude, *Die Messianischen Vorstellungen*, 55.

[55] Debate has raged as to whether this figure should be regarded as past or future. See the recent treatment by M. Knibb, "The Interpretation of Damascus Document VII,9b–VIII,2a and XIX,5b–14," *Revue de Qumran* 15(1991) 248–50.

[56] Van der Woude, *Die Messianischen Vorstellungen*, 55. C. Rabin, *The Zadokite Fragments* (Oxford: Oxford University Press, 1954) 30, suggested a reference to 2 Kgs 8:7 and Elisha.

[57] Justin, *Dialogue with Trypho*, 49.

[58] Brooke, *Exegesis at Qumran*, 204.

[59] J. A. Fitzmyer, " '4QTestimonia' and the New Testament," in Fitzmyer, *Essays on the Semitic Background of the New Testament* (Missoula: Scholars Press, 1974) 82–84.

[60] J. C. VanderKam, "Jubilees and the Priestly Messiah of Qumran," 363.

[61] On the messiahs of Aaron and Israel see Talmon, "Waiting for the Messiah," 111–37.

[62] Brooke argues that this passage is an interpolation, intended to introduce the notion of two messiahs into CD (*Exegesis at Qumran*, 302–4).

[63] Puech, "Fragments d'un apocryphe de Lévi," 2.449–501.

[64] Note however that Moses is said to atone for the sin of Israel in 4Q504 (the Words of the Heavenly Luminaries) 2:9–10.

[65] See the comments on the views of Starcky and Brooke in Chapter Four above. The sketchy views of P. R. Davies, "Eschatology at Qumran," *Journal of Biblical Literature* 104(1985) 39–55 do not withstand scrutiny. The whole question of chronological development will have to be reopened when the full corpus of Scrolls has been edited and studied.

[66] Molin, "Elijahu," 84–85, notes that Elijah is frequently called *kahana rabba* in the Targumim. See also Ginzberg, *An Unknown Jewish Sect*, 245–47; N. Wieder, "The Doctrine of the Two Messiahs among the Karaites," *Journal of Jewish Studies* 6(1955) 14–23; van der Woude, *Die Messianischen Vorstellungen*, 55–57; J. Jeremias, " Ἡλ(ε)ίας," 932–33.

[67] Note however John Strugnell, "Moses-Pseudepigrapha at Qumran," in Lawrence H. Schiffman, ed., *Archaeology and History in the Dead Sea Scrolls* (Sheffield: Journal for the Study of the Old Testament, 1990) 234, who points out that 4Q375–376 describes a ritual for testing a prophet that involves bringing him before the High Priest, and so the two figures must have been distinct. It is not certain, however, whether this work refers to an *eschatological* prophet.

[68] See Teeple, *The Mosaic Eschatological Prophet*.

[69] Mal 4:5 is probably an addition to the original prophecy. It may have been added by the editor of the prophetic corpus. For the identification of Elijah with the messenger see Beth Glazier-McDonald, *Malachi: The Divine Messenger* (Society of Biblical Literature Dissertation Series 98; Atlanta: Scholars Press, 1987) 261–70.

[70] Cf. 1 Macc 4:46 where the stones from the altar that had been profaned by the Gentiles are stored "until a prophet should come to tell what to do with them." M. Philonenko, "'Jusqu'à ce que se lève un prophète digne de confiance' (1 Maccabées 14,41)," in *Messiah and Christos. Studies in the Jewish Origins of Christianity presented to David Flusser* (Ithamar Gruenwald, Shaul Shaked and Gedaliahu G. Stroumsa, eds.; Tübingen: Mohr [Siebeck], 1992) 95–98, argues that the prophet in 1 Maccabees 14 is the "prophet like Moses."

[71] Moore, *Judaism*, 2.357. See also J. Jeremias, "Ἠλ(ε)ίας," 928–41.

[72] Mark 9:11; Matt 17:10. In John 1:19–21, the Baptist denies that he is either the Messiah, Elijah, or "the prophet." Note also Rev 11:4–7, where one of the two witnesses who prophesy before the end either is Elijah or is modeled on him. (He has authority to shut the sky, so that no rain may fall during the days of their prophesying.)

[73] Morris M. Faierstein, "Why do the Scribes say that Elijah Must Come First?" *Journal of Biblical Literature* 100(1981) 75–86, concludes that "almost no evidence has been preserved which indicates that the concept of Elijah as forerunner of the Messiah was widely known or accepted in the first century C.E." This conclusion was challenged by Dale C. Allison, "Elijah Must Come First," *Journal of Biblical Literature* 103(1984) 256–58, but defended by J. A. Fitzmyer, "More About Elijah Coming First," *Journal of Biblical Literature* 104(1985) 295–96. See also Fitzmyer, "The Aramaic 'Elect of God' Text from Qumran Cave 4," in Fitzmyer, *Essays on the Semitic Background of the New Testament*, 137. Joel Marcus, *The Way of the Lord. Christological Exegesis of the Old Testament in the Gospel of Mark* (Louisville: Westminster, 1992) 110, agrees with Allison that Mark attributes to the scribes a belief that Elijah must come before the messiah, but Mark's narrative is shaped by his perception of John the Baptist as precursor of Jesus.

[74] See Ginzberg, *An Unknown Jewish Sect*, 209–56; Volz, *Die Eschatologie der Jüdischen Gemeinde*, 195–97.

[75] A "messenger" (*nuntius*) plays the role of avenger when the kingdom of God is manifested in the *Assumption (Testament) of Moses* 10:2. This figure, however, is usually taken to be an angel. J. Tromp, "Taxo, the Messenger of the Lord," *Journal for the Study of Judaism* 21(1990) 200–9, takes the messenger as Taxo, the man from the tribe of Levi, with seven sons, who appears in the previous chapter.

[76] J. J. Collins, "The Sibylline Oracles," in Charlesworth, ed., *Old Testament Pseudepigrapha* 1.330–34.

[77] David Frankfurter, *Elijah in Upper Egypt. The Apocalypse of Elijah and Early Egyptian Christianity* (Minneapolis: Fortress, 1993).

[78] Robert L. Wilken, *The Land Called Holy. Palestine in Christian History and Thought* (New

Haven, CT: Yale University Press, 1992) 207–8; Frankfurter, *The Apocalypse of Elijah*, 49–50. For further Elijah pseudepigrapha see Michael Stone and John Strugnell, *The Books of Elijah, Parts 1 and 2* (Missoula: Scholars Press, 1979).

[79] Jean Starcky, "Les quatres étapes du messianisme à Qumran," *Revue Biblique* 70(1963) 498. Starcky identified the fragment as 4QarP. It is now identified as 4Q558 (Sy papVision ar[b] [PAM 43.580–83]). See now Puech, *La Croyance des Esséniens en la Vie Future*, 676–771; also J. A. Fitzmyer, "The Aramaic 'Elect of God' Text from Qumran," in Fitzmyer, *Essays on the Semitic Background of the New Testament*, 137.

[80] Emile Puech, "Une Apocalypse Messianique (4Q521)," *Revue de Qumran* 15(1992) 475–519; *La Croyance des Esséniens en la Vie Future*, 627–92. The text is certainly not formally an apocalypse, as it lacks any description of the manner of revelation. On the characteristics of an apocalypse see J. J. Collins, *The Apocalyptic Imagination* (New York: Crossroad, 1984) 2–8.

[81] Eisenman and Wise, *The Dead Sea Scrolls Uncovered*, 19–23. See further my article "The Works of the Messiah," *Dead Sea Discoveries* 1(1994).

[82] Puech, "Une Apocalypse Messianique," 477.

[83] Wise and Tabor, "The Messiah at Qumran," reconstruct the messiah as the subject of line 12. They read line 11 as "and as for the wonders that are not the work of the Lord" (instead of "that have not taken place, the Lord will do;" they read מעשה, work, where Puech reads יעשה, will do). To suggest that the works of the messiah are "not the works of the Lord," however, makes no sense.

[84] Pierre Grelot, "Sur Isaie lxi: la première consecration du grand-prêtre," *Revue Biblique* 97(1990) 414–31, argues that the speaker is the High Priest. David Noel Freedman suggests that he is Cyrus, who is called משיח, anointed, in Isa 45:1. The speaker of a prophetic oracle, however, must be presumed to be a prophet unless there is compelling evidence to the contrary. In view of the proposed anointing of Elisha and of the usage of "anointed ones" in the Scrolls, the claim to be anointed does not necessarily require that the speaker be either a priest or a king.

[85] My position here differs from that of Wise and Tabor in so far as I do not see the agency of God and of the messiah as mutually exclusive.

[86] Puech, "Une Apocalypse Messianique," 509.

[87] Ibid.

[88] P. J. Kobelski, *Melchizedek and Melciresaʿ* (Catholic Biblical Quarterly Monograph Series 10; Washington, D.C.: Catholic Biblical Association of America, 1981) 21; Puech, *La Croyance des Esséniens en la Vie Future*, 523. The restoration was originally suggested by J. A. Fitzmyer.

[89] In 1QH 18:14 it is apparently the hymnist himself who is said to preach good news to the poor. The beginning of this hymn, 1QH 17:26, which praises God for shedding his Holy Spirit on his servant, suggests that the hymnist was applying the prophecy of Isaiah 61 to himself. Whether this entails a claim to be the eschatological prophet is not clear, however. The speaker is anonymous.

[90] Puech, "Une Apocalypse Messianique," 501.

[91] Jacob Neusner, *Messiah in Context* (Philadelphia: Fortress, 1984) 86–98, claims that there was a "prevalent notion that the Messiah would raise the dead" but cites no evidence in support of this view.

[92] Neusner, *Messiah*, 86–87; Moore, *Judaism*, 2.384.

[93] The relevance of this passage is noted by Puech, "Une apocalypse messianique," 492.

[94] E. Puech, "Ben Sira 48:11 et la Résurrection," in H. Attridge, J. J. Collins and T. H. Tobin, eds., *Of Scribes and Scrolls. Studies on the Hebrew Bible, Intertestamental Judaism and Christian Origins* (Lanham, MD: University Press of America, 1990) 81–90; Puech, *La Croyance des Esséniens en la Vie Future,* 74–76.

[95] Sir 41:4: "Whether life is for ten or a hundred or a thousand years, there is no inquiry about it in Hades."

[96] Rev 11:4–6. See R. H. Charles, *A Critical and Exegetical Commentary on the Revelation of St. John* (New York: Scribners, 1920) 1.284–5.

[97] Puech, "Une Apocalypse Messianique," 496. Less persuasive is his suggestion that "the precept of your mercy" reflects Mal 3:22, "precepts and commandments."

[98] Ibid., 496.

[99] Ibid., 497. Cf. Puech, *La Croyance des Esséniens en la Vie Future,* 669–81, where he argues for Elijah as the precursor of the royal messiah and attempts to reconcile this text with the dual messianism attested elsewhere in the Scrolls.

[100] Puech, "Une Apocalypse Messianique," 497.

[101] Puech, *La Croyance des Esséniens en la Vie Future,* makes a sustained argument that belief in resurrection was a standard element in Essene eschatology. The only clear references, however, are in 4Q521 and 4Q Second Ezekiel(= 4Q385). See my review of Puech's book in *Dead Sea Discoveries* 1(1994).

[102] Puech, *La Croyance des Esséniens en la Vie Future,* 666–69. On the "poor" in the Hodayot see Norbert Lohfink, *Lobgesänge der Armen: Studien zum Magnifikat, den Hodajot von Qumran und einigen Psalmen* (Stuttgart: Katholisches Bibelwerk, 1990).

[103] J. A. Fitzmyer, *The Gospel According to Luke I–IX* (Anchor Bible 28; Garden City, NY: Doubleday, 1981) 664.

[104] 1 Kings 17; 2 Kings 4. Elisha was said to heal a leper (2 Kings 5), cause blindness, and give sight (2 Kings 6:18, 20).

[105] Relations between Jesus and the Baptist are too complex to be unraveled here. For a recent study see Robert Webb, *John the Baptizer and Prophet. A Socio-Historical Study* (Journal for the Study of the New Testament Supplement 62; Sheffield: Journal for the Study of the Old Testament, 1991).

[106] Higgins, "Jewish Messianic Belief in Justin Martyr's Dialogue with Trypho," 189.

[107] There is no consensus on the identity of the servant in the original context of Deutero-Isaiah. The most popular views are that the servant represents an ideal Israel, or the prophet himself, or the Israelite king in the exile. For older interpretations see H. H. Rowley, *The Servant of the Lord and Other Essays* (London: Lutterworth, 1952); for recent views R. N. Whybray, *Thanksgiving for a Liberated Prophet* (Sheffield: Journal for the Study of the Old Testament, 1978), P. Grelot, *Les Poèmes du Serviteur* (Paris: Cerf, 1981).

[108] J. Jeremias, "παῖς θεοῦ," in G. Friedrich, ed., *Theological Dictionary of the New Testament* (Grand Rapids, MI: Eerdmans, 1967) 5.677–700.

[109] See M. D. Hooker, *Jesus and the Servant* (London: SPCK, 1959); Sam K. Williams, *Jesus' Death as a Saving Event* (Missoula: Scholars Press, 1975) 111–20; Marinus de Jonge, *Jesus, The Servant-Messiah* (New Haven, CT: Yale University Press, 1991) 48–50.

[110] Starcky, "Les quatres étapes," 492.

[111] Puech, "Fragments d'un apocryphe de Lévi," 492–99. Puech is followed closely by G. J. Brooke, "4QTestament of Levi^d(?) and the Messianic Servant High Priest," in M. de Boer, ed., *From Jesus to John. Essays on Jesus and New Testament Christology in Honour of Marinus de Jonge* (Journal for the Study of the New Testament Supplement 84; Sheffield:

Journal for the Study of the Old Testament, 1993) 83–100. See also the comment of Martin Hengel, "Jesus der Messias Israels," in *Messiah and Christos*, 164.

[112] For the Akkadian background of "servant" as a royal title see M.-J. Seux, *Épithètes Royales Akkadiennes et Suomériennes. Ouvrage publié avec le concours du Centre National de la Recherche Scientifique* (Paris: Letouzey et Ané, 1967) 360–63.

[113] *4 Ezra* 7:28, 29; 13:32, 37, 52; 14:9. See M. E. Stone, *Fourth Ezra* (Hermeneia; Minneapolis: Fortress, 1990) 208. The Arabic version sometimes reads servant instead of son.

[114] The distinction of four servant songs is associated above all with Bernhard Duhm, *Das Buch Jesaja* (Göttingen: Vandenhoeck & Ruprecht, 1892). It is no longer universally accepted. See Richard J. Clifford, *Fair Spoken and Persuading. An Interpretation of Second Isaiah* (New York: Paulist, 1984) 84–93, 146–55, 156–64, who argues that the first three songs are parts of longer poetic units.

[115] "He will be despised," (53:3); "he gave up his soul to death," (53:12). See Jeremias, "παῖς θεοῦ," 695.

[116] Jeremias, *Der Lehrer*, 79–126; Hartmut Stegemann, *Die Entstehung der Qumrangemeinde* (Bonn: published privately, 1971) 41–53.

[117] 1QH 4, trans. Vermes, *The Dead Sea Scrolls in English*, 174–75.

[118] Puech, "Fragments d'un apocryphe de Lévi," 475–76.

[119] Puech, "Fragments d'un apocryphe," 477–78, discusses other possible translations such as "diadem," (Aramaic ṣyṣ').

[120] Ibid., 499. The Aramaic words for "afflict" and "weak" that are used in fragment 34 also occur in the Targum on Isaiah with reference to the servant, but there are no direct allusions to the vocabulary of Isaiah.

[121] Martin Hengel, *Crucifixion* (Philadelphia: Fortress, 1977).

[122] Josephus, *Antiquities* 13.377–79; *War* 1.92–95.

[123] Horgan, *Pesharim*, 176–79.

[124] A number of scholars claimed that the Teacher of Righteousness modeled himself on the Suffering Servant. So M. Black, *The Scrolls and Christian Origins* (New York: Scribners, 1961) 143–44, argued that the Teacher described his sufferings in language reminiscent of the Suffering Servant in 1QH 9. W. H. Brownlee saw allusions to the Servant in 1QH 8:26–27, 35–36 and 1QH 7:10 ("Messianic Motifs of Qumran and the New Testament," *New Testament Studies* 3[1956–57] 12–30). None of these passages, however, attach atoning significance to suffering, or claim messianic status for the speaker. See J. Carmignac, "Les citations de l'Ancien Testament et spécialement des Poèmes du Serviteur dans les Hymnes de Qumrân," *Revue de Qumran* 2(1960) 357–94; Jeremias, *Der Lehrer*, 299–307.

[125] G. H. Dalman, *Der leidende und der sterbende Messias der Synagoge* (Berlin: Reuther, 1888); S. Hurwitz, *Die Gestalt des sterbenden Messias* (Stuttgart: Rascher, 1948); Klausner, *The Messianic Idea*, 483–501.

[126] Joseph Heinemann, "The Messiah of Ephraim and the Premature Exodus of the Tribe of Ephraim," *Harvard Theological Review* 68(1975) 1–15 (reprinted in Landman, ed., *Messianism in the Talmudic Era*, 339–53. Less persuasive is Heinemann's argument that Bar Kokhba became associated with Ephraim because the legend of a premature Exodus by the tribe of Ephraim was found to be reflected in the Bar Kokhba revolt. (This legend is also adduced by Ginzberg, *An Unknown Jewish Sect*, 237). The association of the dying messiah with Ephraim or Joseph remains obscure. Perhaps it hearkens back to the old

division between northern Israel (Ephraim) and Judah. Since the victorious Davidic messiah comes from Judah, the dying messiah is assigned to Ephraim.

[127] Klausner, *The Messianic Idea*, 483.

[128] Jeremias, "παῖς θεοῦ," 690. According to Jerome, Aquila translated as "leprous" instead of "afflicted." E. E. Urbach, *The Sages, Their Concepts and Beliefs* (Jerusalem: Magnes, 1975) 1.683, comments that this story does not lack humor and irony, and implies that it shows some skepticism about messianic expectation.

6

A THRONE IN THE HEAVENS

The expectations surrounding an eschatological teacher/priest such as we find in 4Q541 (Aaron A) may also provide the context for interpreting one of the more enigmatic fragments discovered in Qumran Cave 4. This piece was published as part of a manuscript of the War Rule (4QM) by Maurice Baillet in 1982 and dubbed "cantique du Michel," on the hypothesis that the speaker should be identified with the archangel Michael.[1] The passage is especially interesting, because it speaks of a throne in heaven, and the speaker claims to be reckoned with the אלים, divine beings. Morton Smith has challenged Baillet's interpretation and argued instead that the speaker is a human being who has ascended to heaven.[2] On Smith's interpretation, the fragment raises the issue of the divinization of a human being, in some sense, in a Jewish context, prior to the rise of Christianity.

A Canticle of Michael?

This fragment begins by stating that the righteous will exult because of the power of God, but then it goes on to boast of the glory of the speaker.[3] First it refers to "a mighty throne in the congregation of the gods. None of the kings of the East shall sit in it and their nobles shall not.... No Edomite[4] shall be like me in glory. And none shall be exalted save me, nor shall come against me. For I have taken my seat ... in the heavens.... I shall be reckoned with gods and established in the holy congregation." The remainder of the fragment is rendered difficult by lacunae. I cite only phrases that seem reasonably clear: "my desire is not like flesh ... all that is precious to me is in glory (or: in the glory of ...) ... who has been deemed as plunder because of me,[5] and who is like to me in glory? ..." The passage appears to boast of the speaker's ability to endure evil ("who ... troubles like me and who ... evil like me") and speaks more clearly of his incomparable prowess as a teacher and legal expert ("who will restrain the utterance of my lips and who will arraign me and equal my judgment?"). The end of the passage affirms "I shall be reckoned with gods, and my glory, with [that of] the king's sons."

Baillet placed the fragment immediately before the account of battle in columns 16–17 of 1QM, but admitted that the placement is "only probable." He identified the speaker as the archangel Michael, who is given dominion among the *'ēlîm*, gods, in 1QM 17:7. This proposal was rejected with characteristic vehemence by Morton Smith, who has published the only other study of the passage to date. We need not accept all Smith's objections, e.g. that an archangel would not compare himself to such small fry as the Edomite Herod.[6] Assumptions about what an archangel may or may not do in this kind of literature are risky. It is true, however, that Michael never speaks in the War Scroll, and nothing in the text requires the identification. The hymn gives the impression that the speaker has come to be reckoned among the gods but was not of heavenly origin.[7] The reference to prowess as a teacher also suggests a human speaker. Indeed, if Baillet's positioning of the fragment is correct, then it is most probably a hymn recited by the High Priest before the battle. According to 1QM 15:4 the priest is to read aloud the prayer and hymns in time of war, and this passage is reflected in the fragments of 4QM 10:2, which immediately precede the "canticle of Michael" in Baillet's edition. The "canticle," then, was not necessarily composed as part of the War Rule, but may have been an independent hymn, comparable to the Hodayot. Indeed Smith has questioned the association of this fragment with the War Rule at all.[8] Instead, he "thinks immediately of the author of the Hodayot" and lists the similarities, noting especially the fellowship with the angels in the hymns.[9]

EXCURSUS: PARALLELS IN THE HODAYOT

The affinity of this fragment with the Hodayot has now been confirmed by the discovery of parallels in two other fragments, 4Q427 7 and 4Q471b.

4Q427 7 is a large fragment that has preserved substantial sections of two consecutive columns.[10] There are clear overlaps with Hodayot passages from Cave 1 and Cave 4, which firmly identify the fragment as belonging to the Hodayot. The first column of this fragment preserves the end of a poem written in the first person singular, in which the speaker describes his exalted rank in heaven among the angels. This passage overlaps with 4Q491. The parallels are closest between the end of 4Q491 11 and 4Q427 7 11–12. The phrase "as for me, my station is with the gods" in 4Q427 may be regarded as a variant of "I am reckoned with gods" in 4Q491, and both texts use the words כתם and פז to refer to gold.[11]

4Q471b overlaps with both 4Q491 and 4Q427. This fragment was assigned to the War Rule by John Strugnell but its current editor, Esti Eshel, considers it an independent composition.[12] Fragment 6 line 6 reads ידיד המלך רע לק[. The phrase can be completed from 4Q427 as לקדושים, so "beloved of the king, friend of the h[oly ones]." The following two lines also contain words that appear in 4Q427 7 i 11. 4Q471b also contains a distinctive parallel to 4Q491. Fragment 6 line 5 reads "who will restrain my lips" (the lacuna can be restored to correspond to 4Q491 11, "who will restrain the utterance of my lips"). The word teaching (הוריה) also occurs in both fragments. 4Q491 has no parallel, however, for 4Q471b 6 4: "who is like me among the gods?" Without pressing the details of reconstruction, it appears that 4Q427 7 and 4Q471 6 are copies of the same text, which have only minor variants in the few overlapping lines. 4Q491 11 has more substantial variants, but still represents the same text. The verbal correspondences between 4Q491 and 4Q471b are too close to be merely variants on a common theme.

All three fragments attest the notion of fellowship with the angels. This notion was already familiar from the Hodayot. The most intriguing aspect of 4Q491 11, however, is not paralleled in either 4Q427 or 4Q471b. This is the mention of "a mighty throne in the congregation of the gods" and the claim to have "taken a seat" in the heavens, presumably on this throne.[13] We cannot be sure whether these boasts were also part of 4Q427 and 4Q471, but the question in 4Q471b, "who is like me among the gods?" implies a level of exaltation that is unparalleled in the Hodayot, echoing as it does Exod 15:11, "who is like thee among the gods, O Lord?" Since this boast is more likely to have been added in 4Q471b than omitted in 4Q491, we may suggest that 4Q491 preserves the older form of the text, and that the throne in heaven was an original element in the composition, but this suggestion is obviously very tentative.

Smith commented on the distinctive aspect of the text as follows: "This speaker's claim to have been taken up and seated in heaven and counted as one of the gods (*'ēlîm*) is more direct and explicit than anything I recall in the Hodayot or in any other of the Dead Sea documents hitherto published." Smith takes it as an illustration of "speculation on deification by ascent towards or into the heavens, speculation which may have gone along with some practices that produced extraordinary experiences understood as encounters with gods or angels."[14] Already in his controversial book, *Clement of Alexandria and a Secret Gospel of Mark*, Smith had claimed that "the notion of ascent to the heavens was an important element in Jesus' Palestinian background and had led to the development of a technique for ascent which Jesus might have practised." He had also claimed that "those who ascended were thought to become like the gods in form . . . and to be enthroned in the heavens," which he declared to be the goal of the *Hekhalot* mystics.[15] He now claims to have found in 4Q491 a "clear and complete" example of this phenomenon in a pre-Christian text.

It is not necessary here to discuss all aspects of Smith's theses, especially those regarding a technique for ascent, which are closely bound up with the controversial *Secret Gospel of Mark*. It is necessary, however, to consider the motif of heavenly enthronement, in the context of Judaism in the Hellenistic period, and consider its possible relation to the messianic expectations of the time.

Ascent in Pre-Christian Judaism

Evidence of ascents in pre-Christian Judaism is scarce. In part, this may be due to ideological reasons. The editors of the Hebrew Bible were not sympathetic to accounts of ascent to heaven. The Deuteronomist insisted that the divine commandment was neither too difficult nor too far away: "It is not in heaven that you should say, 'who will go up to heaven for us, and get it for us so that we may hear it and observe it?'" (Deut 30:12). The sages tended to be skeptical. "Who has ascended to heaven and come down?" asked Agur, son of Jakeh (Prov 30:4). Enoch and Elijah do not count, here, since in the Hebrew Bible they are not said to have come back down. The closest we come to a description of a heavenly ascent in the Hebrew Bible (as distinct from an allusion to one) is in the Sinai narrative in Exodus 24. There Moses, Aaron, Nadab, Abihu, and the seventy elders "went up and they saw the God of Israel. Under his feet there was something like a pavement of sapphire stone, like the very heaven for clearness" (Exod 24:9–10). Even this is not quite an ascent to heaven, since God has come down on Mount Sinai. There is a long tradition of prophetic visions of the divine throne, dating back to the pre-exilic period with Micaiah ben Imlah (1 Kings 22) and Isaiah (Isaiah 6).[16] We might assume that the prophet who stands in the council of the Lord has been transported to heaven, but the ascent of the prophet is never the subject of description in the Hebrew Bible. The location of the vision is not an issue. Isaiah apparently had his vision in the Temple in Jerusalem; Ezekiel "in the land of the Chaldeans by the river Chebar." In no case does a prophetic vision of the divine throne imply that the visionary himself will be enthroned or divinized in any way. These visions typically serve two functions: they establish the credentials of the visionary, thereby legitimating him as an intermediary between heaven and earth, and they provide revealed information, typically about the future course of events.

Accounts of ascents to heaven become more common in the Hellenistic period, and are associated especially with the ante-diluvian patriarch, Enoch, and to a lesser degree with Levi, one of the twelve patriarchs, sons of Jacob.[17] The most influential explanations of this phenomenon have been associated with the names of Wilhelm Bousset and Gershom Scholem. Bousset argued that the ascent of the visionary is an anticipation of the ascent of the soul after death.[18] This theory can be supported from many apocalypses of the Christian era, but it does not seem to apply to the earliest ascents of Enoch and Levi.[19] Scholem accorded the ascent a central place in Jewish mysticism and saw its goal as the perception of God's appearance on the throne and knowledge of the mysteries of the heavenly world.[20] Scholem was primarily concerned with the so-called *Hekhalot* literature, Hebrew mystical texts of uncertain date.[21] Scholem argued that the phenomenon represented by this literature was very old, and that it was a development of trends in the apocalyptic literature of the Hellenistic and early Roman periods. Other scholars, however, see the *Hekhalot* literature as a later phenomenon, which developed after the rabbinic period (second to sixth centuries CE).[22]

The earliest Jewish description of a "round trip" ascent to heaven is found in the "Book of the Watchers" in *1 Enoch*.[23] While such ascents eventually became the dominant medium of revelation in apocalypses, they are quite rare in the pre-Christian period. Apart from *Enoch*, the only account of an ascent in a Semitic language is that of Levi in the Aramaic Levi Apocryphon from Qumran, of which a later form is found in the Greek *Testaments of the Twelve Patriarchs*.[24] These early ascent accounts seem to function in much the same way as the call visions of the Hebrew prophets. The ascent of Enoch establishes his role as mediator between heaven and earth. When Enoch presents his petition to the Most High he is told "go say to the Watchers of heaven who sent you to petition on their behalf: 'you ought to petition on behalf of men, not men on behalf of you'" (*1 Enoch* 15:2).[25] The ascent also has a revelatory aspect, as it provides the point of departure for further revelations, which Enoch receives in his subsequent tour of the ends of the earth.[26] It does not, however, involve the enthronement of Enoch, nor is it, at least explicitly, an anticipation of his final assumption in glory.

Similar comments might be made about the ascent of Levi, although in that case the specific purpose of the ascent is rather different, at least as these are presented in the Greek *Testament of Levi*.[27] When Levi enters the heavenly temple and sees the throne of glory, he is told by the Most High: "Levi, I have given to you the blessings of the priesthood." The angel who brings him down to the earth gives him a sword and tells him to execute vengeance on Shechem (*T. Levi* 5:1–3). The function of the ascent then is quite transparent: to confirm the priesthood of Levi and authorize the destruction of Shechem. There is also a revelatory aspect of the vision, which may be the result of secondary expansion. There is no suggestion, however, of enthronement for Levi, or that his ascent is an anticipation of the afterlife.

Heavenly Enthronement

The paradigm case for the view that visionary ascent had its goal in heavenly enthronement is provided by Enoch in the Hebrew *Book of Enoch* or *3 Enoch*.[28] There Rabbi Ishmael narrates that when he ascended on high to behold the vision of the chariot he was greeted by Metatron, who has several names, including Enoch son of Jared. Metatron tells him how he was taken up from the generation of the Flood, and how "the Holy One, blessed be he, made for me (i.e. Metatron) a throne like the throne of glory" (10:1).[29]

There are problems with any attempt to regard Enoch/Metatron as paradigmatic for visionary ascent in the Hellenistic period. First and most obvious is the late date. While the Hebrew *Book of Enoch* may contain old traditions it is unlikely to be older than the sixth century CE. Even in *3 Enoch* it is not suggested that Rabbi Ishmael was given a throne. Indeed the book contains evidence that the enthronement of Metatron was controversial. In a passage that is probably a secondary addition, we read that when *Ahēr* came to behold the chariot and saw Metatron he exclaimed "there are indeed two powers in heaven."[30] Then Metatron was given sixty lashes of fire and made to stand on his feet.

There are, however, several older traditions in which beings other than God are said to be enthroned in heaven.

Perhaps the first candidate to come to mind is the Davidic messiah. The antiquity of the idea that the Davidic king had a throne in heaven is a matter of debate. In Psalm 89:36–37, "His line will continue forever, and his throne endure before me like the sun; It shall be established forever like the moon, an enduring witness in the skies," the analogy between the throne and the heavenly bodies lies in its permanence, not in its location.[31] In the context of pre-exilic Jerusalem, Psalm 110, "The Lord said to my Lord, sit at my right hand," probably meant that the king was seated to the right of the ark, on which God was invisibly enthroned.[32] In the New Testament, however, a messianic interpretation is assumed, and the psalm is taken to imply ascension to heaven.[33] The psalm does not figure prominently in pre-Christian Jewish literature.[34] Melchizedek, who is mentioned in Psalm 110 as the prototypical priest-king, appears as a heavenly judge in 11QMelchizedek, but there is no allusion to Psalm 110 in the surviving fragments. The first clear attestation of the idea that the Davidic messiah should be enthroned in heaven is found in the New Testament in Acts 2:34–36 ("for David did not ascend into the heavens, but he himself says, 'The Lord said to my Lord, sit at my right hand...'").[35]

Heavenly enthronement is probably implied in the vision of "one like a son of man" and the Ancient of Days in Daniel 7. Dan 7:9 says that "thrones were set, and an Ancient of Days took his seat." Then the "one like a son of man" is ushered in, and he is given "dominion and glory and kingship." He is not explicitly said to be enthroned, but it is reasonable to infer that one of the thrones was set for him. Rabbi Akiba is said to have expounded the plural "thrones" as "one for God, one for David,"[36] implicitly identifying the "one like a son of man" as the messiah. The original referent of this figure is a matter of perennial dispute. For much of

Jewish and Christian tradition, he was assumed to be the messiah. The beasts in Daniel's vision represent the kings or kingdoms of the Gentiles, so it was natural enough to assume that the human figure was the king of Israel, especially since a kingdom is conferred on him. Nonetheless, this interpretation is only rarely defended in recent times. There is no clear reference to a Davidic king elsewhere in the book of Daniel. When the word משיח is used it refers to a High Priest (9:25, 26). I have argued elsewhere that the "one like a son of man" should be interpreted as the archangel Michael, the heavenly "prince" who fights for Israel (10:21) and rises in victory at the end (12:1).[37] The messianic interpretation, however, arose very early, and is reflected in the New Testament and in the *Similitudes of Enoch*.

In the *Similitudes*, the "Son of Man" figure of Daniel's vision sits on the throne of glory (*1 Enoch* 62:5; 69:27; 29; compare 45:3; 47:3; 51:3; 55:4; 60:2; 61:8; 62:2, 3 where the "Elect One," another name for the same figure, is enthroned).[38] This figure is also called "messiah" in the *Similitudes* (*1 Enoch* 48:10), but he is a heavenly preexistent figure, rather than an exalted human king.[39] The Son of Man is similarly enthroned as judge in Matt 19:28; 25:31. (In Daniel 7 the "one like a son of man" arrives after the judgment.) A further adaptation of this tradition is found in the *Testament of Abraham* where Abel (son of Adam) sits on a throne to perform judgment.[40] The enthronement of the Son of Man as messiah is also implied in Mark 14:62 ("you will see the son of Man seated at the right hand of the Power and coming with the clouds of heaven"), a passage that combines Daniel 7:14 with Ps 110:1.[41] These scriptural warrants also underlie other New Testament passages that refer to the enthronement of Jesus in heaven. When Heb 8:1 declares that "we have such a high priest, one who is seated at the right hand of the throne of the Majesty in the heavens," the allusion is to Psalm 110. Hebrews presents Jesus as priest and king "after the order of Melchizedek" (Heb 6:20, cf. Ps 110:4). It does not presuppose a tradition of heavenly enthronement that was peculiar to a priestly messiah.[42]

Righteous human beings are also promised thrones in heaven as an eschatological reward. 4Q521 fragment 2, the passage that speaks of a messiah whom heaven and earth will obey, promises that God will glorify the pious on the throne of an eternal kingdom.[43] In *1 Enoch* 108:12, an appendix to *1 Enoch* of uncertain provenance,[44] God "will bring out into shining light those who love my holy name, and I will set each one on the throne of his honour." In the Gospels, the apostles are promised that they will sit on thrones judging the twelve tribes of Israel.[45] Rev 3:21

promises that the one who conquers will "sit on my throne with me," and in Rev 20:4 the visionary sees "thrones, and those seated on them were given authority to judge." According to the Ascension of Isaiah 9:24–26, those who believe will receive "robes and thrones and crowns." Enthronement bespeaks heavenly glory. The function of judgment is often associated with enthronement but is not necessarily implied.

All the instances of heavenly enthronement we have considered thus far are eschatological and relate either to the final judgment or to the final destiny of the just. To my knowledge, there is only one scene of heavenly enthronement in pre-Christian Judaism that is not, or is not necessarily, eschatological. This is found in the Hellenistic Jewish tragedy, the *Exagoge* of Ezekiel the tragedian, whose work was excerpted by Alexander Polyhistor in the early first century BCE, and who most probably wrote in Alexandria, at some time in the second century BCE. One excerpt concerns a dream of Moses:

> "I dreamt there was on the summit of mount Sinai
> A certain great throne extending up to heaven's cleft,
> On which there sat a certain noble man
> Wearing a crown and holding a great scepter
> In his left hand. With his right hand
> He beckoned to me, and I stood before the throne.
> He gave me the scepter and told me to sit
> On the great throne. He gave me the royal crown
> And he himself left the throne.
> I beheld the entire circled earth
> Both beneath the earth and above the heaven,
> And a host of stars fell on its knees before me;
> I numbered them all,
> They passed before me like a squadron of soldiers.
> Then seized with fear, I rose from my sleep."[46]

Jethro then interprets the dream:

> "You will raise up a great throne
> And it is you who will judge and lead humankind;
> As you beheld the whole inhabited earth,
> The things beneath and the things above God's heaven,
> So will you see things present, past, and future."[47]

This dream occurs in a self-conscious literary work. There is no question of a reflection of an actual experience of ascent. In fact, what is described is not really an ascent in any case. Moses sees the throne on top of Mount Sinai, not in the heavens. What is intriguing, however, is that the figure on the throne vacates it for Moses. Jethro's interpretation does not comment on this figure but the one enthroned on top of Mount Sinai can hardly be other than God. Moses then gets to sit on the divine throne. What is implied in the vision is the virtual apotheosis of Moses.

Wayne Meeks has traced the relevant traditions in his article "Moses as God and King."[48] Meeks took his starting point from a passage in Philo's *Life of Moses*: "For he was named god and king of the whole nation. And he was said to have entered into the darkness where God was, that is, into the formless and invisible and incorporeal archetypal essence of existing things, perceiving things invisible to mortal nature."[49] The notion that Moses was named god has a clear basis in Exod 7:1: "I have made you a god to Pharaoh." Since king is one of the attributes of God, this is also taken to mean that Moses was made king. The kingship of Moses is affirmed again in the midrashim (citing Deut 33:5, "he became king in Jeshurun")[50] and in Samaritan tradition.[51] The passage in Ezekiel the Tragedian shows that the tradition is much older than Philo. In Philo the apotheosis is further linked with Moses' ascent of Mount Sinai, into the cloud (Exod 20:21). In Ezekiel, the dream occurs early in the drama (before the burning bush) but the fact that the throne is on Mount Sinai may reflect a similar tradition. Although our earliest sources for this tradition are in Greek, from the Egyptian Diaspora, its later emergence in the midrashim suggests that it had its origin in the exposition of the book of Exodus in the land of Israel.

Here then we have at least one example of the enthronement of a visionary. The visionary in question is Moses, and his case is exceptional. It is warranted, to a degree, by the biblical text that made him a god to Pharaoh. Nonetheless, it involves a considerable extrapolation beyond the biblical text. While the enthronement of Moses can be grounded exegetically, it is not demanded by exegesis, and would hardly have occurred to an exegete who was not already familiar with some traditions of heavenly exaltation, though not necessarily the particular ones that are attested in the Christian era.[52]

The function of Moses' enthronement bears some similarity to the ascents of Enoch and Levi. The vision establishes the authority of Moses. In Psalm 110 the king is given authority by being seated at God's right hand. Moses is seated on God's own throne and promised dominion over men. In addition, he is given knowledge of "things past, present and future," a formula describing prophecy.[53] The manner in which his dominion is to be exercised is not described. One supposes that it was through the medium of the law. The drama, however, seems to have stopped short of the giving of the law on Mount Sinai and concluded with the arrival at the palm trees of Elim, an area of a shaded meadow and well-watered trees. Near this place they see a strange bird, usually identified as the phoenix.[54] The introduction of the phoenix here is suggested by the Greek word for palm tree, φοινιξ. The phoenix, however, had ancient symbolic significance in Egypt, where it was created with the creator god and the renewal of life, but also with Osiris and the renewal of life through death.[55] The symbolism of the scene at Elim suggests that the drama concluded with the intimation of immortality. The enthronement of Moses in his vision may well be an anticipation of his elevation to an immortal state after death.

The enthronement of Moses, then, has some of the functions commonly associated with the call visions of prophets, and with the ascents of Enoch and Levi, but may also include the kind of eschatological anticipation that Bousset thought intrinsic to ecstatic experience.

The Text from Qumran

We return, now, to the text from Qumran Cave 4. Despite the fragmentary nature of the text, it seems clear that the author claims to have sat on the mighty throne in the congregation of the gods and to have been reckoned with the gods, to have undergone a virtual apotheosis. As we have seen, such a claim was not typical in the texts that describe ascents. The author refers to his heavenly enthronement. He does not describe how it took place or give any account of the heavenly geography. He does not describe an ascent. We may assume that someone who has sat on a throne in the heavens has somehow been transported upwards, but the cosmology receives no attention here. Contrary to the claim of Morton Smith, the visionary ascents do not provide the context for the interpretation of this text.

A more promising context is provided by the Hodayot, with their frequent claim to fellowship with the angels. We read in 1QH 3:21–22: "I walk on limitless level ground, and I know there is hope for him whom

Thou hast shaped from dust for the everlasting Council. Thou hast cleansed a perverse spirit of great sin that it may stand with the host of the Holy Ones and that it may enter into community with the congregation of the Sons of Heaven." Or again in 1QH 11:10–12: "And for the sake of your glory, you have cleansed man from sin . . . that he might be joined [with] the sons of your truth and in a lot with your holy ones." This conception is rightly recognized as a kind of realized eschatology.[56] The members of the community enjoy in the present what is promised to the righteous after death in the apocalypses of Daniel and Enoch. These hymns are usually assigned to the "hymns of the community" as distinct from the "hymns of the Teacher."[57] The "I" of these hymns is the typical member of the community, not a unique individual. Similarly, the congregation is said to mingle with the heavenly host in the eschatological war (1QM 8–10). The promise in 4Q521 that God will glorify the pious on the throne of an eternal kingdom can also be understood in this context.[58]

Should 4Q491 also be understood as typical of the community?[59] There are reasons to think that it should not. As Smith noted, there is a stronger and more explicit claim here than elsewhere in the Hodayot. The verb ישבתי (I have sat, or I have dwelt) is most naturally taken to mean that the speaker has sat on the "mighty throne." The questions "who is like me in glory?" (4Q491) and "who is like me among the gods?" (4Q471b) imply a higher level of exaltation than anything we find in the hymns of the community. Moreover, the latter part of the fragment, which speaks of teaching, and asks "who will restrain the utterance of my lips and who will arraign me and equal my judgment?" is more appropriate for an individual who enjoys some authority than for a typical member of the community. It is difficult to classify this passage as a hymn of the community. The speaker surely qualifies as "a clearly recognizable personality," one of the criteria for distinguishing the Teacher hymns.[60] In fact, the vocabulary of this hymn matches the profile of neither the hymns of the community nor those of the Teacher as distinguished by Jeremias,[61] and, while it is incorporated into the Hodayot in 4Q427, it may have originated independently of the rest of the corpus.[62]

The possibility that the speaker is a royal messiah is raised briefly by the statement that "none of the kings of the east" will sit on this throne, and the possible contrast with an "Edomite." Insofar as the passage depicts the activities of the speaker, however, there is little analogy with the Davidic messiah. There are no warlike features, and there is no mention of defeating the enemies of Israel. Instead we find (admittedly elliptical) references to "teaching," "the utterance of my lips," and "my judgment." The speaker, then, seems to be a teacher rather than a king, and Moses rather than David seems to provide the best analogue for heavenly enthronement.

The references to teaching inevitably bring to mind the Teacher of Righteousness. The author of the so-called "Teacher hymns" in the Hodayot is "the man whose mouth Thou hast confirmed" (2:17) and whose mouth is a fount of living waters that shall not fail (8:16). In the Damascus Document, the Teacher must be identified with the *meḥōqōq*, the Interpreter of the Law (CD 6:7). If he is not a new Moses, at least he is the complement of Moses. If Moses had a throne in heaven, we can understand how the Teacher might claim one, too.

There is, however, a striking difference in tone between this hymn and the alleged Teacher hymns of the Hodayot. While the author of this hymn boasts of his ability to bear troubles, he does not complain about persecution, as does the author of the Hodayot. Neither does this hymn show the sense of human sinfulness typical of 1QH, the sense of being snatched from the pit and of being a creature of clay. The tone of this hymn is more confident, and the exaltation of the speaker surpasses anything found in the Hodayot. Moreover, if Smith is correct in reading a reference to the "Edomite" Herod, the hymn is likely to be much later than the time of the original Teacher. There must have been other teachers in the history of the Qumran community, but perhaps the best candidate for identification with the exalted teacher of this hymn is the one who would "teach righteousness at the end of days" (CD 6:11) or the eschatological "Interpreter of the Law" of the Florilegium (4Q174).[63] We have already argued that this figure should also be associated with the eschatological priest of 4Q541 (Aaron A) fragment 9, of whom it is said that "His word shall be as the word of heaven and his teaching shall be according to the will of God." That figure, like the historical teacher, is said to encounter opposition, a fact that may explain the obscure references to "troubles" and "evil" in 4Q491.

Baillet placed 4Q491 11 in the War Rule, before the account of the battle corresponding to 1QM 16–17. It should be noted that 1QM 15 contains an exhortation to be spoken by the High Priest, and the end of column 16 contains the introduction to another exhortation on his part. The High Priest of the War Scroll is *de facto* the eschatological High Priest or Messiah of Aaron. While our canticle was not necessarily composed for this context, this placement is highly compatible with the view that the implied speaker is the eschatological priest/teacher. The claim that he has a throne in heaven is a validation of his authority, and serves the purpose of exhortation in the face of the tribulation of the eschatological battle.

⬡ *Conclusion*

The primary interest of this fragment does not lie in the specific identification of the speaker, which can never be certain, but in the notion of a human figure enthroned in heaven, in a Jewish context. We have seen that this notion is not as strange as it might have seemed initially. The apocalyptic literature offered the prospect of a heavenly afterlife with the stars or angels (Dan 12:3; *1 Enoch* 104:2, 4),[64] even of heavenly enthronement (*1 Enoch* 108:12). The author of the Hodayot claimed to walk already on "limitless level ground" and mingle with the host of heaven. Stronger more distinctive claims were made for the Davidic messiah and Danielic "Son of Man," and also for Moses. The fact that Moses is called "god" by Philo is not an aberration of Greek-speaking Judaism. The figure in 4Q491 is also reckoned among the gods, אלים. In no case does this "divinization" impinge on the supremacy of the Most High, the God of Israel. But it clearly involves the exaltation of some human figures to a status that is envisaged as divine and heavenly rather than human and mortal. The sharp distinction between heaven and earth that was characteristic of the Deuteronomic tradition and of much of the Hebrew Bible was not so strongly maintained in the Hellenistic age, even in the Hebrew and Aramaic speaking Judaism represented by the Dead Sea Scrolls.

NOTES

[1] M. Baillet, *Qumrân Grotte 4. III (4Q482–4Q520)* (Discoveries in the Judaean Desert 7; Oxford: Clarendon, 1982) 26–30. The official designation of the fragment is 4Q491 11.
[2] M. Smith, "Ascent to the Heavens and Deification in 4QMᵃ," in Schiffman, ed., *Archaeology and History in the Dead Sea Scrolls*, 181–88; and "Two Ascended to Heaven," in J. H. Charlesworth, ed., *Jesus and the Dead Sea Scrolls* (New York: Doubleday, 1991) 290–301.
[3] The following translation is adapted from that of M. Smith, "Ascent to the Heavens."
[4] So Smith, reading א דומי as one word. There is a space between the א and the rest of the word, so Baillet reads דומי, silence, and takes the א as the conclusion of the missing preceding word. It is not apparent, however, what sense "silence" could make in this passage.
[5] Or: deemed worthy of contempt (so Baillet; Heb. לבוז נחשב). Smith translates: "I do not

desire [gold] as would a man of flesh; everything precious to me is in the glory of [my God]. [The status of a holy temple,] not to be violated, has been attributed to me." He comments: "he was given the status of a *hieron asylon* . . . a legal status much sought after in the late Roman Republic" (p. 186). There is no parallel for such an idea at Qumran, and it must be regarded as highly implausible.

[6] Smith, "Ascent," 186. As we have noted already (note 4) the reading "Edomite" is not certain. Whether "Edomite" would necessarily refer to Herod is also questionable, since Edom was a traditional enemy of Judea.

[7] In a discussion at the Annenberg Institute in Philadelphia, on May 13, 1993, Devorah Dimant defended Baillet's identification of the speaker as an angel. She pointed to the presence of a number of terms found only in the *Songs of Sabbath Sacrifice*, e.g. the use of בני המלך, sons of the king, and the locution כתם אופיר, gold of Ophir. These terms, however, do not bear on the identity of the speaker, but show that 4Q491 shared the interest of the *Songs of Sabbath Sacrifice* in the angelic world.

[8] Smith, "Two Ascended to Heaven," 295: "it is likely that the same scribe with the same hand may have written several different texts on different pieces of the same skin."

[9] Smith, "Ascent," 187. The fellowship with the angels is discussed by H. W. Kuhn, *Enderwartung und gegenwärtiges Heil* (Göttingen: Vandenhoeck & Ruprecht, 1966) 44–78.

[10] Eileen Schuller, "A Hymn from a Cave Four Hodayot Manuscript: 4Q427 7 i+11," *Journal of Biblical Literature* 112(1993) 605–28.

[11] See further Schuller, "A Hymn from a Cave Four Hodayot Manuscript."

[12] So Stephen A. Reed, *Dead Sea Scroll Inventory Project: Lists of Documents, Photographs and Museum Plates* (Claremont: Ancient Biblical Manuscript Center, 1992) fascicle 9, p. 22. For the text see B. Z. Wacholder and M. Abegg, *A Preliminary Edition of the Unpublished Dead Sea Scrolls. The Hebrew and Aramaic Texts from Cave Four. Fascicle Two* (Washington, D.C.: Biblical Archaeology Society, 1992) 296. The relevance of this fragment to 4Q491 was noted already by Baillet, "Le volume VII de 'Discoveries in the Judaean Desert.' Présentation," in Delcor, ed., *Qumrân*, 79, n.19, where he referred to 4Q471b as 4QSl 86.

[13] It is possible to take ישבתי in a more general sense as "dwelt," and not to associate it with the throne. Puech, "Une Apocalypse Messianique," 489, takes this passage to refer to the exaltation of the council of the poor and the perfect of conduct on a mighty throne in the congregation of the gods, but there is no preposition before throne in the Hebrew. In view of the boasts of the individual author in the remainder of the passage and his claims of exaltation, it is surely he who occupies the throne.

[14] Smith, "Ascent," 187.

[15] Smith, *Clement of Alexandria and a Secret Gospel of Mark* (Cambridge, MA: Harvard University Press, 1973) 238.

[16] I. Gruenwald, *Apocalyptic and Merkavah Mysticism* (Leiden: Brill, 1980) 31.

[17] For an overview of the ascent literature see Martha Himmelfarb, *Tours of Heaven* (New York: Oxford, 1993).

[18] W. Bousset, "Die Himmelsreise der Seele," *Archiv für Religionsgeschichte* 4(1901) 136.

[19] For illustrations from the Christian era, M. Himmelfarb, "Revelation and Rapture: The Transformation of the Visionary in the Ascent Apocalypses," in J. J. Collins and J. H. Charlesworth, eds., *Mysteries and Revelations. Apocalyptic Studies after the Uppsala Colloquium* (Sheffield: Journal for the Study of the Old Testament, 1991) 89–102.

[20] G. Scholem, *Major Trends in Jewish Mysticism* (New York: Schocken, 1961) 40–79.

[21] The *hekhalot* are the heavenly palaces or halls through which the mystic passes *en route* to the divine throne.

[22] P. Schäfer, *Gershom Scholem Reconsidered. The Aim and Purpose of Early Jewish Mysticism* (Oxford: Oxford Centre for Postgraduate Hebrew Studies, 1986) 17. See further Schäfer's study of the *Hekhalot* literature, *The Hidden and Manifest God* (Albany: State University of New York Press, 1992) 7–8. Schäfer grants that ascent is an important motif but questions its centrality in Jewish mysticism.

[23] For a fuller discussion see my essay "A Throne in the Heavens. Apotheosis in pre-Christian Judaism," in John J. Collins and Michael Fishbane, eds., *Death, Ecstasy and Otherworldly Journeys* (Albany: State University of New York Press, 1995).

[24] See Chapter Four above.

[25] Since the priests were the official intercessors, and Enoch was a scribe but not a priest, there may be anti-priestly polemic here. See D. Suter, "Fallen Angel, Fallen Priest: The Problem of Family Purity in 1 Enoch 6–16," *Hebrew Union College Annual* 50(1979) 115–35. G. W. Nickelsburg, "Enoch, Levi, and Peter, Recipients of Revelation in Upper Galilee," *Journal of Biblical Literature* 100(1981) 586, sees *1 Enoch* 12–16 as polemic against the Jerusalem priesthood.

[26] J. D. Tabor, *Things Unutterable. Paul's Ascent to Paradise in its Greco-Roman, Judaic, and Early Christian Contexts* (Lanham, MD: University Press of America, 1986) 75, classifies Enoch's ascent as "ascent to receive revelation."

[27] For the vision in the Aramaic Apocryphon of Levi see Stone and Greenfield in Hollander and de Jonge, *The Testaments of the Twelve Patriarchs*, 460. The passage is very fragmentary.

[28] P. Alexander, "3 (Hebrew Apocalypse of) Enoch," in Charlesworth, ed., *The Old Testament Pseudepigrapha*, 1.223–315; Schäfer, *The Hidden and Manifest God*, 123–38.

[29] Trans. Alexander, "3 (Hebrew Apocalypse of) Enoch," 263. See nos. 13, 894 in P. Schäfer, with M. Schlüter and H. G. von Mutius, *Synopse zur Hekhalot-Literatur* (Texte und Studien zum Antiken Judentum 2; Tübingen: Mohr-Siebeck, 1981).

[30] For the controversy on this topic see A. Segal, *Two Powers in Heaven* (Leiden: Brill, 1977).

[31] Despite the arguments of P. Mosca, "Once Again the Heavenly Witness of Ps 89:38," *Journal of Biblical Literature* 105(1986) 33–36.

[32] H. J. Kraus, *Psalms 60–150 A Commentary* (Minneapolis: Augsburg, 1989) 348. The view of Bernard Duhm, *Die Psalmen* (2nd ed.; Tübingen: Mohr, 1922) 398, 400, that the psalm is a piece of Maccabean propaganda, is now universally rejected. Smith, *Clement of Alexandria*, 238, sees here a claim of ascent on behalf of Simon Maccabee, but this is highly implausible.

[33] See David M. Hay, *Glory at the Right Hand: Psalm 110 in Early Christianity* (Society of Biblical Literature Monograph Series 18; Nashville: Abingdon, 1973); M. Hengel, "'Setze dich zu meiner Rechten!' Die Inthronisation Christi zur Rechten Gottes und Psalm 110,1," in M. Philonenko, ed., *Le Trône de Dieu* (Tübingen: Mohr-Siebeck, 1993) 108–94.

[34] Hay, *Glory*, 21–27. Some echoes of the psalm can be found in the Apocryphon of Levi. See Chapter Four above. Hengel argues that motifs from Daniel 7 and Psalm 110 are combined in the *Similitudes of Enoch* ("Setze dich zu meiner Rechten!" 161–64).

[35] Compare Col. 3:1: "where Christ is seated at the right hand of God." Also Heb 1:3; 12:2.

[36] b. Ḥag 14a; b. Sanh. 38b.

[37] J. Collins, *The Apocalyptic Vision of the Book of Daniel* (Harvard Semitic Monographs 16; Missoula: Scholars Press, 1977) 123–47; and *Daniel* (Hermeneia; Minneapolis: Fortress, 1993) 304–10.

[38] Johannes Theisohn, *Der auserwählte Richter* (Göttingen: Vandenhoeck & Ruprecht, 1975) 68–98; Johannes Friedrich, *Gott im Brüder* (Stuttgart: Calwer, 1977) 127–34.

[39] See further Chapter Eight below.

[40] *Testament of Abraham* 13:1–4.

[41] Compare Acts 7:56 where Stephen sees "the Son of Man standing at the right hand of God." See further Norman Perrin, *A Modern Pilgrimage in New Testament Christology* (Philadelphia: Fortress, 1974) 12–13.

[42] On Melchizedek in Hebrews see Harold W. Attridge, *The Epistle to the Hebrews* (Hermeneia; Philadelphia: Fortress, 1989) 186–97.

[43] Puech, "Une apocalypse messianique," 485–86.

[44] G. W. Nickelsburg, *Jewish Literature Between the Bible and the Mishnah* (Philadelphia: Fortress, 1981) 151; M. Black, *The Book of Enoch or 1 Enoch* (Leiden: Brill, 1985) 323.

[45] Matt 19:28; Luke 22:30.

[46] Eusebius, *Praeparatio Evangelica*, 9.29.4–5. Trans. C. R. Holladay, *Fragments from Hellenistic Jewish Authors II. Poets* (Atlanta: Scholars Press, 1989) 363–65. See also H. Jacobson, *The Exagoge of Ezekiel* (Cambridge: Cambridge University Press, 1983).

[47] Eusebius, *Praeparatio Evangelica* 9.24.6; Holladay, *Fragments*, 367.

[48] W. Meeks, "Moses as God and King," in J. Neusner, ed., *Religions in Antiquity. Essays in Memory of Erwin Ramsdell Goodenough* (Leiden: Brill, 1968) 354–71.

[49] Philo, *Vita Mosis* 1.155–58.

[50] *Bamidbar R.* 15.13, *Tanḥuma*, ed. S. Buber, 4.53–54; cited by Meeks, "Moses as God and King," 356.

[51] *Memar Marqah* 4.6; Meeks, "Moses as God and King," 358.

[52] See P. W. van der Horst, "Moses' Throne Vision in Ezekiel the Dramatist," *Journal of Jewish Studies* 34(1983) 21–29.

[53] Ibid., 28.

[54] On the identification, see H. Jacobson, "Phoenix Resurrected," *Harvard Theological Review* 80(1987) 229–33.

[55] M. Walla, *Der Vogel Phoenix in der antiken Literatur und in der Dichtung des Laktanz* (Wien: Notring, 1969) 1–50; R. van den Broek, *The Myth of the Phoenix According to Classical and Early Christian Traditions* (Leiden: Brill, 1972).

[56] Cf. 1QS 11:5–9. Kuhn, *Enderwartung und gegenwärtiges Heil*, 44–78; G. W. Nickelsburg, *Resurrection, Immortality and Eternal Life in Intertestamental Judaism* (Cambridge, MA: Harvard University Press, 1972) 146–56. This interpretation of the Hodayot is disputed by Puech, *La Croyance des Esséniens en la Vie Future*, 327–419, who reads the verbs in the hymns as "prophetic perfects," anticipating a state of salvation that is not yet present. The eschatology of the Hodayot would then be no different from that of the book of Daniel. Puech's interpretation, however, does not do justice to the distinctive language of the Hodayot.

[57] Kuhn, *Enderwartung und gegenwärtiges Heil*, 23, lists the most widely accepted Teacher hymns as 2:1–19; 4:5–29; 5:5–19; 5:20–6:36; 7:3–25; 8:4–40. See also G. Jeremias, *Der Lehrer der Gerechtigkeit*, 168–267. Jeremias includes 2:31–39 and 3:1–18, and extends two other hymns, 4:5–5:4 and 5:20–7:5.

[58] Puech, "Une Apocalypse Messianique," 485–86.

[59] So Puech, ibid., 489.

[60] Jeremias, *Der Lehrer der Gerechtigkeit*, 171.

[61] Ibid., 172–73.

[62] So Schuller, "A Hymn from a Cave Four Hodayot Manuscript," 627.

[63] So Hengel, "Setze dich zu meiner Rechten!" 176. Puech, *La Croyance des Esséniens en la Vie Future*, 494, identifies this figure as "Maître/Instructeur/Sage/Messie roi-prêtre (?)" I do not see the basis for referring to this figure as a king, but the rest of the titles seem appropriate.

[64] See further J. H. Charlesworth, "The Portrayal of the Righteous as an Angel," in J. J. Collins and G. W. Nickelsburg, eds., *Ideal Figures in Ancient Judaism* (Chico, CA: Scholars Press, 1980) 135–51.

7

THE MESSIAH AS THE SON OF GOD

The divine, or quasi-divine status of a messianic figure is again at issue is a controversial Aramaic fragment designated as 4Q246, better known as the "Son of God" text.[1] The controversy surrounding this text was due in part to the delay in publication. It was acquired in 1958, and entrusted to J. T. Milik. Fourteen years later, in December 1972, Milik presented it in a lecture at Harvard University and promised to publish it in the *Harvard Theological Review*. The publication did not follow. Part of the text was published by Joseph Fitzmyer in an article on "Qumran Aramaic and the New Testament" in 1974.[2] While the text was still unpublished, it was the subject of articles by David Flusser[3] and F. García Martínez,[4] and numerous passing references in other studies. It was finally published by Emile Puech in 1992, in the centenary volume of *Revue Biblique*.[5]

The fragment was dated by Milik to the last third of the first century BCE.[6] It consists of two columns, of nine lines each. Column 1 is torn vertically, so that one third to a half of each line is missing, but column 2 is substantially intact. Since column 2 ends with a construct form (תהומי, depths, or possibly תחומי, boundaries), there was apparently a third column. There may also have been another column before column 1. The fragmentary opening verse says that someone "fell before the throne." The following verses are apparently addressed to a king, and refer to "your vision." The passage goes on to say that "affliction will come on earth . . . and great carnage among the cities." There is reference to kings of Asshur and Egypt. Then the second half of verse 7 reads ". . . will be great on earth." This could possibly continue the affliction described in the previous verses. It could also refer forward, to the figure who is the subject of the following lines. Line 8 says that "all will serve . . ." and line 9 that "by his name he will be named." Then column 2 continues as follows:

> " 'Son of God' he shall be called, and they will name him 'Son of the Most High.' Like sparks which you saw (or: of the vision), so will be their kingdom. For years they will rule on earth, and they will trample all. People will trample on people and city on city, [VACAT]until the people of God arises, [or: until he raises up the people of God][7] and all rest from the sword. His [or its] kingdom is an everlasting kingdom and all his [or its] ways truth. He [or it] will judge the earth with truth and all will make peace. The sword will cease from the earth, and all cities will pay him [or it] homage. The great God will be his [or its] strength.[8] He will make[9] war on his [or its] behalf; give nations into his [or its] hand and cast them all down before him [it]. His [or its] sovereignty is everlasting sovereignty and all the depths. . . ."

The interest of the fragment for our purpose centers on the figure who will be called "Son of God." The correspondences with the infancy narrative in Luke are astonishing. Three phrases correspond exactly: "will be great," "he will be called son of the Most High" (both in Luke 1:32) and "he will be called Son of God" (Luke 1:35). Luke also speaks of an unending reign. It is difficult to avoid the conclusion that Luke is dependent in some way, whether directly or indirectly, on this long lost text from Qumran.

⬚ *Proposed Interpretations*

The correspondences with Luke might be taken as *prima facie* evidence for a messianic interpretation, but the fragmentary state of the text leaves many points of uncertainty. At least five distinct interpretations have already been proposed.

Milik, in his presentation at Harvard, argued that the figure was a historical king, Alexander Balas, son of Antiochus Epiphanes.[10] He could be called "son of God" because he is identified on coins as *theopator*, or

Deo patre natus. Milik suggested that the name by which he was called was that of Alexander the Great. Ingenious though this interpretation is, it has found no followers to date, although Puech now allows the possibility of a reference to a Seleucid king, whether Alexander Balas or Antiochus Epiphanes.[11]

As early as 1961, Arthur Darby Nock reported the opinion of Frank Moore Cross that "there is further evidence forthcoming from Qumran for the use of royal ideology, expressing the messiah's relation to God in terms of sonship."[12] Apparently, the reference was to this text.[13] A messianic interpretation is also allowed by Puech.[14] Fitzmyer's interpretation would also be classified as messianic by most scholars, although he resists this terminology, since such terms as messiah or anointed one are not used.[15] He sees the text as "properly apocalyptic," and takes the enthroned king who is addressed as "someone on the Jewish side rather than on the Seleucid side." He then takes the Son of God figure as "a 'son' or descendant of the enthroned king who will be supported by the 'Great God,'" "possibly an heir to the throne of David."[16] In his most recent treatment of the subject he reformulates his interpretation as "a coming Jewish ruler, perhaps a member of the Hasmonean dynasty, who will be a successor to the Davidic throne, but who is not envisaged as a Messiah. The text should be understood as a sectarian affirmation of God's provision and guarantee of the Davidic dynasty."[17] Seyoon Kim, in his book *The 'Son of Man' as the Son of God*, follows Fitzmyer's interpretation, but has no reservations about calling it messianic.[18]

David Flusser countered Fitzmyer's comments by observing that there is a blank space immediately before the rise of the people of God in column 2, line 4. He argues that this is the turning point in the eschatological drama, and that everything preceding it pertains to the afflictions and tribulations. Unlike Milik, however, Flusser referred these titles not to a historical figure, but to the Antichrist. He pointed out that in Christian tradition the Antichrist lays claim to such titles, and he argued that the idea of an Antichrist is surely Jewish and pre-Christian. He claimed to find a close Jewish parallel in the little-studied *Oracle of Hystaspes*, referring to a future king who will be "a prophet of lies, and he will constitute, and call himself God and will order himself to be worshipped as the Son of God."[19] The *Oracle of Hystaspes*, however, is only known in so far as it is cited by Lactantius, and the extent of the citations and their ultimate provenance is in dispute. Many scholars think that Hystaspes was in fact a Persian-Hellenistic oracle, but in any case this passage about the Antichrist is very probably Christian.[20] There are plenty of

The Messiah as the Son of God

Jewish texts, at Qumran and elsewhere, that refer to an eschatological adversary of some sort, but the figure in question is always described in negative terms in the Jewish texts.[21] (One of the paradigmatic texts in this regard is found in Daniel 11, where "the king shall act as he pleases. He shall exalt himself and consider himself greater than any god and shall speak horrendous things against the God of gods" [Dan 11:36]. We are left in no doubt about the negative character of the king in question.) The idea of an Antichrist, however, who mimics the titles and power of Christ, the messiah, is found only in Christian texts, and cannot safely be inferred from this Qumran fragment.[22]

García Martínez agrees with Fitzmyer on the eschatological character of the text, and on the positive character of the nomenclature, but he seeks to interpret the text primarily in the light of other Qumran documents. He draws his parallels primarily from 11QMelchizedek and the War Scroll, and concludes that the mysterious "Son of God" is the figure designated elsewhere as Melchizedek, Michael or the Prince of Light.[23] This conclusion, however, is asserted rather than argued, and requires critical examination.

Finally, the possibility of a collective interpretation in terms of the Jewish people has been noted by Martin Hengel.[24] To my knowledge, no one has actually argued for such an interpretation, but Hengel is correct that it cannot be ruled out in principle.

The Literary Context

Fundamental to any interpretation of the Son of God figure is an analysis of the structure of the text and his place therein. It is apparent that most of the fragment is the interpretation of a vision, apparently the vision of a king, interpreted by someone else, who falls before the throne in the opening verse. We do not know whether the vision was described in an earlier part of the document. The general situation of an interpreter before a king suggests a relationship to the Daniel literature. The content of the interpretation also has some points of contact with Daniel. The clearest points are at 2:5, "its kingdom is an everlasting kingdom," compare Dan 3:33; 7:27, and at 2:9, "his sovereignty will be an everlasting sovereignty," compare Dan 4:31; 7:14. The conflict between the nations in column 1 is reminiscent in a general way of Daniel 11, but such conflict is a commonplace in apocalyptic literature. (See, for example, Mark 13:8: "nation will rise against nation and kingdom against kingdom;" also *Sib Or* 3:635–36; *4 Ezra* 13:31). Another possible allusion to Daniel lies in the use of the word to trample (דוש) at 2:3. The same verb is used with reference to the fourth beast in Daniel 7.[25] These verbal contacts are most simply explained by positing influence of the book of Daniel on the Qumran document. Puech, however, speaks only of proximity of theme and language, and suggests that 4Q246 was roughly contemporary with Daniel.[26]

The reminiscences of Daniel may provide clues to some of the problems presented by the text. The kings for whom Daniel provided interpretations were, of course, Gentile kings, not kings "on the Jewish side." There is no necessary relationship, however, between the enthroned king and the figure mentioned later.[27] A more important issue concerns the relationship between the Son of God figure and the people of God. As we have seen, the introduction of the Son of God figure is followed by a reference to the transience of human kingdoms and the conflict between peoples. Milik and Flusser inferred that the Son of God figure belonged to this era of tumult, whether as a historical king or as an eschatological Antichrist. We have also seen that the honorific language is hard to reconcile with such an interpretation. Some light may be thrown on the sequence of events by analogy with Daniel 7. There the sequence of tribulation followed by deliverance is fully laid out in Daniel's vision. Then the interpretation gives a brief summary of the same sequence in other terms (vss. 17–18) and finally the tribulation and deliverance are reviewed again, with more emphasis on the fourth beast. The conferral of the kingdom is repeated three times: first it is given to the "one like a son of man," then to the holy ones of the Most High, finally to the people of the holy ones of the Most High. The chapter does not proceed in simple chronological sequence. Rather it goes over the same ground in slightly different ways, and this, in fact, is a well-known feature of apocalyptic writing.[28] I suggest that the Son of God text can be understood in much the same way. The description of the conflict between the peoples in column 2 is redundant, but such redundancy is a feature of apocalyptic style. If this is correct, then the mutual trampling of the nations in column 2 is simply an alternative formulation, or another aspect, of the carnage between the nations in column 1, and the rise of the people of God is parallel to the advent of the "Son of God" or "Son of the Most High."

Another major problem of interpretation is presented by the use of the third person masculine suffix in the lines that follow the rise of the people of God. The suffix could, in principle, refer back either to an individual (the Son of God, so "his kingdom is an everlasting kingdom") or to the people (so "its kingdom is an everlasting kingdom"). The immediate antecedent is certainly the people. Yet the people is an unlikely antecedent for the statement "he will judge the earth with truth." In the Hebrew Bible, it is the Lord himself who is judge of the earth (Gen 18:25; 1 Sam 2:10; Pss 7:9; 9:9, etc). Judgment is a royal function, and the Davidic king transmits the divine justice to the people of Israel (Ps 72:1–2). The ideal king of the future has a wider role. He will "judge the poor with righteousness, and decide with equity for the meek of the earth" (Isa 11:4). In the *pesher* on Isaiah at Qumran, his sword will judge all the peoples.[29] Again in the *Psalms of Solomon*, the eschatological king will "judge peoples and nations in the wisdom of his righteousness" (*Ps Sol* 17:29). In no case, however, is the function of judgment given to the people collectively.

Here again the analogy of Daniel 7 may be helpful. There the four beasts from the sea are interpreted as "four kings" (vs. 17), yet the fourth is "a fourth kingdom" (vs. 23). The eternal kingdom is explicitly given both to the "one like a son of man" and to the people of the holy ones. A king can stand for a kingdom, and a representative individual can stand for a people. The ambiguity of the third person suffixes in column 2 of our Qumran fragment can be explained most satisfactorily if the one who is called "Son of God" is understood as the ruler or representative of the people of God. The everlasting kingdom, then, belongs to both, and the "Son of God" exercises universal judgment on behalf of his people.

In light of these analogies, it is tempting to suggest that the "Son of God" represents an early interpretation of the "one like a son of man" in Daniel 7, who also stands in parallelism to the people.[30] This is, indeed, a possibility, but a word of caution is in order. The "Son of God" text is not simply an exposition of Daniel 7. While some words and phrases are drawn from that source, most elements of the biblical vision are ignored (the sea, the beasts, the clouds, the judgment, etc.). The vision interpreted here is a vision of a king, not Daniel's vision, and it is presented as an original revelation.

Moreover, Daniel is not the only book of which we find reminiscences here. There are at least two echoes of the Qumran War Scroll: the reference to the kings of Asshur and Egypt (1:6; cf. 1QM 1:2, 4, where there is a reference to the *Kittim* of Asshur and the *Kittim* of Egypt) and the rare word נחשיר/נחשירון, carnage (a Persian loan word found in 1QM 1:9). As is well known, the War Scroll itself makes extensive use of Daniel, which was apparently understood to refer to the eschatological war.[31] The echoes of the War Scroll here suggest that the "Son of God" text makes use of Daniel in a similar context. We cannot assume that it reproduces the message of Daniel in any essential way, but comparison with Daniel is, nonetheless, a promising key to the text.

The parallels with the War Scroll raise the question whether the Son of God text comes from a sectarian milieu. There is no reference in the extant text to a separate community such as the יחד of the Community Rule, or even to distinctively sectarian terminology such as "Sons of Light." Most scholars, however, would grant that the War Scroll is sectarian, whether it was originally composed at Qumran or not.[32] The terminological echoes of the War Scroll here suggest that the Son of God text also comes from a sectarian milieu. The evidence is not clear-cut and does not warrant any sweeping assumptions that the text is in conformity with other sectarian compositions. Comparison with other scrolls, however, is not only valid but necessary, if it is pursued as a heuristic exercise. In short, the text must be viewed not only against the backdrop of Daniel, but also against the backdrop of other eschatological scenarios, especially those attested in the Scrolls.

The analogy with Daniel 7 suggests that there is a parallelism between the Son of God and the people. Parallelism, however, admits of different relationships. In the case of Daniel 7, everyone agrees that there is parallelism between the one like a son of man and the people of the holy ones, but scholars are sharply divided as to what that parallelism entails. Some argue for simple identity, taking the "son of man" as a collective figure,[33] others for an individual figure who is representative of the people. The latter group again is split between those who take the son of man as the archangel Michael,[34] who is explicitly identified as the prince of Israel in Daniel 10–12, and those who hold to the messianic interpretation, which was standard for many centuries but has fallen into disfavor in recent times.[35] A similar range of possibilities is present in the relationship between the Son of God and the people of God in the fragmentary text from Qumran.

The Collective Interpretation

In fact, these three interpretations, communal, angelic, and messianic, are all well attested for the expression "son of God" in the Hebrew Bible.[36] The prophet Hosea speaks of Israel as the son of God in the famous passage: "When Israel was a child, I loved him, and out of Egypt I called my son." Already in Exod 4:22b–23, Moses is instructed to say to Pharaoh: "Thus says the Lord: Israel is my firstborn son. I said to you, 'let my son go that he may worship me.'" Closer to the period of the Scrolls, Sirach prays: "Have mercy, O Lord, on the people called by your name, on Israel, whom you have named your firstborn" (36:17). This latter instance is especially interesting here because of the element of being called by the name.

A collective interpretation is not impossible in the text from Qumran, but nonetheless it seems unlikely. As we have noted already, there is no parallel for the notion that the people, collectively, will judge the earth. Moreover, although Israel is often said to *be* God's son, "Son of God" is scarcely used as a title with reference to the people. The eschatological kingdom of Israel, which is well attested, is usually associated with an eschatological ruler under God, whether an angel, such as Michael in Daniel and the War Scroll, or a messianic figure. While certainty is not possible because of the fragmentary state of column 1, an interpretation that allows for such an individual ruler here should be preferred.

The Angelic Interpretation

The sons of El, in the plural, are most often heavenly beings in the Hebrew Bible. Examples include Genesis 6 and Psalm 82; also Deut 32:8–9, where the Greek reading, according to which the Most High fixed the boundaries of the people according to the number of the sons of God, (not of Israel), is supported now by a manuscript from Qumran.[37] In Daniel 3, when the king sees a fourth man in the fiery furnace, who looks like "a son of gods," this is evidently an angelic being. It must be admitted, however, that the use of the singular in this sense is rather unusual. Despite the proliferation of names and titles for "principal angels" in the Hellenistic period (Michael, Melchizedek, Prince of Light, Son of Man in the *Similitudes of Enoch*) in no case is one of them called "the son of God."

García Martínez has proposed that the "Son of God" in the Qumran fragment should be identified with the figure known in other texts as Michael, Melchizedek or Prince of Light.[38] While his argument is not developed, it would seem to rest on the assumption that the document is sectarian and that its eschatology is coherent with that of such compositions as the War Scroll and 11QMelchizedek. While that assumption is open to question, I am prepared to grant it, in view of points of contact already noted between the Son of God text and the War Scroll. The great carnage involving the Kings of Asshur and Egypt can plausibly be identified with the great battle described in the War Scrolls. In that battle, God himself fights for Israel from heaven (1QM 11:17). He has also appointed a Prince of Light to come to its support (1QM 13:10). In the final phase of the battle "He will send eternal succor to the company of His redeemed by the might of the princely Angel of the princedom of Michael" (17:6) and "raise up the princedom of Michael in the midst of the gods and the dominion of Israel among all flesh." It is evidently possible to read the Son of God text in the light of this scenario. It is still God who comes to the aid of Israel, but there is also a role for another heavenly figure under God in the defeat of the nations.

11QMelchizedek is more directly midrashic than either the "Son of God" text or the War Scroll. Its starting point is not the eschatological battle, but the year of Jubilee, as proclaimed in Leviticus 25. The description of Melchizedek is of interest here, however. The document applies Ps. 82:1 to him:

> "'Elohim stands in the assembly [of El], in the midst of Elohim he judges.' And concerning it, he sa[id], 'Above it to the heights, return! El judges the nations.'"

It goes on to say that "Melchizedek will exact the ven[geance] of E[l's] judgments." We have seen that the Son of God is said to judge the earth, a function usually reserved for God in the Hebrew Bible. 11QMelchizedek provides an instance where the divine judgment is executed by a figure other than the Most High, the heavenly *ʾelohim*, Melchizedek.

One other text should be considered in support of the angelic interpretation of the "Son of God." The *Similitudes of Enoch* are not found at Qumran, and are probably the product of a different sect, although their apocalyptic worldview is similar in many respects to that of the community. A central role in this document is filled by a figure called "that Son of Man," who is patently meant to recall the "one like a son of man" of Daniel 7. This figure is enthroned on "the throne of glory" and the kings of the earth fall down and worship before him, and entreat him for mercy.[39] It is reasonable to infer that he shares in the divine function of judge. The fact that the kings of the earth worship before him deserves special notice, since such homage is seldom given to anyone under God in Jewish texts.

These parallels lend substance to the angelic interpretation of the

Son of God text, but they are not decisive. At least two aspects of the text continue to give pause. First, although the principal angel is known by many names at Qumran, the title "Son of God" is not attested for him. Second, it is surprising that God should be said to be the strength of an angelic figure and to fight on his behalf. Usually, the angel is the agent through whom God gives support to his people on earth. If the third person suffix in column 2 refers back to the Son of God, this presents a problem for the angelic interpretation.

The Messianic Interpretation

The individual most often designated as "the son of God" in the Hebrew Bible is undoubtedly the Davidic king, or his eschatological counterpart.[40] The adoption of David as God's son is clearly stated in 2 Samuel 7:14 ("I will be a father to him and he will be a son to me") and in Psalm 89:26–27 ("He shall cry to me: 'You are my Father' . . . I will make him the firstborn, the highest of the kings of the earth"). The relationship is expressed in more mythological terms in Psalm 2:7–8 ("I will tell of the decree of the Lord: he said to me, 'You are my son; today I have begotten you'"). The statements in the Son of God text, that the great God will be his strength and will give peoples into his hand, can apply equally well to the king in the psalm. Psalm 2 also refers to the king as "His (the Lord's) anointed (מְשִׁיחוֹ)" (2:2).

The title "Son of God" takes on a clear messianic connotation in the New Testament, notably in the Lukan infancy narrative cited earlier. Fitzmyer, however, argues strongly that "Per se, the titles do not connote 'messiah' in the Old Testament, and only a naive interpretation emerging from tradition espouses that connotation. Nor do they do so in any Qumran texts."[41] He further adds that "There were undoubtedly other kings in Israel's history, who had sat on the Davidic throne, but were not accorded the title מָשִׁיחַ, much less "Messiah" in the proper sense."[42] I believe that these statements show confusion in regard to the Old Testament evidence, and fail to do justice to the evidence from Qumran.

First, in the context of the Hebrew Bible, 2 Samuel 7 and Psalm 2 refer to the historical Davidic kings. They are not eschatological, and so not "messianic" in the sense in which we have been using the word. Fitzmyer's strictures against naive traditionalists who read these texts as predictions of the messiah are fair enough if one is speaking about the original meaning of the text. Confusion arises, however, when he claims, without any supporting evidence, that some kings "were not accorded the title מָשִׁיחַ." The word מָשִׁיחַ, anointed one, is an epithet applied to the king, in virtue of the fact that he was anointed.[43] Whether it is regarded as a title is a matter of definition, but the term was clearly applicable to any anointed king. There is no evidence that any king of Israel or Judah was not anointed. Fitzmyer here seems to load the term מָשִׁיחַ, anointed, with a special significance that it does not have in the Hebrew Bible. Correspondingly, a future "successor to the Davidic throne" in an apocalyptic or eschatological context is by definition a Davidic messiah. Fitzmyer's notion of "a sectarian affirmation of God's provision and guarantee of the Davidic dynasty" by a king who is not a "messiah" makes no sense in the context of ancient Judaism.[44]

Second, the claim that "Son of God" does not have messianic significance in any Qumran text overlooks the clear evidence of the Florilegium (4Q174). There we have an exposition of 2 Sam 7:14:

> "The Lord declares to you that He will build you a House. I will raise up your seed after you. I will establish the throne of his kingdom [for ever]. I [will be] his father and he shall be my son. He is the Branch of David who shall arise with the Interpreter of the Law [to rule] in Zion [at the end] of days."

The citation from 2 Samuel 7 provides an explicit basis for identifying the Branch of David as the Son of God. Since the Branch is explicitly called the Messiah of Righteousness in the Patriarchal Blessings (4Q252 = 4QpGen), it is surely justified to speak of him as a Davidic messiah.[45] Fitzmyer's insistence that "There is nothing in the OT or Palestinian Jewish tradition that we know of to show that 'Son of God' had a messianic nuance"[46] cannot be maintained unless "messianic nuance" is equated with explicit use of the word "messiah" in the same passage.

EXCURSUS:
OTHER POSSIBLE "SON OF GOD" PASSAGES

Two other texts may be cited in connection with the view that the Davidic messiah was regarded as Son of God at Qumran, but both are fragmentary and problematic.

The first, and better known, is in 1QSa, the so-called "messianic rule." This passage describes the session of the council of the community at the end of days, when the messiah comes. The words before the mention of the messiah are damaged. The late Patrick Skehan claimed that the word יוליד (causes to be born) could be made out "on the testimony of half a dozen witnesses, including Allegro, Cross, Strugnell, and the writer [Skehan], as of the summer of 1955."[47] The following word would then be restored as אל, God, so "when God causes the messiah to be born...." Cross, however, later accepted Milik's reading, יוליך (brings),[48] and other restorations have also been proposed,[49] so the text remains uncertain.

The second passage is found in an obscure fragment from Cave 4 (4Q369) that says "you made him a firstborn son to you" and goes on to speak of someone "like him for a prince and ruler in all your earthly land."[50] This passage is extremely fragmentary, and the context is quite uncertain, but a prince and ruler who is treated as a firstborn son must surely be related to the Davidic line, whether past or future.

The attestation of "Son of God" as a messianic title in Jewish texts of the Hellenistic and Roman periods is not extensive, but an important instance is found in *4 Ezra*. The Latin and Syriac texts of this pseudepigraphon refer to the messiah as "my son" in a number of passages, in chapters 7 and 13 and finally in 14:9. The originality of this reading has been disputed. Some versions use words that mean "servant" in a few instances, and there are other textual variations.[51] Michael Stone has argued that the Greek version, which has not been preserved, read *pais*, and reflected an original Hebrew "servant" rather than "son."[52] Yet the scene in chapter 13, where the messianic figure takes his stand on a mountain and repulses the attack of the nations, is clearly dependent on Psalm 2, where God sets his anointed king on Zion, his holy mountain, and terrifies the nations, and where the king is also told "You are my son, today I have begotten you." Even if the Greek read *pais*, as the versions that read "servant" require, this term, too, could be used for "son," as is evident from The Wisdom of Solomon, where the righteous man calls himself a child of God (*pais theou*, 2:13) and boasts that God is his father (2:16). The Latin and Syriac reading, "my son," should be accepted as a faithful rendering of the original, at least in chapter 13.

4 Ezra 13 is of considerable interest for the interpretation of the Son of God text from Qumran. Ezra's vision of a man coming up out of the heart of the sea and flying with the clouds is evidently inspired by Daniel 7. In the preceding chapter, *4 Ezra* 12, Ezra had seen an eagle coming up from the sea, and was told that this was "the fourth kingdom that appeared in a vision to your brother Daniel, but it was not explained to him as I now explain to you or have explained it" (*4 Ezra* 12:11–12). A similar comment might be made about the man from the sea in chapter 13, who must equally be identified with the "one like a son of man" from Daniel's vision, but is also interpreted in a new way. As in the Qumran text, the advent of this figure is preceded by conflict between the nations: "They shall plan to make war against one another, city against city, place against place, people against people and kingdom against kingdom" (13:31).

In *4 Ezra* 13, the messiah repulses the attack of the Gentiles with a fiery breath (cf. Isa 11:4) and gathers the dispersed of Israel. He is also said to reprove the assembled nations for their ungodliness (13:37). In the preceding vision of the eagle, the messiah has a more prominent judicial function: "First he will bring them alive before his judgment seat, and when he has reproved them he will destroy them" (12:33). It is clear then that the messiah has taken over some of the function of judging the nations, which was usually reserved for God in the Hebrew Bible. There is no place here, however, for worship of this figure by the nations, since they are destroyed after the judgment, like the fourth beast in Daniel.

The eschatology of *4 Ezra* is considerably different from that of a document like the Qumran War Scroll. It has no place for an angelic deliverer, although the messiah has a transcendent character (He rises from the heart of the sea and flies with the clouds). Heavenly savior figures (Michael, Melchizedek) play a part in the Scrolls, but as we have seen the Davidic messiah also has an established place there. Since Michael or the Prince of Light is never called "Son of God," and since there is a clear basis for applying this title to the Davidic king, whether past or future, the messianic interpretation should be preferred. Indeed the parallel in Luke points strongly in this direction: "He will be great and will be hailed as Son of the Most High, and the Lord God will bestow on him the throne of his father David."[53]

Puech argued that the similarity to Daniel points to a date in the mid-second century BCE.[54] If this were so, the Son of God text would be the earliest witness to the hope for a messianic Davidic king in the Hellenistic era, nearly a century earlier than the *Psalms of Solomon*. Such an early date, however, is not required by the manuscript, and the similarities with Daniel may rather be due to the influence of the biblical book on the Qumran text. Puech's early dating implies that the Son of God text was not originally produced by the Qumran sect. The fact that it is written in Aramaic, and that there is no mention of a priestly messiah such as we often find in the Scrolls, might be taken to lend some support to this view. In favor of the contrary view, that the text originated in sectarian circles, are the few verbal parallels with the War Rule. There is no mention of the *Kittim* in the extant fragments. The only foreign powers mentioned are Assyria and Egypt. This suggests a date before the advent of Rome, while the Seleucids and Ptolemies were still the powers to be reckoned with. There is no reason, however, to push the date back into the second century. There is no evidence that the hope for a Davidic king resurfaced in this period before the assumption of royalty by the Hasmoneans. In view of the fragmentary nature of the text, however, much remains uncertain.

It is difficult to say whether the Son of God figure should be regarded as an interpretation of the "one like a son of man" in Daniel 7. If so, it would probably be the oldest surviving interpretation. No other adaptation or interpretation of that chapter has yet been identified in the Qumran corpus. The two earliest Jewish interpretations of Daniel 7 are found in the *Similitudes of Enoch* and *4 Ezra* 13. Both these passages assume that Daniel's "one like a son of man" is an individual, and both use the term "messiah" with reference to him. In both these documents, the Son of Man figure is pre-existent, and therefore transcendent in some sense. The Son of God in the Qumran text is not identical with either of these figures, but he has much in common with them. It should be emphasized that the extant fragment from Qumran lacks clear allusions to Daniel's "one like a son of man" such as we find in the *Similitudes* and in *4 Ezra*. Nonetheless, it is difficult to avoid the impression that the author had Daniel's figure in mind. The Danielic paradigm becomes an important factor in messianism in the first century of the Common Era. The Son of God text suggests that the messianic interpretation of Daniel 7 had begun already in the Hasmonean period.

The Role and Nature of the Son of God

The role of the figure who is called the "Son of God" is essentially similar to that of the messiah in the *Psalms of Solomon*. He will bring an end to conflict, restore the kingdom of Israel, and establish peace on earth. He will not act by his own power. God will be his strength.[55] Nonetheless, he must be understood as a warrior figure, since the nations will be cast down before him.

The designation "Son of God" reflects the status rather than the nature of the messiah. He is the son of God in the same sense that the king of Israel was begotten by God according to Psalm 2. There is no implication of virgin birth and no metaphysical speculation is presupposed. He may still be regarded as a human being, born of human beings, but one who stands in a special relationship to God. The earliest Gospel, Mark, which begins "The beginning of the good news of Jesus Christ, the Son of God,"[56] but has no account of the birth of Jesus, can also be read in those terms. The Gospels of Matthew and Luke, despite the common language in the latter and the Son of God text, have a more developed notion of what the sonship of the messiah entailed, and express it in a narrative of Jesus' birth. In the Hellenistic world, there were many stories about rulers and heroes who were allegedly begotten by divine beings.[57] There were such legends about Alexander the Great[58] and Augustus,[59] and also about philosophers such as Plato[60] and Pythagoras.[61] Matthew and Luke may have been influenced by their Hellenistic-Roman context, even though the motifs of their infancy narratives are much more clearly indebted to the Jewish Scriptures than to any Hellenistic sources.[62] There was a long process of further development between the Gospels and the Church Councils that defined the Son as a member of a divine Trinity, and this process was definitely influenced by Greek philosophy.[63]

Many scholars have argued that the attribution of divine titles to Jesus was part of what Harnack called "the acute Hellenization of Christianity," and a movement away from Jewish notions of messianism. In the words of Rudolf Bultmann: "Hellenistic-Jewish Christians had brought along the *title 'Son of God'* embedded in their missionary message; for the earliest Church had already called Jesus so. But one must recognize that the title, which originally denoted the messianic king, now takes on a new meaning which was self-evident to Gentile hearers. Now it comes to mean *the divinity of Christ, his divine nature*, by virtue of which he is differentiated from the human sphere; it makes the claim that Christ is of divine origin and is filled with divine power."[64]

One need not subscribe to all aspects of Bultmann's theories to grant that the title "Son of God" took on a new and more exalted meaning in Hellenistic Christianity.[65] Nonetheless, we should bear in mind that even in the Hebrew Bible the king could be addressed as a "god," *'elohim*. The titles "Son of God" and "Son of the Most High" imply that this figure stands in a special relationship to the Deity, and that he is not an ordinary mortal. Here again, as in the "throne in heaven" text considered in the previous chapter, the distinction between divine and human is not so sharply drawn as it was in the Deuteronomic tradition or in rabbinic

The Messiah as the Son of God

Judaism. The notion of a messiah who was in some sense divine had its roots in Judaism, in the interpretation of such passages as Psalm 2 and Daniel 7 in an apocalyptic context. This is not to deny the great difference between a text like 4Q246 and the later Christian understanding of the divinity of Christ. But the notion that the messiah was Son of God in a special sense was rooted in Judaism, and so there was continuity between Judaism and Christianity in this respect, even though Christian belief eventually diverged quite radically from its Jewish sources.

NOTES

[1] An earlier version of this chapter appeared as "The '*Son of God*' Text from Qumran," in M. de Boer, ed., *From Jesus to John*, 65–82.

[2] J. A. Fitzmyer, "The Contribution of Qumran Aramaic to the Study of the New Testament," *New Testament Studies* 20(1973–74) 382–407; reprinted in his *A Wandering Aramean. Collected Aramaic Essays* (Society of Biblical Literature Monograph Series 25; Chico, CA: Scholars Press, 1979) 85–113. See also his comments in *The Gospel According to Luke I–IX* (Anchor Bible 28; Garden City, N.Y.: Doubleday, 1981) 205–6, 347–48.

[3] D. Flusser, "The Hubris of the Antichrist in a Fragment from Qumran," *Immanuel* 10(1980) 31–37; reprinted in his *Judaism and the Origins of Christianity* (Jerusalem: Magnes, 1988) 207–13.

[4] F. García Martínez, "4Q 246: Tipo del Anticristo o Libertador Escatologico?" in *El Misterio de la Palabra* (Homenaje al profesor L. Alonso Schökel: Valencia/Madrid, 1983) 229–44, reprinted as "The eschatological figure of 4Q246," in his *Qumran and Apocalyptic. Studies on the Aramaic Texts from Qumran* (Leiden: Brill, 1992) 162–79.

[5] E. Puech, "Fragment d'une Apocalypse en Araméen (4Q246 = pseudo-Dan^d) et le 'Royaume de Dieu,'" *Revue Biblique* 99(1992) 98–131. See now also J. A. Fitzmyer, "4Q246: The 'Son of God' Document from Qumran," *Biblica* 74(1993) 153–74.

[6] Puech, "Fragment," 105.

[7] See Puech, "Fragment," 117.

[8] Puech, "Fragment," 121. Cf. Ps 88:5. Alternatively, "help, succor."

[9] Puech, "Fragment," 121, reads as participle.

[10] Milik's interpretation is reported by Fitzmyer, *A Wandering Aramean*, 92.

[11] Puech, "Fragment," 127. Puech contends (p. 115) that the terminology could be drawn from the "reformed" Jerusalem cult in the time of Antiochus Epiphanes, but there is no evidence that such titles were ever used with reference to a Seleucid king.

[12] A. D. Nock, review of H.-J. Schoeps, *Die Theologie des Apostels im Lichte der jüdischen Religionsgeschichte*, in *Gnomon* 33(1961) 584.

[13] Cross continues to defend a messianic interpretation in private correspondence.

[14] Puech, "Fragment," 127.

[15] Fitzmyer's objections to the messianic interpretation are developed at length in his article "4Q246," 170–73.

[16] Fitzmyer, *A Wandering Aramean*, 92–93. It is not clear to me how Fitzmyer can simultaneously take the text to refer to an heir to the Davidic throne, in an apocalyptic con-

text, and yet say that "there is no indication that he was regarded as an anointed agent of Yahweh. Hence this text supplies no evidence for the alleged messianic use of the title 'Son of God' in pre-Christian Palestinian Judaism" (ibid., 106).

[17] Fitzmyer, "4Q246," 173–74.

[18] Seyoon Kim, *The 'Son of Man' as the Son of God* (Tübingen: Mohr-Siebeck, 1983) 22.

[19] Flusser, *Judaism and the Origins of Christianity*, 212; Lactantius, *Divinae Institutiones* 7.17.2–4.

[20] See J. R. Hinnells, "The Zoroastrian Doctrine of Salvation in the Roman World: A Study of the Oracle of Hystaspes," in E. J. Sharpe and J. R. Hinnells, eds., *Man and His Salvation: Studies in Memory of S. G. F. Brandon* (Manchester: Manchester University Press, 1973) 125–48. Hinnells defends the Persian origin of the oracle, but does not include this passage among the fragments.

[21] This point is made well by García Martínez, "4Q 246," 242.

[22] See the recent review of the evidence in G. C. Jenks, *The Origin and Early Development of the Antichrist Myth* (Beihefte zur Zeitschrift für die Alttestamentliche Wissenschaft 59; Berlin: de Gruyter, 1991).

[23] García Martínez, "The eschatological figure," 178.

[24] M. Hengel, *The Son of God* (Philadelphia: Fortress, 1976) 44.

[25] Two other verbal reminiscences of Daniel may be noted. The word וּשְׁנוֹךְ (the verb "to change," with a second person pronominal suffix that would normally be attached to a noun) at 1:2 recalls the expression זִיוֹהִי שְׁנוֹהִי (his expression changed) at Dan 5:6, where the suffix is also attached to the verb. (I owe this observation to F. M. Cross.) The verb יְשַׁמְּשׁוּן (will serve) at 1:8 also occurs at Dan 7:10, where the service is rendered to God ("a thousand thousands served him").

[26] Puech, "Fragment," 129. This suggestion is consonant with his suggestion that the Son of God figure may refer to Antiochus Epiphanes.

[27] Against Fitzmyer, *A Wandering Aramean*, 92.

[28] See further Collins, *The Apocalyptic Vision of the Book of Daniel*, 116–17.

[29] 4QpIsᵃ col. 3, fragment 7.26. See Horgan, *Pesharim*, 76.

[30] So Kim, *The Son of Man*, 21.

[31] See A. Mertens, *Das Buch Daniel im Lichte der Texte vom toten Meer* (Stuttgart: Echter, 1971) 79.

[32] See, however, Carol Newsom, "'Sectually Explicit' Literature from Qumran," in W. H. Propp, B. Halpern and D. N. Freedman, eds., *The Hebrew Bible and its Interpreters* (Winona Lake, IN: Eisenbrauns, 1990) 176–77, who questions whether the dualistic terminology of the War Scroll is necessarily sectarian.

[33] So, e.g., L. F. Hartman and A. A. DiLella, *The Book of Daniel* (Anchor Bible 23; Garden City, NY: Doubleday, 1978) 85–102.

[34] So, e.g., Collins, *The Apocalyptic Vision*, 144–46; and *Daniel*, 304–10; A. Lacocque, *The Book of Daniel* (Atlanta: Knox, 1979) 133; C. Rowland, *The Open Heaven* (New York: Crossroad, 1982) 182.

[35] On the traditional interpretation see A. J. Ferch, *The Son of Man in Daniel 7* (Berrien Springs, MI: Andrews University Press, 1979) 4–12; for a recent defense of a messianic interpretation see G. R. Beasley-Murray, "The Interpretation of Daniel 7," *Catholic Biblical Quarterly* 45(1983) 44–58.

[36] P. A. H. de Boer, "The Son of God in the Old Testament," *Oudtestamentische Studiën* 18(1973) 188–201; Fitzmyer, *A Wandering Aramean*, 104; G. P. Wetter, *Der Sohn Gottes*

(Göttingen: Vandenhoeck & Ruprecht, 1916); Jarl Fossum, "Son of God," in Freedman, ed., *The Anchor Bible Dictionary* 6.128–37.

[37] P. W. Skehan, "A Fragment of the 'Song of Moses' (Deuteronomy 32) from Qumran," *Bulletin of the American Schools of Oriental Research* 136(1954) 12–15.

[38] García Martínez, "The Eschatological Figure," 178.

[39] *1 Enoch* 62:5,9, compare 48:5, where all those who dwell on the earth fall down and worship before him.

[40] T. N. D. Mettinger, *King and Messiah. The Civil and Sacral Legitimation of the Israelite Kings* (Lund: Gleerup, 1976) 254–93.

[41] Fitzmyer, "4Q246," 171.

[42] Ibid.

[43] On the anointing of kings, see Mettinger, *King and Messiah*, 165–232.

[44] Fitzmyer, "4Q246," 174.

[45] Despite the contention of Fitzmyer, *The Gospel According to Luke*, 1.206.

[46] Fitzmyer, *The Gospel According to Luke*, 1.206. Consequently, Fitzmyer's argument that the identification of Jesus as God's Son goes beyond his identification as Davidic messiah (ibid. 339) is very dubious. He reaffirms his position in "4Q246," 173.

[47] P. Skehan, "Two Books on Qumran Studies," *Catholic Biblical Quarterly* 21(1959) 74.

[48] Cross, *The Ancient Library of Qumran*, 87.

[49] See Schiffman, *The Eschatological Community of the Dead Sea Scrolls*, 54.

[50] This passage was brought to my attention by Harold W. Attridge.

[51] The evidence is laid out clearly in M. E. Stone, *Fourth Ezra* (Hermeneia; Minneapolis: Fortress, 1990) 208.

[52] Ibid., 207.

[53] On the relation between the titles "son of David" and "son of God" (with reference to Rom 1:3–4), see M. de Jonge, "Jesus, Son of David and Son of God," in *Jewish Eschatology, Early Christian Christology and the Testaments of the Twelve Patriarchs. Collected Essays of Marinus de Jonge* (Leiden: Brill, 1991) 135–44.

[54] Puech, "Fragment," 129.

[55] Compare *Ps Sol* 17:34: "The Lord himself is his king, the hope of the one who has a strong hope in God." God is also said to sustain the "shoot of David" in 4QpIsa[a] column 3, fragment 7.23.

[56] The phrase, "the Son of God" is probably a secondary addition in this verse. On the textual problems involved see Adela Yarbro Collins, "Establishing the Text: Mark 1:1," in David Hellholm and Tord Fornberg, eds., *Texts and Contexts: The Function of Biblical Texts in Their Textual and Situative Contexts* (San Francisco: Mellen, forthcoming).

[57] D. R. Cartlidge and D. L. Dungan, *Documents for the Study of the Gospels* (Philadelphia: Fortress, 1980) 129–36.

[58] Plutarch, *Alexander*, 2.1–3.2.

[59] Suetonius, *Lives of the Caesars*, 2.94.1–7.

[60] Diogenes Laertius, *Lives of Eminent Philosophers*, 3.1–2, 45; Origen, *Against Celsus*, 1.37.

[61] Iamblichus, *The Life of Pythagoras*, 3–10. Iamblichus regards the story that Apollo was the father of Pythagoras as simply a rumor.

[62] For an excellent analysis of the infancy narratives see Raymond Brown, *The Birth of the Messiah* (revised edition; New York: Doubleday, 1993).

[63] See R. M. Grant, *Jesus After the Gospels. The Christ of the Second Century* (Louisville: Westminster, 1990) on the developments down to the time of Irenaeus. A succinct summary

of the debates related to the Church Councils can be found in H. Chadwick, *The Early Church* (Harmondsworth: Penguin, 1967) 192–212.

[64] R. Bultmann, *Theology of the New Testament* (New York: Scribners, 1951) 1.128–29.

[65] For a critique of some aspects of Bultmann's views, and of the History of Religions School from the late nineteenth and early twentieth centuries on which he drew, see Hengel, *The Son of God*, 17–56.

8

THE DANIELIC SON OF MAN

The "Son of God" text from Qumran suggests that Daniel 7 was understood with reference to a Davidic messiah from an early point. Such an interpretation is also reflected in Rabbi Akiba's famous exposition of the plural "thrones" in Dan 7:13 as "one for Him (God) and one for David."[1] It is also assumed in the statement attributed to the Jew Trypho in Justin's Dialogue: "These and other scriptures compel us to await one great and glorious, who receives the everlasting kingdom as son of man from the Ancient of Days."[2] The "one like a son of man" who comes with the clouds of heaven in Dan 7:13, however, also gave rise to a different kind of messianic expectation, which emphasized the heavenly, transcendent character of the savior figure. The heavenly "Son of Man" is attested in the *Similitudes of Enoch* and in *4 Ezra*, and also plays a prominent role in the New Testament.

For much of the twentieth century, the notion of a *Menschensohn*, or Son of Man figure, was thought to be independent of the Jewish scriptures, so that Dan 7:13 was a witness to it, but not the source from which it derived. There was considerable diversity of opinion about the origin and precise nature of this figure. More imaginative scholars, like Sigmund Mowinckel, held that "Conceptions of a more or less divine Primordial Man were widespread in the ancient east. Apparently there is a historical connexion between the varying figures of this type, which seem to be derived, directly or indirectly, from Iranian or Indo-Iranian myths."[3] The Jewish conception of "the Son of Man" was "a Jewish variant of this oriental, cosmological, eschatological myth of Anthropos,"[4] influenced by a syncretistic fusion of Iranian and Mesopotamian concepts. At the least, the phrase "Son of Man" was thought to be a well-known, readily recognizable title for a messiah of a heavenly type, in contrast to the national, earthly, Davidic messiah. As late as 1974 Norman Perrin could claim that all the recent studies of the "Son of Man Problem" he had reviewed agreed on one point: "there existed in ancient Judaism a defined concept of the apocalyptic Son of Man, the concept of a heavenly redeemer figure whose coming to earth as judge would be a feature of the drama of the End time."[5]

In the latter part of the century, however, the pendulum has swung away from this consensus. Already in 1968, Ragnar Leivestadt had declared the apocalyptic Son of Man to be a phantom,[6] and he followed this pronouncement with the directive "Exit the Apocalyptic Son of Man."[7] Perrin argued that "there is no 'Son of Man' concept but rather a variety of uses of Son of Man imagery."[8] The arguments of Geza Vermes on the Aramaic usage of the phrase "son of man" directed the discussion away from the apocalyptic texts. Vermes concluded that "no titular use of the phrase 'the son of man' can be substantiated" from Daniel, *1 Enoch* or *4 Ezra*, and that "the association between *ho huios tou anthropou* and Dan 7.13 constitutes a secondary midrashic stage of development, more understandable in Greek than in Aramaic."[9] Barnabas Lindars is typical of much recent scholarship when he declares the "Son of Man" concept to be "a modern myth."[10]

This critical reaction to the older *religionsgeschichtliche* theories is justified in some respects. The theory that derived the Son of Man from Iranian-Chaldean syncretism rested on the amalgamation of a cluster of different figures both in Judaism and in the Hellenistic Near East. In the Jewish context, the Son of Man figure was constructed by combining features from Daniel, *4 Ezra* and the *Similitudes*. Scholars rightly question the historical validity of such composite pictures. The notion that the Son of Man was a variant of a widespread myth of the Primordial Man has been laid to rest with no regrets. It is also now granted that "Son of Man" was not a title in common usage. The significance of the latter point, however, has been exaggerated, and the whole debate about titular usage has been too narrowly focused. It is, after all, possible to conceive of a figure to whom Daniel 7 and other texts refer even if there is some variation in the manner of reference. Consequently, some issues remain in dispute. There have been some new suggestions in recent years that at least Daniel and *4 Ezra* refer to a figure derived, not from oriental syncretism, but from specific Canaanite or Babylonian sources.[11] These proposals are unconvincing, in my judgment. Daniel 7 remains the source of Jewish expectation of an apocalyptic Son of Man. There is good evidence, however, that by the first century CE there were some common assumptions about the figure in Daniel's vision that go beyond what is explicit in the biblical text. Whether or not these common assumptions are deemed to amount to a Son of Man concept, they are important for our understanding of Jewish eschatology in the first century.

◈ *Daniel 7*

There is no doubt that traditional imagery is used in Daniel 7. I believe that the ultimate source of this imagery can be found in the Canaanite myths of the second millennium, which speak of the rebellion of Yamm, the unruly sea, and the triumph of Baal, the rider of the clouds.[12] This imagery had long been adapted in Israelite religion, and had its *Sitz-im-Leben* in the royal cult in the preexilic period.[13] We do not know precisely from what source Daniel derived it, but that is hardly surprising in the present state of our knowledge of Jewish religion prior to the Maccabean revolt.

The question of traditional imagery must be distinguished from the question of literary sources. One scholarly tradition, represented by Martin Noth, and recently by Rollin Kearns, has held that a pre-Danielic "Son of Man" source can be distinguished in Daniel 7:9–10, 13–14.[14] These verses are marked off from their context as poetry in the standard edition of the Hebrew Bible, *Biblia Hebraica Stuttgartensia*, but many commentators have been reluctant to conclude that a switch from prose to poetry requires a change of authorship. Besides, the poetic character of vss. 13–14 has been questioned.[15] The parallelism of classical Hebrew poetry is lacking in vs. 13, and the whole chapter is written in a rhythmic style. Noth argued that the *Similitudes of Enoch* knew only these verses of Daniel 7,[16] but his conclusion has been questioned on the ground that a number of other allusions are possible.[17] Even if the author does not allude to any other part of Daniel, we cannot safely conclude that he was not acquainted with it, only that he was selective in his allusions. Since he clearly alludes to some verses in Daniel 7, and since these verses are not attested outside of Daniel, the simplest conclusion is that he drew on the Book of Daniel, rather than on its hypothetical source.[18]

Moreover, if the imagery of Daniel 7 is ultimately derived from Canaanite myth, the vision of the Ancient of Days and "one like a son of man" belongs to the same complex of tradition as the beasts from the sea, and so it is very unlikely that these verses circulated in isolation. Even apart from this consideration, many scholars think that the contrast between the beasts from the sea and the human figure is an intrinsic part of the vision, and this, too, militates against a distinct Son of Man source.

I have argued at length elsewhere that the "one like a son of man" in Daniel 7 should be understood as a heavenly individual, probably the archangel Michael, rather than as a collective symbol.[19] The expectation of angelic, heavenly savior figures is well attested in the Dead Sea Scrolls. The "Treatise of the Two Spirits" in the Community Rule declares that God has given humanity "two spirits in which to walk until the time of his visitation, the spirits of truth and falsehood. . . . All the children of righteousness are ruled by the Prince of Light and walk in the ways of light, but all the children of falsehood are ruled by the Angel of Darkness." The Prince of Light reappears in the War Scroll (1QM 13), where he is opposed to "Belial, the angel of Mastema."[20] In 1QM 17:7, God raises up the kingdom of Michael among the gods (אלים) and the kingdom of Israel among all flesh. In 11QMelchizedek, the god (אלהים) who rises in the heavenly council and administers divine judgment is called Melchizedek. It seems likely, however, that Michael, Melchizedek and the Prince of Light were three names for the same figure, and that the dualism of the princes of light and darkness was already laid out in the Testament of Amram in the middle of the second century BCE.[21] This dualism involved a significant development beyond what is found in the book of Daniel[22] but shared with the older apocalypse the expectation of deliverance by the hand of an angel. Quite apart from Qumran dualism we also find an angelic deliverer in the *Testament (Assumption) of Moses*, around the turn of the era ("Then will be filled the hands of the messenger who is in the highest place appointed. Yea, he will at once avenge them of their enemies").[23] These angelic saviors are not properly called messiahs, as they are not anointed and in any case are not human figures. They are, however, immediately relevant to the development of traditions relating to the Son of Man.[24]

▨ *The* Similitudes of Enoch

The earliest Jewish evidence for the interpretation and reuse of Dan 7:13–14 is found in the *Similitudes of Enoch*. The date of this document has been controversial, especially since no fragment of it has been found at Qumran.[25] Absence from Qumran, however, does not require a date after 70 CE. Other pseudepigrapha whose early date is not disputed, such as the *Psalms of Solomon* and the *Testament of Moses*, are also unattested in the Scrolls. It has been suggested that the *Similitudes* would have been unacceptable at Qumran because of the near equality of the sun and the moon in chapter 41.[26] In any case, the "community of the righteous" presupposed in the *Similitudes* (e.g. 38:1) was a different conventicle from that of Qumran. If the document was produced in the latter years of the Qumran sect, in a different community, it is not surprising that it had not found its way into the Dead Sea library. It is doubtful whether a Jewish author would have made such explicit use of the expression "Son of Man" for a messianic figure after that phrase had been appropriated by the Christians. On the other hand, the influence of the *Similitudes* should be recognized in Matt 19:28, 25:31, where the Son of Man is said to sit on his throne of glory.[27] Since the *Similitudes* make no allusion to the fall of Jerusalem, a date prior to that event seems most likely.

It is beyond doubt that the *Similitudes of Enoch* allude to Dan 7:9–10, 13–14. The clearest allusions are in *1 Enoch* 46:1: "And there I saw one who had a head of days, and his head (was) white like wool; and with him (there was) another, whose face had the appearance of a man . . ." and in *1 Enoch* 47:3: "And in those days I saw the Head of Days sit down on the throne of his glory, and the books of the living were opened before him, and all his host, which (dwells) in the heavens above, and his council were standing before him."[28] The "Head of Days" is the Enochic equivalent of the "Ancient of Days" in Daniel 7, and the one who accompanies him is Daniel's "one like a son of man." The Son of Man figure in the *Similitudes* is initially introduced as one "whose face had the appearance of a man" (46:1). Enoch then asks his angelic guide "about that son of man, who he was and whence he was. . . ." The angel responds that he is "the son of man who has righteousness, and with whom righteousness dwells. . . ." The manner in which he is introduced does not presuppose that "Son of Man" is a well-known title; it is simply a way of referring back to the figure "whose face had the appearance of a man," while simultaneously recalling Daniel 7.[29] The same figure can also be referred to as "the Chosen One," or "the Righteous One."[30] He is also said to be "like one of the holy angels" (46:2). Angels are often portrayed in human form in apocalyptic literature (compare Dan 8:15; 9:21; 10:5, 18; 12:6–7). While the "Son of Man" is distinguished from other angels (Michael in 60:4–5; 69:14; 71:3; the four archangels in 71:8, 9, 13), his rank is higher than theirs.[31]

It is generally held that this "Son of Man" is identified with Enoch himself at the end of the *Similitudes*. In *1 Enoch* 71:14, Enoch is greeted by an angel on his ascent to heaven: "You are the Son of Man who was born to righteousness, and righteousness remains over you and the righteousness of the Head of Days will not leave you."[32] As is well known, R. H. Charles removed this anomaly by emending the text, a procedure now universally rejected.[33] The supposed identification, however, remains problematic.[34]

1 Enoch 70–71 constitute an epilogue to the *Similitudes*. First, there is an introductory statement in 70:1–2, in the third person, that "after this" Enoch was lifted up from humankind. Then the narrative switches to the first person, with Enoch as narrator. There is some literary support here for a redactional seam, although the point is not conclusive.[35] The third person narrative, however, clearly distinguishes Enoch from "that Son of Man." In *1 Enoch* 70:1 we are told "And it came to pass after this that his name was lifted up alive to the presence of that Son of Man, in the presence of the Lord of Spirits." Attempts to get rid of this reading are scarcely less tendentious than those of Charles.[36] It is true that one important manuscript, Abbadianus 55 (U), omits the word *baxabehu*,[37] "to the presence," before "that Son of Man,"[38] and can be translated "that the name of that son of man was lifted up alive to the presence of the Lord of Spirits."[39] The omission, however, may be simple mechanical error: R. H. Charles wrote of this manuscript that "the omissions are capriciously made; sometimes words, sometimes phrases, sometimes whole sentences and paragraphs are excised to the entire destruction of the sense."[40] If one thinks in terms of scribal alteration, Abbadianus 55 should be rejected as the easier reading: a scribe is more likely to have harmonized the text of Abbadianus 55 by bringing 70:1 into agreement with 71:14 than to have introduced the apparent contradiction presented by the majority reading.[41]

J. C. VanderKam, who recognizes that the reading in *1 Enoch* 70:1, which seems to distinguish between Enoch and the Son of Man, cannot be eliminated, nonetheless argues that "What the author appears to have intended in 70:1 was that Enoch's name was elevated to the place where those characters whom he had seen in his visions were to be found, namely in the throneroom of the celestial palace. That is, he does not see the son of man here but begins his ascent to the place where he himself will perform that eschatological role."[42] VanderKam's desire to make sense of the text as it stands, without recourse to the hypothesis of redaction, is commendable. It does not seem to me, however, that his suggestion here is a possible interpretation of the Ethiopic text. Enoch's name was lifted to, or *to the presence of* that Son of Man and to the presence of the Lord of Spirits, (Eth *baxabehu*),[43] not to the place where he had seen them or to perform their roles. *1 Enoch* 70:1, then, makes a clear distinction between Enoch and the Son of Man, which cannot be avoided. This distinction, in fact, seems to be presupposed throughout the *Similitudes*, where Enoch sees the Son of Man without any suggestion that he is seeing himself.

The distinction between Enoch and the Son of Man in 70:1 is also crucial for another disputed question in the *Similitudes*: the preexistence of the Son of Man. According to *1 Enoch* 48:3: "Even before the sun and the constellations were created, before the stars of heaven were made, his name was named before the Lord of Spirits." The act of naming is closely related to creation—compare Ps 147:4 where Yahweh names the stars.[44] Also the name often stands for the person, as in *1 Enoch* 70:1 where the *name* of Enoch is raised aloft. Consequently, *1 Enoch* 48:3 seems to mean that the Son of Man was created before the sun and the stars. Moreover, 48:3 adds that "he was chosen and hidden before him before the world was created." It seems reasonable to assume that he had to exist in order to be hidden. Yet a number of scholars have held with T. W. Manson that preexistence here only means "a project in the mind of God."[45] So recently VanderKam suggests that "perhaps, then, the hiding refers to no more than a suppression of his identity." For VanderKam, a crucial question is whether any text shows the Son of Man as already existing in heaven during Enoch's earthly life. Precisely such a text is provided by 70:1, where Enoch, at the end of his life, is exalted to the presence of the Son of Man. If the Son of Man was already present in heaven in the antediluvian period, then the texts in chapter 48 can reasonably be interpreted to mean that he was created, like wisdom, before the creation of the earth.

What then of the apparent identification with Enoch in 71:14? In an earlier study of this passage I took the position that 71:14 was a secondary addition to the *Similitudes*, possibly a Jewish rejoinder to the Christian identification of Jesus with the Danielic Son of Man. This still seems possible. As noted above, the transition from third person to first person at 71:3 lends some support to a redactional theory, even if it doesn't require it. The apparent identification of Enoch with the Son of Man at 71:14 remains a problem, however, even for a redactor. If the two figures are indeed identified, then the author, or redactor, must have regarded Enoch as the heavenly man incarnate, although Enoch was apparently unaware of his own identity throughout his visions, and was separated from his heavenly form during his earthly career.[46] Alternatively, we would have to suppose that Enoch's identity was somehow merged with that of a being from whom he was previously distinct. In the later *Sefer Hekhalot*, or *3 Enoch*, Metatron, "the little Yahweh" declares that he is Enoch, son of Jared, who was taken up in the generation of the Flood (4:3–5), enlarged until he matched the world in length and breadth (9:2) and installed on a throne of glory (10:1).[47] In this case, however, it would seem that the human Enoch is transformed into a new angel, rather than merged with one already in heaven.

It is possible that the *Similitudes* identify Enoch with the Son of Man in a way that has no exact parallel, but it now seems to me that a more plausible solution can be found. *1 Enoch* 71:14 is one of two passages in the *Similitudes* where "son of man" is used in direct address. In 60:10 an angel calls Enoch "son of man" after the manner of Ezekiel, but this passage has usually been discounted as part of a Noahic fragment, and from a different author. It serves to remind us, however, that in itself the phrase "son of man" only means "human being." Usually in the *Similitudes*, the reference is specified by the use of the demonstrative. "That Son of Man" is the figure Enoch saw in chapter 46, and simultaneously the figure of Daniel's vision. Where the demonstrative is lacking, it is usually rendered superfluous by the context: 62:7 follows an occurrence with the demonstrative in 62:5 and 69:27 follows an occurrence in 69:26. The greeting addressed to Enoch in 71:14 is exceptional in this regard. In fact, the Ethiopic greeting *'anta we'etu walda be'esi* could even be translated "you are *a* son of man . . ." since Ethiopic has no definite or indefinite article, and the word *we'etu* here functions as a copula rather than as a demonstrative.[48] The possibility arises, then, that Enoch is not being identified with the Son of Man of his visions at all.[49]

The objection to this view is that 71:14 ("you are the son of man who was born to righteousness, . . . and the righteousness of the Head of Days will not leave you . . .") recalls the first appearance of "that Son of Man" with the Head of Days in 46:3 ("you are the son of man who has righteousness and with whom righteousness dwells").[50] Enoch is not being greeted simply as a human being, but as a very specific human being, in language closely related to that used for the heavenly Son of Man. He is not necessarily identified with the heavenly figure, however. Throughout the *Similitudes*, there is close parallelism between the elect and the holy in heaven and their counterparts on earth.[51] So in 38:1–2 we read "When the community of the righteous appears . . . and when the Righteous One appears before the chosen righteous. . . ." The Son of Man is the preeminent Righteous One in heaven, the supernatural double not of the individual Enoch but of all righteous human beings. Insofar as Enoch is preeminent among righteous human beings he has a unique affinity with the heavenly Son of Man. Moreover, there is a significant variation between 71:14 and the earlier passage. In 46:3 the Son of Man simply "has" righteousness; in 71:14 he "was born to righteousness."[52] Enoch, then, is a human being in the likeness of the heavenly Son of Man, and is exalted to share his destiny. According to *1 Enoch* 62:14 and 71:17, other righteous human beings, too, will enjoy length of days with *that* Son of Man. Enoch is first among the earth-born righteous. He must still be distinguished, however, from his heavenly counterpart.

The figure of the Son of Man in the *Similitudes* shows considerable development over against Daniel's "one like a son of man." In later, rabbinic, tradition the name of the messiah is listed among the things that preceded the creation of the world.[53] The Son of Man is equated with the messiah in *1 Enoch* 48:10 and 52:4. While the title messiah plays a minor role in the *Similitudes*, it is all the more significant that the identification of messiah and Son of Man can be assumed. Daniel's "one like a son of man" appears after the judgment of the beasts/kingdoms. In the *Similitudes* he is said to cast down kings from their thrones and from their kingdoms, and he takes his seat on his throne of glory as judge (62:5; 69:29). He also has the role of revealer.[54] In many respects he seems to be assimilated to the Deity (who also sits on the throne of his glory). In 48:5, people fall down and worship him.[55]

In view of the aggrandizement of the Son of Man in the *Similitudes*, many scholars have assumed that the figure is informed by non-Jewish traditions.[56] This assumption has been seriously challenged in recent years.[57] Some new elements in the *Similitudes* can be seen to arise from ambiguities in the text of Daniel. Some are suggested by other biblical passages, or are required by the context of the *Similitudes* themselves. The fact that "thrones were set" in Dan 7:9 led naturally enough to the inference that one of them was for the "Son of Man" figure. It was a short step from there to the assumption that he had an active role in the judgment. That he will cast down the kings from their thrones corresponds to the destruction of the beasts/kingdoms in Daniel. The books opened in *1 Enoch* 47:3 are not the books of judgment as in Daniel 7 but rather the books of life as in Dan 12:1. The apparition of the figure on the clouds in Daniel could easily suggest preexistence. The portrait of the Son of Man figure was filled out with reminiscences of preexistent Wisdom (Proverbs 8), which was also a revealer, and of the hidden servant of the Lord (Isa 49:2: "in his quiver he hid me away").[58] There are also messianic overtones, even apart from the use of the title messiah. The account of the Chosen One in *1 Enoch* 62:2 ("the spirit of righteousness was poured out on him and the word of his mouth kills all the sinners . . .") recalls Isa 11:2, 4.[59] The motif of a second figure enthroned beside God has its clearest precedent in Psalm 110, another royal passage.[60] Nonetheless, he is not a Davidic messiah in any conventional sense. He does not establish a kingdom on earth. Rather, some attributes traditionally associated with the Davidic messiah are here transferred to a heavenly savior figure.

The Enochic Son of Man cannot be adequately understood only in terms of allusions to texts and traditions. The *Similitudes* were not composed for the sake of expounding Daniel, but to articulate the worldview of a particular group of Jews in the first century CE. The Son of Man is an integral part of the symbolic world of the *Similitudes*. Fundamental to that worldview is the belief in a hidden world where the power structures of this world are reversed. The Son of Man is the heavenly counterpart of the righteous on earth.[61] While they are oppressed and lowly, he is enthroned and exalted. When he is manifested at the eschatological judgment, they will be exalted, too. The *Similitudes*, then, make creative use of Daniel 7 to develop their own new expression of the faith and hope of the righteous.

While they are not primarily a work of interpretation, however, the *Similitudes* remain an important witness to the early understanding of Daniel. They take for granted that Daniel's "one like a son of man" is a heavenly individual of very exalted status. While they offer no reason to think that this figure was known independently of Daniel, they show how the Danielic text inspired visions of a heavenly savior figure in first century Judaism.

▨ Fourth Ezra

Daniel 7 is also reflected in *4 Ezra* 13, a Jewish apocalypse from the end of the first century CE.[62] There Ezra reports:

> "Then after seven days, I had a dream in the night. I saw a wind rising from the sea that stirred up all its waves. As I kept looking, that wind brought up out of the depths of the sea something resembling a man and that man was flying with the clouds of heaven. . . ."

The apocalypse was certainly composed in a Semitic language,[63] but is only extant in several versions, of which the Latin and Syriac are most important. The statement "that wind brought up out of the sea something resembling a man" is missing in the Latin, apparently because of *homoioteleuton*. Most scholars assume that the missing passage read *homo* for "man" since this is what the Latin uses elsewhere in the chapter, and the Ethiopic has *be'esi*, man.[64] The Syriac, however, reads ʾyk ḏmwtʾ ḏbrnšʾ, which suggests that the original may have read "son of man," (בן אדם or בר אנשא), and it can be argued that the author used the longer phrase initially and the shorter "man" thereafter.[65] A further textual problem concerns the relation between the wind and the man. The Ethiopic version reads "this wind came out of the sea in the resemblance of a man." It has been argued that this is the *lectio difficilior*, and that "wind" is a misconstrual of the רוח/רוחא, "spirit."[66] This reading is dubious at best, and most scholars restore the Latin on the basis of the Syriac, which has the wind bring the man up.[67]

Regardless of the precise terminology, most scholars take the man flying with the clouds as a clear allusion here to Daniel 7.[68] There is no doubt that *4 Ezra* knew and used Daniel, and specifically Daniel 7. In *4 Ezra* 12:11 the interpreting angel tells Ezra explicitly: "The eagle you observed coming up out of the sea is the fourth kingdom that appeared in a vision to Daniel your brother. But it was not interpreted to him in the same way that I now interpret it to you." Since this reference to the four-kingdom motif comes in the vision immediately preceding *4 Ezra* 13, it is *prima facie* probable that the vision of the man from the sea is also based on Daniel 7. Moreover, the interpretation in chapter 13 provides an unmistakable allusion to Daniel 2, when it says that the mountain on which the man takes his stand was "carved out without hands"—a detail not mentioned in the vision.

Michael Stone has argued strongly that the vision (*4 Ezra* 13:1–13) is an independent piece, reinterpreted but not composed by the author of *4 Ezra*.[69] The interpretation contains extensive material that is not directly connected to the vision. The description of eschatological woes in vss. 29–38 is introduced to explain the fire and tempest that come from the man's mouth. It refers back to the vision at several points, but is rather circuitous as an interpretation. The host that the man collects is identified as the ten lost tribes, which then become the subject of a digression (vss. 40–46). The companions of the man are introduced in vs. 52 although they were not mentioned in the vision (but cf. 7:28). The order of interpretation is also confused: the sea, which appears at the beginning of the vision is not interpreted until vss. 51–52. Stone notes the contrast with *4 Ezra* 12, where the interpretation follows the vision closely, and concludes that "only the attempt to give a new interpretation to a vision which he had before him" can explain the data.[70]

While it may seem unduly complicated to argue that *4 Ezra* used both Daniel 7 (explicitly in chapter 12) and another source that itself depended on Daniel 7 (in chapter 13), the cumulative weight of Stone's arguments is compelling, especially in view of the contrast with chapter 12.[71] The strongest argument concerns the eschatological woes. These provide the context for the interpretation of the vision, but we should expect that if the same author had composed the vision he would have represented the context therein, and laid an adequate foundation for the interpretation. Even if the vision was originally independent, however, the figure flying on the clouds must still be understood as an allusion to Daniel 7. The vision cannot be taken as evidence for a "Son of Man" concept independent of Daniel 7. Moreover, the allusion to Daniel 7 must have been recognized by the author of *4 Ezra*: hence the placement of the vision immediately after the explicit reference to Daniel in chapter 12.

In the interpretation, the "man" of the vision is identified as "he whom the Most High has been keeping for many ages, who will himself deliver his creation" (vs. 26). This figure is further identified, in the Latin and Syriac versions, as "my son" (13:37, 52) and thereby with the messiah, who is called "my son" in 7:28.[72] We have noted in the preceding chapter that *4 Ezra* 13:33–38, which deal with the assault of the Gentiles on Mount Zion, are reminiscent of Psalm 2.[73] In the Psalm, the Lord says: "I have set my king on Zion my holy mountain," and continues in the next verse: "you are my son, this day I have begotten you." In *4 Ezra* 13, too, the messiah takes his stand on Mount Zion (13:35). In any case, it is clear that the man of the vision is identified with the messiah in the context of *4 Ezra*. This identification is probably implicit already in the vision, where the man takes his stand on a mountain and burns up the attacking multitude with a fiery breath: compare Psalm 2 and Isaiah 11, where the shoot from the stump of Jesse will kill the wicked with the breath of his lips. The motif of gathering the people (13:12–13) is associated with the messiah in *Psalms of Solomon* 17:26.

Stone has written that "even if the man in the dream was the traditional 'Son of Man,' the author had to interpret that figure to his readers. Moreover, the author has shorn the Son of Man of all his particular characteristics in the interpretation and treated him as a symbol. This would be inconceivable if the Son of Man concept was readily recognizable to him and his readers."[74] Presumably, by "the Son of Man concept" Stone means the composite Primordial Man of the old "history of religions school," which is certainly not implied in *4 Ezra*. It can hardly be doubted, however, that an allusion to Dan 7:13 was readily recognizable to both the author of the interpretation and his readers. The fact that an interpretation follows does not necessarily mean that the vision would have been unfamiliar or unintelligible. Interpretations were a conventional part of the apocalyptic genre, and provided an opportunity for the author to give a new twist to familiar, traditional symbolism. The statement that this figure is treated as a symbol also requires some qualification. Apocalyptic symbols may be either allegorical or mythic-realistic. So for example, the beasts in Daniel 7 are allegorical symbols that stand for something else (kings or kingdoms), but the Ancient of Days is a mythic-realistic representation of God, and is identified rather than interpreted. In *4 Ezra* 13 the man is clearly a mythic-realistic representation of the messiah: "then my son will be revealed, whom you saw as a man coming up from the sea" (13:32). So, while the author shows no awareness of a Hellenistic-oriental myth of a "Primordial Man," he is surely offering an interpretation (or reinterpretation) of Daniel's "one like a son of man."

Like the *Similitudes of Enoch*, *4 Ezra* 13 contains much that is not explicit in Daniel's vision. The vision is reminiscent of traditional theophanies of the divine warrior. All who hear the voice of the man melt before it, as the mountains traditionally melted before the Lord. The man then takes a much more active part in the destruction and judgment of the wicked than was the case in Daniel. The interpretation of the figure owes much more to traditional messianic motifs than to Daniel 7.

Unlike the *Similitudes of Enoch*, *4 Ezra* has a developed notion of a Davidic messiah. In 7:28–29 he is called "my son (or servant) the messiah."

He is "revealed with those who are with him," a formulation that seems to imply preexistence. They "rejoice four hundred years." Then the messiah dies, the world reverts to primeval silence for seven days and the resurrection follows. This scenario has no clear precedent in earlier traditions, but has some interesting parallels in other works of the late first century CE. In *2 Baruch* 29–30 the messiah "shall begin to be revealed," and Behemoth and Leviathan shall return from the sea to serve as food for all that survive. A period of wonderful fertility follows, after which the messiah "will return in glory." The Christian book of Revelation naturally gives prominence to the death of the messiah. More remarkably, it also provides for two resurrections rather than one. The elect who share in the first resurrection reign with Christ for a thousand years (Rev 20:4). In each of these apocalypses there seems to be an attempt to combine different eschatological traditions, one of which looks for a kingdom on this earth while the other looks for resurrection of the dead and a new creation, by having each tradition define a stage in the eschatological process.[75]

A more traditional account of the messiah is found in *4 Ezra* 11–12. Here he appears as a lion, symbolizing his Judahite descent (cf. Gen 49:9–10). The lion is interpreted explicitly as "the Messiah whom the Most High has kept until the end of days, who will arise from the offspring of David" (12:32). The lion confronts an eagle, symbolizing Rome, which is further identified as the fourth beast of Daniel's vision (12:11). The messiah will denounce Rome for ungodliness, then "he will bring them alive before his judgment seat, and when he has reproved them, then he will destroy them" (12:33). He will then set free "the remnant of my people." This judgment scene is presumably the same as the one described in chapter 13, which, as we have seen, also draws on traditional messianic imagery. Since the messiah is "revealed" in *4 Ezra*, he can readily be identified with the figure who comes on the clouds. Unlike the *Similitudes*, however, the judgment takes place on earth and is associated with the restoration of the Jewish people. In short, the messianic imagery defines the savior figure here to a much greater degree than in the *Similitudes*.

Yet the understanding of the messiah is also modified by the correlation with the "Son of Man" figure. As Stone has noted, "Kingship nowhere figures in the concept of the Messiah" in *4 Ezra*, and his Davidic descent (12:32) is "a traditional element and not at all central to the concepts of the book."[76] Rather, he is a preexistent, transcendent figure, whom the Most High has been keeping for many ages.

The Danielic Son of Man

The relation of *4 Ezra* 13 to the *Similitudes of Enoch* is also complex. On the whole, the "man from the sea" is very different from the Enochic Son of Man. The one is a warrior who takes his stand on a mountain and is concerned with the restoration of Israel and Zion. The other is a judge enthroned in heaven. There is no allusion to the *Similitudes* in *4 Ezra*, and there is no reason to posit literary influence between them.[77]

◈ *Common Assumptions*

Nonetheless, the *Similitudes* and *4 Ezra* have some common features that are significant for the understanding of Daniel 7 in the first century.

First, both assume that the "one like a son of man" in Daniel refers to an individual, and is not a collective symbol. In fact, the collective interpretation is not clearly attested in Jewish sources until Ibn Ezra.[78]

Second, this figure is identified in both works as the messiah, and the understanding of "messiah" is thereby qualified. The title messiah has only minor importance in the *Similitudes*, but the fact that it is still used there shows that it must have been commonly associated with the Danielic "Son of Man." This again is in accordance with the prevalent interpretation in early Jewish tradition.[79]

Third, he is preexistent: "the one whom the Most High has kept for many ages,"[80] and therefore a transcendent figure of heavenly origin, even if he also has a Davidic ancestry in *4 Ezra*. Both figures, in different ways, appropriate imagery traditionally reserved for God: the Enochic Son of Man sits on the throne of glory, and the figure in *4 Ezra* is portrayed in terms of the theophany of the divine warrior.[81] Even the association with the clouds in Daniel was a motif traditionally associated with the Deity.[82]

Fourth, this figure takes a more active role in the destruction of the wicked than was explicit in Daniel.

If "servant" rather than "son" is the original designation of the messiah in *4 Ezra*, then the possibility arises that both documents associate this figure with the Isaianic "servant of the Lord." In neither document, however, does the Son of Man figure undergo suffering. While the *Similitudes* contain some clear allusions to the text of Isaiah (e.g. 48:4, "light of the nations," cf. Isa 49:6), that is not the case in *4 Ezra* 13. At most, the motif of "hiddenness" may be derived from Isa 49:2 ("in his quiver he hid me away"). It would be quite misleading, however, to speak of a "suffering servant" in this connection.

The correspondences between *4 Ezra* and the *Similitudes* point to common assumptions about the interpretation of Daniel 7 in first-century Judaism. It is difficult to say how widespread these assumptions were. Allusions to Daniel 7:13–14 are conspicuously absent at Qumran (apart from the "Son of God" text, 4Q246), despite the heavy use of other parts of Daniel, especially chapter 11, in the Scrolls. However, there is no evidence of influence between the *Similitudes* and *4 Ezra*, and they were certainly not products of a single group. It is reasonable to suppose that their common assumptions were also shared by others in first-century Judaism.

The notion of a heavenly savior king, not explicitly called a messiah, is also found in the fifth *Sibylline Oracle*, a document of Egyptian Judaism from the late first or early second century CE.[83] Three passages in this oracle speak of a savior figure.[84] *Sib Or* 5:108–9 speaks briefly of "a certain king sent from God," (not necessarily from heaven). *Sib Or* 5:256–59 is Christian in its present form: "There will again be one exceptional man from the sky, who stretched out his hands on the fruitful wood, the best of the Hebrews, who will one day cause the sun to stand, speaking with fair speech and holy lips." The structure of the passage, however, requires a saving figure at this point,[85] and only the allusion to crucifixion is necessarily Christian. The notion of a Joshua-*redivivus*, however, might be inspired by the name of Jesus, and so the value of this passage as evidence for Jewish beliefs is suspect. *Sib Or* 5:414–33 speaks of "a blessed man from the expanses of heaven with a scepter in his hands which God gave him" in "the last time of holy ones." This latter passage brings Daniel 7 to mind, especially in view of the allusion to holy ones,[86] but it is not certain whether an allusion is intended. The passage does, in any case, emphasize the heavenly origin of the savior figure.

The notion of a king from heaven is not without parallel in the Hellenistic world outside of Judaism. The *Oracle of Hystaspes*, which is now widely recognized as a Persian-Hellenistic composition of the last century BCE, says that in a time of distress when the righteous are shut in and besieged, God will "send from heaven a great king to rescue and free them, and destroy all the wicked with fire and sword."[87] The identity of the "great king" in a Persian source is disputed. Hinnells argues for the Zoroastrian savior *Sōšyant*.[88] Colpe proposes a native Persian king.[89] There is no reason to posit Persian influence on any of the Jewish texts we have been considering, however. Such similarity in concepts as we find here can be adequately explained as a common reaction to the spread of Roman rule in the Orient.

The Danielic Son of Man

In Jewish writings the emphasis on the heavenly character of the savior king appears in texts of the first century CE, especially in the period after the failure of the first revolt against Rome and the destruction of the Temple (*4 Ezra, Sib Or 5*). We may suspect, then, that it reflects a certain disillusionment with messiahs of human, earthly origin. The disillusionment was not complete, as can be seen from the messianic revolts of the early second century. Also the hope for a heavenly deliverer, under God, is attested in the early apocalyptic literature, notably Daniel 7, and the heavenly messiah of the *Similitudes* is likely to be older than 70 CE. What we find in the writings of the first century CE, however, is a tendency to combine traditions about a Davidic messiah with the expectation of a heavenly savior. There was, then, some flexibility in the use of messianic traditions in this period. Daniel's "one like a son of man" could be understood either as a purely heavenly figure (in the *Similitudes*) or as a messiah who operates on earth to restore Israel (*4 Ezra*). Danielic imagery could be applied to the Davidic messiah to give him a more heavenly, transcendent character than is apparent in other sources. In short, "Davidic messiah" and "Son of Man" were not mutually exclusive concepts. Each involves a cluster of motifs, which could be made to overlap. Rather than two types, we should think of a spectrum of messianic expectation, ranging from the earthly messiah of the *Psalms of Solomon* and several Dead Sea Scrolls, through the transcendent messiah of *4 Ezra* to the heavenly figure of the *Similitudes of Enoch*. Perrin's conclusion that "there is no 'Son of Man' concept but rather a variety of uses of Son of Man imagery,"[90] can be defended, if we recognize that the variety is limited and does not negate the core of common assumptions either about the figure in Daniel's vision or about the Davidic messiah.

NOTES

[1] b. Ḥag 14a, b. Sanh. 38b. See Chrys C. Caragounis, *The Son of Man* (Tübingen: Mohr, 1986) 133–34. The suggestion of Maurice Casey, *Son of Man. The Interpretation and Influence of Daniel 7* (London: SPCK, 1979) 86–87, that the reference is to the historical David, is without any supporting parallel. See the comments of William Horbury, "The Messianic Associations of 'The Son of Man,'" *Journal of Theological Studies* 36(1985) 45–46.
[2] Justin, *Dialogue with Trypho*, 32. Justin's value as a witness to Jewish views remains in question.
[3] Sigmund Mowinckel, *He That Cometh. The Messiah Concept in Israel and Later Judaism* (Nashville: Abingdon, 1955) 422.
[4] Ibid., 425.

[5] Norman Perrin, *A Modern Pilgrimage in New Testament Christology* (Philadelphia: Fortress, 1974) 24.

[6] R. Leivestadt, "Der apokalyptische Menschensohn ein theologisches Phantom," *Annual of the Swedish Theological Institute* 6(1967–68) 49–109.

[7] R. Leivestadt, "Exit the Apocalyptic Son of Man," *New Testament Studies* 18(1971–72) 243–67.

[8] Perrin, *A Modern Pilgrimage*, 26.

[9] G. Vermes, *Jesus and the World of Judaism* (Philadelphia: Fortress, 1984) 96–98.

[10] B. Lindars, *Jesus, Son of Man* (Grand Rapids, MI: Eerdmans, 1983) 3.

[11] Canaanite: Rollin Kearns, *Vorfragen zur Christologie* (3 vols.; Tübingen: Mohr-Siebeck, 1978–82); Babylonian: Helge Kvanvig, *Roots of Apocalyptic* (Neukirchen-Vluyn: Neukirchener Verlag, 1988).

[12] Collins, "Stirring up the Great Sea," 121–36.

[13] See John Day, *God's Conflict with the Dragon and the Sea* (Cambridge: Cambridge University Press, 1985).

[14] Martin Noth, "Zur Komposition des Buches Daniel," *Theologische Studien und Kritiken* 98/99(1926) 143–63; Kearns, *Vorfragen zur Christologie* 2.16.

[15] S. Niditch, *The Symbolic Vision in Biblical Tradition* (Harvard Semitic Monographs 30; Chico, CA: Scholars Press, 1980) 190.

[16] Noth and Kearns claim that the author knew only Daniel's source. Karlheinz Müller, "Beobachtungen zur Entwicklung der Menschensohnvorstellung in den Bilderreden des Henoch und im Buche Daniel," in Ernst C. Suttner and Coelestin Patock, eds., *Wegzeichen. Festschrift H. M. Biedermann* (Würzburg: Augustinus-Verlag, 1971) 258, posits a common written source for the *Similitudes* and Dan 7:9, 10, 13.

[17] E.g. Theisohn, *Der auserwählte Richter*, 26–27, argues that *1 Enoch* 46:7 ("And these are they who judge the stars of heaven") depends on Dan 8:10. The case is stronger if one accepts the emendation of R. H. Charles, *The Ethiopic Version of the Book of Enoch* (Oxford: Clarendon, 1906) 88: "these are they who cast down the stars of heaven." For other possible reminiscences see Casey, *Son of Man*, 107–10.

[18] So also Volker Hampel, *Menschensohn und Historischer Jesus* (Neukirchen-Vluyn: Neukirchener Verlag, 1990) 42. Hampel, however, takes the unusual position that Dan 7:13–14 are secondary in the book of Daniel (ibid., 23).

[19] J. Collins, *Daniel*, 304–10.

[20] On this passage see J. L. Duhaime, "Dualistic Reworking in the Scrolls from Qumran," *Catholic Biblical Quarterly* 49(1987) 32–56.

[21] J. T. Milik, "*Milkî-sedeq et Milkî-resa'* dans les anciens écrits juifs et chrétiens," *Journal of Jewish Studies* 23(1972) 95–144; Kobelski, *Melchizedek*, 49–83.

[22] See my essay, "The Origin of Evil in Apocalyptic Literature and the Dead Sea Scrolls," in J. A. Emerton, ed., *Congress Volume, Paris* (Leiden: Brill).

[23] The consensus of scholarship is that the messenger is an angel. See Nickelsburg, *Resurrection, Immortality and Eternal Life*, 28–31. Tromp, "Taxo, the Messenger of the Lord," 202–5, reviews earlier interpretations, but argues that the messenger is the human figure Taxo.

[24] See Barnabas Lindars, "Re-enter the Apocalyptic Son of Man," *New Testament Studies* 22(1975) 52–72; Kobelski, *Melchizedek*, 130–37.

[25] For a review of the debate see D. W. Suter, "Weighed in the Balance: The Similitudes of Enoch in Recent Discussion," *Religious Studies Review* 7(1981) 217–21.

[26] M. E. Stone and J. C. Greenfield, "The Enochic Pentateuch and the Date of the Similitudes," *Harvard Theological Review* 70(1977) 51–65.

[27] Theisohn, *Der auserwählte Richter*, 149–82; cf. Friedrich, *Gott im Brüder*, 135.

[28] The parallels have often been laid out. See Theisohn, *Der auserwählte Richter*, 14–23; G. K. Beale, *The Use of Daniel in Jewish Apocalyptic Literature and in the Revelation of St. John* (Lanham, MD: University Press of America, 1984) 97–100; Caragounis, *The Son of Man*, 101–2.

[29] The Ethiopic demonstrative could, in principle, be a translation of the Greek definitive article, but this is unlikely here, since the demonstrative is never found with the title "the Elect One" in the *Similitudes*. See Casey, *Son of Man*, 100. Three different Ethiopic phrases are used for "Son of Man" in the course of the *Similitudes*, but these may be only translation variants.

[30] See further Collins, *The Apocalyptic Imagination*, 148. The title "Elect of God" appears in a text from Qumran (4QMess ar), but there it seems to refer to Noah. See J. A. Fitzmyer, "The Aramaic 'Elect of God' Text from Qumran," in idem, *Essays on the Semitic Background of the New Testament*, 127–60; F. García Martínez, "4QMess Ar and the Book of Noah," in idem, *Qumran and Apocalyptic*, 1–44.

[31] On the notion of an exalted angel in apocalyptic literature, see Christopher Rowland, *The Open Heaven. A Study of Apocalypticism in Judaism and Early Christianity* (New York: Crossroad, 1982) 94–113.

[32] Trans. Michael A. Knibb, *The Ethiopic Book of Enoch* (Oxford: Oxford University Press, 1978) 2.166.

[33] Charles, *Apocrypha and Pseudepigrapha of the Old Testament* 2.237.

[34] See Collins, *The Apocalyptic Imagination*, 151–53, and "The Heavenly Representative. The 'Son of Man' in the Similitudes of Enoch," Collins and Nickelsburg, eds., *Ideal Figures in Ancient Judaism*, 111–33.

[35] J. C. VanderKam, "Righteous One, Messiah, Chosen One, and Son of Man" in J. Charlesworth, ed., *The Messiah* (Minneapolis: Fortress, 1992) 169–91, following E. Sjöberg, *Der Menschensohn im Äthiopischen Henochbuch* (Lund: Gleerup, 1946) 164, argues for the unity of chapters 71–72, but does not deal with the transition between vss. 2 and 3.

[36] E.g. Casey, *Son of Man*, 105, appeals to "considerations of intrinsic probability."

[37] I follow the transliteration of T. O. Lambdin, *Introduction to Classical Ethiopic* (Harvard Semitic Series 24; Chico, CA: Scholars Press, 1978) 8.

[38] See M. A. Knibb, *The Ethiopic Book of Enoch* (Oxford: Clarendon, 1978) 1.208.

[39] See Maurice Casey, "The Use of the Term 'Son of Man' in the Similitudes of Enoch," *Journal for the Study of Judaism* 7(1976) 25–26; *Son of Man*, 105; A. Caquot, "Remarques sur les chap. 70 et 71 du livre éthiopien d'Hénoch," in H. Monloubou, ed., *Apocalypses et Théologie de l'Espérance* (Paris: Cerf, 1977) 113. One later manuscript (Abbadianus 197, W) has an identical reading, and another (Abbadianus 99, V) omits some further words but has the same sense. VanderKam, however, correctly notes that even the reading in MS U can be translated as "his name was raised to that son of man" ("Righteous One," 184).

[40] R. H. Charles, "The Book of Enoch," *Apocrypha and Pseudepigrapha of the Old Testament* 2.166.

[41] Matthew Black, *The Book of Enoch or 1 Enoch* (Leiden: Brill, 1985) 250, suggests that a Christian scribe may have altered the text but does not explain why the scribe did not then change 71:14.

[42] VanderKam, "Righteous One," 184. VanderKam arrives at this conclusion because he is reluctant to admit an internal contradiction in chapters 70–71.

[43] Dillmann's lexicon offers 1) apud, juxta, penes; 2) ad, versus, in. (A. Dillmann, *Lexicon Linguae Aethiopicae* [Leipzig: Weigel, 1865]).

[44] Also the opening verses of the Babylonian creation story, the *Enuma Elish*. See further Gottfried Schimanowski, *Weisheit und Messias* (Tübingen: Mohr-Siebeck, 1985) 165–71.

[45] T. W. Manson, "The Son of Man in Daniel, Enoch and the Gospels," *Bulletin of the John Rylands Library* 32(1949–50) 183–85.

[46] A partial parallel for such a concept can be found in the *Prayer of Joseph*, where Jacob declares that "I, Jacob, who is speaking to you, am also Israel, an angel of God and a ruling spirit," and goes on to recall that "when I was coming up from Syrian Mesopotamia, Uriel the angel of God, came forth and said that I, [Jacob-Israel] had descended to earth and I had tabernacled among men and that I had been called by the name of Jacob." (Trans. Jonathan Z. Smith, "Prayer of Joseph," in Charlesworth, ed., *The Old Testament Pseudepigrapha* 2.713). Jacob, however, was apparently aware of his heavenly identity, as he proceeds to tell Uriel's name and rank among the sons of God. Compare also GenR 68.12, where Jacob's features are said to exist in heaven while he is on earth.

[47] See P. Alexander, "3 (Hebrew Apocalypse of) Enoch," in Charlesworth, ed., *The Old Testament Pseudepigrapha* 1.258–63; Schäfer, *The Hidden and Manifest God*, 132–34.

[48] See Lambdin, *Introduction to Classical Ethiopic*, 29.

[49] So also Mowinckel, *He That Cometh*, 442–43. Ephraim Isaac, "1 Enoch," in Charlesworth, ed., *The Old Testament Pseudepigrapha* 1.50, argues for the general sense "human being" here on the grounds that the Ethiopic word is *be'esi*, but *be'esi* is also used in 69:29, where Isaac capitalizes Son of Man.

[50] Different Ethiopic phrases are used in the two passages, *walda sabe'* in 46:3 and *walda be'esi* in 71:14, but these may be only translation variants.

[51] Collins, "The Heavenly Representative," 113. E.g. in 61:4 "the chosen will begin to live with the chosen," i.e. the human chosen ones will begin to live with the heavenly ones.

[52] In *1 Enoch* 62:5 the figure enthroned in heaven is called "that Son of a Woman" but this Ethiopic expression, *walda be'esit*, is almost certainly a corruption of *walda be'esi*, Son of Man.

[53] See Ephraim E. Urbach, *The Sages. Their Concepts and Beliefs* (Jerusalem: Magnes, 1975) 1.684–85; 2.1005–6. Urbach notes that "there are no grounds . . . for a distinction between the pre-existence of his name and the pre-existence of his personality."

[54] For a summary of the roles of the Son of Man, see Caragounis, *The Son of Man*, 116–19.

[55] This, at least, is the most natural reading of 48:5: "All those who dwell upon the dry ground will fall down and worship before him. . . ." It is conceivable, however, that the implied antecedent is the Lord of Spirits.

[56] So especially Sjöberg, *Der Menschensohn im äthiopischen Henochbuch*, 190; compare already Wilhelm Bousset, *Die Religion des Judentums* (Berlin: de Gruyter, 1903) 251.

[57] See especially Theisohn, *Der auserwählte Richter*. Ulrich B. Müller, *Messias und Menschensohn in jüdischen Apokalypsen und in der Offenbarung des Johannes* (Gütersloh: Mohn, 1972) 36–51.

[58] Theisohn, *Der auserwählte Richter*, 114–43. Compare also the motif of the light to the nations in *1 Enoch* 48.4. See also Nickelsburg, *Resurrection, Immortality and Eternal Life in Intertestamental Judaism*, 70–74, on parallels between Isaiah 52–53 and *1 Enoch* 62.

[59] Theisohn, *Der auserwählte Richter*, 63.

[60] In light of these parallels, Casey's argument that the author does not attribute kingship to the Son of Man, because Enoch was not a king, or because of deliberate rejection of the Davidic line, is unconvincing (*Son of Man*, 111).

[61] See further Collins, *The Apocalyptic Imagination*, 142–54.

[62] Ibid., 156.

[63] Most scholars favor Hebrew, but Kvanvig, *Roots of Apocalyptic*, 521, offers a retroversion of chapter 13 into Aramaic.

[64] Kvanvig, *Roots of Apocalyptic*, 517.

[65] Caragounis, *The Son of Man*, 127–28. Compare the *Similitudes*, *1 Enoch* 46:1, which initially refers to "another, whose face had the appearance of a man."

[66] Kvanvig, *Roots of Apocalyptic*, 517–20.

[67] See Jacob M. Myers, *I and II Esdras* (Anchor Bible 42; Garden City, N.Y.: Doubleday, 1974) 302; M. E. Stone, *Fourth Ezra* (Hermeneia; Minneapolis: Fortress, 1990) 381.

[68] See André Lacocque, "The Vision of the Eagle in 4 Esdras, a Rereading of Daniel 7 in the First Century C.E.," in K. H. Richards, ed., *Society of Biblical Literature Seminar Papers* (Chico, CA: Scholars Press, 1981) 237–58. The allusion has been disputed by Kvanvig, *Roots of Apocalyptic*, 522–23. For criticism of his position see my essay "The Son of Man in First Century Judaism," *New Testament Studies* 38(1992) 460–61.

[69] Michael E. Stone, *Features of the Eschatology of 4 Ezra* (Harvard Semitic Studies 35; Atlanta: Scholars Press, 1989) 123–25; "The Concept of the Messiah in IV Ezra," in J. Neusner, ed., *Religions in Antiquity. Essays in Memory of E. R. Goodenough* (Leiden: Brill, 1968) 305–6; and "The Question of the Messiah in 4 Ezra," in Neusner et al., eds., *Judaisms and their Messiahs*, 213. Kearns, *Vorfragen zur Christologie*, 2.53–62, also isolates an independent vision, but his argument depends on imposing unwarranted standards of formal consistency on the material. See the critique of Kearns by Kvanvig, *Roots of Apocalyptic*, 527–29.

[70] Stone, *Features*, 124.

[71] For a contrary view, see Casey, *Son of Man*, 122–29. Casey shows that unity of authorship is not impossible, but the balance of probability favors Stone's arguments.

[72] See Chapter Seven above.

[73] This is also noted by George W. E. Nickelsburg, "Son of Man," in Freedman, ed., *The Anchor Bible Dictionary* 6:141.

[74] Stone, "The Question of the Messiah in 4 Ezra," 213.

[75] Müller, *Messias und Menschensohn*, 91.

[76] Stone, *Features*, 131–32.

[77] Theisohn, *Der auserwählte Richter*, 145, concludes that *4 Ezra* 13 does not reflect the *Similitudes* in any way.

[78] Casey, *Son of Man*, 81–83, claims to find the collective view in two late rabbinic passages, *Midrash on Psalms* 21.5 and *Tanhuma Toledoth* 20, but even he admits that it is not obvious in either case. Casey's further claim that Porphyry held a collective interpretation that he had derived from Syrian tradition (*Son of Man*, 51–70) goes far beyond the evidence. Jerome, in his commentary at 7:14, challenges Porphyry to identify the figure ("Let Porphyry answer the query of whom out of all mankind this language might apply to . . ."), thereby implying that Porphyry had failed to do so.

[79] b. Sanh. 98a; Numbers Rabbah 13.14; *Aggadat Bereshit* 14.3; 23.1 and Rabbi Akiba's explanation of the plural "thrones" as one for God, one for David (b. Hag 14a; b. Sanh. 38b). See Caragounis, *Son of Man*, 131–36.

⁸⁰ *4 Ezra* 13:26. Compare 7:28. Caragounis, *The Son of Man*, 129.

⁸¹ Stone, *Features*, 127–28.

⁸² J. A. Emerton, "The Origin of the Son of Man Imagery," *Journal of Theological Studies* 9(1958) 231–32.

⁸³ Collins, *The Sibylline Oracles of Egyptian Judaism*, 87–89.

⁸⁴ A fourth passage, 155–61, which speaks of a great star that will come from heaven and burn the deep sea, Babylon, and the land of Italy, might arguably be included, but the imagery here is more complex.

⁸⁵ On the structure of *Sib Or* 5 see Collins, *The Sibylline Oracles*, 74.

⁸⁶ Horbury, "Messianic Associations," 44–45.

⁸⁷ Lactantius, *Divine Institutions* 7.17. Since Hystaspes is only transmitted by the Christian Lactantius, there are doubts about the authenticity of some of the material. See John R. Hinnells, "The Zoroastrian Doctrine of Salvation in the Roman World: A Study of the Oracle of Hystaspes," in E. J. Sharpe and J. R. Hinnells, eds., *Man and his Salvation. Studies in Memory of S. G. F. Brandon* (Manchester: Manchester University Press, 1973) 125–48; Hans G. Kippenberg, "Die Geschichte der Mittelpersischen Apokalyptischen Traditionen," *Studia Iranica* 7(1978) 70–75.

⁸⁸ Hinnells, "The Zoroastrian Doctrine of Salvation," 144.

⁸⁹ Carsten Colpe, "Der Begriff 'Menschensohn' und die Methode der Erforschung messianischer Prototypen," *Kairos* 12(1970) 81–112.

⁹⁰ Perrin, *A Modern Pilgrimage*, 26.

9

Messianic Dreams in Action

In the preceding chapters we have seen evidence for four distinct messianic paradigms in Judaism around the turn of the era: king, priest, prophet, and heavenly messiah or Son of Man. These paradigms were not always distinct. Priestly and prophetic motifs merge in the expectation of the eschatological teacher of Qumran. The heavenly messiah can appear in the form of a national king. Philo portrayed Moses as king, priest and prophet.[1] Such a composite figure is exceptional, however. Historically, the Hasmoneans combined priesthood and kingship, and John Hyrcanus was further credited with the gift of prophecy. But as we have seen, this combination of offices was a significant factor in the revival of messianic expectations in the late second and early first centuries BCE and led to a tendency to distinguish the offices and insist on the plurality of messiahs.

The use of the term "messiah" or "anointed" with reference to different kinds of figures in the sources has led to some confusion in modern scholarship, as if these various figures were interchangeable aspects of a messiah concept or *Messiasbild*.[2] Jewish expectations around the turn of the era were not for a generic "messiah," but for a royal messiah who would be the branch of David, or a priestly messiah or Aaron, or a prophet like Moses. While some permutations and combinations were possible, a prophetic figure does not become a king or a priest by virtue of being a "messiah," nor does a royal messiah automatically become a priest or prophet. There were different messianic paradigms, not one composite concept of Messiah.

The messianic texts found in the Scrolls and Pseudepigrapha are inevitably literary sources, the work of a literate, scribal class. As such, their relevance to popular hopes and expectations might be questioned. The messianic exegesis of Qumran or the poetry of the *Psalms of Solomon* do not appear to have led to any popular messianic movement in the first century BCE. This fact, however, may be due more to social circumstances than to any gulf between literate scribes and the common people. We have seen repeatedly that messianic hopes were rooted in the Scriptures, and the content of these Scriptures was part of the oral culture as well as the scribal culture of ancient Judaism.

Prophetic Movements

The influence of scriptural paradigms is most clearly evident in a number of prophetic figures who appear in the first century CE.[3] Josephus tells us of one Theudas, who, when Fadus was governor of Judea (about 45 CE), "persuaded most of the common people to take their possessions and follow him to the Jordan River. He said he was a prophet, and that at his command the river would be divided and allow them an easy crossing" (*Antiquities* 20.97–98). The symbolism of his action most obviously recalls Joshua, before whom the Jordan allegedly parted at the time of the entry into the promised land. It might also recall the parting of the sea at the Exodus, or indeed it might evoke both Exodus and Conquest, which were closely related in any case.[4] Hengel suggests that Theudas may have regarded himself as Moses *redivivus*, in accordance with Deuteronomy 18.[5] He evidently had an extensive following. Josephus says he persuaded "most of the common people" to follow him. The number is given as "about 400" in Acts 5:36, in a speech attributed to Gamaliel, who cites the episode as an example of a movement that failed because it was of human origin. The motif of a new Exodus had biblical precedents in Hosea 2 and Isaiah 40, and reappears around the turn of the era in the Qumran Community Rule and in the career of John the Baptist.[6] There can be no doubt that it intimated imminent divine intervention and the dawn of the eschatological period. It has been suggested that Theudas' followers were armed, by analogy with the Exodus, but this is not indicated by Josephus.[7] The movement was cut short by Fadus, who sent out a contingent of cavalry, had Theudas beheaded and several of his followers executed.

A similar prophetic movement was led by a figure known only as "the Egyptian," in the procuratorship of Festus (52–60 CE). According to Josephus' account in the *Jewish War*, this "false prophet" "made himself credible as a prophet and rallied about thirty thousand dupes and took them around through the wilderness to the Mount of Olives. From there he intended to force an entry into Jerusalem, overpower the Roman garrison and become ruler of the citizen body, using his fellow-raiders" (*Jewish War* 2.261–62). In the *Antiquities*, however, Josephus supplies a different reason for going to the Mount of Olives: "He said that from there he wanted to show them that at his command the walls of Jerusalem would fall down and they could then make an entry into the city" (*Antiquities* 20.169–71). Here again we have the attempted reenactment of one of the greatest paradigms of divine intervention in Israel's history, in this case the destruction of Jericho.

In the *War*, Josephus claims that the Egyptian hoped to enter Jerusalem by force and wanted to "become ruler of the citizen body." The prophetic sign, in the *Antiquities* account, suggests that he relied rather on divine intervention. Accounts of the Egyptian's aspirations must be viewed with some skepticism, in view of Josephus' generally negative attitude towards revolutionary agitators in the *War*.[8] If indeed the Egyptian expected the walls of Jerusalem to fall down, then his expectations can hardly be reduced to the hope that he himself would rule instead of the Romans.[9] The miracle was surely supposed to be the prelude to a definitive transformation. Unfortunately he never got the opportunity to implement his plans for Jerusalem. He himself escaped and "vanished without a trace," but most of his followers were killed by the Roman troops.

There were a number of other prophets, who led movements in the first century CE, of whom we are less well informed. Josephus tells of a Samaritan under Pontius Pilate who led a crowd to Mount Gerizim, promising to show them "the holy vessels buried at the spot where Moses had put them" (*Antiquities* 18.85–87). It is not clear why Moses should be thought to have hidden sacred vessels. By associating himself with Moses, the figure in question may have been putting himself forward as an eschatological prophet, but in this case the evidence is less than clear.[10] Again, Roman cavalry prevented the fulfillment of his promises.

In conjunction with his account of the rise of the *sicarii*, or "dagger-men," in the procuratorship of Festus, Josephus goes on to say:

> "Besides these there arose another body of villains, with purer hands but more impious intentions, who no less than the assassins ruined the peace of the city. Deceivers and impostors, under the pretence of divine inspiration fostering revolutionary changes, they persuaded the multitude to act like madmen, and led them out into the desert under the belief that God would there give them tokens of deliverance. Against them Felix, regarding this as but the preliminary insurrection, sent a body of cavalry and heavy-armed infantry, and put a large number to the sword" (*Jewish War* 2.258–60).

It has been suggested that the "signs" given by these prophets were of a different order from the actions of Theudas and the Egyptian. (Josephus goes on to describe the episode with the Egyptian as "a still worse blow," *Jewish War* 2.261.) The signs of the nameless prophets in the time of Festus were supposedly authenticating miracles, whereas those of Theudas and the Egyptian were liberating acts of God.[11] Josephus calls authenticating miracles signs, but he refers to miracles such as the parting of the sea as epiphanies. The distinction is dubious. The actions of Theudas and the Egyptian presumably were meant to be acts of divine deliverance, but they were also signs that confirmed the credibility of the prophets and indicated to observers that the drama of salvation was underway. The proposed parting of the Jordan by Theudas is of necessity a different kind of event from the original parting by Joshua. The reenactment of a historical paradigm is a "sign" in a way that the original miracle was not. We do not know what kind of signs were intended by the prophets under Festus, but it is unsafe to suppose that they were different in kind from those of Theudas and the Egyptian. We read of another prophet who promised "signs of deliverance" towards the end of the war with Rome in 70 CE (*Jewish War* 6.283–87).

Josephus blames these prophetic figures for stirring up the masses, but he admits that they were not themselves violent revolutionaries. What is of interest for our present purpose is the intersection of scriptural paradigm and political action. In addition to the biblical paradigms of parting the Jordan and causing walls to fall down, it should be noted that these prophets typically led their followers into the wilderness. This might be understood as a guerrilla tactic, but in the case of the prophets it is better understood as a reenactment of the Exodus.[12] In each case there were immediate social and historical circumstances that led to the agitation, but, at least in the cases of Theudas and the Egyptian, Scripture provided the model for the action. The pattern of prophecy and fulfillment was not merely a scribal exercise among the literate few. It had a direct impact on Jewish history in the Roman period.

Royal Pretenders

Josephus, who is virtually our only source for popular movements in Judaism in this period, preserves no stories of priestly messianic pretenders. The ideal of a messiah of Aaron, who would take precedence over the messiah of Israel, was not a common Jewish concern, and appears to have been distinctive to sectarian circles. There are, however, several stories of royal pretenders.

Not everyone who aspired to a crown necessarily qualifies as a *messianic* pretender, but only those who claimed to restore the Davidic line or to bring the biblical prophecies to fulfillment. Josephus tells of a number of people who aspired to kingship after the death of Herod. Judas, son of Hezekiah, whose father had been captured and killed by Herod, is accused by Josephus of causing fear in everyone "by plundering those he encountered in his craving for greater power and in zealous pursuit of royal rank."[13] Simon, a servant of King Herod, a man of imposing size, was proclaimed king by his followers. He set fire to the royal palace in Jericho, but was subsequently defeated and beheaded by the Roman commander Gratus.[14] Another figure, Athronges, had no royal connections, but like Simon, was distinguished by his size and so "dared to aspire to kingship." He and his brothers carried out guerrilla war for a time against the Romans and Herodians, but they were eventually obliged to surrender.[15] Josephus had little sympathy for these figures. He characterized them as "bandits" and commented that "whenever seditious bands came across someone suitable, that person could be set up as king, eager for the ruin of the commonwealth, doing little damage to the Romans, but causing extensive bloodshed among their countrymen."[16] He does not attribute any messianic claims to these figures. It may be that he "studiously avoids" such language, as Horsley suggests,[17] and that they really were messianic pretenders, but we have no real evidence of their aspirations.[18]

According to Josephus, messianic expectation was a significant factor in the outbreak of the revolt against Rome in 66 CE:

"What more than all else incited them to the war was an ambiguous oracle, likewise found in their sacred scriptures, to the effect that at that time one from their country would become ruler of the world. This they understood to mean someone of their own race, and many of their wise men went astray in their interpretation of it. The oracle, however, in reality signified the sovereignty of Vespasian, who was proclaimed Emperor on Jewish soil."[19]

It is not clear what passage in the Scriptures Josephus had in mind.

Two of the rebel leaders appear to have been royal pretenders. Menahem, son of Judas the Galilean, raided the arsenal of Herod the Great on Masada and "returned to Jerusalem as king" (*Jewish War* 2.433–34). Again, we lack information about Menahem's intentions. A legend in *Lamentations Rabbah* 1:16, that the messiah was born in Bethlehem about the time of the destruction of the temple, and that his name was Menahem, son of Hezekiah, has little historical value.[20] Menahem's royal career was short-lived. He visited the Temple "adorned with royal clothing," but was attacked and killed.[21]

A second revolutionary leader had a longer reign. Simon bar Giora was distinguished by his strength and audacity.[22] Initially he gathered his army by proclaiming liberty for slaves and rewards for the free. Josephus admits that his army did not consist of "mere serfs or brigands," but included many men of substance, "subservient to his command as to a king." He was admitted to Jerusalem to throw out John of Gischala and the Zealots, but he himself ruled with a heavy hand. He executed prominent citizens accused of treachery and imprisoned others. When Jerusalem fell, he surrendered to the Romans in dramatic fashion, dressed in a white tunic with a purple mantle, presumably to indicate royalty (*Jewish War* 7.29). He was taken to Rome, displayed in the victory procession and ceremonially executed as the leader of the defeated Jews.

Another Jewish revolt broke out in the Diaspora in the time of Trajan (115–117 CE). It was led by a "king," whose name is variously given as Lukuas or Andreas.[23] According to Eusebius, the Jews arose as if in the grip of some terrible spirit of rebellion. Modern authors have often suggested that the revolt had no more specific cause than the intensity of messianic expectation.[24] The sudden upsurge of messianism, however, also needs an explanation, and points to the general deterioration of Jewish life in Egypt and Cyrene in the period after 70 CE and to the burden of taxation, aggravated by the tax all Jews were obliged to pay to

Rome (the *fiscus Judaicus*).[25] Cassius Dio paints a lurid picture of the ferocity of the rebels: "They would eat the flesh of their victims, make belts for themselves of their entrails, anoint themselves with their blood and wear their skins for clothing; many they sawed in two, from the head downwards; others they gave to wild beasts, and still others they forced to fight as gladiators. In all two hundred and twenty thousand persons perished." It is not necessary to believe that the Jewish rebels did all these things. It is sufficient that the Greeks believed such rumors. A papyrus fragment records the prayer of a Greek mother for her son, "that they may not roast you."[26] The revolt was marked by destruction of pagan temples, including the Ptolemaic Serapeum. On the other side, the Greeks denounced the "impious Jews" (*anosioi Ioudaioi*) as "lawbreakers, once expelled from Egypt by the wrath of Isis," and called on their followers to "attack the Jews."[27] The Alexandrian Jews were massacred early in the revolt. Eventually Egyptian Judaism was virtually wiped out.

There is general agreement that messianism was a significant factor in the revolt.[28] Applebaum wrote: "The spirit of the movement was messianic, its aim the liquidation of the Roman régime and the setting up of a new Jewish commonwealth, whose task was to inaugurate the messianic era."[29] The movement may have had its goal in the land of Israel.[30] We know little of the messianic pretender Lukuas/Andreas. There may be an obscure reference to him in a papyrus, as the "king of the scene and the mime."[31] We know that the Alexandrians performed a satirical mime to mock the Jewish king Agrippa when he visited Alexandria in 38 CE.[32] Lukuas may have been mocked in a similar way.

Some of the spirit of the revolt may be reflected in the fifth *Sibylline Oracle*, which refers more than once to the destruction or dereliction of pagan temples (vss. 52–59, 484–91). The Sibyl expresses hope for "a king sent from God" (vs. 108) or a "man from heaven" (vs. 414). It also mentions "a great star" that "will come from heaven to the wondrous sea and will burn the deep sea and Babylon itself and the land of Italy" (5:158–60).[33] There is no indication that a historical king such as Lukuas is meant, but in fact we know nothing of the imagery associated with him, and the reference of the Sibyl is obscure. In view of the imagery associated with Bar Kochba, it is not impossible that the Sibyl had a messianic king in mind.

The last great Jewish revolt against Rome was led by Simon Bar Kosiba in 132–35 CE. Various causes are given for the outbreak. The most widely held are Hadrian's decision to transform Jerusalem into a pagan city, Aelia Capitolina, and his ban on circumcision. Economic factors may also have played a part.[34] The rebels enjoyed some initial success. It is unclear whether they captured Jerusalem. Bar Kosiba minted his own coins, some of which bear the legend "for the freedom of Jerusalem." This might be understood to celebrate the capture of Jerusalem, but it might also be taken as a programmatic statement of the aim of the revolt.[35] Bar Kosiba's last stand was at Bethar, eleven kilometers southwest of Jerusalem. According to Eusebius, "the siege lasted a long time before the rebels were driven to final destruction by famine and thirst."[36] Cassius Dio says that very few of the Jews survived. "Fifty of their most important outposts and nine hundred and eighty-five of their most famous villages were razed to the ground. Five hundred and eighty thousand men were slain in the various raids and battles, and the number of those that perished by famine, disease and fire was past finding out. Thus nearly the whole of Judaea was made desolate..." (69.12.1–14.3).[37] Archaeology has discovered vivid evidence of the suffering of rebels who were starved to death in caves near the Dead Sea.[38] Cassius Dio adds, however, that "Many Romans perished in this war. Therefore Hadrian in writing to the senate did not employ the opening phrase commonly affected by the emperors, 'If you and your children are in health, it is well; I and the legions are in health.'"

Bar Kosiba is the only royal pretender, other than Jesus, for whom a messianic claim is explicitly made in the sources. Rabbi Akiba is said to have explained the passage "a star shall go forth from Jacob" (Num 24:17), as "Kosiba goes forth from Jacob," and to have hailed him with the pronouncement "This is the king, the messiah." Rabbi Yohanan b. Torta replied, "Aqiba, grass will grow between your cheeks and he still will not have come."[39] Hence Bar Kosiba became known as Bar Kokhba, son of the star, the name by which he was known to his contemporary, Justin Martyr.[40] While the royal messiah was traditionally associated with the scepter of Balaam's oracle, the star lent itself more readily to the wordplay on the name. According to Eusebius, he was "murderous and a bandit, but relied on his name, as if dealing with slaves, and claimed to be a luminary who had come down to them from heaven and was magically enlightening those who were in misery" (*Ecclesiastical History* 4.6.1–4). Whether Bar Kokhba understood himself as messiah is disputed.[41] The claim is attributed to him in the Talmud (b. Sanh. 93b). No such claim is made in his letters. On documents and coins, however, he is called "prince of Israel" (נשיא ישראל).[42] We have seen that the title "prince" (נשיא) had a long history as a messianic title.[43]

Some of the coins bear a star. Some coins also mention Eleazar the Priest, but there is no question of Bar Kochba being subordinate to him, as was the case with the dual messianism of Qumran. Justin says that he had threatened Christians that "if they did not deny and defame Jesus Christ, they would be led away to the most severe punishment."[44] Here two messianic claims confronted each other, and there was no room for compromise.[45] Later Jewish tradition rejected Bar Kochba, and referred to him as Bar Koziba, "son of the lie," as a false messiah.[46] His real name was in doubt until the archaeological discoveries of the 1960s.[47]

Bar Kokhba's letters reveal him as a strict disciplinarian.[48] His messages are frequently accompanied with an admonition such as "and if you do not act accordingly you shall be punished severely."[49] He also shows strict religious piety. One papyrus deals with a request, made towards the end of the war, for palm branches, citrons, myrtles, and willows for the proper observance of Sukkot.[50] Later Jewish legends credited him with might and courage.[51] They also reflect his reputation for cruelty. He is said to have killed Rabbi Eleazar of Modin by kicking him to death.[52] A propensity to violence was perhaps a necessary characteristic of a leader of an armed revolt.

Each of the royal pretenders we have considered was the leader of a violent, armed uprising. Insofar as any of these people had a claim to be regarded as messiahs, the claim was grounded in their military leadership. In this respect, at least, the royal pretenders conformed to the usual paradigm for a royal messiah. The scepter of Balaam's oracle was supposed to smite all the children of Seth. Isaiah's "shoot from the stump of Jesse" was supposed to kill the wicked with the breath of his lips. Despite attempts by some modern scholars to "spiritualize" this image, its violent implications are picked up repeatedly in the Roman period. The Branch of David/Prince of the Congregation has a role in the final battle against the *Kittim* at Qumran. The one who will be called "Son of God" in 4Q246 will bring peace to the earth, but he will do so by military victory: "The great God will be his strength. He will make war on his behalf, give nations into his hand and cast them all down before him." The "son of David" in *Pss Sol* 17 is to "purge Jerusalem from Gentiles," and "smash the arrogance of sinners like a potter's jar." The man from the sea in *4 Ezra* burns up all his adversaries with a stream of fire from his mouth. The messiah in Targum Pseudo-Jonathan "reddens the mountains with the blood of the slain." To be sure, a real life messiah needed more mundane weapons than the breath of his mouth. But the violent destruction of the wicked is a standard element in the repertoire of the Davidic messiah.

Jesus and the Davidic Messiah

Herein lies the anomaly of the messianic claims of Jesus of Nazareth. That he was crucified as "King of the Jews" cannot be doubted. The claim to Davidic kingship also figures prominently in early Christian sources. The title *Christos*, messiah, is treated as a virtual name by Paul. It is unlikely that Jesus' followers would have given him such a politically inflammatory title after his death if it had no basis in his life. Paul says that Jesus was "descended from David according to the flesh, and was declared to be Son of God with power according to the spirit of holiness by the resurrection of the dead."[53] But as Hengel has pointed out, the notion that someone could become messiah by resurrection and elevation to heaven is without parallel in the Jewish sources.[54] It is more likely that Paul is referring to the full realization of Jesus' kingship by his heavenly enthronement. The messianic identity of Jesus must be grounded in some way before his crucifixion.

There is little if anything in the Gospel portrait of Jesus that accords with the Jewish expectation of a militant messiah.[55] The discrepancy has not escaped the attention of scholars. Schweitzer noted "the inconsistency between the public life of Jesus and His Messianic claim," which he attributed to the representation of the Evangelists.[56] We noted in the opening chapter Mowinckel's conclusion that "the Jewish messianic idea" was "the temptation of Satan" that Jesus had to reject. Recent scholars have been less judgmental about Jewish messianism. Yet James D. G. Dunn's conclusion is not far removed from Mowinckel's, when he lists royal messianism as an idea that Jesus reacted against: "In particular, the current view of the royal messiah was one which he did not find helpful as a means of understanding or informing his mission."[57] Donald Juel declares that in light of postbiblical Jewish tradition "to claim Jesus is the Messiah is absurd," and finds Mark's use of *christos* deeply ironic.[58] E. P. Sanders comments that "A teacher who comes into conflict with the Pharisees over the law and who offends the priests by striking at their revenues (the mainline depiction of Jesus), but who appears in visions after his death, does not seem to deserve the title 'Messiah.'" But Sanders adds blithely: "once we grant that the kingdom which Jesus had in mind was actually expected, the problem seems to vanish."[59] He reasons that "if Jesus taught his disciples that there would be a kingdom and that *they* would have a role in it, he certainly, at least by implication, gave himself a role also. 'Messiah' will do perfectly well for the person who is superior to the judges of Israel, even if he was not a warrior."[60] But new meanings of the word "messiah" cannot be coined at will. The claim that Jesus is the royal, Davidic, messiah is a good deal more specific than Sanders allows.

In recent years several scholars have argued that the term "messiah" was originally applied to Jesus as prophet rather than as king.[61] W. C. van Unnik, in his presidential address to the Studiorum Novi Testamenti Societas in 1961 pointed to the quotation from Isa 61:1 in Luke 4:16–21 ("The spirit of the Lord is upon me, because he has anointed me to bring good news to the poor . . .") and to Acts 19:38 ("how God anointed Jesus of Nazareth with the Holy Spirit") and suggested that this motif was not a speciality of Lucan theology.[62] Marinus de Jonge noted the relevance of the herald in 11QMelch 2:18, where the herald (*mebasser*) is identified as "the one anointed of the spirit." He added, however, that he could not find any sign that Jesus' preaching of good news to the poor was connected with "anointing through the Spirit" before Luke, noting that in Jesus' answer to the question of John the Baptist in Q (Matt 11:2–6/Luke 7:18–23) the word *christos* did not occur.[63]

We now have a text from Qumran (4Q521) that has a remarkable parallel to Jesus' answer to the Baptist and that also refers to a messiah, whom heaven and earth obey. While it is apparently God who heals the wounded, gives life to the dead, and preaches good news to the poor in that text, the role of preaching is usually assigned to an agent. The mention of the messiah suggests that God acts through an agent here, too. It is quite likely, then, that these works were considered "works of the messiah," as well as of God, before the Gospels. Since the works in question are typical of what is attributed to Jesus in the Gospels, this text strengthens the case that the epithet "anointed" or "messiah" could have been attached to him because of his words and deeds. The "messiah" in 4Q521 is not perceptibly royal, however, and is best regarded, like the "anointed" speaker in Isaiah 61, as a prophet, not a king. Raising the dead is associated with the prophet Elijah, not with a Davidic king. It is not difficult to see why Jesus, as portrayed in the Gospels, might be recognized as a prophet, and in that sense as "anointed."[64] There are explicit indications in the Gospels that he was so regarded.[65] The parallel with

4Q521 further strengths the case for a prophetic Jesus. It does not explain, however, why he should have been crucified as King of the Jews or regarded as a "Son of David."[66]

We have seen a few cases where royal and prophetic attributes were attached to the same person. John Hyrcanus was a case in point, but his example only discouraged the association, at least in the circles represented by the Dead Sea Scrolls. Philo portrayed Moses as prophet, priest, and king. The figure of Moses may well explain the association of prophet and king in the Gospel of John,[67] but Moses was obviously not a Davidic king, and so he can scarcely illuminate the characterization of Jesus in the Gospels. While David was widely regarded as a prophet, it does not follow that an "anointed" prophet would therefore be accorded royal rank.[68]

The only episode in Jesus' career that fits a scriptural paradigm for a kingly messiah is the triumphal entry into Jerusalem.[69] Matthew and John quote Zech 9:9 here: "Lo your king comes to you, triumphant and victorious is he, humble and riding on a donkey, on a colt, the foal of a donkey." Presumably anyone familiar with the Scriptures would have caught the allusion. The historicity of the incident is questionable, precisely because it fits a biblical paradigm.[70] Yet we have seen that the reenactment of biblical paradigms was typical of eschatological prophets, and the incident fits perfectly with Jesus' execution as King of the Jews. Zech 9:9 is never used as a messianic prophecy in the Scrolls or the Pseudepigrapha.[71] For that reason, the early Christians are perhaps less likely to have invented a story to fulfill it than would have been the case with a better known messianic prophecy. The incident is at least a possible case of a symbolic action by Jesus that fits the mode of operation of an eschatological prophet but that also implies a royal claim. While Jesus functions as a prophet rather than as a royal pretender for most of his career, the manner of his entry into Jerusalem appears to be an enactment of the coming of the Davidic messiah. Here Jesus appears to change roles, from that of prophetic herald of the kingdom to that of king who ushers it in. There is no real parallel for such a progression (unless we take seriously Josephus' claim that the Egyptian aspired to rule in Jerusalem). In the end, any explanation must allow Jesus his historic individuality. If he were indistinguishable from other eschatological prophets and messianic pretenders, he could scarcely have had such an impact on history. It is possible, of course, that Jesus did not intend to identify himself as the messiah, but intended his action as a prophetic sign that the coming of the messiah was imminent. It is easy to see, however, how his followers could make the identification, and how this action might have led to his execution by the Romans. At the very least, the triumphal entry affirms the expectation of the Davidic messiah and in no way rejects it.

Many scholars have noted that Zech 9:9 suggests a different kind of messiah from the victorious king of contemporary Jewish sources.[72] The full context of the passage in Zechariah should be noted, however: "He will cut off the chariot from Ephraim and the war horse from Jerusalem and the battle bow shall be cut off and he shall command peace to the nations; his dominion shall be from sea to sea, and from the River to the ends of the earth" (Zech 9:10). Like the "Son of God" in 4Q246, this king will bring about universal peace, by apparently by military victory. The victory could be achieved by divine power rather than by a human army, but it would involve the overthrow of Gentile power. If this is correct, and Jesus was enacting the paradigm of Zechariah 9, then he did not reject Davidic messianism as utterly as Mowinckel or Dunn have supposed, and his messianic titles in the New Testament are not completely anomalous in light of his actions.

For nonbelievers in antiquity, however, the great objection to the recognition of Jesus as Davidic messiah was not his nonmessianic career, but the shameful defeat of his death.[73] Hence, Trypho in Justin's *Dialogue*: "It is just this that we cannot comprehend, that you set your hope on one crucified" (10.3).[74] The belief in his resurrection, however, opened the way to the retrieval of messianic prophecies unfulfilled in his lifetime. The most explicit claim placed on Jesus' lips by Mark is set in the trial scene, where Jesus answers the direct question, "Are you the messiah, the son of the Blessed One?" by affirming "I am; and you will see the Son of Man seated at the right hand of the Power and coming with the clouds of heaven." The claim of messiahship is supported by two texts, Psalm 110 and Daniel 7, whose messianic import is also recognized in Jewish tradition.[75] Neither prophecy, however, admits of verification in the ordinary course of history. The realization of Jesus' kingship is transferred to heaven or deferred to a second coming, but is still shaped by biblical paradigms. In Matthew 25:31 the Son of Man sits on his throne of glory as judge, just as he does in the *Similitudes of Enoch*. The fullest implementation of the traditional messianic prophecies is found in the book of Revelation, where Jesus comes from heaven on a white horse, wearing a robe dipped in blood. "From his mouth comes a sharp sword with which to strike down the nations, and he will rule them with a rod of iron" (Rev 19:15). The traditional Davidic messianism is qualified here, as it is in the roughly contemporary *4 Ezra* 13.[76] The warrior messiah comes from heaven. But he is a warrior messiah. Jesus of Nazareth shed no Gentile blood in Jerusalem, as the paradigm demanded. In Revelation 19, the scriptural paradigms prevail over anything that might be construed as historical memory in shaping the portrayal of Jesus.[77]

The Christian view of Jesus also departed decisively from the Jewish paradigms in many respects. One such respect was the development of the notion that the messiah should suffer and die. Scriptural warrants for this idea were found. Ps 89:51 tells how the peoples taunted "the footsteps of your anointed." Psalms 22, 31 and 69 are "Psalms of David" that also speak of the humiliation of the speaker. Psalm 22 was especially important in the shaping of the Passion Narratives.[78] The Christian use of these psalms involved a new line of interpretation, however, for which there was no precedent in Judaism. There is surprisingly little use of Isaiah 53 in the New Testament, a fact that would be difficult to explain if that passage had been understood with reference to a suffering eschatological figure in Judaism.[79]

The most significant Christian departure from Jewish notions of the messiah was the affirmation of the divinity of Christ. Trypho speaks for Judaism in Justin's *Dialogue*: "We all expect the messiah to be a man born of men" (49:1). Trypho did not speak for all Jews, however.[80] Already in the Hebrew Bible there were intimations of divinity in some of the royal psalms, most obviously in Ps 45:6, where the king is addressed as *ʾelōhîm*. We have argued that "Son of God" in 4Q246 from Qumran is best understood as a messianic title, and that it had a clear scriptural basis in 2 Samuel 7 and Psalm 2. In a Jewish context, to be sure, the "Son of God" could still be a man born of men; the title refers to status rather than to the manner of begetting. In Daniel 7, however, and in the Son of Man texts in the *Similitudes of Enoch* and *4 Ezra*, we find the expectation of a heavenly savior. The "one like a son of man" in Daniel's vision is described in imagery that normally is reserved for Yahweh in the Hebrew Bible.[81] The Enochic Son of Man is "named," and presumably created, by the Lord of Spirits, but he is named before the creation of the universe, and he is never born on earth. "All those who dwell on dry ground will fall down and worship before him" (*1 Enoch* 48:5). If he is not divine, he is clearly more than human. The messiah in *4 Ezra* is more complex. He will arise "from the offspring of David" (12:32), but he will be "revealed" and he will rise on a cloud from the depths of the sea. His apparition in chapter 13 is described in theophanic language that had been reserved for the divinity in an earlier period. In *Sib Or* 5, the savior king is "a man from the sky" who comes from above, like the savior in the Gospel of John. There were also precedents for the notion of a human being who is exalted to the heavenly world. 4Q491 tells of a throne in heaven, and the speaker claims to have been reckoned with the *ᵓēlîm*. This claim is only an intensification of the fellowship with the heavenly host that is claimed by the typical member of the Dead Sea sect in the Hodayot and an anticipation of the lot of the righteous after death. The belief that Jesus, too, was taken up and enthroned in heaven was not inherently unacceptable in a Jewish context, nor was the idea that he was in some sense "Son of God."

Christian claims for the divinity of Jesus eventually went beyond anything we find in the Jewish texts. The heavenly messiah of the *Similitudes* and the *ᵓēlîm* of the Scrolls are all clearly subordinate to the Most High God. Insofar as we know, Jesus of Nazareth was the only historical figure who was eventually identified with Daniel's Son of Man. Eusebius claims that Bar Kokhba "claimed to be a luminary who had come down to them from heaven" (*Ecclesiastical History* 4.6). That claim, however, cannot be substantiated from Jewish sources, and we cannot be sure what the name "son of the star" entailed. Some claim of heavenly origin would not be out of line with Jewish messianic expectations of the time. Only in the case of Jesus, however, do we have a clear example of a messiah who was believed to have come down from heaven and expected to come again as eschatological judge.

Conclusion

We return, then, to Scholem's antithesis between Jewish and Christian understandings of messianism. The contrast is not without basis, but it is overdrawn. As we have seen, Jewish ideas of messianism were not uniform. There was a dominant notion of a Davidic messiah, as the king who would restore the kingdom of Israel, which was part of the common Judaism around the turn of the era. There were also, however, minor messianic strands, which envisaged a priestly messiah, or an anointed prophet or a heavenly Son of Man. Christian messianism drew heavily on some of the minor strands (prophet, Son of Man) and eventually developed them into a doctrine of Christology that was remote from its Jewish origins.

The Christology of the early Church was shaped by various factors.

The crucifixion of Jesus led to a searching of the Scriptures and to a new, creative exegesis of messianic prophecy. There was a deliberate attempt to claim more for Jesus than had been claimed for any other agent of God. Eventually the creedal formulations were influenced by Greek philosophy. Despite the divergence of their branches, however, Christian and Jewish messianism were rooted in common ground. The importance of the Dead Sea Scrolls for the ancient conflict between Judaism and Christianity lies in the light they shed on that common ground of pre-Christian, pre-rabbinic Judaism.

NOTES

[1] Book 1 of Philo's *De Vita Mosis* is devoted to kingship, 2.8–65 to priesthood, and 2.187–91 to prophecy. See Wayne Meeks, *The Prophet King. Moses Traditions and the Johannine Christology* (Leiden: Brill, 1967) 100–31.

[2] See e.g. M. Hengel, "Jesus, der Messias Israels," in Gruenwald et al., eds., *Messiah and Christos*, 163–65; C. Thoma, "Entwürfe für messianische Gestalten in frühjüdischer Zeit," ibid., 15–30, unjustifiably fuses the royal and prophetic figures.

[3] P. W. Barnett, "The Jewish Sign Prophets — A.D. 40–70: Their Intentions and Origin," *New Testament Studies* 27(1980-81) 679–97; R. A. Horsley, "Popular Prophetic Movements at the Time of Jesus: Their Principal Features and Social Origins," *Journal for the Study of the New Testament* 26(1986) 3–27; Horsley and Hanson, *Bandits, Prophets, and Messiahs*, 135–89; Martin Hengel, *The Zealots* (Edinburgh: Clark, 1989) 229–33; Rebecca Gray, *Prophetic Figures in Late Second Temple Jewish Palestine* (Oxford: Oxford University Press, 1993) 112–44.

[4] Elijah and Elisha also part the Jordan by striking it with a mantle in 2 Kings 2:8, 14.

[5] Hengel, *The Zealots*, 230.

[6] Cross, *The Ancient Library of Qumran*, 217–8.

[7] Hengel, *The Zealots*, 230, n. 5. Gray, *Prophetic Figures*, 115, points out that according to Josephus the Israelites were unarmed at the time of the Exodus (*Antiquities* 2.321, 326).

[8] Gray, *Prophetic Figures*, 117, comments that Josephus generally tends to "militarize" the sign prophets in the *War*, by assimilating them to armed rebels. He was not alone in this. In Acts 21:38, the tribune who arrests Paul in the Temple asks, "Do you know Greek? Are you not the Egyptian, then, who recently stirred up a revolt and led the four thousand assassins out into the wilderness?"

[9] Gray, *Prophetic Figures*, 143, attempts to dismiss the eschatological implications of his action.

[10] See Meeks, *The Prophet King*, 247–48. Horsley and Hanson interpret the action to mean that the man was "a restorer, Moses' eschatological counterpart" (*Bandits, Prophets, and Messiahs*, 164).

[11] Gray, *Prophetic Figures*, 131.

[12] On the role of the desert in eschatological and revolutionary movements, see Hengel, *The Zealots*, 249–53.

[13] Josephus, *Antiquities* 17.271–72; *Jewish War* 2.56. This Judas is apparently distinct

from "Judas the Galilean," founder of the "Fourth Philosophy" (*Antiquities* 18.3–9, 23–25; *Jewish War* 2.118).

[14] Josephus, *Antiquities* 17.273–76.

[15] Josephus, *Antiquities* 17.278–85,

[16] Ibid.

[17] Horsley and Hanson, *Bandits, Prophets, and Messiahs*, 114.

[18] Hengel, *The Zealots*, 292, argues that the strength of Simon and Athronges is a messianic attribute and points out that Athronges had the same occupation, shepherd, as the young David. His name may be derived from the *ethrog*, the citrus fruit associated with the Feast of Tabernacles. W. R. Farmer, "Judas, Simon and Athronges," *New Testament Studies* 4(1957/8) 147–55, relates these figures to the Hasmoneans rather than to the Davidic dynasty.

[19] Josephus, *Jewish War* 6.312–13. This oracle is also reported in Suetonius, *Vespasian*, 4.5 and Tacitus, *History* 5.13.2. See E. Norden, "Josephus und Tacitus über Jesus Christus und eine messianische Prophetie," *Neue Jahrbücher für das klassische Altertum* 16(1913) 637–66.

[20] See Hengel, *The Zealots*, 295. The Haggadah goes on to say that Menahem was swept away by winds and storms. *Lamentations Rabbah* is not likely to have been composed before 400 CE.

[21] Josephus, *Jewish War* 2.444. Menahem was killed by the followers of Eleazar, the son of the High Priest Ananias, who had been killed by "the brigands" (441).

[22] Josephus, *Jewish War* 4.503. Hengel, *The Zealots*, 297; David Rhoads, *Israel in Revolution* (Philadelphia: Fortress, 1976) 140–48; Horsley and Hanson, *Bandits, Prophets, and Messiahs*, 120–27.

[23] Eusebius, *Ecclesiastical History* 4.2.1–5; Cassius Dio 68.32.1–3. The sources are conveniently presented by L. L. Grabbe, *Judaism from Cyrus to Hadrian. 2. The Roman Period* (Minneapolis: Fortress, 1992) 556–61. See also V. Tcherikover and A. Fuks, *Corpus Papyrorum Judaicarum* (Cambridge, MA: Harvard University Press, 1957) 1.86–93; A. Fuks, "Aspects of the Jewish Revolt in A.D. 115–117," *Journal of Roman Studies* 51(1961) 98–104; S. Applebaum, *Jews and Greeks in Ancient Cyrene* (Leiden: Brill, 1979) 242–344; A Kasher, "A Comment on the Jewish Uprising in Egypt during the days of Trajan," *Journal of Jewish Studies* 27(1976) 147–58; M. Hengel, "Messianische Hoffnung und politischer 'Radikalismus' in der 'jüdisch-hellenistischen Diaspora,'" in Hellholm, ed., *Apocalypticism in the Mediterranean World and the Near East*, 655–86.

[24] Fuks, "Aspects," 98–104; V. Tcherikover and A. Fuks, *Corpus Papyrorum Judaicarum* 1.90; Hengel, "Messianische Hoffnung," 663.

[25] Applebaum, *Jews and Greeks*, 328–31.

[26] Tcherikover and Fuks, *Corpus Papyrorum Judaicarum* 1.89, papyrus no. 437.

[27] Tcherikover and Fuks, *Corpus Papyrorum Judaicarum*, no. 520 (a fragmentary prophecy preserved on papyrus). See Frankfurter, "Lest Egypt's City Be Deserted," 203–20. Another papyrus refers to an annual festival in Oxyrhynchus in celebration of the victory over the Jews.

[28] For an exception see T. D. Barnes, "Trajan and the Jews," *Journal of Jewish Studies* 40(1989) 145–62.

[29] Applebaum, *Jews and Greeks*, 260.

[30] According to some medieval sources, the Jews of Cyrene eventually penetrated Judea

and were crushed by Lusius Quietus. See Applebaum, *Jews and Greeks*, 303. The revolt is remembered as "The War of Quietus" in Jewish tradition.

[31] Tcherikover and Fuks, *Corpus Papyrorum Judaicarum*, no. 158a.

[32] Tcherikover and Fuks, *Corpus Papyrorum Judaicarum* 1.89.

[33] See Collins, *The Sibylline Oracles of Egyptian Judaism*, 89–90.

[34] For a concise summary see B. Isaac and A. Oppenheimer, "Bar Kokhba," *The Anchor Bible Dictionary* 1.598–601; and "The Revolt of Bar Kokhba: Ideology and Modern Scholarship," *Journal of Jewish Studies* 36(1985) 33–60. For a critical treatment of the sources see P. Schäfer, *Der Bar Kokhba Aufstand. Studien zum zweiten jüdischen Krieg gegen Rom* (Tübingen: Mohr-Siebeck, 1981) 29–50.

[35] L. Mildenberg, *The Coinage of the Bar Kokhba War* (Aarau: Verlag Sauerländes, 1984) 29–31.

[36] Eusebius, *Ecclesiastical History* 4.6.1–4.

[37] Legendary Jewish accounts of the slaughter can be found in Midrash Lamentations and b. Gittin. See Y. Yadin, *Bar Kokhba. The Rediscovery of the Legendary Hero of the Second Jewish Revolt against Rome* (New York: Random House, 1971) 256–57.

[38] Y. Aharoni, "Expedition B—The Cave of Horror," *Israel Exploration Journal* 12(1962) 186–99; Yadin, *Bar Kokhba*, 60–65.

[39] j. Ta'anit 4.8. See P. Schäfer, "Aqiva and Bar Kokhba," in W. S. Green, ed., *Approaches to Ancient Judaism* (Brown Judaic Studies 9; Atlanta: Scholars Press, 1980) 2.113–30; Grabbe, *Judaism* 2.579–81.

[40] Justin, *Apology* 1.31.6 = Eusebius *Ecclesiastical History* 4.8.4.

[41] G. S. Aleksandrov, "The Role of Aqiba in the Bar Kokhba Rebellion," in J. Neusner, *Eliezer ben Hyrcanus* (Leiden: Brill, 1973) 2.428–42; Mildenberg, *The Coinage of the Bar Kokhba War*, 73–76.

[42] Schäfer, *Der Bar Kokhba Aufstand*, 67.

[43] See further A. Oppenheimer, "The Messianism of Bar Kokhba," in Z. Baras, ed., *Messianism and Eschatology* (Jerusalem: The Historical Society of Israel, 1983, [Heb]) 153–65; Schäfer, *Der Bar Kokhba Aufstand*, 67–73.

[44] Justin, *Apology* 1.31.6 = Eusebius, *Ecclesiastical History*, 4.8.4.

[45] Hengel, *The Zealots*, 301.

[46] E.g. b. Sanh 93b. See Schäfer, *Der Bar Kokhba Aufstand*, 57.

[47] See J. A. Fitzmyer, "The Bar Cochba Period," in Fitzmyer, *Essays on the Semitic Background of the New Testament*, 312–16.

[48] For the documents, see P. Benoit, J. T. Milik and R. de Vaux, *Les Grottes de Murabba'at* (Discoveries in the Judean Desert 2; Oxford: Clarendon, 1961).

[49] Yadin, *Bar Kochba*, 125. Yadin notes that most of the letters were written toward the end of the revolt when Bar Kochba was already desperate.

[50] Ibid., 128–29.

[51] Midrash Lamentations says that "he would catch the missiles from the enemy's catapults on one of his knees and hurl them back, killing many of the foe." Yadin, ibid., 255.

[52] Ibid. See the comments of Schäfer, *Der Bar Kokhba Aufstand*, 73–74.

[53] Rom 1:3–4. Cf. Acts 2.36: "God has made him both Lord and Messiah, this Jesus whom you crucified."

[54] Hengel, "Jesus, der Messias Israels," 158: "Auferweckung bzw. Entrückung zu Gott haben mit Messianität nichts zu tun." Compare the remarks of A. E. Harvey, *Jesus and the Constraints of History* (Philadelphia: Westminster, 1982) 138.

⁵⁵ Nonetheless, from time to time, scholars have portrayed Jesus as a militant revolutionary, notably S. G. F. Brandon, *Jesus and the Zealots: A Study of the Political Factor in Primitive Christianity* (Manchester: Manchester University Press, 1967). See the critiques of Brandon's thesis by Oscar Cullmann, *Jesus and the Revolutionaries* (New York: Harper & Row, 1970) and Martin Hengel, *Was Jesus a Revolutionist?* (Philadelphia: Fortress, 1971).

⁵⁶ A. Schweitzer, *The Quest of the Historical Jesus* (New York: Macmillan, 1969) 337. (First German edition, *Von Reimarus zu Wrede*, 1906).

⁵⁷ J. D. G. Dunn, "Messianic Ideas and their Influence on the Jesus of History," in Charlesworth, ed., *The Messiah*, 380.

⁵⁸ D. H. Juel, "The Origin of Mark's Christology," in Charlesworth, ed., *The Messiah*, 453.

⁵⁹ E. P. Sanders, *Jesus and Judaism* (Philadelphia: Fortress, 1985) 409, n.49.

⁶⁰ Ibid., 234.

⁶¹ K. Berger, "Zum Problem der Messianität Jesu," *Zeitschrift für Theologie und Kirche* 71(1974) 1–30; and "Die königlichen Messiastraditionen des Neuen Testaments," *New Testament Studies* 20(1973–74) 1–44; Harvey, *Jesus and the Constraints of History*, 120–53.

⁶² W. C. van Unnik, "Jesus the Christ," *New Testament Studies* 8(1961–62) 101–16. Compare Harvey, *Jesus and the Constraints of History*, 141; Dunn, "Messianic Ideas," 377–78: "the attribution of a prophetic role to Jesus and the use made of Isa 61:1–2 in describing his mission is likely to go back to the pre-Easter period; also that Jesus himself probably accepted the category of 'prophet' as a more adequate description of his role (than messiah) and took Isa 61:1–2 as at least to some extent programmatic for his ministry."

⁶³ M. de Jonge, "The Earliest Christian Use of Christos. Some Suggestions," in idem, Jewish Eschatology, Early Christian Christology and the Testaments of the Twelve Patriarchs" (Leiden: Brill, 1991) 116–7. (Originally presented as the presidential address to the *Studiorum Novi Testamenti Societas* in 1985). Matthew adds a reference to "the works of the messiah" (τὰ ἔργα τοῦ χριστοῦ). Mark 1:14–15 portrays Jesus as the herald of the kingdom of God but does not say that he was anointed. The epithet *christos* does occur in Mark 1:1.

⁶⁴ Hengel compares Jesus to leaders of "prophetic-charismatic movements of an eschatological stamp" (*The Charismatic Leader and His Followers* [Edinburgh: Clark, 1981] 20–21). Cf. Sanders, *Jesus and Judaism*, 237–40. Dunn's antithesis of prophet and messiah ("Messianic Ideas," 378) cannot be maintained. Presumably by "messiah" here he means Davidic messiah.

⁶⁵ E.g. Mark 6:4 ("Prophets are not without honor, except in their hometown"); 6:15 ("But others said: 'It is Elijah.' And others said, 'It is a prophet, like one of the prophets of old'"); John 6:14 ("This is indeed the prophet who is to come into the world").

⁶⁶ Compare Juel, "The Origin of Mark's Christology," 453: "When such alleged nonroyal messianic tradition is used to interpret Mark, however, the passion narrative makes no sense."

⁶⁷ See Meeks, *The Prophet King*.

⁶⁸ Hengel, "Jesus, der Messias Israels," 165, attempts to build a cumulative argument: if Jesus were an authoritative prophetic teacher, who spoke of the kingdom of God, and used the expression "son of man" with reference to himself and to an eschatological judge, and if he were from a Davidic family, would he not be regarded as a "messiah" and as "King of the Jews"? It seems to me very doubtful that Jesus was known to be of a Davidic family during his lifetime (despite the arguments of John P. Meier, *A Marginal Jew*.

Rethinking the Historical Jesus [New York: Doubleday, 1991] 216–19), and nothing else in the list would require that Jesus be regarded as a king. Marinus de Jonge also suggests that "Jesus may have understood himself as a prophetic Son of David" (*Jesus the Servant-Messiah* [New Haven, CT: Yale University Press, 1991] 72). See the criticisms of this thesis by H. J. de Jonge, "The Historical Jesus' View of Himself and of His Mission," in de Boer, ed., *From Jesus to John*, 21–37, and W. A. Meeks, "Asking Back to Jesus' Identity," ibid., 38–50.

[69] Matt 21:1–11; Mark 1:1–10; Luke 19:29–38; John 12:12–16.

[70] See the discussion by Sanders, *Jesus and Judaism*, 306–7, who regards the historicity of the incident as probable but not certain.

[71] Harvey, *Jesus and the Constraints of History*, 122. The earliest messianic use in a Jewish context is in b. Sanh 98a.

[72] According to Sanders, *Jesus and Judaism*, 306, the disciples knew that Jesus was to be a special kind of king.

[73] See Adela Yarbro Collins, "From Noble Death to Crucified Messiah," *New Testament Studies* 40(1994).

[74] Hengel, "Christological Titles in Early Christianity," in Charlesworth, ed., *The Messiah*, 426–27.

[75] Much of the evidence is later than Mark but is independent of Christian influence. See D. Juel, *Messianic Exegesis. Christological Interpretation of the Old Testament in Early Christianity* (Philadelphia: Fortress, 1988) 137–39, 162–64.

[76] The similarity between Christ in Revelation 19 and the messiah in *4 Ezra* is noted by Adela Yarbro Collins, "Eschatology in the Book of Revelation," *Ex Auditu* 6(1990) 70.

[77] Müller, *Messias und Menschensohn*, 203–8, argues that Revelation 19 incorporates a Jewish composition, but there are no literary arguments for this position. Müller fails to reckon with the vitality of biblical paradigms in shaping the Christian imagination.

[78] Juel, *Messianic Exegesis*, 89–117; Yarbro Collins, "From Noble Death to Crucified Messiah," *New Testament Studies* 40(1994) 481–503.

[79] Sam K. Williams, *Jesus' Death as a Saving Event* (Harvard Dissertations in Religion 2; Missoula: Scholars Press, 1975) 221–29; Juel, *Messianic Exegesis*, 119–33.

[80] Larry W. Hurtado, *One God, One Lord. Early Christian Devotion and Ancient Jewish Monotheism* (Philadelphia: Fortress, 1988), discusses some of the Jewish precedents for the attribution of divine attributes to figures under God. He treats "Personified Divine Attributes," "Exalted Patriarchs as Divine Agents," and "Principal Angels." Inexplicably, however, he neglects the import of royal messianism.

[81] Rev 1:13–16 goes further, in applying to the Son of Man some of the imagery associated with the Ancient of Days in Daniel 7. See further Adela Yarbro Collins, "The 'Son of Man' Tradition and the Book of Revelation," in Charlesworth, ed., *The Messiah*, 536–68. The Old Greek translation of Daniel says that the one like a son of man came as (*hōs*), rather than to (*heōs*) the Ancient of Days, but this may be due to scribal error. See Sharon Pace Jeansonne, *The Old Greek Translation of Daniel 7–12* (Catholic Bible Quarterly Monograph Series 19; Washington, D.C.: Catholic Biblical Association, 1988) 96–98.

BIBLIOGRAPHY

Abegg, Martin, "Messianic Hope and 4Q285: A Reassessment," *Journal of Biblical Literature* 113(1994) 81–91.

Aharoni, Y., "Expedition B—The Cave of Horror," *Israel Exploration Journal* 12(1962) 186–99.

Aleksandrov, G. S., "The Role of Aqiba in the Bar Kokhba Rebellion," in J. Neusner, *Eliezer ben Hyrcanus* (Leiden: Brill, 1973) 2.428–42.

Alexander, P. S., "3 (Hebrew Apocalypse of) Enoch," in J. H. Charlesworth, ed., *The Old Testament Pseudepigrapha* (Garden City, NY: Doubleday, 1983) 1.223–315.

———, "A Note on the Syntax of 4Q448," *Journal of Jewish Studies* 44(1993) 301–2.

Allegro, J. M., "Further Messianic References in Qumran Literature," *Journal of Biblical Literature* 75(1956) 174–87.

Allison, Dale C., "Elijah Must Come First," *Journal of Biblical Literature* 103(1984) 256–58.

Alt, Albrecht, "Jesaja 8,23–9,6. Befreiungsnacht und Krönungstag," *Kleine Schriften zur Geschichte des Volkes Israel* (Munich: Kaiser, 1953) 2.206–25.

Applebaum, S., *Jews and Greeks in Ancient Cyrene* (Leiden: Brill, 1979).

Attridge, Harold W., *The Epistle to the Hebrews* (Hermeneia; Philadelphia: Fortress, 1989).

Aune, David E., "On the Origins of the 'Council of Yavneh' Myth," *Journal of Biblical Literature* 110(1991) 491–93.

Baillet, Maurice, *Qumrân Grotte 4: 3 (4Q482–4Q520)* (Discoveries in the Judaean Desert 7; Oxford: Clarendon, 1982).

Baras, Z., ed., *Messianism and Eschatology* (Jerusalem: The Historical Society of Israel, 1983 [in Hebrew]).

Barnes, T. D., "Trajan and the Jews," *Journal of Jewish Studies* 43(1992) 203–20.

Barnett, P. W., "The Jewish Sign Prophets — A.D. 40–70: Their Intentions and Origin," in *New Testament Studies* 27(1980–81) 679–97.

Barton, John, *Oracles of God: Perceptions of Ancient Prophecy in Israel after the Exile* (Oxford: Oxford University Press, 1986).

Baumgarten, J. M., "4Q502, Marriage or Golden Age Ritual?" *Journal of Jewish Studies* 34(1983)125–35.

———, "The Qumran-Essene Restraints on Marriage," in L. H. Schiffman, ed., *Archaeology and History in the Dead Sea Scrolls* (Sheffield: Journal for the Study of the Old Testament, 1990) 13–24.

Beale, G. K., *The Use of Daniel in Jewish Apocalyptic Literature and in the Revelation of St. John* (Lanham, MD: University Press of America, 1984).

Beall, T. S., *Josephus' Description of the Essenes Illustrated by the Dead Sea Scrolls* (Studiorum Novi Testamenti Societas Monograph Series 58; Cambridge: Cambridge University Press, 1988).

Beasley-Murray, G. R., "The Interpretation of Daniel 7," *Catholic Biblical Quarterly* 45(1983) 44–58.

Becker, Joachim, *Messiaserwartung im Alten Testament* (Stuttgarter Bibelstudien 83: Stuttgart: Katholisches Bibelwerk, 1977) = *Messianic Expectation in the Old Testament* (trans. David E. Green; Philadelphia: Fortress, 1980).

Beckwith, R., *The Old Testament Canon of the New Testament Church and its Background in Early Judaism* (Grand Rapids, MI: Eerdmans, 1985).

Benoit, P., J. T. Milik and R. de Vaux, *Les Grottes de Murabba'at* (Discoveries in the Judaean Desert 2; Oxford: Clarendon, 1961).

Berger, Klaus, "Die königlichen Messiastraditionen des Neuen Testaments," *New Testament Studies* 29(1973–74) 1–44.

———, "Zum Problem der Messianität Jesu," *Zeitschrift für Theologie und Kirche* 71(1974) 1–30.

Bergmeier, Roland, *Die Essener-Berichte des Flavius Josephus* (Kampen: Kok Pharos, 1993) 114–21.

Beyerlin, W., *Near Eastern Religious Texts Relating to the Old Testament* (Philadelphia: Westminster, 1978).

Black, Matthew, *The Book of Enoch or 1 Enoch* (Leiden: Brill, 1985).

———, "Theological Conceptions in the Dead Sea Scrolls," *Svensk Exegetisk Årsbok* 18–19 (1953/54) 72–97.

———, *The Scrolls and Christian Origins* (New York: Scribners, 1961).

Blenkinsopp, J., *A History of Prophecy in Israel* (Philadelphia: Westminster, 1983).

Bockmuehl, M., "A 'Slain Messiah' in 4Q Serekh Milhamah (4Q285)?" *Tyndale Bulletin* 43(1992) 155–69.

Bibliography

Borgen, Peder, "'There Shall Come Forth a Man': Reflections on Messianic Ideas in Philo," in J. H. Charlesworth, ed., *The Messiah* (Minneapolis: Fortress, 1992) 341–61.

Borger, R., ed., *Die Inschriften Asarhaddons König von Assyrien* (Archiv für Orientforschung 9; Graz: published by the editor, 1956).

Bousset, Wilhelm, "Die Himmelsreise der Seele," *Archiv für Religionsgeschichte* 4(1901) 136–69; 229–73.

———, *Die Religion des Judentums* (Berlin: de Gruyter, 1903).

Brandon, S. G. F., *Jesus and the Zealots: A Study of the Political Factor in Primitive Christianity* (Manchester: Manchester University Press, 1967).

Braude, W. G., trans., *Midrash on Psalms* (New Haven, CT: Yale University Press, 1959).

———, *Pesikta Rabbati* (New Haven, CT: Yale University Press, 1968).

Brooke, George J., *Exegesis at Qumran. 4QFlorilegium in its Jewish Context* (Journal for the Study of the Old Testament Supplement 29; Sheffield: Journal for the Study of the Old Testament, 1985).

———, "4Q252, Pesher Genesis: Structure and Themes," *Jewish Quarterly Review* (forthcoming).

———, "4QTestament of Levi^d(?) and the Messianic Servant High Priest," in M. de Boer, ed., *From Jesus to John. Essays on Jesus and New Testament Christology in Honour of Marinus de Jonge* (Journal for the Study of the New Testament Supplement 84; Sheffield: Journal for the Study of the Old Testament, 1993) 83–100.

———, "The Kittim in the Qumran Pesharim," in L. Alexander, ed., *Images of Empire* (Sheffield: Journal for the Study of the Old Testament, 1991) 135–39.

———, "The Messiah of Aaron in the Damascus Document," *Revue de Qumran* 15(1991) 215–30.

Broshi, Magen, "The Gigantic Dimensions of the Visionary Temple in the Temple Scroll," *Biblical Archaeology Review* 13(1987) 36–37 = H. Shanks, ed., *Understanding the Dead Sea Scrolls* (New York: Random House, 1992) 113–15.

———, "Postscript to 'Qumran, Khirbet and 'Ein Feshka,' by Roland de Vaux" in E. Stern, ed., *The New Encyclopedia of Archaeological Excavations in the Holy Land* (New York: Simon and Schuster, 1993) 1241.

Brown, Raymond E., *The Birth of the Messiah* (Garden City, NY: Doubleday, 1977, revised edition, 1993).

———, "J. Starcky's Theory of Qumran Messianic Development," *Catholic Biblical Quarterly* 28(1996) 51–57.

Brownlee, W. H., "A Comparison of the Covenanters of the Dead Sea Scrolls with Pre-Christian Jewish Sects," *Biblical Archeologist* 13(1950) 50–72.

———, "Messianic Motifs of Qumran and the New Testament," *New Testament Studies* 3(1956–57) 12–30.

Buehler, William W., *The Pre-Herodian Civil War and Social Debate* (Basel: Reinhardt, 1974).

Bultmann, Rudolf, *Theology of the New Testament* (New York: Scribners, 1951).

Caquot, A., "Le messianisme Qumrànien," in M. Delcor, ed., *Qumrân, Sa piété, sa théologie et son milieu* (Bibliotheca Ephemeridum Theologicarum Lovaniensium 46; Paris-Gembloux: Duculot/Leuven University Press, 1978) 231–47.

———, "Remarques sur les chap. 70 et 71 du livre éthiopien d'Hénoch," in H. Monloubou, ed., *Apocalypses et Théologie de l'Espérance* (Paris: Cerf, 1977) 111–22.

Caragounis, Chrys C., *The Son of Man* (Tübingen: Mohr, 1986).

Carmignac, J., "La Notion d'eschatologie dans la Bible et à Qumrân," *Revue de Qumrân* 7(1969) 17–31.

———, "Les citations de l'Ancien Testament et spécialement des Poèmes du Serviteur dans les Hymnes de Qumrân," *Revue de Qumrân* 2(1960) 357–94.

———, "Le Retour du Docteur de Justice à la fin des jours?" *Revue de Qumrân* 1(1958–59) 235–48.

Cartlidge, D. R., and Dungan, D. L., *Documents for the Study of the Gospels* (Philadelphia: Fortress, 1980).

Casey, Maurice, *Son of Man. The Interpretation and Influence of Daniel 7* (London: SPCK, 1979).

———, "The Use of the Term 'Son of Man' in the Similitudes of Enoch," *Journal for the Study of Judaism* 7(1976) 1–29,

Chadwick, Henry, *The Early Church* (Harmondsworth: Penguin, 1967).

Charles, R. H., *Apocrypha and Pseudepigrapha of the Old Testament* (2 vols. Oxford: Clarendon, 1913).

———, *The Book of Enoch, or I Enoch* (Oxford: Clarendon, 1912).

———, *A Critical and Exegetical Commentary on the Revelation of St. John* (New York: Scribners, 1920).

———, *The Ethiopic Version of the Book of Enoch* (Oxford: Clarendon, 1906).

Charlesworth, James H., "From Jewish Messianology to Christian Christology. Some Caveats and Perspectives," in J. Neusner, W. S. Green and E. Frerichs, eds., *Judaisms and Their Messiahs* (Cambridge: Cambridge University Press, 1987) 225–64.

———, "From Messianology to Christology: Problems and Prospects," in J. H. Charlesworth, ed., *The Messiah* (Minneapolis: Fortress, 1992) 3–35.

———, ed., *The Messiah* (Minneapolis: Fortress, 1992).

———, "The Messiah in the Pseudepigrapha," in H. Temporini and W. Haase, eds., *Aufstieg und Niedergang der Römischen Welt* (Berlin: de Gruyter, 1979) *II.19.1*, 188–218.

———, *The Old Testament Pseudepigrapha* (2 vols. Garden City, NY: Doubleday, 1983–85).

———, "The Portrayal of the Righteous as an Angel," in J. J. Collins and G. W. Nickelsburg, eds., *Ideal Figures in Ancient Judaism* (Chico, CA: Scholars Press, 1980) 135–51.

Bibliography

———, "Sense or Sensationalism? The Dead Sea Scrolls Controversy," *The Christian Century* (January 29, 1992) 92–98.

Chester, A., "Jewish Messianic Expectations and Mediatorial Figures," in M. Hengel and U. Heckel, eds., *Paulus und das antike Judentum* (Tübingen: Mohr, 1991) 17–89.

Clifford, Richard J., *Fair Spoken and Persuading. An Interpretation of Second Isaiah* (New York: Paulist, 1984).

Collins, John J., *The Apocalyptic Imagination* (New York: Crossroad, 1984).

———, *The Apocalyptic Vision of the Book of Daniel* (Harvard Semitic Monographs 16; Mossoula, MT: Scholars Press, 1977).

———, *Daniel* (Hermeneia; Minneapolis: Fortress, 1993).

———, "The Epic of Theodotus and the Hellenism of the Hasmoneans," *Harvard Theological Review* 73(1980) 94–104.

———, "Essenes," in D. N. Freedman, ed., *The Anchor Bible Dictionary* 2.619–26.

———, "The Heavenly Representative. The 'Son of Man' in the Similitudes of Enoch," in J. J. Collins and G. W. Nickelsburg, eds., *Ideal Figures in Ancient Judaism* (Chico, CA: Scholars Press, 1980) 111–33.

———, "Method in the Study of Messianism," in M. Wise, N. Golb, J. J. Collins, and D. Pardee, eds., *Methods of Investigation of the Dead Sea Scrolls and the Khirbet Qumran Site: Present Realities and Future Prospects* (New York: New York Academy of Sciences, 1994) 213–29.

———, "Nebuchadnezzar and the Kingdom of God. Deferred Eschatology in the Jewish Diaspora," in C. Elsas and H. G. Kippenberg, eds., *Loyalitätskonflikte in der Religionsgeschichte. Festschrift für Carsten Colpe* (Würzburg: Königshausen & Neumann, 1990) 252–57.

———, "The Origin of Evil in Apocalyptic Literature and the Dead Sea Scrolls," in John A. Emerton, ed., *Congress Volume, Paris* (Leiden: Brill, forthcoming).

———, "The Origin of the Qumran Community. A Review of the Evidence," in M. P. Horgan and P. J. Kobelski, eds., *To Touch the Text. Biblical and Related Studies in Honor of Joseph A. Fitzmyer, S.J.* (New York: Crossroad, 1989) 159–78.

———, "Patterns of Eschatology at Qumran," in B. Halpern and J. D. Levenson, eds., *Traditions in Transformation. Turning Points in Biblical Faith* (Winona Lake, IN: Eisenbrauns, 1981) 351–75.

———, "The Place of the Fourth Sibyl in the Development of the Jewish Sibyllina," *Journal of Jewish Studies* 25(1974) 365–80.

———, "Prophecy and Fulfillment in the Qumran Scrolls," *Journal of the Evangelical Theological Society* 30(1987) 267–78.

———, "The Sage in Apocalyptic and Pseudepigraphic Literature," in J. G. Gammie and L. Perdue, eds., *The Sage in Israel and the Ancient Near East* (Winona Lake, IN: Eisenbrauns, 1990) 343–54.

———, "The Sibyl and the Potter," in L. Borman, K. Del Tredici, and A. Standhartinger, eds., *Religious Propaganda and Missionary Competition in the New Testament World. Essays in Honor of Dieter Georgi* (Leiden: Brill, 1994) 57–69.

——, "The Sibylline Oracles," in J. H. Charlesworth, ed., *The Old Testament Pseudepigrapha* (Garden City, NY: Doubleday, 1983) 1.317–472.

——, *The Sibylline Oracles of Egyptian Judaism* (Society of Biblical Literature Dissertation Series 13; Missoula, MT: Scholars Press, 1974).

——, "The 'Son of God' Text from Qumran," in M. de Boer, ed., *From Jesus to John. Essays on Jesus and the New Testament Christology in Honour of Marinus de Jonge* (Sheffield: Journal for the Study of the Old Testament, 1993) 65–82.

——, "The Son of Man in First Century Judaism," *New Testament Studies* 38(1992) 448–66.

——, "Stirring up the Great Sea: The Religio-Historical Background of Daniel 7," in A. S. van der Woude, ed., *The Book of Daniel in the Light of New Findings* (Bibliotheca Ephemeridum Theologicarum, Lovaniensium 106; Leuven: Leuven University Press, 1993) 121–36.

——, "A Throne in the Heavens. Apotheosis in pre-Christian Judaism," in John J. Collins and Michael Fishbane, eds., *Death, Ecstasy and Otherworldly Journeys* (Albany: State University of New York Press, forthcoming).

——, "The Works of the Messiah," *Dead Sea Discoveries* 1(1994) 98–112.

Colpe, Carsten, "Der Begriff 'Menschensohn' und die Methode der Erforschung messianischer Prototypen," *Kairos* 12(1970) 81–112.

Cook, Stephen L., "The Metamorphosis of a Shepherd: The Tradition History of Zechariah 11:17 + 13:7–9," *Catholic Biblical Quarterly* 55(1993) 453–66.

Crook, M. B., "A Suggested Occasion for Isaiah 9,2–7 and 11,1–9," *Journal of Biblical Literature* 68(1949) 213–24.

Cross, Frank Moore, *The Ancient Library of Qumran and Modern Biblical Studies* (Garden City, NY: Doubleday, 1961).

——, *Canaanite Myth and Hebrew Epic* (Cambridge, MA: Harvard University Press, 1973).

——, "Some Notes on a Generation of Qumran Studies," in J. Trebolle Barrera and L. Vegas Montaner, eds., *The Madrid Qumran Congress* (Leiden: Brill, 1992) 1–21.

Crossan, J. D., *The Historical Jesus* (San Francisco: Harper, 1991).

Cullmann, Oscar, *Jesus and the Revolutionaries* (New York: Harper & Row, 1970).

Dalman, G. H., *Der leidende und der sterbende Messias der Synagoge* (Berlin: Reuther, 1888).

Davenport, G. L., "The 'Anointed of the Lord' in Psalms of Solomon 17," in J. J. Collins and G. W. Nickelsburg, eds., *Ideal Figures in Ancient Judaism* (Chico, CA: Scholars Press, 1980) 67–92.

Davies, Philip R., *Behind the Essenes. History and Ideology in the Dead Sea Scrolls* (Brown Judaic Studies 94; Atlanta: Scholars Press, 1987).

——, "Calendrical Change and Qumran Origins: An Assessment of VanderKam's Theory," *Catholic Biblical Quarterly* 45(1983) 80–89.

————, *The Damascus Covenant. An Interpretation of the "Damascus Document"* (Journal for the Study of the Old Testament Supplement 25; Sheffield: Journal for the Study of the Old Testament, 1983).

————, "Eschatology at Qumran," *Journal of Biblical Literature* 104(1985) 39–55.

————, "War Rule (1QM)," in D. N. Freedman, ed., *The Anchor Bible Dictionary* 6.875–76.

Davies, W. D., *Torah in the Messianic Age and/or the Age to Come* (Society of Biblical Literature Monograph Series 7; Philadelphia: Society of Biblical Literature, 1952).

Day, John, *God's Conflict with the Dragon and the Sea* (Cambridge, MA: Cambridge University Press, 1985).

de Boer, Martinus, ed., *From Jesus to John. Essays on Jesus and New Testament Christology in Honour of Marinus de Jonge* (Journal for the Study of the New Testament Supplement 84; Sheffield: Journal for the Study of the Old Testament, 1993).

de Boer, P. A. H., "The Son of God in the Old Testament," *Oudtestamentische Studiën* 18(1973) 188–201.

Deichgräber, R., "Zur messiaserwartung der Damaskusschrift," *Zeitschrift für die Alttestamentliche Wissenschaft* 78(1966) 333–43.

de Jonge, H. J., "The Historical Jesus' View of Himself and of His Mission," in Martinus de Boer, ed., *From Jesus to John*, 21–37.

de Jonge, Marinus, "The Earliest Christian Use of Christos. Some Suggestions," in M. de Jonge, *Jewish Eschatology*, 102–24.

————, *Jesus, The Servant-Messiah* (New Haven, CT: Yale University Press, 1991).

————, "Jesus, Son of David and Son of God," in M. de Jonge, *Jewish Eschatology*, 135–44.

————, *Jewish Eschatology, Early Christian Christology and the Testaments of the Twelve Patriarchs. Collected Essays of Marinus de Jonge* (Leiden: Brill, 1991).

————, "The Testament of Levi and 'Aramaic Levi,'" *Revue de Qumrân* 13(1988) 367–85 = *Jewish Eschatology*, 244–62.

————, *The Testaments of the Twelve Patriarchs. A Study of Their Text, Composition and Origin* (2nd ed.; Assen: van Gorcum, 1975).

————, "Two Messiahs in the Testaments of the Twelve Patriarchs?" in M. de Jonge, *Jewish Eschatology*, 191–203.

Delcor, M., "Psaumes de Salomon," *Supplément au Dictionnaire de la Bible*, fasc. 48(1973) 214–45.

————, ed., *Qumrân, Sa piété, sa théologie et son milieu* (Bibliotheca Ephemeridum Theologicarum Lovaniensium 46; Leuven: Leuven University Press, 1978).

Dillmann, A., *Lexicon Linguae Aethiopicae* (Leipzig: Weigel, 1865).

Dimant, Devorah, "4QFlorilegium and the Idea of the Community as Temple," in A. Caquot, M. Hadas-Lebel and J. Riaud, eds., *Hellenica et Judaica: Hommage à Valentin Nikiprowetzky* (Paris/Leuven: Peeters, 1986).

Donceel, Robert, and Pauline Donceel-Voûte, "The Archaeology of Qumran," in M. Wise, N. Golb, J. J. Collins, and D. Pardee, eds., *Methods of Investigation of the Dead Sea Scrolls and the Khirbet Qumran Site: Present Realities and Future Prospects* (New York: New York Academy of Sciences, 1994) 1–32.

Donceel-Voûte, Pauline, "'Coenaculum.' La Salle à l'Étage du Locus 30 à Khirbet Qumrân sur la Mer Morte," *Banquets d'Orient. Res Orientales* 4(1992) 61–84.

Donner, H., and W. Rollig, *Kanaanäische und aramäische Inschriften* (3 vols. Wiesbaden: Harrassowitz, 1962–64).

Doran, Robert, "The Non-Dating of Jubilees: Jub 34–38; 23:14–32 in Narrative Context," *Journal for the Study of Judaism* 20(1989) 1–11.

Duhaime, Jean L., "Dualistic Reworking in the Scrolls from Qumran," *Catholic Biblical Quarterly* 49(1987) 32–56.

Duhm, Bernhard, *Das Buch Jesaja* (Göttingen: Vandenhoeck & Ruprecht, 1892).

———, *Die Psalmen* (2nd ed.; Tübingen: Mohr, 1922).

Dunand, F., "L'Oracle du Potier et la formation de l'apocalyptique en Égypte," in F. Raphael, ed., *L'Apocalyptique* (Paris: Geuthner, 1977) 39–67.

Dunn, James D. G., "Messianic Ideas and their Influence on the Jesus of History," in Charlesworth, ed., *The Messiah*, 365–81.

———, *The Partings of the Ways Between Christianity and Judaism and Their Significance for the Character of Christianity* (Philadelphia: Trinity Press International, 1991).

Dupont-Sommer, A., *Aperçus préliminaires sur les manuscrits de la Mer Morte* (Paris: Maisonneuve, 1950).

———, *The Essene Writings from Qumran* (Gloucester, MA: Peter Smith, 1973).

———, "Le mère du Messie et la mère de l'Aspic dans un hymne de Qoumrân," *Revue de l'Histoire des Religions* (1955) 174–88.

Eddy, S. K., *The King Is Dead. Studies in the Near Eastern Resistance to Hellenism 334–332 B.C.* (Lincoln: University of Nebraska Press, 1961).

Eisenman, Robert H., and James M. Robinson, eds., *A Facsimile Edition of the Dead Sea Scrolls* (2 vols.; Washington, D.C.: Biblical Archeology Society, 1991).

Eisenman, R. H., and M. Wise, *The Dead Sea Scrolls Uncovered. The First Complete Translation and Interpretation of 50 Key Documents Withheld for Over 35 Years* (Rockport, MA: Element, 1992).

Ellis, E. Earle, *The Old Testament in Early Christianity* (Tübingen: Mohr-Siebeck, 1991).

Emerton, John A. "The Origin of the Son of Man Imagery," *Journal of Theological Studies* 9(1958) 225–42.

Ephron, J., *Studies on the Hasmonean Period* (Leiden: Brill, 1987).

Eshel, E., and H., and A. Yardeni, "A Scroll from Qumran Which Includes Part

Bibliography

of Psalm 154 and a Prayer for King Jonathan and His Kingdom," (Hebrew), *Tarbiz* 60(1991) 295–324, (English), *Israel Exploration Journal* 42(1992) 199–229.

Eshel, H., "The Historical Background of the Pesher Interpreting Joshua's Curse on the Rebuilder of Jericho," *Revue de Qumrân* 15(1992) 409–20.

Faierstein, Morris M., "Why do the Scribes say that Elijah Must Come First?" *Journal of Biblical Literature* 100(1981) 75–86.

Farmer, William R., "Judas, Simon and Athronges," *New Testament Studies* 4(1957/8) 147–55.

Feldman, Louis H., *Jew and Gentile in the Ancient World* (Princeton, NJ: Princeton University Press, 1993).

Ferch, A. J., *The Son of Man in Daniel 7* (Berrien Springs, MI: Andrews University Press, 1979).

Fishbane, Michael, *Biblical Interpretation in Ancient Israel* (Oxford: Oxford University Press, 1985).

———, "Use, Authority and Interpretation of Mikra at Qumran," in Martin J. Mulder, ed., *Mikra. Text, Translation, Reading and Interpretation of the Hebrew Bible in Ancient Judaism and Early Christianity* (Philadelphia: Fortress, 1988) 339–77.

Fitzmyer, J. A., "The Aramaic 'Elect of God' Text from Qumran Cave 4," in Fitzmyer, *Essays on the Semitic Background of the New Testament*, 127–60.

———, "The Bar Cochba Period," in Fitzmyer, *Essays on the Semitic Background of the New Testament*, 305–54.

———, "The Contribution of Qumran Aramaic to the Study of the New Testament," *New Testament Studies* 20(1973–74) 382–407, reprinted in idem, *A Wandering Aramean*, 85–113.

———, *Essays on the Semitic Background of the New Testament* (Missoula, MT: Scholars Press, 1974).

———, "'4QTestimonia' and the New Testament," in Fitzmyer, *Essays on the Semitic Background of the New Testament*, 59–89.

———, "4Q246: The 'Son of God' Document from Qumran," *Biblica* 74 (1993) 153–74.

———, *The Gospel According to Luke I–IX* (Anchor Bible 28; Garden City, NY: Doubleday, 1981).

———, "More About Elijah Coming First," *Journal of Biblical Literature* 104(1985) 295–96.

———, "The use of explicit Old Testament quotations in Qumran literature and in the New Testament," in Fitzmyer, *Essays on the Semitic Background of the New Testament*, 3–58.

———, *A Wandering Aramean. Collected Aramaic Essays* (Society of Biblical Literature Monograph Series 25; Chico, CA: Scholars Press, 1979).

Flusser, David, "The Four Empires in the Fourth Sibyl and in the Book of Daniel," *Israel Oriental Studies* 2(1972) 148–75.

———, "The Hubris of the Antichrist in a Fragment from Qumran," *Immanuel* 10(1980) 31–37, reprinted in Flusser, *Judaism and the Origins of Christianity* (Jerusalem: Magnes, 1988) 207–13.

Fossum, Jarl, "Son of God," in D. N. Freedman, ed., *The Anchor Bible Dictionary* 6.128–37.

Fraidl, Franz, *Die Exegese der Siebzig Wochen Daniels in der alten und mittleren Zeit* (Graz: Leuschner & Lubensky, 1883).

Frankfurter, David, *Elijah in Upper Egypt. The Apocalypse of Elijah and Early Egyptian Christianity* (Minneapolis: Fortress, 1993).

———, "Lest Egypt's City Be Deserted: Religion and Ideology in the Egyptian Response to the Jewish Revolt (116–117 C.E.)," *Journal of Jewish Studies* 43(1992) 203–20.

Freedman, David Noel, ed., *The Anchor Bible Dictionary* (6 vols.; New York: Doubleday, 1992).

Freedman, H., and M. Simon, trans., *Midrash Rabbah: Genesis* (London: Soncino, 1939).

Friedlander, G., trans., *Pirke de Rabbi Eliezer* (New York: Hermon, 1965).

Friedrich, Johannes, *Gott im Brüder* (Stuttgart: Calwer, 1977).

Fuks, Alexander, "Aspects of the Jewish Revolt in A.D. 115–117," *Journal of Roman Studies* 51(1961) 98–104.

Gager, John, *The Origins of Anti-Semitism. Attitudes Towards Judaism in Pagan and Christian Antiquity* (New York: Oxford University Press, 1983).

García Martínez, Florentino, "4Q246: Tipo del Anticristo o Libertador Escatologico?" in *El Misterio de la Palabra* (Homenaje al profesor L. Alonso Schökel; Valencia/Madrid, 1983) 229–44, reprinted as "The eschatological figure of 4Q246," in García Martínez, *Qumran and Apocalyptic*, 162–79.

———, "Messianische Erwartungen in den Qumranschriften," *Jahrbuch für Biblische Theologie* 8(1993) 171–208.

———, "Nuevos Textos Mesiánicos de Qumran y el Mesias del Nuevo Testamento," *Communio* 26(1993) 3–31.

———, *Qumran and Apocalyptic. Studies on the Aramaic Texts from Qumran* (Leiden: Brill, 1992).

———, "Qumran Origins and Early History: A Groningen Hypothesis," *Folia Orientalia* 25(1989) 113–36.

———, *Textos de Qumrán* (Madrid: Trotta, 1992).

García Martínez, F., and A. van der Woude, "A Groningen Hypothesis of Qumran Origins," *Revue de Qumrân* 14(1990) 521–41.

Gaston, Lloyd, "Paul and the Torah," in A. Davies, ed., *Anti-Semitism and the Foundations of Christianity* (New York: Paulist, 1979).

Gese, Hartmut, "Anfang und Ende der Apokalyptik, dargestellt am Sacharjabuch," *Zeitschrift für Theologie und Kirche* 70(1973) 20–49.

Ginzberg, L., *An Unknown Jewish Sect* (New York: Jewish Theological Seminary, 1976, trans. of the German 1922 edition) 209–56.

Bibliography

Glazier-McDonald, Beth, *Malachi: The Divine Messenger* (Society of Biblical Literature Dissertation Series 98; Atlanta: Scholars Press, 1987).

Golb, Norman, "The Dead Sea Scrolls. A New Perspective," *The American Scholar* 58(1989) 177–207.

———, "Khirbet Qumran and the Manuscripts of the Judaean Wilderness: Observations on the Logic of their Investigation," *Journal of Near Eastern Studies* 49(1990) 103–114.

———, "The Problem of Origin and Identification of the Dead Sea Scrolls," *Proceedings of the American Philosophical Society* 124(1980) 1–24.

———, "Who Hid the Dead Sea Scrolls?" *Biblical Archeologist* 48(1985) 68–82.

Goldman, Y., *Prophétie et royauté au retour de l'exil. Les origines littéraires de la forme massorétique du livre de Jérémie* (Orbis Biblicus et Orientalis 118; Freiburg: Universitätsverlag/Göttingen: Vandenhoeck & Ruprecht, 1992).

Goldstein, Jonathan A., "How the Authors of 1 and 2 Maccabees Treated the 'Messianic' Promises," in Neusner et al., eds., *Judaisms and Their Messiahs*, 69–96.

Grabbe, L. L., *Judaism from Cyrus to Hadrian* (2 vols.; Minneapolis: Fortress, 1992).

Grant, Robert M., *Jesus After the Gospels. The Christ of the Second Century* (Louisville, KY: Westminster, 1990).

Gray, G. B., "The Psalms of Solomon," in Charles, ed., *Apocrypha and Pseudepigrapha of the Old Testament*, 2.625–52.

Gray, Rebecca, *Prophetic Figures in Late Second Temple Jewish Palestine* (Oxford: Oxford University Press, 1993).

Grayson, A. K., *Babylonian Historical-Literary Texts* (Toronto: University of Toronto Press, 1975).

Green, William Scott, "Introduction: Messiah in Judaism: Rethinking the Question," in Neusner et al., eds., *Judaisms and Their Messiahs*, 1–13.

Greenberg, Moshe, *Ezekiel 1–20* (Anchor Bible 22; Garden City, NY: Doubleday, 1983).

Greenfield, J. C., and M. E. Stone, "The Aramaic and Greek Fragments of a Levi Document," in H. W. Hollander and M. de Jonge, eds., *The Testaments of the Twelve Patriarchs: A Commentary* (Leiden: Brill, 1985) 457–69.

———, "Remarks on the Aramaic Testament of Levi from the Geniza," *Revue Biblique* 86(1979) 214–30.

Grelot, Pierre, "Notes sur le Testament araméen de Levi," *Revue Biblique* 63(1956) 391–406.

———, *Les Poèmes du Serviteur* (Paris: Cerf, 1981).

———, "Sur Isaie lxi: la première consécration du grand-prêtre," *Revue Biblique* 97(1990) 414–31.

Griffiths, Gwyn, "Apocalyptic in the Hellenistic Era," in D. Hellholm, ed., *Apocalypticism in the Hellenistic World and in the Near East* (Tübingen: Mohr-Siebeck, 1983) 273–93.

Gruenwald, Ithamar, *Apocalyptic and Merkavah Mysticism* (Leiden: Brill, 1980).

Gruenwald, I., S. Shaked, and G. Stroumsa, eds., *Messiah and Christos: Studies in the Jewish Origins of Christianity* (Tübingen: Mohr-Siebeck, 1992).

Hampel, Volker, *Menschensohn und Historischer Jesus* (Neukirchen-Vluyn: Neukirchener Verlag, 1990).

Hanson, Paul D., "Zechariah 9 and an Ancient Ritual Pattern," *Journal of Biblical Literature* 92(1973) 37–59.

Harrington, D. J., and J. Strugnell, "Qumran Cave 4 Texts: A New Publication," *Journal of Biblical Literature* 112(1993) 491–99.

Hartman, L. F. and A. A. DiLella, *The Book of Daniel* (Anchor Bible 23: New York, NY: Doubleday, 1978).

Harvey, A. E., *Jesus and the Constraints of History* (Philadelphia: Westminster, 1982).

Hay, David, *Glory at the Right Hand: Psalm 110 in Early Christianity* (Society of Biblical Literature Monograph Series 18; Nashville, Abingdon, 1973).

Hecht, R. D., "Philo and Messiah," in Neusner et al., eds., *Judaisms and Their Messiahs*, 139–68.

Heinemann, Joseph, "The Messiah of Ephraim and the Premature Exodus of the Tribe of Ephraim," *Harvard Theological Review* 68(1975) 1–15 (reprinted in Landman, ed., *Messianism in the Talmudic Era*, 339–53).

Hellholm, D., ed., *Apocalypticism in the Mediterranean World and the Near East* (Tübingen: Mohr-Siebeck, 1983).

Hengel, Martin, *The Charismatic Leader and His Followers* (Edinburgh: Clark, 1981).

———, "Christological Titles in Early Christianity," in Charlesworth, ed., *The Messiah*, 425–48.

———, *Crucifixion* (Philadelphia: Fortress, 1977).

———, "Jesus, der Messias Israels," in Gruenwald, Shaked, and Stroumsa, eds., *Messiah and Christos*, 155–76.

———, *Judaism and Hellenism* (Philadelphia: Fortress, 1974).

———, "Messianische Hoffnung und politischer 'Radikalismus' in der 'jüdisch-hellenistischen Diaspora,'" in Hellholm, ed., *Apocalypticism in the Mediterranean World and the Near East*, 655–86.

———, "'Setze dich zu meiner Rechten!' Die Inthronisation Christi zur Rechten Gottes und Psalm 110,1," in M. Philonenko, ed., *Le Trône de Dieu* (Tübingen: Mohr-Siebeck, 1993) 108–94.

———, *The Son of God* (Philadelphia: Fortress, 1976).

———, *Was Jesus a Revolutionist?* (Philadelphia: Fortress, 1971).

———, *The Zealots* (Edinburgh: Clark, 1989).

Hesse, F., "Chrio, etc." in G. Friedrich, ed., *Theological Dictionary of the New Testament* (Grand Rapids, MI: Eerdmans, 1974) 9.501–9.

Higgins, A. J. B., "Jewish Messianic Belief in Justin Martyr's Dialogue with Trypho," in Landman, ed., *Messianism in the Talmudic Era*, 182–89.

Bibliography

Hillers, D., *Micah* (Hermeneia; Philadelphia: Fortress, 1984).

Himmelfarb, Martha, *Tours of Heaven* (New York: Oxford, 1993).

————, "Revelation and Rapture: The Transformation of the Visionary in the Ascent Apocalypses," in J. J. Collins and J. H. Charlesworth, eds., *Mysteries and Revelations. Apocalyptic Studies after the Uppsala Colloquium* (Sheffield: Journal for the Study of the Old Testament, 1991) 89–102.

Hinnells, J. R., "The Zoroastrian Doctrine of Salvation in the Roman World: A Study of the Oracle of Hystaspes," in E. J. Sharpe and J. R. Hinnells, eds., *Man and His Salvation: Studies in Memory of S. G. F. Brandon* (Manchester: Manchester University Press, 1973) 125–48.

Holladay, Carl R., *Fragments from Hellenistic Jewish Authors II. Poets* (Atlanta: Scholars Press, 1989).

Holladay, W., *Jeremiah I* (Philadelphia: Fortress, 1986).

Hollander, H. W., and M. de Jonge, *The Testaments of the Twelve Patriarchs. A Commentary* (Leiden: Brill, 1985).

Holm-Nielsen, S., *Hodayot: Psalms from Qumran* (Aarhus: Universitets-forlaget, 1960).

Hooker, M. D., *Jesus and the Servant* (London: SPCK, 1959).

Horbury, William, "The Messianic Associations of 'The Son of Man,'" *Journal of Theological Studies* 36(1985) 34–55.

Horgan, Maurya P., *Pesharim: Qumran Interpretations of Biblical Books* (Catholic Biblical Quarterly Monograph Series 8; Washington, D.C.: Catholic Biblical Association, 1979).

Horsley, Richard A., "Popular Prophetic Movements at the Time of Jesus: Their Principal Features and Social Origins," *Journal for the Study of the New Testament* 26(1986) 3–27.

Horsley, R. A., and J. S. Hanson, *Bandits, Prophets, and Messiahs. Popular Movements at the Time of Jesus* (Minneapolis: Winston, 1985).

Hultgård, A., *L'Eschatologie des Testaments des Douze Patriarches I. Interprétation des Textes* (Stockholm: Almqvist & Wiksell, 1977).

Hurtado, L. W., *One God, One Lord. Early Christian Devotion and Ancient Jewish Monotheism* (Philadelphia: Fortress, 1988).

Hurwitz, S., *Die Gestalt des sterbenden Messias* (Stuttgart: Rascher, 1948).

Isaac, B. and A. Oppenheimer, "Bar Kokhba," in D. N. Freedman, ed., *The Anchor Bible Dictionary* 1.598–601.

————, "The Revolt of Bar Kokhba: Ideology and Modern Scholarship," *Journal of Jewish Studies* 36(1985) 33–60.

Isaac, Ephraim, "1 Enoch," in Charlesworth, ed., *The Old Testament Pseudepigrapha* 1.5–89.

Jacobson, Howard, *The Exagoge of Ezekiel* (Cambridge: Cambridge University Press, 1983).

————, "Phoenix Resurrected," *Harvard Theological Review* 80(1987) 229–33.

Jenks, G. C., *The Origin and Early Development of the Antichrist Myth* (Beihefte zur

Zeitschrift für die Alttestamentliche Wissenschaft 59; Berlin: de Gruyter, 1991).

Jeremias, G., *Der Lehrer der Gerechtigkeit* (Göttingen: Vandenhoeck & Ruprecht, 1963).

Jeremias, J., "ʿHλ(ε)ίας," in G. Kittel, ed., *Theological Dictionary of the New Testament* (Grand Rapids, MI: Eerdmans, 1964) 2.928–41.

——, "Παις Θεοῦ" in G. Friedrich, ed., *Theological Dictionary of the New Testament* (Grand Rapids, MI: Eerdmans, 1967) 5.677–700.

Juel, D. H., *Messianic Exegesis. Christological Interpretation of the Old Testament in Early Christianity* (Philadelphia: Fortress, 1988).

——, "The Origin of Mark's Christology," in Charlesworth, ed., *The Messiah*, 449–60.

Kasher, Aryeh, "A Comment on the Jewish Uprising in Egypt during the days of Trajan," *Journal of Jewish Studies* 27(1976) 147–58.

——, *The Jews in Hellenistic and Roman Egypt* (Tübingen: Mohr-Siebeck, 1985).

Kaufman, S. A., "Prediction, Prophecy, and Apocalypse in the Light of New Akkadian Texts," in A. Shinan, ed., *Proceedings of the Sixth World Congress of Jewish Studies 1973* (Jerusalem: World Union of Jewish Studies, 1977) 1:221–228.

Kearns, Rollin, *Vorfragen zur Christologie* (3 vols.; Tübingen: Mohr-Siebeck, 1978–82).

Kim, Seyoon, *The 'Son of Man' as the Son of God* (Tübingen: Mohr-Siebeck, 1983).

Kippenberg, H. G., *Garizim und Synagoge* (Berlin: de Gruyter, 1971).

——, "Die Geschichte der Mittelpersischen Apokalyptischen Traditionen," *Studia Iranica* 7(1978) 49–80.

Klausner, Joseph, *The Messianic Idea in Israel* (London: Allen and Unwin, 1956).

Knibb, Michael A., *The Ethiopic Book of Enoch* (Oxford: Oxford University Press, 1978).

——, "The Exile in the Literature of the Intertestamental Period," *Heythrop Journal* 17(1976) 253–72.

——, "The Interpretation of Damascus Document VII,9b–VIII,2a and XIX,5b–14," *Revue de Qumrân* 15(1991) 243–51.

——, *The Qumran Community* (Cambridge: Cambridge University Press, 1987).

——, "The Teacher of Righteousness—A Messianic Title?" in P. R. Davies and R. T. White, eds., *A Tribute to Geza Vermes. Essays on Jewish and Christian Literature and History* (Journal for the Study of the Old Testament Supplement 100; Sheffield: Journal for the Study of the Old Testament, 1990) 51–65.

Knowles, Louis E., "The Interpretation of the Seventy Weeks of Daniel in the Early Church Fathers," *Westminster Theological Journal* 7(1944) 136–60.

Kobelski, Paul J., *Melchizedek and Melchireša'* (Catholic Biblical Quarterly Monograph Series 10; Washington, D.C.: Catholic Biblical Association of America, 1981).

Bibliography

Koch, K., "Ezra and the Origins of Judaism," *Journal of Semitic Studies* 19(1974) 190–93.

Koenen, Ludwig, "Die Adaptation Ägyptischer Königsideologie am Ptolemäerhof," in W. Peremans, ed., *Egypt and the Hellenistic World* (Studia Hellenistica 27; Leuven: Leuven University Press, 1983) 152–70.

———, "Die Prophezeiungun des 'Töpfers,'" *Zeitschrift für Papyrologie und Epigraphik* 2(1968) 178–209.

Kratz, R. G., *Kyros im Deuterojesaja-Buch* (Tübingen: Mohr-Siebeck, 1991).

Kraus, H. J., *Psalms 1–59. A Commentary* (Minneapolis: Augsburg, 1988).

———, *Psalms 60–150. A Commentary* (Minneapolis: Augsburg, 1989).

Kugel, James, "Levi's Elevation to the Priesthood in Second Temple Writings," *Harvard Theological Review* 86(1993) 1–64.

———, "The Story of Dinah in the Testament of Levi," *Harvard Theological Review* 85(1992) 1–34.

Kuhn, H.-W., *Enderwartung und gegenwärtiges Heil* (Göttingen: Vandenhoeck & Ruprecht, 1966).

Kuhn, K. G., "The Two Messiahs of Aaron and Israel," in K. Stendahl, ed., *The Scrolls and the New Testament* (New York: Harper, 1957) 54–64.

Kvanvig, Helge, *Roots of Apocalyptic* (Neukirchen-Vluyn: Neukirchener Verlag, 1988).

Laato, Antti, *The Servant of YHWH and Cyrus* (Stockholm: Almqvist & Wiksell, 1992).

Lacocque, André, *The Book of Daniel* (Atlanta: Knox, 1979).

———, "The Vision of the Eagle in 4 Esdras: A Rereading of Daniel 7 in the First Century CE," in K. H. Richards, ed., *Society of Biblical Literature 1981 Seminar Papers* (Chico, CA: Scholars Press, 1981) 237–58.

Lamarche, P. *Zacharie IX-XIV. Structure littéraire et messianisme* (Paris: Gabalda, 1961).

Lambdin, Thomas O., *Introduction to Classical Ethiopic* (Harvard Semitic Series 24; Chico, CA: Scholars Press, 1978).

Landman, Leo, *Messianism in the Talmudic Era* (New York: Ktav, 1979).

Leiman, S. Z., *The Canonization of Hebrew Scripture* (Hamden, CT: Archon Books, 1976).

Leivestadt, Ragnar, "Der apokalyptische Menschensohn ein theologisches Phantom," *Annual of the Swedish Theological Institute* 6(1967–68) 49–109.

———, "Exit the Apocalyptic Son of Man," *New Testament Studies* 18(1971–72) 243–67.

Levenson, Jon D., *Theology of the Program of Restoration of Ezekiel 40–48* (Harvard Semitic Monographs 10; Missoula, MT: Scholars Press, 1976).

Levey, Samson H., *The Messiah: An Aramaic Interpretation. The Messianic Exegesis of the Targum* (Monographs of the Hebrew Union College 2; Cincinnati, OH: Hebrew Union College/Jewish Institute of Religion, 1974).

Lewis, J. P., "What Do We Mean by Jabneh?" *Journal of Bible and Religion* 32(1964) 125–32.

Licht, J., מגילת הסרכים (Jerusalem: Mosad Bialik, 1965).

Lim, Timothy, "The Chronology of the Flood Story in a Qumran Text (4Q252)," *Journal of Jewish Studies* 43(1992) 288–98.

Lincoln, Bruce, *Discourse and the Construction of Society* (New York: Oxford University Press, 1989).

Lindars, Barnabas, *Jesus, Son of Man* (Grand Rapids, MI: Eerdmans, 1983).

———, "Re-enter the Apocalyptic Son of Man," *New Testament Studies* 22(1975) 52–72.

Liver, J., "The Doctrine of the Two Messiahs in Sectarian Literature in the Time of the Second Commonwealth," *Harvard Theological Review* 52(1959) 149–85 (reprinted in Landman, ed., *Messianism in the Talmudic Era*, 354–90).

Lohfink, Norbert, *Lobgesänge der Armen: Studien zum Magnifikat, den Hodajot von Qumran und einigen Psalmen* (Stuttgart: Katholisches Bibelwerk, 1990).

Lohse, E., *Die Texte aus Qumran* (Darmstadt: Wissenschaftliche Buchgesellschaft, 1971).

Lust, Johan, "Messianism and Septuagint," in J. A. Emerton, ed., *Congress Volume Salamanca (1983)* (Leiden: Brill, 1985) 174–91.

Mack, Burton L., *A Myth of Innocence. Mark and Christian Origins* (Philadelphia: Fortress, 1988).

———, "Wisdom and Apocalyptic in Philo," *The Studia Philonica Annual. Studies in Hellenistic Judaism* 3(1991) 21–39.

MacRae, George, "Messiah and Gospel," in Neusner et al., eds., *Judaisms and Their Messiahs*, 169–85.

Maier, Johann, "The Temple Scroll and Tendencies in the Cultic Architecture of the Second Commonwealth," in L. H. Schiffman, ed., *Archaeology and History in the Dead Sea Scrolls* (Sheffield: Journal for the Study of the Old Testament, 1990) 67–82.

Malamat, Abraham, "The Historical Setting of Two Biblical Prophecies on the Nations (Zech 9:1–6, Jer 47)," *Israel Exploration Journal* 1(1951) 149–59.

Manson, T. W., "The Son of Man in Daniel, Enoch and the Gospels," *Bulletin of the John Rylands Library* 32(1949–50) 171–95.

Marcus, Joel, *The Way of the Lord. Christological Exegesis of the Old Testament in the Gospel of Mark* (Louisville, KY: Westminster, 1992).

Mayes, A. D. H., "Amphictyony," in D. N. Freedman, ed., *The Anchor Bible Dictionary*, 1.212–16.

McCarter, P. K., *2 Samuel* (Anchor Bible 9; Garden City, NY: Doubleday, 1984).

Meeks, Wayne A., "Asking Back to Jesus' Identity," in M. de Boer, ed., *From Jesus to John*, 38–50.

———, "Moses as God and King," in J. Neusner, ed., *Religions in Antiquity. Essays in Memory of Erwin Ramsdell Goodenough* (Leiden: Brill, 1968) 354–71.

Bibliography

——, *The Prophet King. Moses Traditions and the Johannine Christology* (Leiden: Brill, 1967).

Meier, John P., *A Marginal Jew. Rethinking the Historical Jesus* (New York: Doubleday, 1991).

Mendels, Doron, "The Five Empires. A Note on a Hellenistic Topos," *American Journal of Philology* 102(1981) 330–37.

——, *The Land of Israel as a Political Concept in Hasmonean Literature* (Tübingen: Mohr-Siebeck, 1987).

——, *The Rise and Fall of Jewish Nationalism* (New York: Doubleday, 1992).

Mertens, A., *Das Buch Daniel im Lichte der Texte vom Toten Meer* (Stuttgart: Echter, 1971).

Mettinger, T. N. D., *King and Messiah. The Civil and Sacral Legitimation of the Israelite Kings* (Lund: Gleerup, 1976).

Metzger, B., "The Furniture of the Scriptorium at Qumran," *Revue de Qumrân* 1(1959) 509–15.

Meyers, C. L. and E. M., *Haggai, Zechariah 1–8* (Anchor Bible 25B; Garden City, NY: Doubleday, 1987).

——, *Zechariah 9–14* (Anchor Bible 25C; New York: Doubleday, 1993).

Mildenberg, L., *The Coinage of the Bar Kokhba War* (Aarau: Verlag Sauerländes, 1984).

Milik, J. T., *The Books of Enoch* (Oxford: Oxford University Press, 1976).

——, "4Q Visions de 'Amram et une citation d'Origène," *Revue Biblique* 79(1972) 77–97.

——, "Milkî-sedeq et Milkî-reša' dans les anciens écrits juifs et chrétiens," *Journal of Jewish Studies* 23(1972) 95–144.

——, "Les Modèles Araméens du Livre d'Esther dans le Grotte IV de Qumrân," *Revue de Qumrân* 15(1992) 321–99.

——, *Ten Years of Discovery in the Wilderness of Judaea* (London: SCM, 1959).

Molin, G., "Elijahu der Prophet und sein Weiterleben in den Hoffnungen des Judentums und der Christenheit," *Judaica* 8(1952) 65–94.

Momigliano, Arnaldo, "La Portata Storica dei Vaticini sul Settimo Re nel Terzo Libro degli Oracoli Sibillini," in *Forma Futuri: Studi in Onore del Cardinale Michele Pellegrino* (Turin: Erasmo, 1975).

Moore, George Foot, *Judaism in the First Centuries of the Christian Era* (2 vols.; New York: Schocken, 1971, original copyright, 1927).

Morenz, S., "Ägyptische und davidische Königstitular," *Zeitschrift für ägyptische Sprache* 79(1954) 73–74.

Mosca, Paul, "Once Again the Heavenly Witness of Ps 89:38," *Journal of Biblical Literature* 105(1986) 33–36.

——, "Ugarit and Daniel 7: A Missing Link," *Biblica* 67(1986) 496–517.

Mowinckel, S., *He That Cometh. The Messiah Concept in the Old Testament and Later Judaism* (Nashville: Abingdon, 1955).

——, *The Psalms in Israel's Worship* (Nashville: Abingdon, 1967).

Müller, Karlheinz, "Beobachtungen zur Entwicklung der Menschensohn-vorstellung in den Bilderreden des Henoch und im Buche Daniel," in Ernst C. Suttner and Coelestin Patock, eds., *Wegzeichen. Festschrift H. M. Biedermann* (Würzburg: Augustinus-Verlag, 1971) 253–612.

Müller, Ulrich B., *Messias und Menschensohn in jüdischen Apokalypsen und in der Offenbarung des Johannes* (Gütersloh: Mohn, 1972).

Murphy-O'Connor, J., "The Damascus Document Revisited," *Revue Biblique* 92(1985) 225–45.

———, "La genèse littéraire de la Règle de la Communauté," *Revue Biblique* 76(1969) 528–49.

———, "The Original Text of CD 7:9–8:2 = 19:5–14," *Harvard Theological Review* 64(1971) 379–86.

———, "Qumran, Khirbet," in D. N. Freedman, ed., *The Anchor Bible Dictionary* 5.590–93.

Myers, Jacob M., *I and II Esdras* (Anchor Bible 42; Garden City, NY: Double-day, 1974).

Neusner, Jacob, *Messiah in Context* (Philadelphia: Fortress, 1984).

Neusner, J., W. S. Green, and E. Frerichs, eds., *Judaisms and Their Messiahs* (Cambridge: Cambridge University Press, 1987).

Newsom, Carol A., "The 'Psalms of Joshua' from Qumran Cave 4," *Journal of Jewish Studies* 39(1988) 56–73.

———, "'Sectually Explicit' Literature from Qumran," in W. H. Propp, B. Halpern, and D. N. Freedman, eds., *The Hebrew Bible and Its Interpreters* (Winona Lake, IN: Eisenbrauns, 1990) 167–87.

Nickelsburg, G. W., "Enoch, Levi, and Peter: Recipients of Revelation in Upper Galilee," *Journal of Biblical Literature* 100(1981) 575–600.

———, *Jewish Literature Between the Bible and the Mishnah* (Philadelphia: Fortress, 1981).

———, *Resurrection, Immortality and Eternal Life in Intertestamental Judaism* (Cambridge, MA: Harvard University Press, 1972).

———, "Salvation without and with a Messiah," in Neusner et al., eds., *Judaisms and Their Messiahs*, 49–68.

———, "Son of Man," in D. N. Freedman, ed., *The Anchor Bible Dictionary* 6.137–50.

Nickelsburg, G. W., and M. E. Stone, *Faith and Piety in Early Judaism* (Philadelphia: Fortress, 1983).

Niditch, Susan, *The Symbolic Vision in Biblical Tradition* (Harvard Semitic Monographs 30; Chico, CA: Scholars Press, 1980).

Niehr, H., "נשׂא," in G. J. Botterweck and H. Ringgren, eds., *Theologisches Wörterbuch zum Alten Testament* (Stuttgart: Kohlhammer, 1986) 5.647–57.

Nikiprowetzky, Valentin, *La Troisième Sibylle* (Paris: Mouton, 1970).

Nock, A. D., Review of H. J. Schoeps, *Die Theologie des Apostels in Lichte der jüdischen Religionsgeschichte* in *Gnomon* 33(1961) 584.

Norden, Eduard, "Josephus und Tacitus über Jesus Christus und eine messianische Prophetie," *Neue Jahrbücher für das klassische Altertum* 16(1913) 637–66.

Noth, Martin, *Das System der Zwölf Stämme Israels* (Stuttgart: Kohlhammer, 1930).

———, "Zur Komposition des Buches Daniel," *Theologische Studien und Kritiken* 98/99(1926) 143–63.

Oegema, Gerbern S., *Der Gesalbte und sein Volk* (Göttingen: Vandenhoeck & Ruprecht, 1994).

Oppenheimer, A., "The Messianism of Bar Kokhba," in Z. Baras, ed., *Messianism and Eschatology*, 153–65.

Pace Jeansonne, Sharon, *The Old Greek Translation of Daniel 7–12* (Catholic Biblical Quarterly Monograph Series 19; Washington, D.C.: Catholic Biblical Association, 1988).

Paul, Shalom, *Amos* (Hermeneia; Minneapolis: Fortress, 1991).

Perrin, Norman, *A Modern Pilgrimage in New Testament Christology* (Philadelphia: Fortress, 1974).

Petersen, David, *Haggai and Zechariah 1–8* (Old Testament Library; Philadelphia: Westminster, 1984).

Philonenko, M., "'Jusqu'à ce que se lève un prophète digne de confiance' (1 Maccabées 14:41)," in Gruenwald, Shaked, and Stroumsa, eds., *Messiah and Christos*, 95–98.

Ploeger, Otto, *Theocracy and Eschatology* (Richmond: Knox, 1968).

Porter, Paul A., *Metaphors and Monsters. A Literary-Critical Study of Daniel 7 and 8* (Lund: Gleerup, 1983).

Pouilly, J., *La Règle de la Communauté de Qumrân. Son évolution littéraire* (Paris: Gabalda, 1976).

Puech, Emil, "Une Apocalypse Messianique (4Q521)," *Revue de Qumrân* 15(1992) 475–519.

———, "Ben Sira 48:11 et la Résurrection," in H. W. Attridge, J. J. Collins, and T. H. Tobin, eds., *Of Scribes and Scrolls. Studies on the Hebrew Bible, Intertestamental Judaism, and Christian Origins* (Lanham, MD: University Press of America, 1990) 81–90.

———, *La Croyance des Esséniens en la Vie Future: Immortalité, Résurrection, Vie Éternelle?* (2 vols.; Études Bibliques 21; Paris: Gabalda, 1993).

———, "Fragment d'une Apocalypse en Araméen (4Q246 = pseudo-Dan^d) et le 'Royaume de Dieu,'" *Revue Biblique* 99(1992) 98–131.

———, "Fragments d'un apocryphe de Lévi et le personnage eschatologique. 4QTestLévi(c–d)(?) et 4QAJa," in J. Trebolle Barrera and L. Vegas Montaner, eds., *The Madrid Qumran Congress* (Leiden: Brill, 1992) 2.449–501.

———, "Le Testament de Qahat en Araméen de la Grotte 4 (4QTQah)," *Revue de Qumrân* 15(1991) 23–54.

Purvis, J. D., *The Samaritan Pentateuch and the Origin of the Samaritan Sect* (Cambridge, MA: Harvard University Press, 1968).

Qimron, E., and J. Strugnell, *Qumran Cave 4. V. Miqṣat Maʿaśē Ha-Torah* (DJD10; Oxford: Clarendon, 1994) 400–7.

Rabin, C., *The Zadokite Fragments* (Oxford: Oxford University Press, 1954).

Redditt, Paul, "Israel's Shepherds: Hope and Pessimism in Zechariah 9–14," *Catholic Biblical Quarterly* 51(1989) 631–42.

Reed, Stephen A., *Dead Sea Scroll Inventory Project: Lists of Documents, Photographs and Museum Plates* (Claremont: Ancient Biblical Manuscript Center, 1992).

Rhoads, David, *Israel in Revolution* (Philadelphia: Fortress, 1976).

Roberts, J. J. M., "The Old Testament's Contribution to Messianic Expectations," in Charlesworth, ed., *The Messiah*, 39–51.

Rosen, Debra, and Alison Salvesen, "A Note on the Qumran Temple Scroll 56:15–18 and Psalm of Solomon 17:33," *Journal of Jewish Studies* 38(1987) 99–101.

Rowland, Christopher, *The Open Heaven. A Study of Apocalypticism in Judaism and Early Christianity* (New York: Crossroad, 1982).

Rowley, H. H., *The Servant of the Lord and Other Essays* (London: Lutterworth, 1952).

Ryle, H. E., and M. R. James, *Psalmoi Salomontos. Psalms of the Pharisees commonly called The Psalms of Solomon* (Cambridge: Cambridge University Press, 1891).

Saldarini, A. J., *Pharisees, Scribes and Sadducees in Palestinian Society. A Sociological Approach* (Wilmington: Glazier, 1988).

Sanders, E. P., *Jesus and Judaism* (Philadelphia: Fortress, 1985).

———, *Judaism. Practice and Belief. 63 BCE–66 CE* (Philadelphia: Trinity Press International, 1992).

Schäfer, Peter, "Aqiva and Bar Kokhba," in W. S. Green, ed., *Approaches to Ancient Judaism* (Brown Judaic Studies 9; Atlanta: Scholars Press, 1980) 2.113–30.

———, *Der Bar Kokhba Aufstand. Studien zum zweiten jüdischen Krieg gegen Rom* (Tübingen: Mohr-Siebeck, 1981).

———, *Gershom Scholem Reconsidered. The Aim and Purpose of Early Jewish Mysticism* (Oxford: Oxford Centre for Postgraduate Hebrew Studies, 1986).

———, *The Hidden and Manifest God* (Albany: State University of New York Press, 1992).

Schäfer, P., M. Schlüter, and H. G. von Mutius, *Synopse zur Hekhalot-Literatur.* Texte und Studien zum Antiken Judentum 2 (Tübingen: Mohr-Siebeck, 1981).

Schechter, Solomon, *Fragments of a Zadokite Work* (Cambridge: Cambridge University Press, 1910).

Schiffman, L. H., "The Deuteronomic Paraphrase of the Temple Scroll," *Revue de Qumrân* 15(1992) 543–67.

Bibliography

———, *The Eschatological Community of the Dead Sea Scrolls* (Society of Biblical Literature Monograph Series 38; Atlanta: Scholars Press, 1989).

———, "The Sadducean Origins of the Dead Sea Scroll Sect," in H. Shanks, ed., *Understanding the Dead Sea Scrolls* (New York: Random House, 1992) 35–49.

Schimanowski, Gottfried, *Weisheit und Messias* (Tübingen: Mohr-Siebeck, 1985).

Scholem, Gershom, *Major Trends in Jewish Mysticism* (New York: Schocken, 1961).

———, *The Messianic Idea in Judaism and Other Essays on Jewish Spirituality* (New York: Schocken, 1971).

Schuerer, Emil, *The History of the Jewish People in the Age of Jesus Christ* (rev. and ed. by G. Vermes, F. Millar, and M. Black; 3 vols.; Edinburgh: Clark, 1973–87).

Schuller, Eileen, "A Hymn from a Cave Four Hodayot Manuscript: 4Q427 7 i + 11," *Journal of Biblical Literature* 112(1993) 605–28.

Schüpphaus, J., *Die Psalmen Salomos: Ein Zeugnis Jerusalemer Theologie und Frömmigkeit in der Mitte des vorchristlichen Jahrhunderts* (Leiden: Brill, 1977).

Schwartz, D. R., "The Three Temples of 4QFlorilegium," *Revue de Qumrân* 10(1979–81) 83–91.

Schweitzer, Albert, *The Quest of the Historical Jesus* (New York: Macmillan, 1969).

Seebass, H., "אחרית/'acharîth," in G. J. Botterweck and H. Ringgren, eds., *Theological Dictionary of the Old Testament* (Grand Rapids, MI: Eerdmans, 1974) 1.207–12.

———, *Herrscherverheissungen im Alten Testament* (Neukirchen-Vluyn: Neukirchener Verlag, 1992).

Segal, Alan, *Two Powers in Heaven* (Leiden: Brill, 1977).

Seux, M.-J., *Épithètes Royales Akkadiennes et Sumériennes. Ouvrage publié avec le concours du Centre National de la Recherche Scientifique* (Paris: Letouzey et Ané, 1967).

Sjöberg, Erik, *Der Menschensohn im Äthiopischen Henochbuch* (Lund: Gleerup, 1946).

Skehan, Patrick W., "A Fragment of the 'Song of Moses' (Deuteronomy 32) from Qumran," *Bulletin of the American Schools of Oriental Research* 136(1954) 12–15.

———, "The Period of the Biblical Texts from Khirbet Qumran," *Catholic Biblical Quarterly* 19(1957) 435–40.

———, "Two Books on Qumran Studies," *Catholic Biblical Quarterly* 21(1959) 71–78.

Smith, J. Z., "A Pearl of Great Price and a Cargo of Yams: A Study in Situational Incongruity," *History of Religions* 16(1976) 1–19.

———, "Prayer of Joseph," in Charlesworth, ed., *The Old Testament Pseudepigrapha* 2.699–714.

Smith, Morton, "Ascent to the Heavens and Deification in 4QM^a," in L. H. Schiffman, ed., *Archaeology and History in the Dead Sea Scrolls* (Sheffield: Journal for the Study of the Old Testament, 1990) 181–88.

———, *Clement of Alexandria and a Secret Gospel of Mark* (Cambridge, MA: Harvard University Press, 1973).

———, "Two Ascended to Heaven," in J. H. Charlesworth, ed., *Jesus and the Dead Sea Scrolls* (New York: Doubleday, 1991) 290–301.

———, "What Is Implied by the Variety of Messianic Figures?" *Journal of Biblical Literature* 78(1959) 66–72.

Starcky, J., "Les quatres étapes du messianisme à Qumrân," *Revue Biblique* 70(1963) 481–505.

Stegemann, Hartmut, "Die Bedeutung der Qumranfunde für die Erforschung der Apokalyptik," in David Hellholm, ed., *Apocalypticism in the Mediterranean World and the Near East* (Tübingen: Mohr-Siebeck, 1983) 495–530.

———, *Die Enstehung der Qumrangemeinde* (Bonn: published privately, 1971).

———, "The Institutions of Israel in the Temple Scroll," in D. Dimant and U. Rappaport, eds., *The Dead Sea Scrolls. Forty Years of Research* (Leiden: Brill, 1992) 156–85.

———, "Some Remarks to 1QSa, 1QSb, and Qumran Messianism," paper presented at the meeting of the *International Organization of Qumran Studies* in Paris, July 1992.

Stemberger, G., "Die sogenannte 'Synode von Jabne' und das frühe Christentum," *Kairos* 19(1977) 14–21.

Stendahl, Krister, *The Scrolls and the New Testament* (New York: Harper, 1957).

Steudel, Annette, *Der Midrasch zur Eschatologie aus der Qumrangemeinde (4QMidrEschat^{a, b})* (Leiden: Brill, 1994).

———, "4QMidrEschat: 'A Midrash on Eschatology' (4Q174 + 4Q177)," in Julio Trebolle Barrera and Luis Vegas Montaner, eds., *The Madrid Qumran Congress. Proceedings of the International Congress on the Dead Sea Scrolls, Madrid, 18–21 March 1991* (Leiden: Brill, 1992) 531–41.

Stone, Michael E., "The Concept of the Messiah in IV Ezra," in J. Neusner, ed., *Religions in Antiquity. Essays in Memory of E. R. Goodenough* (Leiden: Brill, 1968) 295–312.

———, "Enoch, Aramaic Levi and Sectarian Origins," *Journal for the Study of Judaism* 19(1988) 159–70.

———, *Features of the Eschatology of 4 Ezra* (Harvard Semitic Studies 35; Atlanta: Scholars Press, 1989).

———, *Fourth Ezra* (Hermeneia; Minneapolis: Fortress, 1990).

———, "The Question of the Messiah in 4 Ezra," in Neusner et al., eds., *Judaisms and Their Messiahs*, 209–24.

Stone, M. E., and J. C. Greenfield, "The Enochic Pentateuch and the Date of the Similitudes," *Harvard Theological Review* 70(1977) 51–65.

———, "The Prayer of Levi," *Journal of Biblical Literature* 112(1993) 247–66.

Bibliography

Stone, M. E., and John Strugnell, *The Books of Elijah, Parts 1 and 2* (Missoula, MT: Scholars Press, 1979).

Strugnell, John, "Moses-Pseudepigrapha at Qumran," in Lawrence H. Schiffman, ed., *Archaeology and History in the Dead Sea Scrolls* (Sheffield: Journal for the Study of the Old Testament, 1990) 221–56.

———, "Notes en marge du volume V des 'Discoveries in the Judaean Desert of Jordan,'" *Revue de Qumrân 7*(1970) 163–276.

Sussman, Y., "The History of the Halakha and the Dead Sea Scrolls: Preliminary Observations of the Miqsat Ma'ase Ha-Torah," *Tarbiz* 59(1990) 11–76 (Hebrew).

Suter, David, "Fallen Angel, Fallen Priest: The Problem of Family Purity in 1 Enoch 6–16," *Hebrew Union College Annual* 59(1979) 115–35.

———, "Weighed in the Balance: The Similitudes of Enoch in Recent Discussion," *Religious Studies Review 7*(1981) 217–21.

Swain, J. W., "The Theory of the Four Monarchies: Opposition History under the Roman Empire," *Classical Philology* 35(1940) 1–21.

Tabor, James D., "A Pierced or Piercing Messiah? — The Verdict is Still Out," *Biblical Archeology Review* (November/December 1992) 58–59.

———, *Things Unutterable. Paul's Ascent to Paradise in Its Greco-Roman, Judaic, and Early Christian Contexts* (Lanham, MD: University Press of America, 1986).

Talmon, Shemaryahu, "The Concept of Māšîaḥ and Messianism in Early Judaism," in J. Charlesworth, ed., *The Messiah*, 79–115.

———, "Types of Messianic Expectation at the Turn of the Era," in Talmon, ed., *King, Cult and Calendar in Ancient Israel* (Jerusalem: Magnes, 1986) 202–24.

———, "Waiting for the Messiah at Qumran," in Talmon, *The World of Qumran from Within* (Leiden: Brill, 1989) 273–300.

———, "Waiting for the Messiah: The Spiritual Universe of the Qumran Covenanters," in Neusner et al., eds., *Judaisms and Their Messiahs*, 111–37.

Tcherikover, Victor, and Alexander Fuks, *Corpus Papyrorum Judaicarum* (3 vols. Cambridge, MA: Harvard University Press, 1957–64).

Teeple, H. M., *The Mosaic Eschatological Prophet* (Society of Biblical Literature Monograph Series 10; Philadelphia: Society of Biblical Literature, 1957).

Theisohn, Johannes, *Der auserwählte Richter* (Göttingen: Vandenhoeck & Ruprecht, 1975).

Thoma, Clemens, "Entwürfe für messianische Gestalten in frühjüdischer Zeit," in Gruenwald, Shaked, and Stroumsa, eds., *Messiah and Christos*, 15–30.

Tiller, Patrick A., *A Commentary on the Animal Apocalypse of 1 Enoch* (Atlanta: Scholars Press, 1993).

Tollington, Janet E., *Tradition and Innovation in Haggai and Zechariah 1–8* (Journal for the Study of the Old Testament Supplement 150; Sheffield: Journal for the Study of the Old Testament, 1993).

Tov, Emanuel, and Stephen J. Pfann, *The Dead Sea Scrolls on Microfiche* (Leiden: Brill, 1993).

Tromp, Johannes, "Taxo, the Messenger of the Lord," *Journal for the Study of Judaism* 21(1990) 200–9.

———, "The Sinners and the Lawless of Psalm of Solomon 17," *Novum Testamentum* 35(1993) 344–61.

Trump, S., ed., *Millennial Dreams in Action* (Hague: Mouton, 1962).

Turner, Victor, *Dramas, Fields, and Metaphors* (Ithaca: Cornell University Press, 1974).

Ulrichsen, J. H., *Die Grundschrift der Testamente der zwölf Patriarchen* (Stockholm: Almqvist & Wiksell, 1991).

Urbach, E. E., *The Sages, Their Concepts and Beliefs* (Jerusalem: Magnes, 1975).

van der Broek, R., *The Myth of the Phoenix According to Classical and Early Christian Traditions* (Leiden: Brill, 1972).

van der Horst, P. W., "Moses' Throne Vision in Ezekiel the Dramatist," *Journal of Jewish Studies* 34(1983) 21–29.

VanderKam, J. C., *The Dead Sea Scrolls Today* (Grand Rapids, MI: Eerdmans, 1994).

———, *Enoch and the Growth of an Apocalyptic Tradition* (Catholic Biblical Quarterly Monograph Series 16; Washington, D.C.: Catholic Biblical Association, 1984).

———, "Enoch Traditions in Jubilees and Other Second Century Sources," in P. J. Achtemeier, ed., *Society of Biblical Literature 1978 Seminar Papers* (Missoula, MT: Scholars Press, 1978) 229–51.

———, "Jubilees and the Priestly Messiah of Qumran," *Revue de Qumrân* 13(1988) 353–65.

———, "The Origin, Character and Early History of the 364-Day Calendar: A Reassessment of Jaubert's Hypotheses," *Catholic Biblical Quarterly* 41(1979) 390–411.

———, "The People of the Dead Sea Scrolls: Essenes or Sadducees?" in H. Shanks, ed., *Understanding the Dead Sea Scrolls* (New York: Random House, 1992) 50–62.

———, "Revealed Literature of the Second Temple Period," forthcoming.

———, "Righteous One, Messiah, Chosen One, and Son of Man," in Charlesworth, ed., *The Messiah*, 169–91.

———, *Textual and Historical Studies in the Book of Jubilees* (Harvard Semitic Monographs 14; Missoula, MT: Scholars Press, 1977) 217–238.

———, "The 364-Day Calendar in the Enoch Literature," in K. H. Richards, ed., *Society of Biblical Literature 1983 Seminar Papers* (Chico, CA: Scholars Press, 1983) 157–65.

VanderKam, J. C., and J. T. Milik, "The First Jubilees Manuscript from Qumran Cave 4: A Preliminary Publication," *Journal of Biblical Literature* 110(1991) 243–70.

van der Ploeg, J., "Eschatology in the Old Testament," *Oudtestamentische Studiën* 17(1972) 89–99.

Bibliography

van Unnik, W. C. "Jesus the Christ," *New Testament Studies* 8(1961–62) 101–16.

de Vaux, Roland, *Archaeology and the Dead Sea Scrolls* (London: Oxford University Press, 1973).

———, "Qumran, Khirbet and ʿEin Feshka," in E. Stern, ed., *The New Encyclopedia of Archaeological Excavations in the Holy Land* (New York: Simon and Schuster, 1993) 4.1235–41.

Vermes, Geza, "Brother James's heirs? The Community at Qumran and its relations to the first Christians," *Times Literary Supplement* 4 December 1992, 6–7.

———, *The Dead Sea Scrolls in English* (London: Penguin Books, 1987).

———, *The Dead Sea Scrolls. Qumran in Perspective* (Philadelphia: Fortress, 1977).

———, *Jesus the Jew* (Philadelphia: Fortress, 1973).

———, *Jesus and the World of Judaism* (Philadelphia: Fortress, 1984).

———, "The Oxford Forum for Qumran Research Seminar on the Rule of War from Cave 4 (4Q285)," *Journal of Jewish Studies* 43(1992) 85–90.

———, *Post-Biblical Jewish Studies* (Leiden: Brill, 1975).

———, "Preliminary Remarks on Unpublished Fragments of the Community Rule from Qumran Cave 4," *Journal of Jewish Studies* 42(1991) 250–55.

———, The So-Called King Jonathan Fragment (4Q448)," *Journal of Jewish Studies* 44(1993) 294–300.

Vermes, Geza, and Martin D. Goodman, *The Essenes According to the Classical Sources* (Sheffield: Journal for the Study of the Old Testament, 1989).

Volz, P., *Die Eschatologie der Jüdischen Gemeinde* (Tübingen: Mohr, 1934; reprint, Hidesheim: Olms, 1966).

Wacholder, B. Z., *The Dawn of Qumran: The Sectarian Torah and the Teacher of Righteousness* (Cincinnati: Hebrew Union College, 1983).

Wacholder, B. Z., and M. Abegg, *A Preliminary Edition of the Unpublished Dead Sea Scrolls. The Hebrew and Aramaic Texts from Cave Four. Fascicle Two* (Washington, D.C.: Biblical Archaeology Society, 1992).

Walla, M., *Der Vogel Phoenix in der antiken Literatur und in der Dichtung des Laktanz* (Wien: Notring, 1969).

Webb, Robert, *John the Baptizer and Prophet. A Socio-Historical Study* (Journal for the Study of the New Testament Supplement 62; Sheffield: Journal for the Study of the Old Testament, 1991).

Weinfeld, Moshe, "The Covenant of Grant in the Old Testament and in the Ancient Near East," *Journal of the Americal Oriental Society* 90(1970) 184–203.

Wetter, G. P., *Der Sohn Gottes* (Göttingen: Vandenhoeck & Ruprecht, 1916).

White, Sidnie A., "A Comparison of the 'A' and 'B' Manuscripts of the Damascus Document," *Revue de Qumrân* 48(1987) 537–53.

Whybray, R. N., *Thanksgiving for a Liberated Prophet* (Sheffield: Journal for the Study of the Old Testament, 1978).

Wieder, N., "The Doctrine of the Two Messiahs among the Karaites," *Journal of Jewish Studies* 6(1955) 14–23.

———, "The 'Law Interpreter' of the Sect of the Dead Sea Scrolls: The Second Moses," *Journal of Jewish Studies* 4(1953) 158–75.

Wildberger, H., *Isaiah 1–12* (Minneapolis: Augsburg, 1991).

Wilken, Robert L., *The Land Called Holy. Palestine in Christian History and Thought* (New Haven, CT: Yale University Press, 1992).

Williams, Sam K., *Jesus' Death as a Saving Event* (Harvard Dissertations in Religion 2, Missoula, MT: Scholars Press, 1975).

Wills, Lawrence M., *The Jew in the Court of the Foreign King* (Harvard Dissertations in Religion 26; Minneapolis: Fortress, 1990).

Wilson, Bryan, *Magic and the Millenium* (London: Heinemann, 1973).

Wilson, G. H., "The Qumran Psalms Scroll Reconsidered: Analysis of the Debate," *Catholic Biblical Quarterly* 47(1985) 624–42.

Wise, Michael O., "Bar Kochba Letters," in D. N. Freedman, ed., *The Anchor Bible Dictionary* 1.601–606.

———, *A Critical Study of the Temple Scroll from Qumran Cave 11* (Studies in Ancient Oriental Civilization 49; Chicago: The Oriental Institute of the University of Chicago, 1990).

———, "The Eschatological Vision of the Temple Scroll," *Journal of Near Eastern Studies* 49(1990) 155–72.

———, "4QFlorilegium and the Temple of Adam," *Revue de Qumrân* 15(1991) 103–32.

———, "The Teacher of Righteousness and the High Priest of the Intersacerdotium: Two Approaches," *Revue de Qumrân* 14(1990) 587–613.

———, "The Temple Scroll and the Teacher of Righteousness," in Z. J. Kapera, ed., *Mogilany 1989. Papers on the Dead Sea Scrolls, Vol. 2* (Kraków: Enigma, 1991) 121–47.

Wise, Michael, and J. D. Tabor, "The Messiah at Qumran," *Biblical Archeology Review* (November/December 1992) 60–65.

Wolff, Hans Walter, *Joel and Amos* (Hermeneia; Philadelphia: Fortress, 1977).

van der Woude, A. S., *Die Messianischen Vorstellung der Gemeinde von Qumrân* (Assen: van Gorcum, 1957).

Wright, Robert B., "Psalms of Solomon," in Charlesworth, ed., *The Old Testament Pseudepigrapha* 2.639–70.

Yadin, Yigael, *Bar Kokhba. The Rediscovery of the Legendary Hero of the Second Jewish Revolt Against Rome* (New York: Random House, 1971).

———, "Le Rouleau du Temple," in Delcor, ed., *Qumrân*, 115–19.

———, *The Scroll of the War of the Sons of Light Against the Sons of Darkness* (Oxford: Oxford University Press, 1962).

———, *The Temple Scroll: The Hidden Law of the Dead Sea Sect* (London: Weidenfeld and Nicolson, 1985).

———, *The Temple Scroll, Volume One: Introduction* (Jerusalem: Israel Exploration Society, 1977).

Bibliography

Yarbro Collins, Adela, *The Combat Myth in the Book of Revelation* (Harvard Dissertations in Religion 9; Missoula, MT: Scholars Press, 1976).

———, "Eschatology in the Book of Revelation," *Ex Auditu* 6(1990) 63–72.

———, "Establishing the Text: Mark 1:1," in D. Hellholm and T. Fornberg, eds., *Texts and Contexts. The Function of Biblical Texts in Their Textual and Situative Contexts* (San Francisco: Mellen, forthcoming).

———, "From Noble Death to Crucified Messiah," *New Testament Studies* 40(1994) 481–503.

———, "The 'Son of Man' Tradition and the Book of Revelation," in Charlesworth, ed., *The Messiah*, 536–68.

Zimmerli, Walther, *Ezekiel 2* (Hermeneia; Philadelphia: Fortress, 1983).

CHRONOLOGICAL TABLE

I. *Maccabean and Hasmonean Period*

167–154 BCE	The Maccabean Revolt
164–161	Judas Maccabee
161–143/2	Jonathan Maccabee, *de facto* ruler and High Priest (Some scholars date the origin of the Qumran sect to this time)
143/2–135/4	Simon Maccabee formally acknowledged as ruler and High Priest
134/2–104	John Hyrcanus, ruler, priest and prophet Qumran sect in existence
104–103	Aristobulus, first to assume the title "king"
103–76	Alexander Jannaeus, called "King Jonathan" on coins Violent break with the Pharisees
76–67	Salome Alexandra
67–63	Aristobulus II Conflict with Hyrcanus II Intervention of Romans
63	Capture of Jerusalem by Pompey

Chronological Table

II. *Roman Period*

37–4	Herod the Great
31 BCE–14 CE	Roman Emperor Augustus
4 BCE	Death of Herod. Activity of messianic pretenders, Judas, Simon and Athronges
4 BCE–6 CE	Archelaus ruler of Judaea Herod Antipas and Philip inherit other provinces of Herod's kingdom
6–41	Judaea under Roman governors
14–37	Roman Emperor Trajan
26–36	Pontius Pilate governor of Judaea Execution of Jesus of Nazareth Activity of Samaritan prophet
37–41	Roman Emperor Gaius (Caligula)
41–54	Roman Emperor Claudius
41–44	Herod Agrippa I, ruler of restored kingdom of Herod the Great
44–46	Governorship of Fadus Activity of Theudas
52–60	Governorship of Festus Activity of the Egyptian prophet (c. 56 CE)
54–68	Roman Emperor Nero
66–70	First Jewish revolt Messianic(?) activity of Menahem and Simon bar Giora Destruction of Qumran settlement Galba, Otho and Vitellius, Roman emperors in quick succession
69–79	Roman Emperor Vespasian
79–81	Titus Emperor
81–96	Domitian
96–98	Nerva
98–117	Trajan
115–117	Revolt in Libya and Egypt Activity of Lukuas/Andreas
117–138	Hadrian Roman Emperor
132–135	Revolt of Bar Kokhba

ABBREVIATIONS

Biblical Books

Gen	Hab	Luke
Exod	Zeph	John
Lev	Hag	Acts
Num	Zech	Rom
Deut	Mal	1–2 Cor
Josh	Ps (plural: Pss)	Gal
Judg	Job	Eph
1–2 Sam	Prov	Phil
1–2 Kgs	Ruth	Col
Isa	Cant	1–2 Thess
Jer	Eccles (or Qoh)	1–2 Tim
Ezek	Lam	Titus
Hos	Esth	Philemon
Joel	Dan	Heb
Amos	Ezra	Jas
Obad	Neh	1–2 Pet
Jonah	1–2 Chron	1–2–3 John
Mic	Matt	Jude
Nah	Mark	Rev

Abbreviations

Apocrypha and Pseudepigrapha

2 Bar	Second (Syriac) Baruch
3 Bar	Third (Greek) Baruch
1 Enoch	Ethiopic Enoch
2 Enoch	Slavonic Enoch
3 Enoch	Hebrew Enoch (= Sepher Hekhalot)
4 Ezra	= 2 Esdras 3–14
Jub	Jubilees
1–2–3–4 Macc	First–Second–Third–Fourth Maccabees
Pss Sol	Psalms of Solomon
Sib Or	Sibylline Oracles
Sir	Sirach
T. Judah	Testament of Judah
T. Levi	Testament of Levi
T. Moses	Testament of Moses (= Assumption of Moses)
T. 12 Patr.	Testaments of the Twelve Patriarchs
Tob	Tobit
Wis	The Wisdom of Solomon

Dead Sea Scrolls and Rabbinic Sources

Ar. Levi	The Aramaic Levi Apocryphon
b.	Babylonian Talmud
b. Ḥag.	tractate Ḥagiga, Babylonian Talmud
Bamidbar R.	Midrash on Numbers
b. Sanh.	tractate Sanhedrin, Babylonian Talmud
CD	The Damascus Document from the Cairo Geniza (Cairo Document)
j.	Jerusalem Talmud
m.	Mishnah tractate
p.	Pesher
Q	Qumran Cave (e.g. 4Q = documents from Qumran Cave Four)
1QapGen	The Genesis Apocryphon from Qumran Cave 1
1QH	The Hodayot, or Hymns Scroll
1QM/4QM	Serekh-ha-milhamah, the War Rule
1QpHab	The commentary on Habakkuk from Cave 1
1QS	Serekh-ha-yahad, the Community Rule

1QSa	The Messianic Rule
1QSb	The Scroll of Blessings
4QCatena	Exegetical text from Cave 4 (4Q177)
4QFlor	The Florilegium from Cave 4 (4Q174)
4QMMT	Miqsat Ma'aseh Torah from Qumran Cave 4 = the Halakhic letter
4QMess ar	Aramaic "Messianic" text from Cave 4 = the Elect of God text
4QpIsa	The commentary on Isaiah from Qumran Cave 4
4QpMic	The commentary on Micah from Cave 4
4QpNah	The commentary on Nahum from Cave 4
4QpPss	The commentary on Psalms from Cave 4
4QTest	The Testimonia from Qumran Cave 4
11QMelch	The Melchizedek Scroll from Cave 11
11QShir Shabb	The Songs of Sabbath Sacrifice
11QTemple	The Temple Scroll from Cave 11
T. 'Amram	The Testament of 'Amram
T. Kohath	The Testament of Kohath

INDEX OF SCRIPTURAL CITATIONS

New Testament

Index of Scriptural Citations

Index of Ancient Sources

Dead Sea Scrolls

Hellenistic Jewish Authors

Ezekiel the Tragedian

Josephus

Index of Ancient Sources

INDEX OF AUTHORS

Index of Authors

Index of Authors

INDEX OF SUBJECTS

Index of Subjects

Index of Subjects